BARRON'S

S0-AAZ-848

ACCOUNTING

Fourth Edition

THE EASY WAY

BARRON'S

ACCOUNTING

Fourth Edition

THE EASY WAY

Peter J. Eisen
Assistant Principal, Accounting and Business Practice
New York City Department of Education
New York, New York

BARRON'S

All inquiries should be addressed to:
Barron's Educational Series, Inc.
250 Wireless Boulevard
Hauppauge, NY 11788
http://www.barronseduc.com

Library of Congress Catalog Card Number 2003043542
International Standard Book Number 0-7641-1976-1

Library of Congress Cataloging-in-Publication Data

Eisen, Peter J.
    Accounting the easy way / Peter J. Eisen.—4th ed.
      p. cm.
    Includes index.
    ISBN 0-7641-1976-1
    1. Accounting.   I. Title.
  HF5635.E34   2003
  657—dc21   2003043542

PRINTED IN THE UNITED STATES OF AMERICA
9 8 7 6 5 4 3 2 1

CONTENTS

11 ACCOUNTING FOR PAYROLL

12 PARTNERSHIP ACCOUNTING

13 CORPORATE ACCOUNTING

EXERCISE SOLUTIONS

PREFACE

Accounting the Easy Way is designed for individuals with some knowledge of accounting as well as those with none at all. This book presents the subject matter in a logical sequence, with exercises after every appropriate topic within each chapter. These exercises allow you to apply knowledge just learned and then check your work against the solutions at the back of the book. This fourth edition also includes supplementary exercises for each chapter, presented together in a separate section at the back of the book. The first supplementary exercise for each chapter consists of questions relating to information presented in the text for that chapter. Your ability to answer the questions to the first supplementary exercise provides an indication of how well you understand the material in the chapter. The remaining supplementary exercises are meant to be used to reinforce your understanding or to assist you in cases in which the initial exercise proved inadequate. The organization of these supplementary exercises is similar to the original exercises presented in the body of the text. Key figures are provided, where appropriate, to assist in verifying whether you answered the supplementary exercises correctly. Finally, a comprehensive glossary includes definitions of important accounting terms.

Since no prior knowledge of accounting is needed to master the subject matter in *Accounting the Easy Way*, the student will find this book an excellent self-study guide and an invaluable companion to any textbook required in a survey-level college course on principles of accounting. Unlike traditional college textbooks that present accounting principles for various forms of business organizations at the same time, *Accounting the Easy Way* concentrates on accounting for sole proprietorships and thus gives a simpler, more direct presentation of the subject. The partnership and corporation forms of business organizations are discussed briefly in the last two chapters of the book.

This fourth edition of *Accounting the Easy Way* presents the most up-to-date information on the new tax code as it relates to this elementary course. The most up-to-date withholding tax tables are used and illustrated. This book may also be used as a college accounting textbook on the high school level. The presentation and organization meets the traditional first term college accounting course curriculum.

I would like to take this opportunity to thank my wife, Amy, for her continuing support and encouragement in the original writing and in this most recent revision of the book. A special thanks to my son Howard for his invaluable patience and assistance in instructing me in the use of the microcomputer and word processing software used in the original and latest edition of this book.

Peter J. Eisen

CHAPTER 1

THE ACCOUNTING EQUATION

Some Basics

WHAT IS ACCOUNTING?

Accounting is the art of organizing, maintaining, recording, and analyzing financial activities. Accounting is generally known as the "language of business." The accountant translates this accounting information into meaningful terms that are used by interested parties. Every organization, whether organized for profit, nonprofit, charitable, religious, or governmental purposes requires accountants.

Accounting may be divided into three areas: (1) public accounting, (2) private accounting, and (3) governmental accounting. The public accountant, usually an employee of a CPA firm, is employed as an independent contractor by a business to perform an auditing function: to review the accounting system used by the business, check the correctness of financial statements, and give an opinion. The public accountant also prepares income tax returns and provides management advisory services. The private accountant, usually employed by a business, records business activities and prepares periodic financial statements. The governmental accountant performs the same functions as a private accountant but is employed by a federal, state, or local governmental agency.

WHO USES ACCOUNTING INFORMATION?

Accounting information is used by everyone. The manager of an organization, who is charged with the responsibility of seeing that the enterprise is properly directed, calls upon the accounting information provided to make appropriate decisions. Investors in an enterprise need information about the financial status and future prospects of an organization. Bankers and suppliers grant loans and extend credit to organizations based on their financial soundness as evidenced by accounting information. Customers are concerned about a company's ability to provide a product or service. Employees are concerned about the ability of the employer to pay wages and fringe benefit packages.

WHAT INFORMATION DOES AN ACCOUNTANT GATHER?

The accountant keeps track of all "business transactions." A business transaction is any business activity that affects what a business owns or owes, as well as the ownership of that business.

What Are Assets?

Those things that are owned by any business organization are known as ASSETS. In order for an item to be considered an asset, it must meet two requirements: (1) it must be owned by the organization, and (2) it must have money value. OWNERSHIP is the exclusive right to possess, use, enjoy, and dispose of property. MONEY VALUE exists if a buyer is willing to pay money to a seller for the property.

EXERCISE 1   From the following list of items, indicate by checking the appropriate box which items are or are not assets.

Item	Yes	No
Cash		
Automobile		
Rented Apartment		
Checks		
Computer		
Library Book On Loan		
Clothing		
Postage Stamps		
Grocery List		
Food		

EXERCISE 2   Prepare a list of ten assets that you personally own. You may include the assets listed in Exercise 1, but attempt to list as many other personal assets as you can.

EXERCISE 3   Prepare a list of ten assets that a business organization would own. Attempt to list business assets that an individual might not have.

KEEPING TRACK OF ASSETS

Since there apparently are so many different kinds of assets, how does the accountant keep track of all of the assets? The accountant does not keep track of all of the assets individually, but rather combines assets of a similar nature into common groups. For example, an individual or business organization may have such assets as coins, bills, money orders, and checks. These assets would be placed in a category or grouping known as CASH. Thus, any money, regardless of its actual form, would be known and categorized as cash. Cash also includes money in bank accounts of the individual that is available for payment of bills.

EXERCISE 4   Test your ability to assign specific assets to categories. Place the assets listed below under the asset category headings that follow.

Traveler's checks, tables, truck, typewriter, adding machine, lamp, pencils, chairs, stationery, wrapping paper, automobiles, coins, money in bank, light bulbs, desk, pens, currency, showcases, computer, software programs, computer printer, and toner cartridge.

Cash	Office Supplies	Furniture and Fixtures	Office Equipment	Delivery Equipment

1. What is the difference between office supplies and office equipment?
2. A toner cartridge is considered an office supply, even though it is an integral part of the computer printer. Why?
3. Will we replace a typewriter as frequently as a typewriter ribbon? Why or why not?
4. What type of asset is a supply? (Short-life or long-life?)
5. What type of asset is a computer? (Short-life or long-life?)

TYPES OF ASSETS

As the previous exercises indicated, assets may take many forms. While they may be grouped together into categories as in Exercise 4, they may also be considered to be tangible and intangible assets as well. A tangible asset is one that can be readily seen, and possibly touched, such as those previously illustrated. They are physical assets. An intangible asset is without physical qualities, but has a value based on rights or privileges belonging to the owner.

The assets of an organization are usually divided into four categories: (1) current assets, (2) investments, (3) property, plant, and equipment, and (4) intangible assets.

CURRENT ASSETS are defined as cash and other assets that can reasonably be expected to be converted to cash, used up, or sold within one year or less. Examples of current assets include cash, accounts receivable (obligations due from customers), and supplies.

INVESTMENTS are generally of a long-term nature, are not used in the normal operations of the organization and are not expected to be converted to cash within the year. Examples of investments are stocks and bonds of other organizations.

PROPERTY, PLANT, AND EQUIPMENT are long-term or long-life assets that are used in the continuing operations of the organization and are expected to be used by the organization for more than a year. These kinds of assets are also known as "Plant Assets." Examples of these assets are land, building, machinery, and equipment.

INTANGIBLE ASSETS are usually of a long-term nature and have no physical substance but are of value to the owners of the organization. Examples of these assets are patents, copyrights, goodwill, franchises, and trademarks.

EXERCISE 5 Place the following assets in the appropriate columns of the form following them: cash in bank, office equipment, First National City bonds, patents, accounts receivable, office supplies, notes receivable (due in ninety days), building, office machines, furniture and fixtures, mortgage notes receivable (due in six years), store equipment, petty cash, goodwill, factory supplies, and merchandise.

Current Assets	Investments	Plant Assets	Intangible Assets

A COMMON WAY TO EXPRESS ASSETS

We have indicated that the accountant keeps track of all business transactions. So far, the only business transactions we have discussed are things that the organization owns, namely assets. In order to keep track of these assets, there must be a common way of expressing these assets. The common way of expressing the value of items in a business is known as the MONETARY PRINCIPLE. All business transactions are recorded in terms of money. Money is the only factor that is common to all assets as well as to other items we will shortly be discussing. If we were to say that we have the asset "office supplies," the accountant would express the ownership of this asset in terms of a money value assigned to it. The money value assigned would be based on what the office supplies had cost when they were purchased. If we acquired office supplies that had cost us $50, we would then say that the value of the asset office supplies is $50. All things owned by and owed to an organization, as well as the ownership of the organization, will be expressed in terms of money value. Money or cash becomes the common denominator in presenting accounting information.

Determining Money Value of Assets

In the case of the office supplies illustrated, the value assigned was based on the cost of the item. This is known as the COST PRINCI-PLE. The cost assigned to the asset not only includes the purchase price, but also transportation charges, installation charges, and any other costs associated with placing the asset into use by the organization.

While every form of organization previously mentioned uses accounting information, we will assume from this point on that we are dealing with a profit-making business. We will further assume that the business is that of a single owner (also proprietorship). A SOLE PROPRIETORSHIP is a business that is formed by one individual. This individual is considered the owner of the business and receives any profits that the business earns and sustains any losses that the business may incur. The assets which the business owns are separate and apart from the assets that the owner may personally own. This is known as the BUSINESS ENTITY CONCEPT.

EXERCISE 6   Mr. Regal, the owner of a limousine service, purchases an automobile from a local car dealer. The purchase price of the automobile is $32,450. There are make-ready charges of $385, delivery charges of $265, and applicable state sales tax amounting to $2,731.

1. Determine the cost at which the new automobile should be recorded on the books of Mr. Regal's business.
2. If, upon leaving the dealership, Mr. Regal was offered $35,500 for the automobile, at what price should the new automobile be recorded on his records? Why?
3. Does Mr. Regal own the asset automobile? Why or why not?

EXERCISE 7   Mr. Glenn is negotiating to buy a parcel of property for his business. The seller of the property is asking $170,000 for the property. The assessed value of the property for property tax purposes is $125,000. The property is presently insured by the owner for $135,000. Mr. Glenn originally offered the seller $130,000 for the property. Mr. Glenn and the seller have agreed on a purchase price of $150,000. Shortly after the purchase is made by Mr. Glenn, he is offered $175,000 for the same property. At what price would Mr. Glenn record the property on the books of his business?

Recognizing the Proprietor's Ownership

The proprietor in beginning a business contributes assets to the business. These assets contributed may consist of cash, supplies, or equipment. Each asset is assigned a money value based on the cost of the asset to the proprietor. Since the proprietor is also the owner of the business, those assets contributed represent the proprietor's ownership or equity in the business. A record is set up by the accountant to represent the proprietor's ownership in the business. This record is called CAPITAL.

CAPITAL is the ownership of the assets of the business by the proprietor. For every asset that the proprietor contributes to the business there is a corresponding value assigned to the record of proprietor's capital. A term frequently used interchangeably with capital is EQUITY. In this instance, equity represents the ownership of the assets of the business by the proprietor.

EXERCISE 8 Ms. Taylor began a business on April 1, 200-, contributing to the business the following assets: Cash, $3,000; Office Supplies, $275; Office Equipment, $700; Furniture and Fixtures, $2,100. Determine the value of Ms. Taylor's ownership (CAPITAL) in the business.

1. What is the total value of the assets that Ms. Taylor contributed to the business?
2. What is the value of Ms. Taylor's ownership in the business?

Assets = Capital

From the above relationship we can develop a simple equation which relates assets to capital. This equation will be expressed as: ASSETS = CAPITAL. Thus, if Ms. Taylor contributed to the business assets valued at $6,075, the equation would be expressed as:

$$\text{ASSETS} = \text{CAPITAL}$$
$$\$6,075 \quad = \quad \$6,075$$

If at some future date the proprietor contributes additional assets to the business, both the value of the total assets and the value of the capital will increase by the same amount, thus the equation would remain in balance. Should the proprietor decide to take an asset out of the business for personal use, this will cause a corresponding decrease in the value of the total assets and the value of the total capital.

EXERCISE 9 Using the chart presented below, show the effects on the equation caused by the following business transactions. After you have recorded the transactions on the chart, add the individual columns and verify that the equation is still in balance. (Remember that assets are set up in various categories depending upon the nature of the asset. If a business uses an existing asset to acquire another asset, this will only cause a change in assets. There will be no effect on the proprietor's capital. Transactions 4 and 5 should not affect capital; they represent an EXCHANGE OF ASSETS.)

1. The proprietor invested $5,000 cash in the business.
2. The proprietor invested a typewriter valued at $250.
3. The proprietor took $200 out of the business as a permanent reduction in investment.
4. The proprietor purchased supplies for the business, paying for the supplies with $75 in cash from the business.
5. The proprietor purchased an adding machine for $50, paying with cash from the business.

	ASSETS			=	CAPITAL
No.	CASH +	SUPPLIES +	EQUIPMENT	=	CAPITAL
1					
2					
3					
4					
5					
TOTAL					

EXERCISE 10

List the following headings on a sheet of paper. Cash + Accounts Receivable + Store Supplies + Office Supplies + Furniture and Fixtures + Equipment = Capital.

Record the following business transactions in the appropriate columns. Identify each by number and after each transaction is recorded, verify that the equation is in balance by FOOTING (adding) the columns. The proprietor of the business:

1. Invested $20,000 in the business.
2. Purchased furniture and fixtures for use in the business paying $1,200 in cash.
3. Purchased store supplies paying $170 in cash.
4. Purchased equipment for use in the business paying $1,500 in cash.
5. Loaned a business associate $750 in cash which he promised to repay in ten days.
6. Contributed office supplies to the business that had a value of $60.
7. Received a check for $300 in partial payment of the amount that his associate has owed him.
8. Permanently reduced his investment in the business by taking out a desk worth $100 and $900 in cash.
9. Returned equipment previously purchased and received a cash refund of $175.
10. Bought office supplies paying $65 in cash.

Expressing Borrowed Assets

In the previous two exercises we practiced recording business transactions that affected assets and capital of the business. The owner of a sole proprietorship will use the assets he or she contributed to the business to acquire other assets that the business needs to function. In some circumstances there may be inadequate assets available to meet the needs of the business. When this situation occurs, it may be necessary for the business to obtain the needed assets from other sources.

The most obvious way in which additional assets can be obtained for the business is by borrowing. When cash or any other asset is borrowed, the firm is said to have incurred a debt or liability. Regardless of what is borrowed, it is customary to repay the obligation in cash. When the obligation is initially incurred, the business obtains the asset borrowed. At the same time, a liability is incurred which has to be recognized as an obligation of the business. Until the debt is paid, the creditor (the person to whom the money is owed) is said to have a claim upon the assets originally loaned. A LIABILITY is defined as the ownership of the assets of a business by its *creditors*. Notice that this definition of a liability is identical to the definition of capital, except for the last word. (Capital is the ownership of the assets of a business by the *proprietor*). Since a liability is, by definition, not an asset or ownership as evidenced by capital, it becomes necessary to establish a third classification of items, namely that of liabilities. Since a liability is closely associated with the ownership of the business assets, it is shown on the equation on the same side as capital. The term *equity* as previously discussed was used synonymously with *capital*. *Equity* signifies ownership, thus it represents both capital and liabilities in this case. The final form of the equation, which is generally known as the ACCOUNTING EQUATION, is:

$$ASSETS = LIABILITIES + CAPITAL$$

Liabilities may take many forms. If the owner of a business has to borrow money and orally promises to pay back the obligation, this obligation would be known as an ACCOUNT PAYABLE. If the promise made took the form of a written document, such as an IOU or a promissory note, then the obligation would be known as a NOTE PAYABLE. Regardless of the form that the actual obligation takes, its placement in the accounting equation would remain the same. Let's assume the following information:

$$
\begin{array}{ccccc}
ASSETS & = & LIABILITIES & + & CAPITAL \\
\$14,000 & = & -0- & + & \$14,000
\end{array}
$$

The business borrows $6,000 from a local bank. What would happen to the various classifications within the accounting equation? Show the new totals (balances) as a result of recording the transaction.

$$
\begin{array}{ccccc}
ASSETS & = & LIABILITIES & + & CAPITAL \\
\$14,000 & = & 0 & + & \$14,000 \\
+\ \$\ 6,000 & = & +\ \$6,000 & + & 0 \\
\hline
\$20,000 & = & \$6,000 & + & \$14,000
\end{array}
$$

If at a later date the loan is repaid, determine the effects of the repayment on the total value of the assets, liabilities, and capital.

EXERCISE 11

Calculate the value of the missing element of the accounting equation in each of the numbered situations:

	ASSETS	=	LIABILITIES	+	CAPITAL
1.	$6,000	=	$2,000	+	?
2.	$5,500	=	?	+	$2,300
3.	?	=	$4,500	+	$3,650
4.	$10,550	=	$485	+	?
5.	$8,400	=	?	+	$8,400

EXERCISE 12

A. L. Brandon is the owner of the Brandon Small Appliance Repair Shop. On January 1, 200-, the assets, liabilities, and proprietor's capital in the business were: Cash, $2,000; Accounts Receivable, $400; Supplies, $500; Equipment, $6,000; Accounts Payable, $900; A. L. Brandon, Capital, $8,000. The business transactions for the month of January were as follows:

1. Paid $300 of the outstanding accounts payable.
2. Received $100 on account (part payment) from customers.
3. Purchased $250 worth of supplies on account (on credit).
4. Returned a defective piece of equipment that was purchased last month and received a cash refund of $1,200.
5. Borrowed $1,000 from a supplier, giving word to repay the loan in thirty days.
6. Paid creditor $200 on account (part payment).
7. Purchased equipment for $800, giving $200 cash and promising to pay the balance in sixty days.
8. Bought supplies paying $65 cash.
9. Received a $250 check from customer on account.

Set up a chart using a form similar to that in Exercise 10. Record the January 1 balances immediately under the various assets, liability, and capital item headings. Record the business transactions listed above. Be certain to label each transaction with the corresponding number assigned, and foot the columns after each transaction has been recorded to verify the balance of the equation. Notice that every business transaction has a minimum of two changes. Transaction 7 has three changes, but notice that the dollar change is equal, thus the equation in this case, as with all the business transactions, remains in balance.

What Are Revenue, Expenses, and Profit?

Every business exists primarily to earn a profit. This profit is realized through REVENUE received by an organization as a result of the sale of a service or product by that business. Our primary concern will be with a business that provides a service. Examples of persons in service-oriented occupations are accountants, lawyers, doctors, beauticians, real estate and insurance brokers, and travel agents. The resulting profits of a service business belong to the owner (sole proprietor) of the enterprise. The revenue generated through the services provided are recognized as an increase in the capital of the owner. This is justified because the profits that the business earns belong to the owner of the business, and the revenue received should be reflected in the record of ownership.

RECORDING REVENUE

If revenue of $500 cash is received by the business, this revenue should be recorded as an increase in cash of $500 and a resulting increase in proprietor's capital of $500. Revenue may be received in forms other than cash. An organization may receive payment for services rendered in the form of other assets such as supplies, equipment, and even someone's word to pay at a future time (accounts receivable). The effects on the accounting equation will still result in an increase in the specific asset received and a corresponding increase in capital.

An increase in the proprietor's capital will result from not only an investment by the owner, but also as a result of revenue received for services provided.

RECORDING EXPENSES

Profit and revenue are not the same. PROFIT represents the income that a business has earned after certain adjustments have been made. Revenue is one component which permits the recognition of profit. Every business, regardless of its nature, must incur certain costs in order to operate. These costs are known as EXPENSES. Expenses are generally referred to as the "costs of doing business." Examples of expenses that businesses incur are rent expense, insurance expense, salary expense, and supplies expense. Expenses are also known as "necessary evils," because they must be incurred in order to obtain revenue which ultimately will be translated into profits for the business. While we learned that revenue causes an increase in capital, an expense will have the opposite effect and result in a decrease in capital.

If rent expense for the month amounting to $300 is paid, this will result in a decrease in the asset cash and a corresponding decrease in proprietor's capital.

A decrease in the proprietor's capital will result from a permanent reduction in the owner's investment in the business, from the proprietor taking assets out of the business, and now as a result of the payment of an expense.

Transaction	Effect on Proprietor's Capital
Owner's investment	Increase
Owner's withdrawals	Decrease
Revenues	Increase
Expenses	Decrease

HOW REVENUE AND EXPENSES AFFECT CAPITAL

When the proprietor makes the initial investment or subsequent investments in the business, this investment is said to be PERMANENT in nature. An assumption is made that the assets contributed through the investment will be used in the business on an ongoing basis to maintain the business and contribute toward future growth. The revenue and expenses which affect capital are also used to determine if the business has earned a profit. Since profit is determined periodically, these records (revenue and expenses) are considered to be TEMPORARY in nature. Also, when the proprietor borrows assets from the business, this withdrawal is considered temporary.

PERMANENT CAPITAL = Proprietor's Capital (Investment)
TEMPORARY CAPITAL = Revenue, Expenses, Withdrawals

In order to distinguish temporary capital from permanent capital, the accountant maintains separate records for each specific kind of temporary capital account. An ACCOUNT is a separate record maintained for each category of asset, liability, permanent, and temporary capital record. The proprietor's capital account is only affected by changes which are considered to be permanent in nature. Business transactions which result in the receipt of revenue or the payment of expenses will be recorded in separate specific accounts. These accounts will increase and decrease in the same way as if the changes were made directly to the proprietor's capital account. Just as revenue would be considered as an increase in the proprietor's capital, it is expressed as an increase in the specific revenue account. An expense, as a cost of doing business, has a decreasing effect on the proprietor's capital. Business transactions directly affecting these expenses, while increasing the value of the individual expense, still have a decreasing effect on the proprietor's capital.

EXERCISE 13

Upon finishing law school, Carolyn Goldstein set up a law practice. During the first month, she completed the following business transactions:

1. Invested $3,000 cash in the business.
2. Purchased a law library for $1,200 cash.
3. Received $500 for services rendered.
4. Purchased office supplies on credit for $150.
5. Paid Rent for the month amounting to $300.
6. Sent a bill for $1,100 for services rendered.
7. Sent a check for $50 in part payment of accounts payable.
8. Received $200 from customers as a result of services previously rendered and recognized.
9. Sent a check for $60 to the local utility company for costs incurred in beginning service.
10. Borrowed $200 from the business (show the effect of this loan in the Carolyn Goldstein drawing account).

Set up a chart using a form similar to that in Exercise 12. The following account headings are to be used: Assets—Cash, Accounts

Receivable, Office Supplies, Law Library; Liabilities—Accounts Payable; Capital—Carolyn Goldstein, Capital; Carolyn Goldstein, Drawing; Income from Services; Rent Expense; Utilities Expense. Record the business transactions listed above making certain to verify the balance in the accounting equation as a result of each business transaction. Remember, revenue increases capital. Expenses decrease capital. Drawing decreases capital.

Summing Up

Accounting is the art of organizing, maintaining, recording, and analyzing financial activities.

Accounting information is used by managers of all business organizations. Others who may have an indirect financial interest in the organization also make use of accounting information.

Business transactions represent economic events that affect the financial condition of the business. The position of the organization is represented by assets, liabilities, and capital.

Assets represent anything that is owned and has money value. Assets are organized into groups. These groups are current assets; investments; property, plant, and equipment; and intangible assets.

The assignment of costs to all noncurrent assets is based upon the cost principle. The cost to be assigned to the asset includes all costs necessary to make the asset operational for the business.

Liabilities are the claims upon the assets of the business by its creditors. Liabilities may either be short-term or long-term obligations. Accounts payable expected to be paid within a year are short-term obligations. Notes payable, if not payable within a year, are considered long-term liabilities.

Capital is the ownership of the assets of the business by the proprietor.

The accounting equation is:

$$ASSETS = LIABILITIES + CAPITAL$$

Capital may be divided into two categories: permanent and temporary. Permanent capital represents the investment that the owner makes in the business. Temporary capital represents revenue, expenses, and drawing (withdrawal).

All businesses are in business for the purpose of earning a profit. This profit can be determined by comparing revenue with expenses. The excess of revenue over expenses represents profit. If expenses exceed revenue, the result is known as a loss. Resulting profit or loss will cause a change in the proprietor's capital.

CHAPTER 2

FINANCIAL STATEMENTS

What Are Financial Statements?

We learned that one of the functions of the accountant is to keep track of accounting information. The accountant is also called upon to prepare various reports from the accounting information. There are three basic reports that the business organization uses on a regular basis. These reports are the:

INCOME STATEMENT

STATEMENT OF CAPITAL

BALANCE SHEET

These financial statements present the accounting information in formal reports that tell interested groups, such as managers, creditors, prospective investors, and governmental agencies, how the business is doing. These reports are prepared from information obtained from the various business transactions that the business recorded. Thus, transactions involving assets, liabilities, permanent and temporary capital become the data used in the preparation of the financial statements.

Financial statements are prepared at least once a year. The period of time covered in a statement is known as the "accounting period." An accounting period may follow the calendar, in which case it begins on January 1 and ends on December 31 of the same year. A business having such a system is said to have a calendar-year accounting period. Any business that has an accounting period consisting of twelve months other than a calendar year is generally known as having a fiscal-year accounting period. Organizations may prepare financial statements for periods of time that are less than the one-year accounting period. When such statements are prepared they are generally known as "interim statements." An interim statement is prepared for a period of time other than a fiscal year or calendar year. Examples of interim statements would be statements prepared for six-month, three-month, or even monthly periods. Regardless of the period of time covered by the individual financial statements, the kind of information presented by the various statements does not change.

The Income Statement

The income statement is a report that presents the revenue, expenses, and resulting net income or net loss for a business for a period of time. The income statement is divided into two parts. The first part is known as the "heading" and the second part is known as the "body" of the report. The heading of the income statement asks three questions:

Whose business is it?

What statement is being prepared?

When is it being prepared?

The body of the income statement lists the revenue and expenses. A comparison of these two items will result in either a net income or net loss. Where total revenue exceeds total expenses, the excess represents the net income. Where the total of the expenses exceeds the total revenue, then the difference represents a net loss.

Note the form of the following income statement.

Regal Limousine Service
Income Statement
For the Year Ended December 31, 200-

Revenue:		
Limousine Rental		$24,000
Expenses:		
Repairs Expense	$ 2,350	
Salaries Expense	14,500	
Gas and Oil Expense	3,000	
Total Expenses		19,850
Net Income		$ 4,150

Notice that the date assigned to the income statement covers a period of time. This is true of all income statements regardless of whether they are prepared for a one-year accounting period or for an interim period.

EXERCISE 1   Referring to the Regal Limousine Service income statement, answer the following questions:

1. What is the period of time covered by the income statement?
2. What is the source of the revenue?
3. What are the total revenues?
4. What are the total expenses?
5. Why is there a resulting net income?
6. Is this statement an interim statement? Why or why not?
7. Who does the net income belong to? Why or why not?

EXERCISE 2   Bambi Sands owns the New Wave Beauty Parlor. From the information listed below, prepare an income statement for the month ending January 31, 200-.

Revenue from Sales	$1,350	Rent Expense	$175
Salaries Expense	500	Supplies Expense	300
Service Revenue	4,580	Advertising Expense	850

The Statement of Capital

We learned in an earlier discussion that the proprietor's capital account represents his or her ownership in the assets of the business. Part of the discussion centered around the fact that whatever net income the business earns also belongs to the owner. The owner has the right either to withdraw the profits that the business earns or to reinvest the income in the business. If the latter approach is chosen, then the profits would be added to the proprietor's capital record. If the proprietor withdraws from the business more than the business earns, this results in a decrease in proprietor's capital. Whichever approach is taken, it must be reflected in the record of the proprietor's ownership. The statement of capital shows the changes that take place in the proprietor's capital over a period of time (usually an accounting period).

Because some information used in the statement of capital comes from the income statement, the statement of capital is prepared after the income statement. The statement of capital consists of two parts: the heading and the body of the statement. The heading answers the same three questions as the income statement did: Whose statement? What statement? When is it prepared?

Note the form of the following statement of capital.

Regal Limousine Service
Statement of Capital
For the Year Ended December 31, 200-

Avery Regal, (Beginning) Capital, Jan. 1, 200-		$23,200
Plus: Net Income for the Year	$4,150	
Less: Avery Regal, Drawing	3,200	
Net increase in Capital		950
Avery Regal, (Ending) Capital, Dec. 31, 200-		$24,150

The body of the statement of capital shows what has happened to the proprietor's record of ownership in the business during the year. If the proprietor had made an additional investment in the business, this would have appeared as an additional increase, in a fashion similar to showing the income for the year. Changes in the proprietor's capital from the beginning of an accounting period to the end of that period, or a period as indicated by an interim statement, will occur as a result of the following situations:

1. A permanent increase in the proprietor's investment in the business. (Addition to Capital)
2. A permanent decrease in the proprietor's investment in the business. (Subtraction from Capital)
3. The proprietor's withdrawal of assets from the business, usually in anticipation of profits. (Subtraction from Capital)
4. The recognition of net income for the period. (Addition to Capital)
5. The recognition of a net loss for the period. (Subtraction from Capital)

In the Regal Limousine Services statement of capital, if the subtraction from capital had exceeded the addition to capital, this would have resulted in a net decrease in capital, which would have been subtracted from the original capital to arrive at the new capital balance.

EXERCISE 3   Prepare a statement of capital for the New Wave Beauty Parlor for the month ending January 31, 200-. The proprietor, Bambi Sands, had a beginning capital balance of $14,500. During the month she withdrew $1,600 in anticipation of profits. The net income earned for the month amounted to $4,105.

EXERCISE 4   Albert Bradley owns the Bradley Cleaning Service. On January 1, 200-, Mr. Bradley's capital balance is $20,500. During the year the following activities affected his ownership (equity) in the business: net income for the year was $18,300; on March 23, 200-, the proprietor made an additional permanent investment in the business of $5,000; during the year the proprietor withdrew assets worth $15,600 from the business. Prepare a statement of capital for the year ended December 31, 200-.

The Balance Sheet

The balance sheet shows the financial position of a business on a specific date. It represents a detailed presentation of the accounting equation. In chapter 1 the final form of the accounting equation was:

$$\text{ASSETS} = \text{LIABILITIES} + \text{CAPITAL}$$

The balance sheet provides a detailed listing of the various assets that a business owns, the liabilities that are owed to the creditors, and the value of the proprietor's ownership of the assets of the business. It is known as the balance sheet, because upon its completion it must be in balance. In other words, the total value of the business's assets must be in agreement with the total value of the liabilities and capital (total equity) of the business. It is cumulative in nature in that it reports the results of all the financial activities of the business since its formation.

The balance sheet may be prepared at any moment in time. However, it is usually prepared following the preparation of the income statement and the statement of capital. This is due to the fact that the balance sheet relies on the information obtained from the statement of capital in order for it to be properly and completely prepared. The capital balance found on the balance sheet is obtained from the new capital found on the last line of the statement of capital. While the heading of the balance sheet is basically the same as that of the previous financial statements discussed, it does differ in one important respect. The date assigned to the balance sheet does not cover a period of time, but rather represents a moment in time. If we were to prepare a balance sheet on January 31, 200-, it would reflect the financial position of the business at that time. This balance sheet would be different from one prepared on the previous or the following day.

THE REPORT AND ACCOUNT FORMS

There are two forms that the balance sheet takes: (1) the report form and (2) the account form. While both forms provide identical information, their appearance differs according to the use to be made of the forms by the accountant.

REPORT FORM

Regal Limousine Service
Balance Sheet
December 31, 200-

Assets

Cash	$16,000	
Accounts Receivable	2,500	
Automobile Supplies	1,200	
Limousines	38,000	
Total Assets		$57,700

Liabilities and Capital

Accounts Payable	$ 3,200	
Notes Payable	30,350	
Total Liabilities		$33,550
Avery Regal, Capital		24,150
Total Liabilities and Capital		$57,700

ACCOUNT FORM

Regal Limousine Service
Balance Sheet
December 31, 200-

Assets		**Liabilities and Capital**	
Cash	$16,000	Accounts Payable	$ 3,200
Accounts Receivable	2,500	Notes Payable	30,350
Automobile Supplies	1,200	Total Liabilities	33,550
Limousines	38,000	Avery Regal, Capital	24,150
Total Assets	$57,700	Total Liabilities & Capital	$57,700

EXERCISE 5   Referring to either form of the balance sheet just illustrated, answer the following questions:

1. When was the balance sheet prepared?
2. How does the date on this balance sheet differ from the date on the statement of capital or the income statement?
3. Can Avery Regal purchase another limousine for the business paying cash of $19,900? Why or why not?
4. What is the total equity of the Regal Limousine Service?
5. What is the total amount of Avery Regal's claim against the total assets of the business?
6. What is the amount of the creditors' claims against the assets of the business?
7. What is the net income for the period?
8. What was the value of Avery Regal's ownership in this business on January 1, 200- (beginning of the accounting period)?
9. In order to prepare this financial statement, which business reports had to precede it and why?
10. What is the difference between the account form and the report form of the balance sheet?

EXERCISE 6   The New Wave Beauty Parlor had the following assets, liabilities, and proprietor's capital as of January 31, 200-: Cash, $2,380; Accounts Receivable, $1,400; Beauty Equipment, $15,000; Bambi Sands, Capital,?; Notes Payable, $2,275; Beauty Supplies, $800; Accounts Payable, $300. Prepare an account-form balance sheet for the New Wave Beauty Parlor. Note that the proprietor's capital account balance is not provided. Using the accounting equation will enable you to determine the capital balance.

EXERCISE 7   Betty Brody is the owner of the City-Wide Tax Service. For the year ended April 30, 200-, this service business had the following information; Cash, $12,500; Accounts Receivable, $3,700; Office Furniture and Fixtures, $11,300; Office Machines and Computers, $15,000; Automobile, $9,500; Accounts Payable, $1,700; Betty Brody, Capital, $32,000; Betty Brody, Drawing, $18,600; Revenue from Income Tax Preparation, $21,300; Revenue from Monthly Clients, $43,800; Salaries Expense, $12,500; Advertising Expense, $900; Rent Expense, $6,000; Automobile Expense, $1,300; General Office Expenses, $7,500.

Prepare the City-Wide Tax Service's income statement, statement of capital, and balance sheet for the year ended April 30, 200-.

EXERCISE 8   Based on your reading and the completion of the exercises in chapter 2, answer the following questions:

1. What specific names have been given to the three accounting reports we have discussed?
2. What is the order of the preparation of the accounting reports? Why?

3. What is the name of the accounting report that may show either a net profit or net loss for an accounting period?
4. What are the two main parts of the body of the income statement known as?
5. If total revenue exceeds total expenses for an accounting period, what is the difference called?
6. What accounting report shows the change that may take place in proprietorship during the accounting period?
7. What are the two primary items that bring about a change in proprietorship during the accounting period?
8. What business record shows the results of the proprietor's borrowing assets from the business, usually in anticipation of profits?
9. What temporary capital records are found in the income statement?
10. What temporary capital record appears on the statement of capital?
11. In the body of a balance sheet, what are the two sections called?
12. Of the two forms of the balance sheet, which form more closely approximates the accounting equation in form?

THE CLASSIFIED BALANCE SHEET

Regardless of the form of the balance sheet prepared, every balance sheet we have prepared so far has been classified according to categories of items. Assets, liabilities, and capital were grouped separately.

Classifying Assets

Assets we have learned may be further grouped according to the degree of liquidity or the expected conversion to cash or the time it takes to use up the asset. For analytical purposes, assets are classified as follows:

CURRENT ASSETS are cash and other assets that can reasonably be expected to be converted to cash, used up, or sold within one year or less. Thus, on the classified balance sheet, current assets would be listed first, based on their relative degree of liquidity (readily converted to cash).

INVESTMENTS may be either short- or long-term assets depending on the nature of the investments. Generally, bonds are considered long-term investments, whereas stocks may be either long- or short-term investments. They generally appear immediately following current assets on the classified balance sheet.

PROPERTY, PLANT, AND EQUIPMENT are long-term in nature and are used in the continuing operations of the business and are expected to have a useful life of more than one year. They are also known as plant assets and as fixed assets.

INTANGIBLE ASSETS are usually long-term in nature and are traditionally shown after plant assets. Examples are patents, copyrights, and goodwill.

Classifying Liabilities

Liabilities are classified in a similar manner. Liabilities are considered to be CURRENT LIABILITIES if the obligation is to be settled within one year or within the current accounting period. These debts are usually settled with the payment of current assets. Examples of current liabilities are accounts payable, taxes payable, salaries payable, and notes payable (if the obligation is due within one year). Following current liabilities on the balance sheet are LONG-TERM LIABILI-TIES, which are usually payable in more than a year. Examples of long-term liabilities include bonds payable and mortgages payable. In the year in which a long-term liability becomes payable, it is usually converted to a current liability (appearing under the current liability heading of the balance sheet).

CLASSIFIED BALANCE SHEET—REPORT FORM

Regal Limousine Service
Balance Sheet
December 31, 200-

Assets

CURRENT ASSETS		
Cash	$16,000	
Accounts Receivable	2,500	
Automobile Supplies	1,200	
Total Current Assets		19,700
FIXED ASSETS		
Limousines		38,000
Total Assets		$57,700

Liabilities and Capital

CURRENT LIABILITIES		
Accounts Payable	$ 3,200	
Notes Payable (current)	3,035	
Total Current Liabilities		$ 6,235
LONG-TERM LIABILITIES		
Notes Payable		27,315
Total Liabilities		33,550
Avery Regal, Capital		24,150
Total Liabilities and Capital		57,700

EXERCISE 9 Prepare a classified balance sheet for the North Shore Realty Co. As of December 31, 200-, the following assets, liabilities, and proprietor's capital appeared for the business:

Cash	$2,960
Office Equipment	2,005
Insurance	30
Office Salaries Payable	60
Samuel Fields, Capital	6,900
Office Supplies	75
Accounts Payable	65
Automobile	2,030
Accounts Receivable	125
Mortgage Payable	200

Summing Up

All businesses are organized and maintain records based on an accounting period. An accounting period covers a twelve-month period based either on the calendar year or any other complete twelve-month period known as a fiscal period. Whether the business is on a calendar or fiscal year, it must prepare various statements to satisfy the needs of governmental organizations (federal, state, and local), as well as other interested parties. In addition, the accountant may be called upon to prepare these statements for a period of time less than a complete accounting period. These reports are known as interim reports. There are basically three financial reports that are prepared: the income statement, the capital statement, and the balance sheet. Each statement provides different information.

The income statement compares the revenue earned for a period of time with the expenses incurred for the same period. If the revenue exceeds the expenses, the excess is known as net income. When total expenses are greater than revenue, the resulting difference is known as a net loss.

The capital statement reflects the change that takes place in the proprietor's capital account as a result of business activities of the firm. A change in the investment, the recognition of net income or loss, the recognition of proprietor's drawing in anticipation of profit, all have an effect on the proprietor's capital account at the end of the specific accounting period.

The balance sheet shows the financial position and condition of the organization at a specific moment in time. A balance sheet consists of a detailed listing of the values of the various assets, liabilities, and proprietor's capital at a specific date. The balance sheet relies on the preparation of the statement of capital for the determination of the new proprietor's capital balance. The statement of capital also relies on the income statement preparation for the determination of the change in capital for the particular period. Thus, the order of preparation of the financial statement will never change due to this relationship.

In addition to listing assets, liabilities, and proprietor's capital, a more detailed balance sheet known as a classified balance sheet may be prepared. The primary benefit of the classified balance sheet is that it categorizes assets and liabilities in significant groups according to the useful life of the items. In general, assets that can be expected to be used up or converted to cash within one year, and liabilities which will be paid within one year, are classified as current items. Those assets and liabilities that are expected to exist for more than one year are generally grouped as long-term items.

Remember that up to this point we have been dealing exclusively with a sole proprietorship form of business. The form and content of financial statements vary according to the nature of a particular business organization. At this point, however, it would be counterproductive to illustrate corporate or partnership financial statements. They will be presented in future chapters dealing specifically with those forms of business organizations.

RECORDING BUSINESS TRANSACTIONS

What Are Business Transactions?

Business transactions are any business activities that affect what a business owns and owes, as well as the ownership of the business. We have learned in chapter 1 to keep track of business transactions by using an expanded form of the accounting equation. Most businesses, however, are involved in daily business transactions so numerous as to make this method unwieldy. Since we cannot expect an accountant to remember everything that has happened to the value of a specific asset or keep a mental note of all the numerous records of an organization, another method must be devised to record business transactions.

INFORMATION TO KEEP TRACK OF

When we added a business transaction to the accounting equation, we showed the change that took place in the specific record. This increase or decrease is an important part of our record, but we also want to keep track of the *date* that a particular transaction takes place. Some form of explanation is also helpful, especially if the specific item acquired might not be apparent from the title of the record we maintain for it. Thus, the three kinds of information that every business transaction should contain are:

1. The date of the transaction;
2. An explanation of the transaction (where necessary);
3. The amount of the transaction and whether it represents an increase or a decrease.

CHANGES RESULTING FROM A BUSINESS TRANSACTION

Every business transaction involves at least two changes. A review of the business transactions affecting the accounting equation will vividly illustrate this statement. If we were to acquire the asset equipment and give in payment the asset cash, we can see that both records are affected.

This is known as double entry. If we were to acquire the asset supplies and at the same time also acquire the asset equipment as a result of paying cash, this would also be considered double entry. This is known as double entry because the total value of the two assets obtained would be equal to the value of the asset cash given up.

WHERE TO RECORD BUSINESS TRANSACTIONS

Business transactions are recorded in a record that is known as an ACCOUNT. Each asset, liability, and capital record that we maintain would be kept on a separate account page. The purpose of the account is to facilitate the recording of the essential information generated by the business transaction. The account is represented by a separate page for each asset, liability, and capital record. These individual account pages are kept in a bound or looseleaf type binder known as a LEDGER. If we were to record the purchase of equipment and a resulting payment of cash, it would be necessary to set up two accounts in the ledger. The first ledger account would be headed with the name "Cash." The second ledger account would have the heading "Equipment." Changes made to these respective assets would then be recorded on the specific account pages.

The Account

THE STANDARD FORM

The standard form of the ledger account is very similar to the basic account form of the balance sheet. The account form of the balance sheet consists of two sides. In its simplest form the ledger account is known as the "T" account because it looks like the capital letter "T," just as the account form of the balance sheet does. The standard form of the account is illustrated below. This is the most widely used form.

Account Name   Account No.

Date	Item	PR	Debit	Date	Item	PR	Credit

The three major parts of the account form are: (1) the account title, (2) the DEBIT side, and (3) the CREDIT side. The account is divided into two equal parts. The left, or debit, side has provisions for the date, item (explanation), and amount. The right, or credit, side also has provisions for the date, item (explanation), and amount.

MAKING ENTRIES IN LEDGER ACCOUNTS

Each part of a business transaction will have an affect on a specific ledger account. The effect will either be an increase or a decrease in the existing account. In order for an account to exist it must have a Balance. This BALANCE represents the value or worth of the specific account at a moment in time. When a balance sheet is prepared, it represents the balances from the accounting equation at a moment in time. The value of each asset, liability, and proprietor's capital as shown on the balance sheet can then become the basis for establishing the individual accounts in the ledger. Using the account form of the balance sheet provides an outline of how the balances in the individual ledger accounts should be shown. The following simple balance sheet will be used to illustrate recording the beginning balances in the ledger accounts:

Regal Limousine Service
Balance Sheet
December 3, 200-

Assets		Liabilities and Capital	
Cash	$16,000	Accounts Payable	$ 3,200
		A. Regal, Capital	12,800
Total Assets	$16,000	Total Liabilities & Capital	$16,000

Note the side of the balance sheet on which the assets are shown. Since the assets are shown on the left side of the balance sheet, we will show this balance on the left side of the ledger account for this asset and *all* assets. The beginning balance of all asset accounts are shown on the left side (debit side) of the account.

Cash
_____
$16,000 |

The liability and proprietor's capital account balances are shown on the right side of the balance sheet. The beginning balances of *all* liability and proprietor's permanent capital accounts will be shown on the same side as they appear on the balance sheet. Thus the beginning balances of *all* liabilities and proprietor's permanent capital accounts will be shown on the right side (credit side) of the ledger account.

Accounts Payable   A. Regal, Capital
_____   _____
| $3,200 | $12,800

RECORDING ASSET CHANGES

The beginning balances for all assets are recorded on the debit or left side of the account. This balance on the ledger account will appear in the same position as it appears on the balance sheet. The asset account cash is said to have a debit balance.

When we wish to record an increase in any asset account, the increase is shown on the same side as the beginning balance of the account. If we were to show an increase in the asset cash, this increase appears on the same side of the ledger account as did the original balance.

Since the balance and any subsequent increase is shown on the debit or left side of the ledger account, any decrease in an asset account will be shown on the opposite side of the account. A decrease in any asset account will be shown on the right, or credit, side of the account. The following illustrative account will apply to all assets:

Asset Accounts

Beginning Balance Increases	Decreases

If we wished to know the new balance in the account after changes have taken place in it, we would add both sides of the account and determine the difference between the totals. The excess of debits over credits would give us a resulting balance known as a DEBIT BALANCE. This is a normal balance for an asset account. If the resulting balance was zero, this would indicate that total debits equaled total credits and that the asset has no value at that point in time. It is possible for an asset account to have a credit balance. This, however, is quite unusual, so we will defer this discussion to a later chapter.

RECORDING CHANGES IN LIABILITY AND PERMANENT CAPITAL ACCOUNTS

The beginning balance of the proprietor's permanent capital account and all liability accounts are shown on the same side of the account as the side that they appear on in the balance sheet. To record an increase in capital or a liability account we would credit the account. An increase in a capital or liability account is shown on the same side as the beginning balance in that account. If we were to record an additional obligation in the form of an accounts payable, this would be credited to the liability account, accounts payable. Any time a liability account is credited, this results in an increase in the value of that account. Should the proprietor make an additional investment in the company, this would result in an increase in the ownership as reflected in the proprietor's capital account. To record this increase, the proprietor's capital account would be credited. The beginning balance and any increase in a liability and permanent capital account are recorded as credits to the account. When an account is being credited, you are recording the entry to the right side of the account.

When a liability or permanent capital is to be decreased, this reduction is shown as an entry on the left side or debit side of the particular account. Any time there is to be a decrease in the value of a liability or permanent capital, it is recorded as a debit. The following account illustrates where changes take place in the ledger account:

All Liability and Permanent Capital Accounts

Decrease	Beginning Balance Increase

If we are interested in finding the new balance for any liability or permanent capital account, we would total both the debit and credit columns of each account. If we were then to subtract the total debits from the total credits, the resulting difference would either represent a credit balance or a zero balance. When total credits exceed total debits, the resulting difference is called a credit balance. When total credits are equal to total debits, a zero balance will result.

EXERCISE 1 Answer the following questions to test your understanding of the materials just presented:

1. Where does the accountant keep track of the changes in the value of specific assets, liabilities, and the proprietor's capital?
2. What is the bound or looseleaf type book in which individual records of assets, liabilities, and proprietor's capital are kept?
3. What are the three kinds of information that appear on each side of the "T" account?
4. What is the left side of the ledger account known as?
5. What is the right side of the ledger account called?
6. On which side of the account are the beginning balances for assets shown?
7. On which side of the account do we show increases in assets?
8. On which side of the account do we show the beginning balances for the proprietor's permanent capital and all liabilities?
9. On which side of the account do we show increases in the value of the various liabilities and proprietor's permanent capital?
10. Where are decreases in the value of assets, liabilities, and proprietor's permanent capital recorded in the account?
11. What does the term "balance" refer to?
12. What does the term "double entry" mean?
13. What document may assist us in remembering where to record the beginning balance for an item?
14. How may we determine the balance in a ledger account after transactions have been recorded in it?

EXERCISE 2 From the following balance sheet, set up the ledger accounts in "T" form and record the beginning balances. Be certain to head up the account properly and also date each entry in the individual accounts to correspond with the date of the balance sheet.

Jill Baxter
Balance Sheet
January 1, 200-

ASSETS

Cash	$ 4,000
Service Supplies	2,000
Furniture and Fixtures	7,000
Total Assets	$13,000

LIABILITIES AND CAPITAL

Accounts Payable	$ 2,000
Jill Baxter, Capital	11,000
Total Liabilities and Capital	$13,000

EXERCISE 3   Using the ledger accounts completed in Exercise 2, record the following business transactions for the month of January 200-

Jan.   **4**   Received cash amounting to $5,000 as a result of returning furniture and fixtures that had recently been purchased.

   8   Sent out a check for $600 in partial payment of the accounts payable.

   14   Jill Baxter, the proprietor made an additional investment in the business by contributing furniture and fixtures valued at $1,500.

   26   Purchased additional service supplies for $200. Agreed to pay the obligation in thirty days.

   31   Purchased service supplies paying cash of $50.

After you have recorded the transactions in the appropriate ledger accounts, find the balances in the respective accounts. After you have found the balances, prepare a balance sheet for Jill Baxter, dated January 31, 200-. Remember to use the balances that you have just determined from the individual ledger accounts.

ANALYZING BUSINESS TRANSACTIONS

The process of recording business transactions as in Exercise 3 should be done using the process of analyzing the various business transactions. To merely debit cash and credit furniture and fixtures for $5,000 on January 4, 200- is not sufficient. While the entry is correct, there is no indication of what has taken place.

The analysis for the January 4 entry should be:

1. The asset cash increased; therefore, we debit the account.
2. The asset furniture and fixtures decreased; therefore, we credit the account.

Analysis will always entail classifying the account as either an asset, liability, or form of capital. Then it is necessary to indicate the change and whether the change is a debit or a credit.

The analysis of the transaction on January 26 would be:

1. The asset service supplies increased; therefore, we debit the account.
2. The liability account, accounts payable increased; therefore, we credit the account.

The analysis of the transaction of January 15 would be as follows:

1. The asset furniture and fixtures increased; therefore, we debit the account.
2. The capital account, Jill Baxter, capital, increased; therefore, we credit the account.

It is obvious that the accountant must be thoroughly familiar with how to record an increase and a decrease in the various accounts.

RECORDING TRANSACTIONS IN TEMPORARY CAPITAL ACCOUNTS

Ledger accounts, in addition to being established for all assets, liabilities, and proprietor's capital, must also be set up for temporary capital accounts. The temporary capital accounts for a sole proprietorship consists of revenue, expenses, and the proprietor's drawing account. Since these accounts are directly related to permanent capital, and will affect proprietorship as evidenced by the statement of capital, changes in these accounts will mirror the changes in permanent capital.

An *increase* in permanent *capital* is recorded as a *credit* to the account. Since revenue represents an increase in capital, all *revenue* entries in the ledger account will be recorded as a *credit*.

A. Regal Capital		Income from Services	
	$10,000		$200

The preparation of the income statement compares revenue with expenses. If the resulting difference is net income, it is the net income that is shown as an increase in capital. If there were no expenses, then total revenue would cause a direct increase in capital. Since the accountant must keep track of expenses as well as revenue, specific expense accounts are established. Since expenses have a decreasing effect on net income, they would also cause an indirect reduction in permanent capital. Just as a *decrease* in proprietor's *capital* is recorded as a *debit*, the recognition of an *expense* on the ledger account will be recorded as a *debit*. All expenses recorded in their respective accounts are recorded as debits. As the amount of the same expense is recorded numerous times during the month (e.g., salaries expense), each entry is recorded as a debit. As the total value of the expense increases, the proprietor's capital decreases.

The proprietor's drawing or personal account will also decrease the proprietor's permanent capital, as evidenced by the statement of capital. The proprietor uses the DRAWING ACCOUNT to take cash and other assets out of the business, for personal use, in anticipation of profits. If the business were to neither recognize a profit, nor sustain a loss, the drawing account would cause a reduction in permanent capital. Entries to the drawing account would be recorded as a debit. The following "T" accounts illustrate the entries as they would appear in the drawing and expense accounts. Notice their relationship to the normal balance in the proprietor's permanent capital account.

A. Regal, Capital	A. Regal, Drawing	Salaries Expense
\$10,000	\$100	\$50
		50

To find the balances in these ledger accounts, it would simply be a matter of adding (footing) the column in which the amounts appear. The balance in income from services is a credit balance of \$200. The balance in A. Regal, drawing is a debit balance of \$100. The balance in the salaries expense account is a debit balance of \$100.

THE RULE OF DOUBLE-ENTRY ACCOUNTING

We have learned that every business transaction involves at least two changes. The two changes must agree as to amount. The change must cause the accounting equation to maintain its equality. Now that we are recording transactions directly in the ledger accounts, the concept of double-entry accounting must be applied completely.

For every debit entry, there must be a corresponding credit entry of the same amount. When recording a simple business transaction, such as an investment of \$1,000 in the business by the proprietor, the following entries in the ledger accounts would be recorded: Debit the asset cash for \$1,000; credit the permanent proprietor's capital account for \$1,000.

If a compound business transaction such as the purchase of supplies for \$100, equipment for \$300, and the payment of \$400 cash takes place, the following entries to the ledger accounts would be recorded: Debit the asset supplies for \$100; debit the asset equipment for \$300; credit the asset cash for \$400. The requirements of double-entry accounting have been met because the total debits are equal in amount to the total credits. A compound entry may represent any number of accounts being debited and credited at the same time. The important concept to remember is that *total debits* (dollar amounts) *must equal total credits* (dollar amounts) for every business transaction. In this compound entry the \$100 and \$300 (debit entries) = \$400 (credit entry).

EXERCISE 4 Refer to the Regal Limousine Service balance sheet previously presented on page 24. Set up "T" accounts for each item presented on the balance sheet. Be sure to include the date, an explanation, and the amount of the entry in the individual ledger accounts. Also verify double-entry accounting based on the beginning balances in the ledger accounts.

STANDARD FORM FOR THE LEDGER ACCOUNT

Checking your work on Exercise 4 with the solution provided, notice the manner in which the information is placed in the account. The current year is placed at the top of the date column. It does not take up a line, but rather is inserted at the very top of the date column. The month is then abbreviated followed by the day of the month. If another entry debiting cash were to follow, the year and month would not be repeated on the next line. Only the day of the month would appear. If the next entry was in a new year, then the year would appear followed by the month and the day of the month.

Since the information used to set up the ledger accounts came from the balance sheet, the explanation indicates "balances." This entry was *not* the result of a daily business transaction, but was rather an existing balance from the December 31, 200- balance sheet. Subsequent business transactions recorded in these accounts would contain information in the explanation area of the account. In practice where an entry in the ledger account is not unusual, the accountant may choose to omit any explanation.

The amount areas of the ledger account does not include dollar signs. Since the "T" account form does not provide specially ruled columns, it is appropriate to use a comma to separate thousands from hundreds of dollars and a decimal point to distinguish dollars from cents.

The following standard form of the ledger account does not use dollar signs, commas, or decimal points. The specific columnar format differentiates these areas.

Cash

Date		Explanation	PR	Debit Amount	Date		Explanation	PR	Credit Amount
200- Jan.	1	Balance	✓	5000 00	200- Jan.	3			200 00
	4			600 00		9			125 00
	7	6975.50		900 00					325 00
	12	− 325.00 6,650.50		475 50					
				6975 50					

EXERCISE 5   In Exercise 13 in chapter 1 you recorded Carolyn Goldstein's business transactions for her first month in business in the expanded accounting equation. Assume that Ms. Goldstein established her law practice on July 1, 200-. Further assume that the numbered business transactions represented days in the month of July. Set up "T" accounts as needed. Record the ten business transactions in the appropriate ledger accounts. Working with the narrative to the exercise and the accounting equation solution will assist you in successfully completing this exercise.

Remember: The beginning balance and increases in all assets are recorded on the debit side of the account. All decreases in assets are recorded as credits to the account.

The beginning balance and all increases in liability and permanent capital accounts are recorded on the credit side of the account. Decreases are recorded on the debit side of the account.

The recognition of a revenue transaction is recorded to the credit side of the account.

The recognition of an expense or proprietor's drawing is recorded on the debit side of the account.

OTHER FORMS OF THE LEDGER ACCOUNT

There are basically two other forms that the ledger account will take: the three-column, or Boston ledger and the four-column ledger account.

THREE-COLUMN LEDGER ACCOUNT

Cash

Date		Explanation	PR	Debit	Credit	Balance
200- Jan.	1	Balance	✓			5000 00
	3				200 00	4800 00
	4			600 00		5400 00
	7			900 00		6300 00
	9				125 00	6175 00
	12			475 50		6650 50

FOUR-COLUMN LEDGER ACCOUNT

Cash

Date		Explanation	PR	Debit	Credit	Balance Debit	Balance Credit
200- Jan.	1	Balance	✓			5000 00	
	3				200 00	4800 00	
	4			600 00		5400 00	
	7			900 00		6300 00	
	9				125 00	6175 00	
	12			475 50		6650 50	

In order to determine the balance in the account form of the ledger, it is necessary to foot both the debit column and the credit column and then find the difference in the amounts to ascertain the balance. Using the three-column or four-column form of the ledger enables you to maintain a running balance in each account. If we wanted to know the balance in any account at a particular moment, we would simply refer to the account and the last figure found in the balance column, which represents the balance in the account. When the three-column account is used, it is assumed that the amount shown in the balance column represents the normal balance in the account. Should an unusual balance appear, it will be shown either in brackets or encircled. When the four-column ledger account is used the nature of the balance will be shown either in the debit-balance column or the credit-balance column. Unusual balances, such as a credit balance in an asset account, will be shown in the credit-balance column of the account. The four-column ledger account, while used as part of a manual accounting system, was more appropriately used with accounting posting machines.

EXERCISE 6   Using either a three-column or four-column ledger account, record the following business transactions for the month of October 200-:

Oct. 1   The proprietor, John Graves, began the Graves Delivery Service by investing the following: Cash, $12,000; Delivery Equipment, $8,000.

3   Received $3,000 in revenue as a result of delivery service income.

5   The proprietor made an additional investment in the business consisting of delivery equipment valued at $2,500 and warehouse supplies worth $500.

8   Paid $500 in rent for the warehouse for the month of October.

15   Paid $250 for repairs and gasoline expenses for the first half of the month of October.

19   Received a check for $1,200 from a customer for delivery services rendered.

25   Sent a check for $50 to pay for deposits required by the local utilities company for electricity. Designated this payment as a utilities expense.

30   Paid employees' salaries for the month amounting to $450.

After recording the business transactions in the various ledger accounts, prepare a listing of the accounts and their various balances. If the total debit balances equal the total credit balances, this should indicate that we recorded the transactions correctly in the various ledger accounts.

PROVING THE ACCURACY OF RECORDED TRANSACTIONS

At regular intervals, such as once a month, the accountant would want to prove that the requirements of double-entry accounting have been adhered to. In order to do so, a form is prepared that will prove the accuracy of the ledger. This form is known as a TRIAL BALANCE. A trial balance represents a listing of the ledger account balances as of a moment in time. Following the listing of the account balances, the footing of the debit column and the credit column of the trial balance should agree. If the two columns agree, the trial balance is said to be in balance, which means that the ledger is in balance. This does not mean that the individual business transactions were recorded to the appropriate ledger account; it merely means that for every debit there was a corresponding credit of the same amount. The actual form of the trial balance is illustrated below. This trial balance represents one that would be prepared for Exercise 6, if one had been called for:

John Graves
Trial Balance
October 30, 200-

	DEBIT	CREDIT
Cash	$14,950	
Delivery Equipment	10,500	
John Graves, Capital		$23,000
Delivery Service Income		4,200
Warehouse Supplies	500	
Rent Expense	500	
Repairs and Gasoline Expense	250	
Utilities Expense	50	
Salaries Expense	450	
	$27,200	$27,200

After you have completed the trial balance and have totaled the debit column and the credit column to prove that they both agree, the final procedure is to double underscore the debit column and the credit column. The process of double underlining the two totals indicates that the ledger is in balance and the work has been appropriately recorded for the month. Keep in mind that this trial balance does not indicate that the entries were recorded in the proper accounts; it merely indicates that double-entry accounting has been followed correctly.

The Journal

Each business transaction has at least two parts to it. There is an entry that is recorded as a debit to a ledger account and a corresponding credit to another account. While a date and possibly an explanation are assigned to the transaction, there are still aspects of the transaction that are not readily apparent from this entry system. If you were to refer back to a transaction that took place last month involving the receipt of cash, the debit portion of the entry would be obvious. The problem might center around the reason for the receipt of cash. Was the receipt of cash the result of the recognition of revenue, the result of an additional investment, the result of a customer paying off an obligation, or was it the result of a loan obtained from a local bank, and if so, was that loan evidenced by an oral or a written promise? It should be obvious that this receipt of cash could have resulted from many activities on one given day. A deficiency inherent in merely using the ledger account is that the entire transaction is not recorded together. Also, the ledger account lacks a dated order of transactions as would be found in a diary or some other record of dated events. While an explanation can be written into the ledger, it is often not practical to do so because of the lack of adequate room. To correct the inadequacies of the ledger account system, a record known as the journal, or businessperson's diary, is used.

THE PURPOSE AND FORM OF THE JOURNAL

The JOURNAL is known as the book of original or first entry. All business transactions are first recorded in this journal. The journal has three basic advantages over the ledger:

1. It shows the complete business transaction in one place. Regardless of the number of debits or credits to a particular business transaction, all parts of the transaction are shown together in one place.
2. All business transactions are recorded in the journal in chronological order. This is the reason that it is known as the businessperson's diary. Like a diary that records events in dated order, the journal records business transactions in dated order.
3. The journal provides for an adequate explanation of what took place. Regardless of the nature of the transaction being recorded,

provision is made for as detailed an explanation as the accountant feels is necessary.

The following represents the typical form of the journal. It is sometimes referred to as the general journal because of the fact that *all* business transactions are first recorded in it.

General Journal

Date	Account and Explanation	PR	Debit	Credit

RECORDING BUSINESS TRANSACTIONS

Since the information to be recorded in the journal is basically the same as that which we have been recording in the individual ledger accounts, we must start by briefly reviewing that which we are already doing:

1. Recording the date of the entry;
2. Debiting the ledger account for the amount of the debit;
3. Crediting the ledger account for the amount of the credit;
4. Recording a brief explanation where necessary and appropriate.

We will continue doing the above four steps, but now they will be done directly in the general journal, rather than through the individual ledger accounts.

If on January 3, 200-, the proprietor was to send a check for $500 in payment of the January rent to the Able Realty Co., the general journal entry would be as follows:

General Journal

Date	Account and Explanation	PR	Debit	Credit
200- Jan. 3	Rent Expense		500 00	
	Cash			500 00
	Paid Able Realty Co.			
	for month of January			

Note that a separate line was used for each debit and credit entry. The debit entry began at the margin, followed by the credit entry that was indented. The explanation followed the business transaction and provided the necessary information that the actual accounts being debited and credited could not provide. It was not necessary to indicate in the explanation that this transaction was in payment of *rent*, for this was understood. The month that the payment represented and the company being paid were not part of the transaction itself; thus, it was included as part of the explanation.

Regardless of the kind of business transaction to be recorded, it must first be recorded in the book of original entry—that is, the journal. Each transaction begins with the date of the entry, followed by the debit entry or entries, then the credit entry or entries which are indented. This is all followed by an explanation on the next available line.

Record the following compound journal entry using the proper accounting form: On June 22, 200-, the business acquired office furniture at a cost of $1,200 and related office supplies costing $75. The entire amount was paid by issuing check No. 345 to the Green Office Equipment and Supply Co. of Andover, Mass.

General Journal

Date		Account and Explanation	PR	Debit	Credit
200- June	22	Furniture and Fixtures		1200 00	
		Office Supplies		75 00	
		Cash			1275 00
		Sent check No. 345 to Green Office			
		Equipment and Supply Co. of Andover, Mass.			

While the above illustrations show the explanation starting at the margin immediately following the credit entry, some accountants will indent the explanation and still others will indent the explanation and show it in brackets. The form of the explanation is not as important as its use. It serves as an important part of the recording process and should not be omitted.

EXERCISE 7   Record the following business transactions in the general journal of the Albert Kranz Trucking Service.

200-

Aug. **1**   Purchased a used delivery truck, paying A-1 Used Truck Co. $2,300 cash.

4   Received a check from the Stevens Department Store in payment of trucking charges as evidenced by a bill sent today for $900.

6   Proprietor withdrew $200 from the business for personal use.

9   Paid radio station WPBB $300 for advertising services for the week.

10   Sent a check in payment of an outstanding obligation to the Ready Repair Shop amounting to $230. The form of the obligation was an oral promise (accounts payable).

16   Paid salaries for the two weeks ending today, amounting to $370.

19   Sent a bill to May's department store for $340 for goods transported.

23   Paid $120 for gasoline and oil used in trucks for the three-week period ending this date.

27   The proprietor took $150 home for personal use.

29   Paid salaries for the two weeks ending today, amounting to $385.

31   Received payment from May's department store for obligation of August 19.

Recording Transactions in Both Journal and Ledger

While it may appear that recording transactions in both the journal and the ledger duplicates work, there are important reasons for doing so. Let us briefly review the purpose of each record.

The journal is the book of original entry, all business transactions are first recorded in it. All transactions are recorded in chronological order. All parts of the transaction are recorded together and an adequate explanation is provided.

The ledger is a bound or looseleaf type book that contains various records called accounts. Each account represents individual assets, liabilities, and forms of capital. Changes in the various accounts are recorded as debit and credit entries. At any moment in time, the accountant may easily determine the balance of the account. From the accounts found in the ledger, the accountant can prepare a trial balance. This trial balance will verify that double-entry accounting has been adhered to. From the trial balance, the accountant may prepare various financial statements as needed by the organization and other interested parties.

It should be obvious from this discussion that both the journal and the ledger represent important documents that a business organization must maintain.

TRANSFERRING TRANSACTIONS FROM THE JOURNAL

The journal was defined as the book of original or first entry. This indicates that business transactions are first recorded in the general journal. The ledger may then be defined as the book of secondary or final entry. The daily business transactions are transferred from the journal to the ledger. The process of accomplishing this transfer is known as POSTING. The process of posting is similar to mailing a letter. The writer of a letter places the addressed letter in a mailbox, where it is then transferred by the postal service to the person named on the face of the envelope. When a business transaction is posted, the information recorded in the journal is transferred to the specific ledger accounts involved. The process of analyzing the business transaction doesn't change, but the record of the business transaction can now be found in two places. If the accountant, after posting a business transaction from the journal to the ledger, wishes to know the effect of a business transaction on a specific account, there is an easy way to do this. This is accomplished by using the POST REFERENCE or REFERENCE columns found in both the ledger account and the journal. Each journal page is assigned a page number, usually in consecutive or numerical order. A designation such as J-1 would indicate page 1 of the journal. Each page in the ledger would be given a number as well. The ledger account page number would usually represent a specific kind of account. The account "Cash" might be assigned the number 1, the account "Supplies" might be assigned the number 2, and so forth. The reference columns in the journal and ledger account would then be used to indicate, respectively, where the information had been transferred to and where it had been obtained from. A series of numbers may be assigned to a group of accounts. As in the above illustrations, the numbers 1–10 might represent assets. If more asset account numbers are needed, then the 100 series might be used to represent assets. The 200 series might represent liabilities, etc. (Refer to Exercise 8 for series of account numbers assigned.) The following business transaction will illustrate the process of posting the information:

200-
Jan. 10 Paid $50 for supplies acquired today.

General Journal					Page 1	
Date		Account and Explanation	PR	Debit	Credit	
200- Jan.	10	Supplies	2	50 00		
		Cash	1		50 00	
		Acquired today				

Cash — Account No. 1

Date		Explanation	PR	Debit	Date		Explanation	PR	Credit	
200- Jan.	1	Balance	✓	300 00	200- Jan.	10		J-1	50 00	

Cash — Account No. 2

Date		Explanation	PR	Debit	Date		Explanation	PR	Credit	
200- Jan.	10		J-1	50 00		10				

The check mark indicates that the balance in the cash account on January 1 is a result of previous business transactions resulting in this remaining amount.

EXERCISE 8   Set up the following ledger accounts for the Speedy Car Wash Co. Include the account numbers and balances. Use the June 1, 200- date: Cash (#101), $2,000; Accounts Receivable (#102), $1,500; Supplies (#110), $300; Car Wash Equipment (#115), $5,000; Accounts Payable (#201), $500; Ralph Speedy, Capital (#301), $8,300; Ralph Speedy, Drawing (#302); Car Wash Revenue (#410); Salaries Expense (#520); Rent Expense (#521); Laundry Expense (#522); Utilities Expense (#523).

Prepare a trial balance dated June 1, 200-. Having verified that the ledger is in balance, journalize and post to the ledger accounts the following business transactions for the month of June 200-.

200-

June 3   Paid monthly rent of $200 to Ajax Realty Co. in cash.

5   Received a check for $500 from Adams Bros. in part payment of their obligation to us. (Cr. A/R)

8   Received $1,000 for car wash revenue for the week ending today.

9   Paid salaries for the two weeks ending today amounting to $480.

14   Sent a check for $300 in payment of our obligation to Randolph Supply Co. due today. (Dr. A/P)

15   The proprietor took $500 out of the business for personal use.

22   Sent a bill today for $200 to the Granger Trucking Co. for services provided on credit. (Dr. A/R)

26   Paid monthly water bill amounting to $85.

27   Sent the Clean Towel Co. a check for $60 for the monthly laundry expense.

29   Purchased a new wind machine for $1,200 and agreed to pay Car Wash Equipment Co. in thirty days. (Cr. A/P)

30   Bought car wash supplies consisting of soap powder and liquid wax, paying $120 cash.

After you have journalized and posted the transactions, find the balances in the ledger accounts and prepare a trial balance dated June 30, 200-.

Verifying Ledger Balances

The balances in the ledger are verified by preparing a trial balance. A trial balance may be prepared at any time, such as at the end of a month, three months, six months, or a year. A trial balance must be prepared at least once a year; however, it is more practical for the accountant to prepare the trial balance more frequently. This enables the accountant to verify that the requirements of double-entry accounting have been met. It also reduces the amount of checking that may be necessary in the event that the trial balance does not balance.

Before we discuss what to do when the trial balance is not in balance, let's review the accounting process from the business document to the preparation of the trial balance. An accountant takes the following steps in recording a business transaction:

1. Record the business transaction from the business document into the journal.
2. Post the journal entry to the specific ledger account and note the posting in the journal and ledger reference columns.
3. Find the balance in the standard "T" account or verify the balances in the three- or four-column ledger accounts.
4. Prepare the trial balance.

In Exercise 8, you had an opportunity to follow through with the steps enumerated above. Hopefully, you were able to get the trial balance to balance. If you were not, be aware that this situation is not unusual and can occur even with the most experienced accountant. If your trial balance did not balance, there are specific steps that are followed to locate the error, correct it, and get the trial balance to balance.

To correct a trial balance that is out of balance, you use basically the same steps followed in recording the transactions initially, except now you do them in reverse order.

The accountant will begin by:

1. Re-adding the debit and credit columns of the trial balance to check the totals obtained.
2. Verifying that the amounts carried to the trial balance from the accounts are the same amounts and have been recorded in the appropriate column of the trial balance. It is not uncommon for a *transposition* (reversing numbers—i.e., 45 becomes 54) or a *slide* (mistakenly adding or deleting zeroes—i.e., $3,000 becomes $30,000 or $300) to occur.
3. Verifying that the balances in the individual ledger accounts were correctly determined.
4. Verifying the posting process by first checking to see if all post references are indicated in the journal.
5. Verifying that all journal entries have been properly posted to the appropriate ledger account and the correct side of the account (e.g., a debit posting may have inadvertently been recorded on the credit side of the account), and that all journal entries have actually been posted to accounts.
6. Verifying that each business transaction recorded in the journal has met the requirements of double-entry accounting. When you originally journalize and you reach the bottom of the journal page, it is customary to foot the debit and credit columns. Both columns should have the same totals. This is a way of verifying double-entry accounting even prior to posting. Remember, errors made in journalizing will be compounded if not corrected prior to posting.

The six steps listed above may not all be necessary. Once you have located an error, you then correct it and indicate the correction on the trial balance. By readding the trial balance you may find it to be in balance, unless there are other errors that you have not yet located. If you were unsuccessful in getting your trial balance to balance in Exercise 8, use the above procedures to locate and correct your error(s).

Summing Up

The accountant is called upon to keep track of changes that occur as a result of business transactions. Every business transaction involves at least two changes. Changes in assets causing an increase are recorded as *debits*. Decreases are recorded as *credits*. Increases in all liabilities and proprietor's capital are recorded as *credits*. Decreases are recorded as *debits*. Changes in temporary capital accounts are recorded so as to reflect their change in permanent capital. Thus, revenue causing an increase in permanent capital is credited, while expenses and drawing are debited, causing a decrease in permanent capital. If ledger accounts are established based on an existing balance sheet, the beginning balances in the individual accounts would be shown on the same side of the account as increases in those specific accounts would be.

Business transactions are recorded in two sets of books. Each business transaction is first recorded in the journal (book of original entry), and then posted (transferred) to the individual accounts found in the ledger (book of final entry).

Every business transaction must meet the requirements of double-entry accounting—i.e., for every debit entry, there must be a corresponding credit entry of the same amount. A compound entry may involve numerous account debits and/or credits. The total amount of the debits must equal the total amount of the credits for each transaction in order to meet the requirements of double-entry accounting.

Each journal page is assigned a page number. Transactions are recorded in the journal in chronological order, using each page in numerical order. Each ledger account is also assigned a specific page number that is unique to that particular account. Business transactions are first recorded in chronological order in the journal and then posted daily to the specific numbered ledger account. The reference columns in both the journal and the individual ledger accounts are used to verify posting. The reference column in the account indicates the source of the posting; thus, "J-12" in the reference column of the cash account indicates that the entry came from page 12 of the journal. The number "1" placed in the reference column of the journal (on page 12) indicates that the amount was posted to the cash account. When a transaction has been recorded in the journal and the reference column is blank, this indicates that posting has not as yet taken place. The posting reference in the journal indicates that posting has taken place and also indicates which account the individual entry has been posted to.

The process of journalizing and posting is an ongoing, daily activity. Frequently, it becomes necessary during the accounting cycle to verify the accuracy of this activity. Even though financial statements may not necessarily be needed, the process of checking the accuracy of the ledger should take place. Most accountants will verify the accuracy of the ledger once a month by preparing a trial balance. The trial balance is a listing of the ledger account balances as of a specific date. If the total of the debit and credit columns agree, the ledger is said to be in balance. A trial balance that is not in balance requires the accountant to locate errors by redoing the steps of preparation in reverse order until the error has been located and corrected.

CHAPTER 4

RECORDING ADJUSTING, CLOSING, AND REVERSING ENTRIES

Adjusting Entries

The business transactions that have been recorded represent activities that affect the accounting period in which they are recorded. There may be transactions, however, that will not only affect the current period, but possibly a prior or future period. In order for the ledger accounts to properly reflect the activities for the current accounting period, it may be necessary for the accountant to prepare adjusting entries. ADJUSTING ENTRIES are journal entries that are recorded in order to properly reflect the appropriate balances in the various ledger accounts for a specific accounting period. Although these entries are usually prepared at the end of the accounting period, they could be prepared at any time that the accountant feels that it would be appropriate to do so. Let us assume that we will only prepare adjusting entries at the end of the accounting period.

TYPES OF ADJUSTING ENTRIES

There are basically two categories of adjusting entries that must be considered—accruals and deferrals.

In order to understand how the above adjustments are used it is first necessary to be familiar with the nature of a particular business. Most businesses are on what is called the ACCRUAL BASIS. This system assumes that revenue is recognized when earned, regardless of when the revenue is actually received in the form of cash, and that expenses are recognized when incurred (e.g., rent for December is an expense for December, even if it isn't paid until January), regardless of when payment in the form of cash is actually made. This concept is known as the PRINCIPLE OF MATCHING COSTS AND REVENUE. Individuals, unlike businesses, are on the CASH BASIS. This means that revenue is recognized when received and expenses are recognized when paid. While there are situations where a business may be on the cash basis, we will assume here that all businesses are on the accrual basis.

Accruals

The word "accrual" means to accumulate. In accounting it is necessary to recognize that although certain items may have accumulated, they may not have been recognized as of yet.

Accrued Expenses

Frequently, expense items have been incurred but have not necessarily been recorded, either because the business is not obligated to pay the expense yet or for any number of reasons has failed to do so. When this situation occurs, it is necessary to record an adjusting entry.

EXAMPLE Let's say that the December 200-, rent is due to be paid at the beginning of December. The amount of the payment should be $500. The business fails to pay the rent by December 31, which is the end of the accounting period. The following journal entry represents the adjusting entry that the accountant would prepare on December 31, 200-.

```
200-
Dec. 31   Rent Expense                              500
              Rent Payable                                   500
          To recognize the expense for December
```

The recording of this adjusting entry enables the business to recognize an expense that was incurred during the accounting period that includes the month of December, even though the actual expense will not be paid until the following accounting period. The principle of matching costs and revenue has been met. When an income statement for the year ending December 31, 200-, is prepared, it will properly include rent expense for the year, including the expense for December. In this situation when the rent is actually paid in the new year, the following entry would be recorded in the journal:

```
200-
Jan. 4    Rent Payable                             500
              Cash                                         500
          To pay December rent past due.
```

In our earlier discussion on current assets, it was stated that a current asset is one that will be used up or converted to cash within a year or less. The asset supplies, for instance, is generally classified as a current asset. It is anticipated that part if not all of the asset supplies will be used up within the course of an accounting period. The ledger account for supplies records the beginning balance in the account as well as increases due to purchases and decreases as a result of supplies being returned. If the accountant takes a physical count of the supplies at the end of the accounting period, this count will probably represent a dollar cost assigned to the supplies that is less than the value as stated in the ledger account. The reason for this is that the supplies were probably used up in part during the period. A supply that is used up is considered to have become an expense. It becomes necessary to recognize this expense on the books, thus the need for an adjusting entry.

EXAMPLE   The balance in the supplies ledger account on December 31, 200- indicates a balance in the account of $1,200. An actual physical count of the supplies on hand indicates that the value of the supplies is actually $750. The difference between the supplies on hand and the balance in the account indicates that $450 worth of supplies has been used up. It becomes necessary for the accountant to record the following adjusting entry to recognize the expense and at the same time to adjust the supplies account so that it shows the true value of the supplies on hand.

200-
Dec. 31   Supplies Expense   450
                   Supplies   450
           To recognize the supplies used up.

Let us examine the ledger account affected as a result of the posting of this adjusting entry.

Supplies			Supplies Expense	
200-	200-		200-	
Dec. 31 1,200	Dec. 31 450		Dec. 31 450	

As a result of the adjusting entry, the supplies used up ($450) have been recognized as an expense, and at the same time the value of the asset supplies have been reduced by the amount of the supplies no longer in existence.

These two examples illustrate UNRECORDED EXPENSES that have been adjusted at the end of the accounting period. Any current asset that is subject to use and thus becomes an expense is treated in the same manner as in the supplies illustration. Where an expense has been incurred, but not yet paid as in the case of the rent expense, it is treated in a similar fashion. Note that the rent expense was *not* paid in December, so it became necessary to set up a liability when recognizing the rent expense.

EXERCISE 1   Record the appropriate adjusting journal entries for the following situations. Assume that the accounting period ends on December 31, 2002, and that all adjusting entries are made as of that date.

1. A physical count of office supplies indicates that $250 worth of office supplies had been used up during the accounting period.
2. Rent totaling $800 for the months of November and December has not been paid by December 31, 2002.
3. You received a bill from the *Daily Standard News* for advertisements placed in the newspaper during the second week of November. The bill is for $200, not to be paid until January 15, 2003.
4. On December 1, 2002, you borrowed $1,000 from the First City Bank. The bank charges you interest at an annual rate of 10% on the obligation, and interest is not to be repaid for ninety days. Record the adjusting entry to recognize the interest expense on the loan from December 1 to December 31, 2002.

5. On July 1, 2002, you took out a fire insurance policy on the business premises. At that time you recorded this insurance premium in an asset account entitled Prepaid Insurance for the amount of the yearly premium of $600. On December 31, 2002, record the adjusting entry for this asset. Remember, an asset that has been used up becomes an expense.

6. Salaries are paid on Fridays for the week ending on the same day. The salaries for the week amount to $5,000. The last day of the accounting period is Wednesday, December 31, 2002. Record the adjusting entry necessary to recognize the salaries expense for the last three days of the year. The actual payment of the week's salaries will not take place until January 2, 2003.

Accrued Revenue

In Exercise 1, adjusting entries resulting in the recognition of expenses were highlighted. In each adjusting entry an accrual was made to recognize the expense. In some cases the expense had not been paid; thus, to recognize it a liability had to be set up. In other situations a current asset that was used up was converted to an expense through the adjusting process. The principle of accrued expenses can also apply to ACCRUED REVENUE. When income has been earned as a result of a service provided but payment is not due from the customer yet, we record the transaction as a credit sale of services. In doing so we are accruing revenue. This kind of transaction is not normally considered an adjusting entry because of the nature of credit transactions. When we provide a service on credit, it is important for us to record the revenue and the resulting accounts or notes receivable, so that we have a record of who owes us money as a result of the credit sale. There are situations where revenue earned has not been recognized because it hasn't been received. Accrued revenue represents revenue that has been accumulating during the accounting period and that will probably be received during a future accounting period. Thus, it has not been recognized in the current accounting period. It is the accountant's responsibility to recognize this UNRECORDED REVENUE and see to it that an appropriate adjusting entry is made.

EXAMPLE A customer borrowed $1,000, giving you a ninety-day promissory note that called for interest at the annual rate of 8%.

The note began to earn interest on December 1, 2002, which was the date the note was given to you. The agreement calls for the interest on the note to be paid to you on the date that the note becomes due. Since the interest income on the note will not be received until the note is due, it is necessary to record an adjusting entry to recognize the unrecorded revenue. Assuming that the accounting period ends on December 31, 2002, it will be necessary to recognize accrued revenue from December 1 through December 31 of the current year. The income earned but not received and not recognized would be calculated as $1,000 (amount owed) × 8% (interest rate) × 1/12 (30 days as compared to a banking year, which consists of 360 days) = $6.67 (accrued interest). The appropriate journal entry is:

2002
Dec. 31 Interest Receivable   6.67
                 Interest Income   6.67
         For interest earned but not yet
         received on 90-day note.

Note that this entry is very similar to the first example of an unrecorded expense. In that situation a liability was established in order to recognize the expense. In this case an asset interest receivable is set up. It would not be appropriate to debit the notes receivable account because the face value of the note has not changed. When the note becomes due on March 1, 2003, of the new accounting period, the following entry will be made:

2003
Mar. 1   Cash   1,020.00
                 Interest Receivable   6.67
                 Interest Income   13.33
                 Notes Receivable   1,000.00
         Customer paid maturity value of
         promissory note due today.

If the interest-bearing promissory note had come due in the same accounting period as when it was issued, there would have been no need for an adjusting entry. The above entry would have combined the interest receivable and the interest income entry with the $20 being credited to interest income.

Deferrals

We have seen that adjusting entries can result from unrecorded expenses and unrecorded revenue. The accumulation of these items and their subsequent adjusting entries are known as accruals. The required adjusting entries affect liabilities and/or assets. It is also possible to encounter situations in which expenses that have been recorded during an accounting period have not actually been used up to the extent indicated in the account. Revenue recognized during an accounting period may not have been entirely earned, even though recorded as such. When the accountant becomes aware of these facts, he or she must record an adjusting entry known as a "deferral." A DEFERRAL represents the postponement of the recognition of either an expense or a revenue item.

Certain business transactions may be interpreted differently depending on the accountant, the philosophy of the business, as well as the nature of the transaction. A simple business transaction, such as the payment of the monthly rent, can be handled in two different ways:

1. Since the rent payment represents a right use property that will be used up at the end of each month, the rent should initially be recorded as an expense; or,
2. Since the rent payment represents a right to use property and that property has a money value, the rent can be considered a form of an asset. Since rent is usually payable at the beginning of the month and the rights to use the property extend to the end of the month, it is an asset.

Both approaches are reasonable and appropriate given the circumstances. If the first approach is used and the rent is recognized as an expense, then no adjusting entry would be necessary except in the following situation:

EXAMPLE   The terms of the one-year lease on the premises that was signed and became effective on November 1, 200-, were:

The annual rent is $6,000. It is to be paid in two installments of 50% each. The first installment is due November 1, 200-. The entry made to reflect this transaction is as follows:

```
200-
Nov. 1   Rent Expense                        3,000
             Cash                                    3,000
         For 6-month prepayment.
```

Notice that the rent expense recognized is for six months. The number of months remaining in this accounting period is two. If we were not to prepare an adjusting entry, the rent expense for the year will be overstated. Ask yourself three questions:

1. For what period of time did we prepay the rent? (six months)
2. How many months and what amount should actually be recognized as an expense through the end of the accounting period? (Two months, $1,000)
3. What adjusting entry should be made and what will the deferral of the expense create? (It should be obvious that the existing expense is overstated to the extent of four months and $2,000. To correct this situation the following entry is made:

```
200-
Dec. 31   Prepaid Rent                        2,000
              Rent Expense                            2,000
          To defer 4 months' rent.
```

The credit to rent expense reduces the expense to be recognized for the accounting period (a postponement). The debit entry converts the expense to an account that is generally known as a "prepaid expense." The term PREPAID EXPENSE is somewhat confusing because of its literal meaning. It represents an expense that was paid in advance. Since it was paid in advance and at this point not used up, it is actually classified as an *asset*.

If the accountant had used the second approach, considering the rent payment to represent an asset or initially a prepaid expense, then the entry for the payment would have been the following:

```
200-
Nov. 1   Prepaid Rent (or Rent)              3,000
             Cash                                    3,000
         For 6-month prepayment.
```

This approach assumes that the item initially is an asset and that by the end of the accounting period, that portion of prepaid rent that has been used up will be converted to an expense in a similar fashion to the conversion of supplies to an expense. In this case the adjusting entry would be:

```
200-
Dec. 31   Rent Expense                           1,000
               Prepaid Rent                              1,000
          To recognize the expense for
          the 2 months.
```

Note that the adjustment permits the recognition of the proper expense for the period and at the same time corrects the asset prepaid rent to show a proper balance of $2,000 for the remaining four months. This approach is an accrual.

When an expense previously paid has not been fully used up, it is necessary to defer that portion not used and convert it to an asset. The usual title of such an asset has the term "prepaid" placed before it. Accounts such as Prepaid Insurance, Prepaid Supplies, Prepaid Rent, and Prepaid Commissions were all created as a result of an adjusting entry when it became necessary to postpone the recognition of an expense already paid for. When revenue has been received but not earned entirely within the accounting period, you must defer the recognition of the revenue. UNEARNED REVENUE represents revenue received but not earned within the accounting period and the accountant must record an adjusting entry to defer this income. The principle of matching costs and revenue requires that revenue be recognized when earned, regardless of when received. Here the situation is that the revenue has been received, and yet it may not be earned until some future period. This is an example of a deferral.

EXAMPLE You receive a rent check from your tenant on November 1, 2002. The check is for $800 and is payment of four months' rent beginning with November. The entry recorded upon the receipt of the check was as follows:

```
2002
Nov. 1   Cash                                    800
               Income from Rental                       800
          Four months' rent beginning
          this date.
```

At the end of the accounting period, what adjusting entry would the accountant have to make? Obviously, if the income received represents four months' rental income, then part of the income should be recognized; however, the balance would have to be deferred. The following adjusting entry would be recorded:

```
2002
Dec. 31   Income from Rental                     400
               Unearned Rental Income                   400
          To defer unearned rent.
```

The deferral of the income permits the income for the period to be properly stated. The adjustment also results in the recognition of a liability for the income received, but at this point not earned. The tenant has the right to use the premises for the months of January and February. The landlord has an obligation to supply the premises; thus, a liability exists as a result of the adjusting entry.

During the next accounting period (2003), when the income actually becomes earned, the following entry would be made. This entry could be made at the very beginning of the new year (as will be discussed shortly) or at the time the income actually becomes fully earned.

```
2003
Jan. 1   Unearned Rental Income                          400
                Income from Rental                                400
         To recognize income earned in the New Year.
```

EXERCISE 2   Record the following adjusting entries to reflect the accrual and deferral of expenses and revenue for the calendar year ending December 31 of the current year.

1. Recognized the interest income accumulated on a $5,000 note bearing interest of 9% dated November 2.
2. Recorded an adjusting entry to recognize that income from commissions previously received but not yet earned to the extent of 40% of the $800 commission.
3. Determined that the balance in the ledger account for office supplies was $990, but that an inventory showed only $260 worth of office supplies remaining.
4. Accrued salaries for the last three days in the old year amounting to $1,500.
5. Showed a balance of $2,270 in the prepaid insurance account. Insurance records indicate that $1,245 of the insurance expired during the year.
6. Borrowed $6,000 for ninety days, with interest payable at an annual rate of 12%. The loan was taken out forty-five days before the end of the accounting period and is due to be paid in full 45 days into the new year.

Adjusting Noncurrent Assets

Noncurrent, or plant, assets are subject to a loss in value due to the item being used. Current assets such as supplies obviously lose value because the item is used up. The loss in value of plant assets is not obvious because the asset still exists in its complete form at the end of the accounting period. It is necessary, however, to recognize a loss in value due to use. This loss in value is known as DEPRECIATION, which is the recognition of a loss in value of a plant asset due to wear and tear over its useful life. When depreciation is recognized as an adjusting entry at the end of the accounting period, an expense is charged. Since the expense does not represent an actual outlay of cash, and the cost principle prevents us from reducing the value of the asset directly, it becomes necessary to credit a new account. This account is known as "Accumulated Depreciation." The following entry illustrates depreciation being recognized on office equipment at the end of the accounting period.

```
200-
Dec. 31   Depreciation Expense—Office Equip.             300
                 Accumulated Depreciation                       300
          To record annual depreciation.
```

This adjusting entry recognizes the expense and records a credit entry to the accumulated depreciation account. This account is classified as a "contra-asset." The purpose of this account is merely to offset the plant asset account. The net or book value of the plant asset will be determined by subtracting the accumulated depreciation account from the value of the plant asset. The most common form of depreciation that is used is known as "straight-line depreciation." Under this method, the value of the asset is divided by its useful life in years to determine the amount of depreciation to be recognized annually.

EXAMPLE   The original cost of a truck is $20,000. It is expected to have a useful life of ten years and at the end of ten years to have no value. To determine the annual depreciation on the truck, the following would be done:

$$\frac{\text{COST OF ASSET}}{\text{USEFUL LIFE}} = \frac{\$20,000}{10 \text{ YEARS}} = \frac{\$2,000 \text{ ANNUAL}}{\text{DEPRECIATION}}$$

The method used to determine depreciation may change, but the adjusting entry to recognize depreciation is the same. We indicated that adjusting entries could be made as frequently as once a month or whenever necessary. We are still assuming that these accruals and deferrals are being made annually. To find depreciation for one month, we would first find it for one year and divide the results by twelve. When a plant asset is expected to have a "residual value" or scrap value at the end of its useful life, this value is not subject to depreciation. If the asset in the preceding example had a scrap value of $1,000, then the annual depreciation recognized would amount to $1,900. After the asset has been fully depreciated, the book value and the residual value would be the same. The following calculation would be made assuming scrap value of $1,000.

$$\frac{\text{COST OF ASSET} - \text{SCRAP VALUE}}{\text{USEFUL LIFE}} = \frac{\$20,000 - \$1,000}{10 \text{ YEARS}} = \frac{\$1,900 \text{ ANNUAL}}{\text{DEPRECIATION}}$$

EXERCISE 3   Office equipment was purchased at a cost of $3,400. It has an expected useful life of six years, and after it has been fully depreciated, it will have a scrap value of $400.
Determine:

1. How much of the asset is subject to depreciation?
2. What will be the annual depreciation recognized?
3. Assuming that the asset was acquired at the beginning of the year, record the adjusting entry to recognize depreciation for the first full year.
4. Determine the book value of the asset after the first year's adjusting entry.
5. What is the book value of the asset after it has been depreciated for six years?
6. What happens to the book value of the asset during each year of its useful life? Why?
7. When recording annual depreciation, why doesn't the accountant credit the asset account directly?

RECORDING ADJUSTING ENTRIES

Preparing the Worksheet

Adjusting entries recorded at the end of the accounting period permit revenue to be recognized when earned and expenses to be recognized when incurred. Since the adjustment process can take place monthly as well as annually, the accountant may be called upon to prepare financial statements following the adjusting process. To expedite the preparation of financial statements and the preparation of adjustments prior to statement preparation, the WORKSHEET is prepared.

In an earlier chapter we illustrated and discussed the preparation of the trial balance. The trial balance was used to verify that the ledger was in balance. The trial balance is prepared prior to recording adjusting entries and becomes the backbone of the worksheet. Some accountants define a worksheet as an expanded trial balance, which it literally is. Unlike financial statements, the worksheet is used and viewed by the accountant only, so it is usually prepared in pencil. The form consists of a column to list the accounts from the ledger followed by eight money columns.

The preparation of the worksheet precedes the recording of adjusting entries. At the end of the accounting period or a month, a trial balance is prepared on the worksheet. Necessary adjusting entries are recorded directly on the worksheet using the adjustments columns. The information in the adjustments column is then extended along with the trial balance information to the remaining two sets of the worksheet columns. The remaining sets of columns are the income statement and balance sheet columns.

Assets, liabilities, permanent capital, and the proprietor's drawing account are extended from the trial balance columns through the adjustments columns and recorded in the appropriate balance sheet column. Revenue and expenses are extended from the trial balance columns through the adjustments columns to the appropriate income statement column. (See accompanying illustration.) The function of the adjustments columns is to adjust the balances in the ledger accounts to match costs and revenue for the specific accounting period covered by the worksheet. No journal entries or related postings are made at this time, although these adjusting entries made on the worksheet will later become the basis for recording adjusting journal entries and related postings at the end of the accounting period. If the accountant is preparing interim statements from the worksheet, no adjusting journal entries or related postings would be made. The worksheet merely becomes the vehicle for preparing the interim statements.

The following worksheet is illustrated prior to recording adjusting entries on it.

Avery Rental Services
Worksheet
For the Year Ended December 31, 2002

Accounts	Trial Balance		Adjustments		Income Statement		Balance Sheet	
	Debit	Credit	Debit	Credit	Debit	Credit	Debit	Credit
Cash	5600 00							
Accounts Receivable	1000 00							
Equipment	4500 00							
Accumulated Depreciation		1000 00						
Accounts Payable		500 00						
Avery, Capital		5000 00						
Avery, Drawing	900 00							
Rental Income		6200 00						
Salaries Expense	39000 00							
Supplies Expense	650 00							
Rent Expense	1100 00							
	6850 00	6850 00						

The accountant gathers information relevant to the adjusting process. The adjusting entries are then recorded directly on the worksheet. The following exercise is based on the illustrative worksheet presented. Accompanying this exercise is a completed worksheet based on the exercise.

EXERCISE 4   Record in journal form the following adjusting entries using the information provided in the worksheet previously presented.

a. Depreciation for the year amounting to $500.

b. Salaries are paid on Friday for the week including the payday. December 31, 2002, falls on a Thursday this year. The daily payroll amounts to $130. Record the adjusting entry to recognize the accrual of salaries for four days.

c. Included in the rental income account is income received but not yet earned amounting to $1,200. Record the necessary adjusting entry.

d. Supplies recognized as an expense amounting to $600 have not been used up during the current accounting period. Make the necessary adjusting entry.

Verify the correctness of your journal entries by comparing the entries with the adjustments that appear on the completed worksheet presented that follows.

Avery Rental Services
Worksheet
For the Year Ended December 31, 2002

Accounts	Trial Balance Debit	Trial Balance Credit	Adjustments Debit	Adjustments Credit	Income Statement Debit	Income Statement Credit	Balance Sheet Debit	Balance Sheet Credit
Cash	560000						560000	
Accounts Receivable	100000						100000	
Equipment	450000						450000	
Accumulated Depreciation		100000		(a)50000				150000
Accounts Payable		50000						50000
Avery, Capital		500000						500000
Avery, Drawing	90000						90000	
Rental Income		6200000	(c)120000			6080000		
Salaries Expense	3900000		(b)52000		3952000			
Supplies Expense	650000			(d)60000	590000			
Rent Expense	1100000				1100000			
	6850000	6850000						
Depreciation Expense			(a)50000		50000			
Salaries Payable				(b)52000				52000
Unearned Rental Income				(c)120000				120000
Prepaid Supplies			(d)60000				60000	
			282000	282000	5692000	6080000	1260000	872000
Net Income					3880000			388000
					6080000	6080000	1260000	1260000

How to Record Adjusting Entries on the Worksheet

The trial balance only contains those accounts that have balances as of December 31, 2002. When adjustments are recorded to the worksheet where accounts are needed, such as adjustment (a), then the needed account is added below the trial balance. Notice that letters are used to relate debit adjustments to corresponding credits. Once the adjustments have been recorded in the adjustments column, the accountant will foot the debit and credit adjustments column. If the totals are in agreement, they are then double underscored. Those accounts not having adjustments are simply extended to the appropriate set of columns. Assets and the proprietor's drawing account are extended to the debit column of the balance sheet. Liabilities and proprietor's capital are extended to the credit column of the balance sheet. Revenue and expense accounts that were not adjusted are extended to the credit and debit columns respectively. The extensions of the accounts that were affected by the adjustments are treated according to the specific adjustment.

Adjustment (a) causes a change in the accumulated depreciation account that began with a credit balance on the trial balance. There was a credit adjustment to it that caused it to increase to $1,500. This new *adjusted* balance is carried to the credit side of the balance sheet column. (Remember, this account is a contra-asset.) The debit entry to adjustment (a) recognizes a depreciation expense and extends the amount to the debit or expense side of the income statement columns.

Adjustment (b) causes an increase in salaries expense that is extended to the debit side of the income statement section. The corresponding credit to salaries payable establishes this liability that was not previously on the books and extends the amount to the credit side of the balance sheet.

Adjustment (c) reduces rental income as a result of its not having been earned, causing the balance in the account to be reduced and extended to the credit or income side of the income statement columns. The corresponding credit establishes the liability unearned rental income, which is extended to the credit side of the balance sheet.

Adjustment (d) recognizes that what had been considered to be entirely an expense apparently is still in inventory. This caused a reduction in the supplies expense, the new balance of which was extended to the debit side of the income statement columns and created the prepaid supplies account (an asset) with the extension to the debit side of the balance sheet.

Following the extensions of the trial balance and adjustments to entry amounts, the four remaining columns are footed. Note that the results of the footing causes four different totals. A comparison of the difference between the income statement and balance sheet column totals are the same, however. The reason that the same difference appears is that this difference will either represent a net income or a net loss. In the above worksheet, note that there is an excess of credit on the income statement column as compared with debits. This excess represents net income that is shown on the debit side of the income statement to allow the two columns to be balanced. Note that the debit total exceeds the credit total on the balance sheet columns. This is the case because the income earned by the business has not yet been transferred to the owner of the business (it is not reflected in Avery's capital account). Remember, temporary capital accounts are eventually transferred to the proprietor's capital account. If the balances in the income statement and the balance sheet had been reversed, this would mean that the business had sustained a loss. A credit entry to get the income statement columns to balance would indicate that the total expenses (debits) exceeded the total revenues (credits). This loss would be reflected in a debit entry to get the balance sheet columns to agree. The debit entry would represent the net loss that would have to be taken out of the proprietor's capital account.

The extension of the drawing account is made to the debit side of the balance sheet columns. This is done because the drawing account has a reducing effect on proprietor's permanent capital.

Using the Completed Worksheet

If the accountant had been requested to prepare interim financial statements, the information needed could be taken directly from the worksheet. There would be no need to journalize and post adjusting entries. This is especially important if a company normally adjusts its books only at the end of the accounting period. If the worksheet is prepared at the end of the accounting period, this enables the accountant to record and post the adjusting entries properly after preparing the worksheet. Financial statement preparation is greatly expedited by the preparation of the worksheet. The actual adjustment to the books can take place at any future time without holding up the preparation of these statements. In preparing the statements from the worksheet, the income statement is taken directly from the income statement columns of the worksheet. The preparation of the statement of capital requires the accountant to obtain the beginning capital balance from the balance sheet, as well as the drawing and net income figures. The preparation of the balance sheet uses all the information in the balance sheet columns, except for the drawing, net income or loss, and proprietor's capital balances. The statement of capital will provide the new capital balance for the proprietor.

EXERCISE 5   The following trial balance was prepared for the Beldon Service Co. as of December 31, 200-.

Beldon Service Co.
Trial Balance
December 31, 200-

	Debit	Credit
Cash	$16,900	
Accounts Receivable	2,000	
Prepaid Insurance	600	
Supplies	300	
Furniture	13,500	
Accumulated Depreciation		$ 500
Accounts Payable		1,500
Notes Payable		8,000
L. Beldon, Capital		12,000
L. Beldon, Drawing	4,000	
Service Revenue		21,000
Rental Revenue		1,600
Salaries Expense	5,000	
Rent Expense	1,400	
Utilities Expense	900	
	$44,600	$44,600

The following information is provided for adjustment purposes:

a. An analysis of the insurance files indicates that there is a balance in the insurance account of $400.
b. Supplies used during the year amounted to $175.
c. Depreciation expense on the furniture amounted to $500 for the year.
d. Of the service revenue recorded, it has been determined that $400 of it has not been earned for the current year.
e. Salaries earned but not paid for the last week in the fiscal year amounted to $300.
f. Interest expense incurred but not yet paid on a promissory note amounted to $40.

Directions:

1. Set up an eight-column worksheet using the trial balance presented above.
2. Record the adjusting entries directly on the worksheet using the letters assigned.
3. Complete the worksheet.
4. Using the completed worksheet prepare an income statement, statement of capital, and balance sheet.

Chart of Accounts

If you wanted to find where a particular topic was covered in this book, you would use the table of contents at the beginning of the book. The accountant in organizing the ledger will also establish a CHART OF ACCOUNTS, which is comparable to a table of contents. The purpose of the chart of accounts is to provide the user of the ledger with a means of determining the accounts found in the ledger and their location within the ledger. The organization of the chart of accounts follows the accounting equation format very closely, in that the chart lists asset accounts first, followed by liability accounts, then proprietor's capital, drawing, revenue, and expense accounts. In every ledger and trial balance form previously presented this format has been followed. Note that the numbering of the account pages also follows this format. The asset accounts are assigned the numbering series beginning with 100. Liabilities are assigned the 200 series, and capital accounts use the 300 series.

The following represents a typical chart of accounts found on the first page of a ledger:

CHART OF ACCOUNTS

Assets

Cash	101
Accounts Receivable	102
Supplies	105
Equipment	120

Liabilities

Accounts Payable	201
Notes Payable	205

Capital

J. Jones, Capital	300
J. Jones, Drawing	301
Service Revenue	310
Rental Revenue	320
Commission Revenue	330
Rent Expense	350
Salaries Expense	355
Supplies Expense	356
Insurance Expense	357
Utilities Expense	358
Miscellaneous Expense	370
Income Summary	400

Notice that even though the accounts are listed in numerical order, not all numbers have been used. This is to allow for future expansion when additional accounts will need to be inserted in the correct area of the ledger.

Closing Entries

In an earlier chapter we distinguished between permanent and temporary capital accounts. Temporary capital accounts consisted of the proprietor's drawing account and all of the revenue and expense accounts.

The word "temporary" means NOT permanent or subject to change. These temporary accounts are eventually eliminated and the contents of the accounts transferred to permanent capital. We accomplish this through the preparation of the statement of capital. The statement of capital compares the drawing account with the net income or loss shown by the income statement. The resulting balance causes either an increase or a decrease in the proprietor's capital. While this process is necessary in order to prepare financial statements, it must also be reflected in the various ledger accounts. This is accomplished through the recording of closing entries.

The CLOSING ENTRY involves transferring the balances of the temporary capital accounts to the proprietor's permanent capital account. In order to accomplish this, each temporary capital account must be either debited or credited to eliminate its balance, while a corresponding debit or credit is summarized in another temporary account designed exclusively for that purpose. This new temporary account is known as the INCOME SUMMARY or NET EARNINGS SUMMARY. The name of the account may vary from business to business, but the closing process remains basically the same.

The procedure for closing the ledger accounts is as follows:

1. All revenue accounts are closed to the income summary account.
2. All expense accounts are closed to the income summary account.
3. Proprietor's drawing is closed to the income summary account.
4. The income summary account is closed to the proprietor's permanent capital account.

EXAMPLE The following partial trial balance is illustrated for Mary Rodriguez Co. (after adjusting entries have been recorded and posted to the ledger):

Mary Rodriguez Co.
Trial Balance
December 31, 2002

	Debit	Credit
Mary Rodriguez, Capital		$5,000
Mary Rodriguez, Drawing	$ 645	
Service Revenue		2,000
Rental Revenue		1,200
Salaries Expense	800	
Rent Expense	450	
Miscellaneous Expenses	1,250	

The following closing entries would be recorded in the ledger of the Mary Rodriguez Co.:

2002

Dec. 31	Service Revenue	2,000	
	Rental Revenue	1,200	
	Income Summary		3,200
	To close revenue to income summary.		

```
2002
Dec. 31    Income Summary                          2,500
               Salaries Expense                              800
               Rent Expense                                  450
               Miscellaneous Expenses                      1,250
           To close expense to income summary.

       31  Income Summary                            645
               Mary Rodriguez, Drawing                       645
           To close drawing to income summary.

       31  Income Summary                             55
               Mary Rodriguez, Capital                        55
           To close income summary to capital.
```

Notice the effects on the individual ledger accounts as a result of these closing entries being posted. The word "Balance" in the individual ledger accounts refers to the pencil footed balance in the individual accounts as of December 31. December 31 entries represent the posting of the closing entries.

Mary Rodriguez, Capital			
	2002		
	Balance	5,000	
	Dec. 31	55	

Mary Rodriguez, Drawing			
2002		2002	
Balance	645	Dec. 31	645

Services Revenue			
2002		2002	
Dec. 31	2,000	Balance	2,000

Rental Revenue			
2002		2002	
Dec. 31	1,200	Balance	1,200

Salaries Expense			
2002		2002	
Balance	800	Dec. 31	800

Rent Expense			
2002		2002	
Balance	450	Dec. 31	450

Miscellaneous Expenses			
2002		2002	
Balance	1,250	Dec. 31	1,250

Income Summary			
2002		2002	
Dec. 31	2,500	Dec. 31	3,200
31	645		
31	55		

After the closing entries have been journalized and posted, the only accounts that will have balances in the ledger will be the permanent accounts—namely, the assets, liabilities, and proprietor's permanent capital. The temporary accounts will still be found in the ledger; however, these accounts will now have no balances. The process of closing the ledger takes place at the end of the accounting period, so that at the beginning of the next accounting period the accountant can begin to accumulate information in the temporary accounts again. Remember that the income statement covers a period of time. The closing process permits the elimination of one accounting period's temporary accounts, and thus the accumulation of revenue, expenses, and proprietor's drawings begin again in the following period.

EXERCISE 6   Using the worksheet prepared from Exercise 5 set up "T" accounts for each account found in the trial balance. Record the balances in the individual "T" accounts. Journalize the adjusting entries from the worksheet and post to the "T" accounts. Take the information as to proprietor's drawing, as well as the information in the income statement, journalize and post the closing entries.

Post-Closing Trial Balance

End-of-the-year activities involve the preparation of the worksheet, including the making of any necessary adjusting entries. The accountant will then journalize and post these adjusting entries. Closing entries are then journalized and posted. The adjusting and closing process has a dramatic effect on the ledger, in that the trial balance prepared to verify that the ledger was in balance is no longer valid. It then becomes necessary to prove that the ledger is still in balance. In order to do so the accountant will prepare another trial balance that is called a "post-closing trial balance." Prepared at the end of the accounting period, the POST-CLOSING TRIAL BALANCE differs significantly from the previous trial balance in that its accounts reflect adjusting entries that have been made and its temporary accounts no longer have balances. The successful completion of the post-closing trial balance will prove that the ledger is in balance at the end of the accounting period. Prior to recording any business transactions for the new accounting period, this post-closing trial balance must be prepared.

EXERCISE 7   Having completed Exercise 6, prepare a post-closing trial balance for the Beldon Service Co.

Steps in the Accounting Cycle

We will assume that the accountant is called upon to prepare financial statements once a year at the end of the accounting period. Given this fact the following steps would be followed in maintaining accounting records for the accounting cycle:

a. Journalize daily business transactions.
b. Post to the various ledger accounts.
c. Prepare a trial balance monthly.
d. Prepare a worksheet with necessary adjusting entries at the end of the accounting period.
e. Prepare financial statements.
f. Journalize and post adjusting entries.
g. Journalize and post closing entries.
h. Prepare a post-closing trial balance.

When the accountant is requested to prepare interim financial statements, the procedures just presented are slightly modified. Since in most business organizations adjusting entries are journalized and posted at the end of the accounting period, to do so during the year would entail additional unnecessary work. An interim statement is prepared at any time other than the end of the accounting period. The accountant could prepare these statements monthly, quarterly, semi-annually, or for any period of time of less than one year. Generally accepted accounting principles require that adjustments take place to reflect properly revenue and expenses; however, for interim purposes these adjustments do not have to be reflected in the journal or ledger.

The accountant in preparing interim statements would prepare the worksheet with adjusting entries reflecting the specific period of time covered by the statement, but would not journalize or post the adjusting entries nor prepare closing entries. Journalizing and posting adjusting and closing entries would only take place at the end of the accounting period.

Reversing Entries

The process of recording adjusting entries creates certain ledger accounts that are not normally recorded in the accounting period. For example, in the process of recognizing accrued salaries, the salaries payable account is established. Note the following adjusting entry:

2002			
Dec. 31	Salaries Expense	1,800	
	Salaries Payable		1,800
	To recognize accrued salaries		

While the salaries payable account will be listed on the chart of accounts and an actual page for it will be found in the ledger, no entries are normally made in this account during the year, with the exception of the adjusting entry just illustrated. The payroll clerk or bookkeeper in charge of preparing the payroll at the end of the week is familiar with the basic procedure of recording the salaries expense and reducing the amount of cash.

The following example will illustrate the need for a reversal entry.

EXAMPLE   Salaries are paid on Friday for the week ending that day. December 31 ends on a Tuesday and salaries are not to be paid until Friday of that week. Accrued salaries for those two days amounts to 1,800. The following adjusting entry is recorded by the accountant as part of the adjusting process:

```
2002
Dec. 31   Salaries Expense                      1,800
               Salaries Payable                         1,800
          To recognize accrued salaries
```

As a result of closing the ledger at the end of the accounting period, the salaries expense account will have a zero balance going into the new accounting period. We recognize that salaries payable, being a liability, will appear on the post-closing trial balance and will have a balance at the beginning of the new accounting period. When the payroll entry is made on January 3 of the new year, the amount of the payroll is 4,500. The payroll clerk is used to recording the following entry and would normally do so on January 3.

```
2003
Jan. 3   Salaries Expense                       4,500
              Cash                                       4,500
         For the week ending today
```

How much of this expense should be recognized in the new year? (Only $2,700 representing three days' earnings in the new year.)

How much of this expense has already been recognized in the preceding year? ($1,800 as a result of the December 31 adjusting entry.)

How much of the expense was recognized by the bookkeeper on January 3? ($4,500)

Since the bookkeeper or payroll clerk are not expected to be involved with the adjusting entry process, the above problem can be solved by recording a REVERSING ENTRY on the first day of the new accounting period. The ledger accounts following the preparation of the post-closing trial balance appear as follows:

Salaries Expense	Salaries Payable
	2002
	Dec. 31 1,800

Since the salaries payable account is not one of the accounts found to have a balance during the year, the accountant will record the following reversal entry:

```
2003
Jan. 1   Salaries Payable                       1,800
              Salaries Expense                          1,800
         To reverse adjusting entry
```

Note: The reversal entry is the exact opposite of the adjusting entry recorded on December 31. Notice the effect this entry has when posted to the ledger accounts.

Salaries Expense			Salaries Payable		
2003			2003		2002
Jan. 1	1,800		Jan. 1 1,800		Dec. 31 1,800
(New Year)			(New Year)		

The balance in the salaries payable account has been eliminated and the balance transferred to the salaries expense account as a CREDIT BALANCE, which, in effect, says that this expense account is temporarily being classified as a liability. When the bookkeeper makes the entry paying the payroll on January 3 (as shown above), the effect of the posting on the salaries expense account is as follows:

Salaries Expense	
2003	2003
Jan. 3 Payment 4,500	Jan. 1 (reversal) 1,800

What is the balance in the salaries expense account on January 1? (credit balance, $1,800)

What is the total salaries expense that should be paid for the week ending January 3? ($4,500)

What was the salaries expense recognized for the old year as a result of the adjusting entry? ($1,800)

What is the salaries expense that is being recognized for the new year as of January 3? ($2,700)

WHEN TO USE REVERSING ENTRIES

A reversal entry is required whenever an adjusting entry results in the establishment of an account on the books that normally does not carry a balance during the year. The reversal entry will take place on the first day of the new accounting period and the entry will be the exact reverse of the previous adjusting entry recorded.

EXAMPLE   At the end of the accounting period, the balance in the supplies expense account is $900. After a physical inventory, it is determined that $125 in supplies have not been used up and have to be adjusted.

1. Record the necessary adjusting entry.
2. Record the closing entry necessary based on the information provided.
3. Record the reversal entry.

(Old Year)

Dec. 31   Prepaid Supplies (Asset)   125
           Supplies Expense   125
           To recognize the expense not used
           up during the accounting period.

     31   Income Summary   775
           Supplies Expense   775
           To close the expense account.

(New Year)

Jan. 1   Supplies Expense   125
           Prepaid Supplies   125
           To record the reversal entry.

Note the effects on the accounts after these entries have been posted.

Supplies Expense					Prepaid Supplies			
Old		Old			Old		New	
Balance	900	Dec. 31	125		Dec. 31	125	Jan. 1	125
New		31	775					
Jan. 1	125							

What was the supplies expense recognized in the old year? ($775)

What account did the adjusting entry establish and how is it classified? (Prepaid supplies are classified as an asset.)

What did the reversing entry convert the asset prepaid supplies into? (Supplies expense.)

What benefit does the reversing entry provide in this instance? (The supplies expense has been reestablished with a balance of $125, which represents a probable expense in the new year.)

The process of recording reversing entries is left up to the discretion of the accountant. We have previously discussed situations where adjusting entries created balances in accounts that are not normally used during the accounting period. While it is advisable to utilize reversal entries, it is not mandatory to do so. In a situation where the bookkeeper is not familiar with these reversible accounts, it is advisable to record reversal entries. When the bookkeeper or accounting clerk is familiar with the accounts established as a result of adjusting entries and can properly record future period transactions involving them, then reversal entries may not be needed.

EXERCISE 8   Based on the following information, record the necessary adjusting entries. Having done so, record the necessary reversal entries.

1. Salaries for the week amounted to $3,500. For the week ending January 4 (payday) record the adjusting entry needed for the old year.
2. The office supplies account has a balance before adjustments of $530; the office supplies inventory at the end of the year is $160.

3. The insurance expense on the trial balances has a balance of $1,350. An analysis of the various policies shows that $450 in unexpired premiums remain at the end of the year.

4. You sign a new lease with a tenant that requires that the tenant pay his rent for a six-month period at $100 per month. The effective date of the lease was November 1. At that time you received a check for $600 that you credited to the rental income account. Make an adjusting and reversal entry, if needed.

Summing Up

The accounting period or cycle consists of a twelve-month period. If the accounting period follows the calendar, the company is said to be on a calendar-year basis. If the company's year begins on any date other than January 1, the business is said to be on a fiscal-year basis. Regardless of these factors, every business must maintain records that provide detailed information on the business's activities for the accounting period. Maintenance of adequate and appropriate records is accomplished through the following procedures:

1. Business transactions are journalized on a daily basis.
2. These transactions are then posted to appropriate ledger accounts.
3. A trial balance proving that the ledger is in balance is usually prepared monthly.
4. A worksheet is prepared whenever interim financial statements are needed by the organization.
5. At the end of the accounting period, a worksheet is prepared with the necessary adjusting entries for the year.
6. Financial statements are prepared from the year-end worksheet.
7. Adjusting entries on the year-end worksheet are then journalized and posted to the ledger.
8. Closing entries are then journalized and posted causing the temporary capital accounts to be closed to income summary, and the resulting balance closed to proprietor's permanent capital.
9. The balance in the ledger is then verified by the preparation of the post-closing trial balance.
10. At the beginning of the new accounting period, reversal entries are recorded to eliminate those accounts established as a result of the adjusting process.

Adjusting entries are usually recorded at the end of the accounting period. The purpose of these entries is to see that the principle of matching costs and revenue is followed. Adjusting entries may represent accruals or deferrals. They generally affect the recognition of unrecorded expenses and revenue as well as the need to postpone the recognition of expenses and revenue.

Closing entries are recorded at the end of the accounting period. These entries close the temporary capital accounts, and the resulting balances either increase or decrease the proprietor's permanent capital.

Reversing entries are recorded at the beginning of the new accounting period. The completion of these entries makes it easier for the accountant to monitor the recording of the daily business transactions by the bookkeepers and accounting clerks. By recording reversal entries, the accountant does not have to rely on the bookkeeper's knowledge of the adjusting process.

Many tools are developed for use by the accountant that enable the accurate and timely preparation of business data. The use of a *chart of accounts* in the ledger enables the user to locate a specific account quickly due to the logical organization of the chart. A *worksheet* is an invaluable tool in preparing financial statements. When the worksheet is prepared in the interim, the work involved in adjusting journalization and posting is not necessary. A year-end worksheet expedites the preparation of the financial statements, as well as the journalizing and posting of adjusting and closing entries. The preparation of a *trial balance* and a *post-closing trial balance* enables the accountant to check that the ledger is in balance as a result of the balance documents.

CHAPTER 5

ACCOUNTING FOR A TRADING BUSINESS

How Service and Trading Businesses Differ

There are primarily two functions of businesses: service and trading.

Service businesses sell knowledge while trading businesses sell a particular product or group of products. Obviously, there are businesses that specialize in the manufacture of the product that the trading business sells; however, this business organization will be presented in a more advanced course.

Up to now we have been concentrating exclusively on accounting for a service business. The accounting for a trading business is primarily the same as that for a service business, except that in a trading business a product is being sold. Service companies, such as law firms, accounting firms, and advertising agencies, perform services and the compensation received for those services is recorded in various accounts such as: income from fees, commissions income, and income from services. These revenue totals, when compared with total expenses, enable the accountant to determine whether the service business has earned a profit or sustained a loss. The determination of profit or loss for a trading business is somewhat more involved, however, because of a significant added component. That component is the cost of purchasing the product being sold. As a result of this cost, it is necessary to be familiar with a number of ledger accounts that are only used by organizations that sell products.

SPECIAL ACCOUNTS FOR A TRADING BUSINESS

Since a trading business's primary reason for existence is to sell a product, it is necessary to talk in terms of the product being sold. In order to sell the product, it is first necessary to acquire it. Since these goods that we are purchasing are not being bought for use but rather for resale, we usually maintain records on them separate from records on traditional assets that are bought for use.

The account title used for goods that are bought for resale is usually called "Merchandise Purchases." Merchandise purchases are all goods bought exclusively for the purpose of resale. This account is classified as an *expense*. It is expected that as the goods are sold, the

69

cost will be recognized as an expense that is known as the "Cost of Goods Sold."

From time to time goods that are purchased may not meet the owner's expectations. When this happens, the buyer will request the right to return the good. The goods being returned are recorded in a separate account entitled "Purchases Returns and Allowances." This account is classified as a contra-expense account because it directly offsets the merchandise purchases account. In order for goods to be available for sale, it is necessary to have those goods transported to the retailer's establishment. By agreement, the cost of transporting the goods can be borne by either the buyer or the seller. If the cost is the responsibility of the buyer, this cost is recorded in an account entitled "Freight on Purchases" or "Freight In." It is appropriate to maintain a separate record for freight charges so that an accurate analysis of the accounting data can be made.

As an incentive to pay their obligations early, buyers of goods may be offered discounts by the seller. This discount is only recognized if and when it is taken by the buyer. This discount is recorded in a ledger account called "Purchases Discount" or "Discount on Purchases." Thus, the discount represents a reduction in cost due to early payment and is a form of revenue to the buyer of the goods. It is recognized only when taken by the buyer.

METHODS OF DETERMINING INCOME

The primary difference between a service business and a trading business is the product sold by the trading business. The primary expense of a trading business is usually the cost of the item being sold. Because of this fact, a trading business's income statement is traditionally broken down into a number of sections. The following represents a skeletal form of an income statement for a trading business:

> Net Sales
> − Cost of Goods Sold
>
> Gross Profit
> − Expenses
>
> Net Income

Determining Net Sales

Merchandise sold by a trading (retail) business are usually recorded in an account called "Sales." This revenue account may have other titles, such as Income from Sales, Sales Income, Sales Revenue, or other titles that provide a greater description of the product being sold. Every sale, whether it is made for cash or on credit, will be credited to the sales account. The balance in the sales account at the end of the accounting period is usually known as GROSS SALES. Gross sales represents the total sales made by the organization for the particular accounting period.

If a customer receives a defective or otherwise unsatisfactory item from the seller, the seller usually provides the customer with a right to return the product. Since the original intent of the buyer was to retain the goods, an assumption is made that the reason for the return was the fault or negligence of the seller. It is important that a record be maintained for the returns of these items. The accountant will set up a separate account to show these returns; the account is called "Sales Returns and Allowances." Since the effect of the return is to offset the original sale, this account can be classified as a contra-revenue account. Entries recorded in the sales returns and allowances account would represent debits.

At the end of the accounting period or for interim statement purposes, the calculation of net sales would result from subtracting sales returns and allowances from the figure for gross sales. The following represents the net sales section of an income statement for a trading business:

Revenue		
Gross Sales	65,000	
Less: Sales Returns and Allowances	2,380	
Net Sales		62,620

Recording Sales, and Sales Returns, and Allowances

Sales both on credit and for cash cause the revenue account (sales) to be credited. The following examples illustrate the journal entries for recording both cash and credit sales:

200-			
July 3	Cash	1,357	
	Sales		1,357
	For merchandise sold for cash.		
7	Accounts Receivable	985	
	Sales		985
	For merchandise sold on credit.		

When a customer wishes to return goods to a seller, this right is usually not automatic. The customer will request the right to return the goods to the seller. If the original sale had been paid for, then the following entry would reflect the refund issued on the books of the seller of the merchandise:

200-			
July 5	Sales Returns and Allowances	78	
	Cash		78

If the original sale was made on credit, the buyer must first request the right to return the goods. The seller's permission to return the goods comes in a form known as a CREDIT MEMORANDUM. This is the authorization needed by the buyer to return the goods. The credit memo becomes the document that is used to record the following entry:

200-			
July 12	Sales Returns and Allowances	102	
	Accounts Receivable		102
	Issued credit memo #453 for defective merchandise returned.		

Recording Sales Discounts

A DISCOUNT is a reduction in price. A SALES DISCOUNT represents a reduction in price related to a sale. The seller of goods has a choice as to how goods are to be sold. Basically, goods may be sold for cash or on credit. Competition among sellers really determines whether an item is to be offered for sale for cash or on credit. Where credit is extended on sales, the terms given the buyer are stated on the sales invoice. Such TERMS (means and methods of payment allowed) are calculated from the date of the invoice. Terms such as "n/30" mean that the entire obligation, the net (n), is due the seller within 30 days of the invoice date. Terms of "n/60 or "n/90" or "n/120" or longer periods of time may be given to the purchaser to pay the obligation. The terms offered usually depend upon the custom of the trade. In some trades, it is customary for invoices to become due and payable 10 days after the end of the month in which the sale occurred. Such a term would be expressed as "n/10 EOM."

When credit periods are long, creditors may offer the buyer a CASH DISCOUNT, which is a price reduction offered by the seller to the buyer as an incentive to pay the obligation to the seller before the buyer is actually required to do so. Terms of "2/10, n/30" may be offered. This term states that a 2% discount will be given if the obligation is paid within 10 days of the invoice date, or the entire amount (net) is due within 30 days from the invoice date. The sales discount is offered by the seller, but it is the buyer who exercises the option of taking the cash discount or not. To the seller this sales discount represents an expense of the business. As such, when it is taken by the buyer, it is recorded on the seller's books as an expense. The account title used to recognize this expense is "Sales Discount" or "Discount on Sales." On the buyer's books this cash discount represents a form of revenue, or a contra-expense, and is generally known as a purchase discount or discount on purchases. When the discount is taken by the buyer it is recorded as a credit to the purchases discount account.

When a customer sends payment within the discount period offered by the seller, the transaction on the seller's books would be recorded as follows, given the following example:

Sale made on credit on January 5, 200-. The amount of the sale was $500, the terms: 2/10, n/30. The following entries were made to record the credit sale and the subsequent payment received from the buyer on January 13, 200-.

200-			
Jan. 5	Accounts Receivable	500	
	Sales		500
	2/10, n/30		
13	Cash	490	
	Sales Discount	10	
	Accounts Receivable		500
	Inv. paid within discount period.		

Sales discounts are accumulated in the expense account. Since this discount represents a cost of doing business and it is directly related to the sale of the product, it is appropriate to show sales discounts as a reduction from gross sales on the income statement. The following section of the income statement illustrates the placement of a sales discount:

Revenue		
Gross Sales		50,000
Less: Sales Returns and Allowances	1,350	
Sales Discount	940	2,290
Net Sales		47,710

EXERCISE 1   The Spencer Department Store bought $2,400 of merchandise, terms 2/10, n/30, from the Gigi Company. Assuming they paid for the goods within the discount period, make the following entries on the books of the seller: (1) the recording of the original sale and (2) the entry for the payment of the liability within the discount period by the customer.

EXERCISE 2   Merchandise is sold on account to a customer for $12,000, terms: 2/10, 1/15, n/30. The date of the invoice is March 6, 200-. The bill is paid by the customer on March 20, 200-. Determine the amount of cash to be received by the seller and record the journal entry on the books of the seller to reflect the receipt of the money on March 200-.

Determining the Cost of Goods Available for Sale

The primary cost in a trading business is the cost of the merchandise sold. In order for the sale of merchandise to take place, the goods must first be available for sale. Goods available for sale consist of two components: net purchases and merchandise inventory.

During the current accounting period, goods that are purchased are charged to the merchandise purchases account. Any goods returned are credited to the purchases returns and allowances account. Delivery charges on purchases are charged to a freight on purchases account. Discounts earned as a result of early payments of credit purchases are credited to the purchases discount account. Net purchases would be determined in the following manner:

Merchandise Purchases		15,000
Less: Purchases Returns and Allowances	400	
Purchases Discount	500	900
		14,100
Add: Freight on Purchases		200
Net Purchases		14,300

Merchandise purchased in a previous accounting period that remains unsold into the current accounting period is known as MER-CHANDISE INVENTORY. This inventory at the beginning of the new accounting period is known as beginning merchandise inventory. During the current accounting period this inventory remains on the books with no changes being recorded to it. At the end of the accounting period the accountant determines the value of the goods sold. Before this can be done, however, the accountant must determine the COST OF MERCHANDISE AVAILABLE FOR SALE. The following section of the income statement for a trading business illustrates this:

Merchandise Inventory, January 1, 2002			4,000
Merchandise Purchases		15,000	
Less: Purchases Returns & Allowances	400		
Purchases Discount	500	900	
		14,100	
Add: Freight on Purchases		200	
Net Purchases			14,300
Cost of Merchandise Available for Sale			18,300

DETERMINING THE MERCHANDISE INVENTORY

The merchandise of a trading business consists of goods on hand at the beginning of the accounting period (beginning merchandise inventory) and goods purchased during the accounting period (merchandise purchases), both being available for resale to customers. The beginning merchandise inventory and the merchandise purchases for the accounting period represent the COST OF MERCHANDISE FOR SALE, as previously illustrated. While the determination of merchandise purchases is obtained from the ledger account, as a result of posting to the account during the accounting period, the determination of the value assigned to MERCHANDISE INVENTORY is obtained by taking a "physical count" of merchandise at a particular time during the accounting period. Companies that sell a great quantity and variety of items such as department stores keep track of their stock of goods by using the PERIODIC INVENTORY METHOD. This method entails taking a physical count of the merchandise on hand at the end of the accounting period. The value of this inventory is determined by multiplying the quantity of each item by its appropriate unit cost. A total cost figure for the entire inventory is then determined by adding the total costs of all the kinds of merchandise in the inventory.

The actual physical inventory is taken at the end of the accounting period. It represents a combination of goods purchased during the year and merchandise the firm had on hand at the beginning of the year but has not sold as of the end of the accounting period. This merchandise inventory is actually an asset, an asset that has to be reflected on the books at the end of the accounting period (year). In order to do so the following adjusting entry is made to establish the ending merchandise inventory on the books of the company:

```
2002
Dec. 31   Merchandise Inventory                      500
              Income Summary                             500
          To establish the ending inventory on the books
```

The debit entry establishes the asset value on the books. The credit entry acts to offset the value of the merchandise purchases and the beginning inventory, which, in combination, represent the cost of merchandise available for sale, but only after the value of the goods remaining is subtracted. The credit entry is necessary to obtain the cost of goods sold, as the next topic will illustrate.

The merchandise inventory determined at the end of the accounting period also represents the beginning merchandise inventory for the next accounting period. This beginning inventory is necessary in order to determine the cost of merchandise available for sale in the next accounting period.

DETERMINING THE COST OF MERCHANDISE SOLD

Cost of goods sold represents the cost assigned to the actual merchandise that was sold during the accounting period. To determine the cost of goods sold under a periodic inventory system, it is necessary to compare the cost of merchandise available for sale with the goods that were not sold. Goods not sold are represented by the ending merchandise inventory. The following section of the income statement provides the value of the goods sold during the accounting period:

```
Cost of Merchandise Available for Sale              18,300
Less: Merchandise Inventory, December 31, 2002       3,500
Cost of Merchandise Sold                            14,800
```

The actual-cost-of-merchandise-sold section of an income statement for a trading business would appear as follows:

```
COST OF MERCHANDISE SOLD
Merchandise Inventory, January 1, 2002                              4,000
Merchandise Purchases                              15,000
Less: Purchases Returns & Allowances       400
      Purchases Discount                   500        900
                                                   14,100
Add: Freight on Purchases                             200
Net Purchases                                                      14,300
Cost of Merchandise Available for Sale                            18,300
Less: Merchandise Inventory, December 31, 2002                     3,500
Cost of Merchandise Sold                                          14,800
```

EXERCISE 3   At the end of the accounting period the following information relating to a trading business was: Sales, $219,180; Merchandise Inventory December 31, 2002, $46,200; Purchases Returns and Allowances $2,500; Merchandise Inventory, January 1, 2002, $52,390; Freight on Purchases, $2,600; Purchases, $97,500. Determine: (1) Net purchases (2) Cost of goods available for sale; (3) Cost of goods sold, and (4) Gross profit on sales.

EXERCISE 4   Prepare an income statement for a trading business through the gross-profit-on-sales section. The following account balances were found in the ledger of the Reliable Dry Goods Co. as of December 31, 2002. Merchandise Inventory, January 1, 2002, $28,650; Sales $172,200; Sales Returns and Allowances, $3,430; Purchases $138,900; Freight on Purchases, $2,300; Purchases Returns and Allowances, $1,820; Purchases Discount, $1,300; Merchandise Inventory December 31, 2002, $31,200.

Recording Daily Business Transactions

As you read through this section, post the journal entries presented to "T" accounts. Set up the following "T" accounts: Cash; Accounts Receivable; Merchandise Inventory; Accounts Payable; Sales; Sales Returns and Allowances; Sales Discounts; Merchandise Purchases; Purchases Returns and Allowances; Purchases Discounts; and Freight on Purchases. Allow four lines for each ledger account.

The following business transactions in narrative form are presented for the Acme Department Store. As you read the narrative analyze the information and determine the appropriate journal entry called for. Compare your entry with the journal entry immediately following the narrative, and then proceed to post the journal entries to appropriate ledger accounts.

On January 1, 2002 the following selected balances appeared in the ledger account for the Acme Department Store: Merchandise Inventory, January 1, 2002, $12,000.

(Jan. 4—Sales on credit amounted to $3,000. Terms: 2/10, n/30).

2002
Jan. 4   Accounts Receivable   3,000
              Sales   3,000
         2/10, n/30

(Jan. 5—Purchased merchandise on credit for $900. Terms: 1/10, n/30.)

Jan. 5   Merchandise Purchases   900
              Accounts Payable   900
         Credit terms offered 1/10, n/30

(Jan. 7—Sent a credit memo to our customer allowing a return of $200 on goods sold on Jan. 4.)

2002
Jan. 7 Sales Returns and Allowances   200
     Accounts Receivable   200
   Issued credit memo #202

(Jan. 13—Received a check from our customer in payment of the invoice of Jan. 4, less the return of Jan. 7, and the discount taken by the customer.)

Jan. 13 Cash   2,744
    Sales Discount   56
     Accounts Receivable   2,800
   Customer paid inv. of Jan. 4, less 2% discount.

(Jan. 15—Sent a check for $891 in payment of purchase made on Jan. 5.)

Jan. 15 Accounts Payable   900
    Purchases Discount   9
    Cash   891
   Paid inv. of Jan. 5, less 1% discount.

(Jan. 18—Cash sales amounted to $5,500)

Jan. 18 Cash   5,500
    Sales   5,500
   Cash sales

(Jan. 25—Purchased merchandise on credit for $1,200. Terms: 1/10, n/30.)

Jan. 25 Merchandise Purchases   1,200
    Accounts Payable   1,200
   Credit terms offered 1/10, n/30

(Jan. 27—Received authorization to return $200 in goods purchased on Jan. 25.)

Jan. 27 Accounts Payable   200
    Purchases Returns & Allowances 200
   Received credit memo for Jan. 25 inv.

(Jan. 31—Paid for freight charges on purchase of Jan. 5. The amount of the bill was $40.)

Jan. 31 Freight on Purchases   40
    Cash   40
   Paid freight charges on January 5 purchase

After you have posted the above transactions to the appropriate ledger accounts, foot the accounts and determine the balances in the accounts as of January 31, 2002. Using the appropriate ledger accounts, prepare an income statement for Acme Department Store (through the gross-profit-on-sales section).

Adjusting and Closing Entries

The adjusting entries previously discussed for service businesses apply as well to trading businesses. There are accounts, however, used in a trading business that were not part of a service business and thus require discussion.

The merchandise inventory account on the chart of accounts is listed as an asset. This account is not recorded to during the accounting period. Any adjustments to the goods available for sale are shown in the merchandise purchases or the purchases returns and allowances account. At the end of the accounting period, the beginning merchandise inventory account is considered to have been sold. Because of this concept, it is necessary to convert the asset to an expense. In order to do so the following journal entry is recorded:

```
2002
Dec. 31   Income Summary                  10,500
               Merchandise Inventory                     10,500
           To close beginning merchandise inventory
```

This adjusting entry eliminates the January 1, beginning balance in the merchandise inventory account and converts the value of the inventory to an expense. The debit side of the income summary account represents all the expenses of the business. At this point it is assumed that all of the goods in the inventory account have been sold.

At the end of the accounting period, the business will take a physical inventory to determine the value of the goods on hand that were not sold. This inventory represents the ending inventory of the period. Since the beginning inventory has been closed to income summary, it is then appropriate to recognize the value of the new ending inventory on the books. The following entry is made to set up the ending inventory on the books:

```
2002
Dec. 31   Merchandise Inventory            9,300
               Income Summary                            9,300
           To set up ending merchandise
           inventory
```

This adjusting entry has brought about two changes. First, the new ending inventory (asset) is recognized on the books. Secondly, the value of the goods not sold reduces the cost of goods available for sale to represent the cost of goods sold.

The following example will illustrate how the adjusting and closing process determines the cost of goods available for sale and the cost of goods sold.

EXAMPLE   The following balances appear in the ledger account: Merchandise Inventory, Jan. 1, 2002, $4,000; Merchandise Purchases, $6,000. The value of the December 31, 2002, inventory is $3,000. The following are entries to adjust and close the accounts:

2002

Dec. 31	Income Summary		6,000	
		Merchandise Purchases		6,000
	To close expenses.			
31	Income Summary		4,000	
		Merchandise Inventory		4,000
	To close beginning inventory.			
31	Merchandise Inventory		3,000	
		Income Summary		3,000
	To set up ending inventory.			

Income Summary

2002	
Dec. 31	6,000
31	4,000

The balance of $10,000 represents the cost of goods available for sale.

Income Summary

2002		2002	
Dec. 31	6,000	Dec. 31	3,000
31	4,000		

The balance of $7,000 represents the cost of goods sold.

PREPARING A WORKSHEET

A trading concern's worksheet contains the same adjusting entries that would characterize a service business's worksheet. The accounts unique to a trading business are merchandise purchases, purchases returns and allowances, purchases discount, freight on purchases, sales returns and allowances, sales discount, and freight on sales. These would be adjusted when necessary and closed to income summary, because they are all temporary accounts. The treatment of the inventory accounts is unique to a trading business and thus requires further discussion.

The daily business transactions just illustrated involved the merchandise inventory account in the adjusting and closing process. These entries, as with all adjusting entries, are preceded by their appearance on the worksheet. The trading organization's first adjusting entry on the worksheet will transfer the beginning merchandise inventory account, located on the trial balance, to income summary. This recognizes that this asset carried during the year is now converted to an expense. This entry causes the balance in the merchandise inventory to become zero. The debit entry to income summary recognizes that this asset is now considered to be an expense. The second adjusting entry establishes the ending merchandise inventory on the books as an asset by debiting merchandise inventory and crediting income summary. The credit to income summary recognizes that *not all* of the purchases or beginning merchandise inventory sent to income summary really represents an expense. The following partial worksheet will illustrate these procedures:

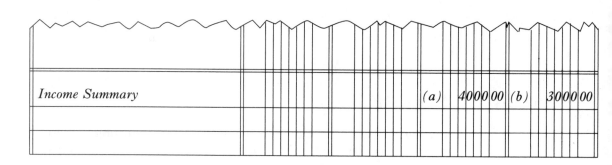

Eversharp Trading Co.
Worksheet
For the Year Ended December 31, 2002

Account	Trial Balance		Adjustments	
	Dr.	Cr.	Dr.	Cr.
Cash	12000 00			
Merchandise Inventory	4000 00		(b) 3000 00	(a) 4000 00

Income Summary			(a) 4000 00	(b) 3000 00

Adjusting entry (a) converts the beginning inventory to an expense. Adjusting entry (b) sets up the asset value of the new ending inventory.

EXERCISE 5   The following trial balance for the Xavier Co. is presented:

Xavier Co.
Trial Balance
June 30, 2003

	DEBITS	CREDITS
Cash	$ 6,500	
Merchandise Inventory, July 1, 2002	3,000	
Notes Receivable	1,500	
Accounts Receivable	2,200	
Office Supplies	500	
Equipment	1,850	
Accounts Payable		$ 1,550
Notes Payable		250
A. Xavier, Capital		10,000
A. Xavier, Drawing	475	
Sales		12,640
Sales Returns and Allowances	150	
Merchandise Purchases	8,025	
Purchases Returns and Allowances		150
Discount on Purchases		340
Discount on Sales	110	
Freight on Purchases	45	
Rent Expense	600	
Interest Income		25
	$24,955	$24,955

The following information was available as of June 30, 2002 the end of the fiscal year:

(a) The ending physical inventory on June 30, 2003 was $3,950.
(b) Office supplies used amounted to $60.
(c) Annual depreciation of equipment was $175.
(d) Interest accrued on notes payable amounted to $11 for the year.
(e) Interest income on notes receivable earned but not received amounted to $75.

Prepare a worksheet for the Xavier Co. Record the adjusting and closing entries to the general journal. Prepare the necessary financial statements for the Xavier Co.

Reversal Entries

The reversal entries we previously discussed apply to a trading form of business as well as a service business. The criterion for recording a reversal entry is whether that particular account, having been set up as a result of an adjusting entry, normally carries a balance in the ledger account during the year. If it does, then no reversal entry is needed. If the account normally does not have a balance in the ledger during the year, the balance in the account is eliminated at the very beginning of the new accounting period through the recording of a reversal entry. Remember that the reversal entry is the opposite of the original adjusting entry made.

EXERCISE 6 The various expenses presented below were incurred by a trading business during the current year. Analyze the numbered items presented and for each item determine in which section of the income statement they should be reported. In which of the following expense sections of the income statement should each be reported: (a) selling (b) general, (c) other?

1. Fire insurance premiums on inventory expired.
2. Advertising materials used.
3. Salary of the general manager paid.
4. Heating and lighting expenses incurred.
5. Gasoline and oil used in the delivery equipment.
6. Depreciation expense on office equipment accrued.
7. Salary of the salespersons paid.
8. Interest expense on notes payable incurred.

EXERCISE 7 From the following information prepare journal entries to: adjust the books at the end of the accounting period, prepare the necessary closing entries, and, where appropriate, prepare the reversal entries needed. Assume the end of the accounting period coincides with the calendar year.

1. Merchandise inventory, Jan. 1, 2002, $35,700; merchandise inventory Dec. 31, 2002, $36,500.
2. Sales salaries are paid for a five-day week ending on Friday. The last payday of the year was Friday, December 26, 2002. If the weekly payroll for a five-day week is $4,500, prepare the adjusting entry to recognize the accrual for the last three days in the year.
3. The prepaid insurance account before adjustments at the end of the accounting period has a balance of $2,396. An analysis of the policies indicates that the actual balance in the account should be $1,800.
4. Interest on a promissory note had been paid one year in advance. The amount of the income recognized was $45 for a period of one year. The income was recognized for the full amount on the day the note was issued, which was July 1, 2002.

Summing Up

There are primarily two forms of business organizations: service and trading. The distinction between a service business and a trading business is found in the accounts of the trading business. Since a trading or merchandising business is concerned with the sale of a product the following accounts are usually an integral part of this business merchandise purchases, purchases returns and allowances, discount on purchases, freight on purchases, sales, sales returns and allowances, and sales discounts. Income determination for a trading business usually takes the following form:

Net Sales
− Cost of Goods Sold
_____
Gross Profit
− Operating Expenses
_____
Net Income

The ledger accounts that characterize a trading business are temporary capital accounts, which are closed out at the end of the accounting period.

In a trading concern using the periodic inventory system, a merchandise inventory account is used. The physical inventory that is taken annually becomes the basis for recognizing the asset value of the goods on hand at the end of the period. This ending inventory for one accounting period becomes the beginning inventory for the following period.

The cost-of-goods-sold section of an income statement for a trading business shows the interaction of the inventory in relation to the goods purchased.

Cost of Goods Sold

Merchandise Inventory, January 1, 200-
+ Merchandise Purchases (Net)
_____
Cost of Goods Available for Sale
− Merchandise Inventory, December 31, 200-
_____
Cost of Goods Sold

The daily activities of a trading business are basically the same as for any business. Transactions involving the acquisition of goods for the purpose of resale are recorded in the merchandise purchases account. Any adjustments related to the acquisition of the goods are usually recorded in separate accounts for analytical purposes. The sale of the product is handled in the same manner as the sale of a service that may either be for cash or on credit. Since goods sold may be returned by the buyer, the seller must record the goods returned in a sales returns and allowances account.

The adjusting process for a trading organization differs from a service business only in respect of the merchandise inventory account. At the end of the accounting period, the accountant must close the beginning inventory to income summary, thus enabling the recognition of the fact that the asset has been converted to an expense. Once the physical inventory has been taken, it is necessary to establish the new inventory on the books. The entry requires a debit to merchandise inventory and a credit to income summary. The debit recognizes the asset value, and the credit recognizes that all the goods available for sale have not been sold. The adjusting, closing, and reversing processes for trading businesses are basically the same as those for service businesses.

CHAPTER 6

SPECIAL JOURNALS AND CONTROLS

What Are Special Journals?

The accountant is responsible for the design and implementation of the accounting system used by the business organization. Whether the accountant is the controller of the business or comes into the organization as an outside consultant, his or her function entails the recording, classifying, and summarizing of data accomplished either manually or by the use of mechanical, electrical, or electronic equipment. While the current trend towards high technology focuses on the use of mini and microcomputers for accounting purposes, it is necessary that the accountant be thoroughly familiar with the manual systems that have been traditionally used. The traditional manual systems are easier to understand and more adaptable to learning through practice. This chapter will focus in part on special journals designed for manual accounting systems. The following special journals can also be readily applied to the microcomputer.

All transactions discussed in previous chapters have been illustrated using the two-column general journal. While the entries have been appropriately recorded and would be done in a similar fashion in most business concerns, there are situations where special journals are used that will take the place of the general journal as illustrated. The need for an alternative approach to the exclusive use of the general journal arises out of the volume of business transactions to be recorded by an organization. In a large business there may be hundreds or even thousands of business transactions to be recorded daily. In order to handle these transactions rapidly and efficiently requires the development of special journals. Special journals divide the labor required with a two-column general journal, so that more than one bookkeeper and or accountant can work on the books of the organization at the same time. SPECIAL JOURNALS are books of original entry that are specifically designed for the purpose of recording similar kinds of transactions. Because of the similarity in the transactions recorded in the individual special journals, the actual recording and posting represents a substantial time- and labor-saving device.

Kinds of Special Journals

There are primarily four special journals that are used by most businesses. These journals are the:

Sales Journal

Cash Receipts Journal

Purchases Journal

Cash Payments Journal

Regardless of the nature of the business enterprise, one or all of the above journals may be used. The criteria for using one or all of the special journals is the volume of business transactions and the need for a division of labor.

The organization of the special journal is tailored to the particular needs of the business. Special columns are used to record repetitive transactions. This procedure permits the posting of transactions or parts to be done in total (summary) at the end of the month, rather than daily. Picture a transaction that may be recorded two or three hundred times per month, such as the receipt of cash. Using a special journal, you can reduce posting to the cash account by two hundred and ninety-nine entries. This can be accomplished by posting the debit to the cash account once at the end of the month, rather than three hundred times during the month.

In addition to special journals, special ledgers will be introduced to show how certain kinds of transactions are posted to separate ledgers, known as SUBSIDIARY LEDGERS. A subsidiary ledger is separate and apart from the general ledger and, like the special journals, will contain specific accounts not specifically found in the general ledger.

SALES JOURNAL

Recording Transactions

Sales of goods and/or services may be made for cash or on credit. While it is more desirable to sell goods and services for cash whenever possible, competition and other factors may force a business to sell their product or service on credit. When the terms of a sale call for payment in thirty, sixty, or ninety days the use of a special journal is appropriate. In fact, any sale of a product or service on credit (regardless of the credit terms) will be recorded in the SALES JOURNAL.

The recording of the following credit sale was made to the general journal:

```
200-
Jan. 10   Accounts Receivable                    400
               Sales                                      400
          R. Jones, terms: n/30
```

This credit sale requires the journalizing of both the debit and credit parts of the entry and subsequent postings. The use of a sales journal will reduce the work in both journalizing and posting. Another disadvantage to using the general journal for this kind of entry that we haven't previously discussed is that the oral promise represented by the debit to accounts receivable does not specify the person who owes the money as a result of the credit sale. The following entry to the sales journal will provide obvious benefits:

Sales Journal

Date		Account Debited	Inv. #	Terms	PR	Amount
200- Jan.	10	R. Jones	101	n/30		400 00

The same basic information previously recorded to the general journal appears in the sales journal. There are certain obvious advantages to the sales journal form. The transaction is recorded on a single line. The debit entry is to a specific customer's name. The amount appears only once and the credit portion of the entry is assumed. Every credit sale is recorded in the sales journal and each credit entry will affect the sales account. It is necessary to present an accounts-debited column because of the many customers that a business will sell to on credit. During the month each sale on credit previously recorded in the general journal had to be posted immediately to the two accounts in the general ledger.

Using the sales journal permits the bookkeeper to refrain from posting the credit portion of the entry until the end of the month.

At that time the total of the amount column will be posted in summary to the credit side of the sales account. The debit postings must be made daily and here is where what we have previously learned has to be modified. The daily postings of the debit entries will be made to a subsidiary (secondary) ledger that is known as an ACCOUNTS RECEIVABLE LEDGER.

The accounts receivable ledger is a separate ledger that contains individual accounts for each customer who has been sold goods on credit. The form of the customer accounts are the same as the previous ledger accounts presented. The customer's name will appear on the top of the account. Increases to the account will be recorded as debit entries and decreases will be recorded as credit entries. Transactions recorded to the sales journal on a daily basis will require daily postings to the various customer accounts found in the accounts receivable ledger. Many business organizations will assign a specific page designation to each customer's account. This page designation is used to indicate that posting has taken place. We will use a page designation that corresponds to the first letter of the last name of the customer. R. Jones's page designation in the accounts receivable ledger would be the letter "J," to correspond to the first letter of his last name. The following illustrates the sales journal and the daily posting to the subsidiary accounts receivable ledger.

Sales Journal　　　　　　　　　　　　　　　　*Page S-1*

Date		Account Debited	Inv. #	Terms	PR	Amount
200- Jan.	10	R. Jones	101	n/30	J	400 00

Accounts Receivable Ledger

R. Jones　　　　　　　　　　　　　　　　　　　　*Page J*

Date			PR	Debit	Credit	Balance
200- Jan.	10	n/30	S-1	400 00		400 00

All credit sales would be recorded to the sales journal in the same manner as the transaction just illustrated. The posting procedure would be the same for each credit sale except that now they would be posted to a specific customer's account. The accounts receivable ledger will contain as many accounts as there are customers. Be particularly aware of the designations used in the post-reference columns of the sales journal as well as the customer's account. The "J" in the post-reference column of the sales journal indicates that posting to the ledger has taken place and that it was made to the account page "J." The S-1 in the post reference (PR) column of the customer's account indicates the source of the information. Notice that the terms given the customer are also shown in the customer's ledger account.

Notice how the following additional credit sales are recorded and posted to the respective accounts:

200-
Jan. 12　Sold goods to D. Lane for $3,000, terms: n/30
　　 15　Sold goods to R. Jones for $500, terms: as had

Sales Journal *Page S-1*

Date		Account Debited	Inv. #	Terms	PR	Amount
200- Jan.	10	R. Jones	101	n/30	J	400 00
	12	D. Lane	102	n/30	L	3000 00
	15	R. Jones	103	n/30	J	500 00

Accounts Receivable Ledger

R. Jones *Page J*

Date			PR	Debit	Credit	Balance
200- Jan.	10	n/30	S-1	400 00		400 00
	15	n/30	S-1	500 00		900 00

D. Lane *Page L*

Date			PR	Debit	Credit	Balance
200- Jan.	12	n/30	S-1	3000 00		3000 00

The notation in the post-reference column (PR), also known as the ledger-reference column, in the sales journal indicates two things. A letter appearing in the column indicates that the transaction has been posted, and secondly, where the posting has been made to. The January 10 entry in the sales journal has been posted to account "J," which represents the page in the accounts receivable ledger that the R. Jones account is found. The same fact would be true for the entry of January 15. The entry of January 12 indicates that the posting was made to the D. Lane account in the accounts receivable ledger. While the format of the general journal is lacking in the sales journal, it is understood that the only part of each entry that must be posted immediately is the debit to the various customer accounts in the subsidiary ledger. This is necessary because of the many different credit customers an organization will be dealing with. Remember, we will no longer debit the accounts receivable account, but will record all credit sales in the sales journal and post the debit part of the entry to the individual customer's account in the accounts receivable ledger. The time- and labor-saving aspects of this journal enable us to post the credit to the sales account, in summary, at the end of the month. No posting to the sales account will take place during the month. The individual customer accounts established for R. Jones and D. Lane reflect the postings made from the sales journal. The source of these postings is evidenced in the post-reference column (also known as the journal-reference column) by the "S-1" notation. This information came from the first page of the sales journal.

The Summary Entry

During the month, only the debit entries are posted from the sales journal. At the end of the month, the summary entry enables us to complete the posting so that double-entry accounting is maintained. Notice that in the sales journal completed below, the total is obtained at the end of the month. This total represents the amount of the credit entry to be posted to the sales journal. The accounts receivable account, found in the general ledger, is known as a CONTROL ACCOUNT. The function of the control account is to provide a summary of the activities posted to the subsidiary ledger. This account is necessary in order to prepare a trial balance at the end of the month. Since individual customers' accounts are not found in the general ledger (the source for the preparation of the trial balance), it is necessary to have a "control" figure in the ledger. The individual in charge of the subsidiary accounts receivable ledger prepares a SCHEDULE OF ACCOUNTS RECEIVABLE. The schedule of accounts receivable is a listing of the balances in the individual customer accounts, in this illustration, at the end of January of the current year. The total of this schedule is used to verify that the control account is in agreement with the subsidiary ledger. The posting to the accounts receivable control account in the general ledger is a direct result of the posting of the debit portion of the summary entry illustrated.

Sales Journal *Page S-1*

Date		Account Debited	Inv. #	Terms	PR	Amount
200- Jan.	10	R. Jones	101	n/30	J	400 00
	12	D. Lane	102	n/30	L	300 00
	15	R. Jones	103	n/30	J	500 00
	31	Dr. Accounts Receivable, Cr. Sales			5/30	3900 00

General Ledger

Accounts Receivable (Control Account)   *Page 5*

Date			PR	Debit	Credit	Balance	
						Debit	Credit
200- Jan.	31		S-1	3900 00		3900 00	

Sales   *Page 30*

Date			PR	Debit	Credit	Balance	
						Debit	Credit
200- Jan.	31		S-1		3900 00		3900 00

The following schedule of accounts receivable would be prepared to verify the control balance.

A Business
Schedule of Accounts Receivable
January 31, 200-

R. Jones	900
D. Lane	3,000
Total	3,900

Once the control account balance has been verified, the trial balance may then be prepared.

EXERCISE 1 The following business transactions took place during the month of February 200-, for the Anderson Stationery Co.:

200-
Feb. 3 Sold stationery supplies to Clearview Mfg. Co. for $680, terms: n/30.

8 Sold 10 reams of bi-fold computer paper to Data Word Associates for $89, terms: n/30.

17 Sold stationery supplies to HAL Corp. for $700, terms: n/30.

28 Sold fifteen cases of rexo-graph paper 8½″ × 11″ to Clearview Mfg. Co. for $180, terms: n/30.

Directions:

1. Rule a sales journal similar to the one illustrated;
2. Set up general ledger accounts for accounts receivable (page 5), and sales (page 40);

3. Set up four customer accounts in the accounts receivable ledger;
4. Journalize and post the transactions presented above;
5. Summarize the sales journal; and
6. Prepare a schedule of accounts receivable.

The accounts receivable ledger contains customer accounts that are organized in a fashion similar to the telephone directory. Some accountants prefer giving individual customer account numbers rather than letters. When this approach is used, the control account is given an account designation such as "5." All customer accounts then use the designation "5.01," "5.02," "5.03," and so on. Either method is acceptable and appropriate. A mere checkmark in the post-reference column of the sales journal will indicate that posting has taken place (and is acceptable), but does not indicate where the posting has been made to. The last method is the least desirable, but is the most common method used.

CASH RECEIPTS JOURNAL

Recording Transactions

The accountant justifies the use of the sales journal based on the substantial volume of credit sales recorded during the month. If the terms of the credit sale call for payment by the customer in thirty days, then the volume of cash receipts will equal and probably substantially exceed the number of credit sale entries. This then justifies the introduction of the multicolumn CASH RECEIPTS JOURNAL. All transactions, regardless of their source, that result in the receipt of cash are recorded in the cash receipts journal. While it is obvious that obligations due a business as a result of prior credit sales will be recorded in the cash receipts journal, the same organization may have as many, if not considerably more, cash sales. These sales, as well as other transactions causing an inflow of cash, would be recorded in the cash receipts journal.

The following cash receipts journal is a typical form used in business:

Cash Receipts Journal

Date		Account Credited	PR	General Acct. Cr.	Sales Cr.	Accounts Receivable Cr.	Sales Discount Dr.	Cash Dr.
200-Feb.	9	R. Jones	J			400 00		400 00
	10	D. Lane	L			3000 00		3000 00
	15	R. Jones	J			500 00	5 00	495 00
	17	Sales	✓		700 00			700 00
	21	Notes Receivable	8	450 00				450 00
	28			450 00	700 00	3900 00	5 00	5045 00
				✓	(40)	(5)	(44)	(1)

The multicolumn cash receipts journal contains special columns representing those accounts that are most frequently encountered in recording cash receipts. The criterion for using a special column is the volume of monthly transactions to that account. The most obvious column needed is a CASH DEBIT COLUMN. Every transaction in this journal will cause a debit to cash to be recorded. As was mentioned earlier, the advantage of this column is that posting to the cash ledger account will only take place once, at the end of the month. During the month, no postings will be made to the cash account in the general ledger. The number in brackets under the total of the cash debit column represents the post reference for the summary entry posted to the cash account in the general ledger at the end of the month.

Every cash receipt results from a number of different kinds of daily business transactions; however, the most common transactions resulting in the debit to cash are from cash sales and from customers paying their outstanding obligations. Thus, two primary special columns are: sales (cr.) and accounts receivable (cr.).

Any time a cash sale is made to customers, the transaction is recorded in the cash receipts journal. Note the February 17 transaction in the cash receipts journal just illustrated. Since both parts of the transaction are recorded in special columns, there is no need for daily postings to take place. In fact, the accountant uses a checkmark in the post-reference column to indicate that no posting is to be made at this time. From the standpoint of labor and time savings, the accountant has eliminated the posting of daily transactions involving cash sales and simply posts the two column totals at the end of the month.

The transactions of February 9, 10, and 15 represent the payment of obligations by customers. Note that in each case the credit entry is recorded in the accounts receivable credit column. Unlike the sales and the cash columns, this accounts receivable column has to be posted daily because each customer's account has to be reduced to the extent of the payments made. Notice that the post-reference column reflects the postings that were made to the various customer accounts that are found in the accounts receivable ledger. At the end of the month, the summary total of the accounts receivable credit column is posted to the accounts receivable control account in the general ledger. The entry of February 15 also involved the taking of a discount by the customer. Apparently the customer paid within the discount period and was entitled to a 1% discount. The effect of this discount caused a reduction in the amount of cash received, the recognition by the seller of an expense, and the elimination of the obligation, in full, by crediting the customer's account. The posting of the sales discount takes place at the end of the month, since only entries involving sales discounts are recorded in that specific column.

Whenever an account is credited in the cash receipts journal and there is no specific column set up for that account, it must be recorded in the general accounts credited column. These accounts are general ledger accounts and since they may be various accounts, it is necessary to post these accounts on a daily basis to the general ledger. The entry in the cash receipts journal for February 21 illustrates how the general accounts credited column is used. Notice at the end of the month, there is a checkmark under the general accounts credit column. This checkmark indicates that no posting is to be made. This is due to the fact that the accounts recorded in this column have been posted during the month and a summary posting is not necessary.

The Summary Entry

At the end of the month the columns of the cash receipts journal are pencil-footed. The debit column totals (sales discount and cash) are then compared with the totals of the credit columns (general accounts, sales, and accounts receivable). If the total of the debit column agrees with the total of the credit column totals, the journal is said to be in balance. The totals are then recorded in ink, the date is assigned, usually the last day of the month, the totals are double underscored, and the posting of the totals takes place. The summary entry in the cash receipts journal involves the posting of the totals of all the columns of the journal, except the general accounts credited column. The general accounts credited column is not posted at the end of the month, since it is posted daily to the general ledger. The sales, accounts receivable, sales discount, and cash columns are all posted at the end of the month to their respective accounts in the general ledger. The accounts receivable credit column had been posted to the individual customer accounts in the subsidiary ledger during the month. The summary entry sees to it that the accounts receivable control account in the general ledger reflects what was shown in the customer's accounts during the month.

EXERCISE 2   Record the following transactions in Estelle Rafferty's sales journal and cash receipts journal for the month of October 200-.

200-
Oct. 1   Received a check for $100 from L. Marin in partial payment of his account.

5   Sent an invoice to T. Ross for sale made today amounting to $100, terms: 2/10, n/30.

9   The proprietor made an additional cash investment in the business amounting to $1,500.

13   Sold goods to R. Adams for $200. Terms: n/30.

15   Received a check from T. Ross in payment of invoice dated October 5, 200-. (Note the terms of October 5 transaction.)

17   Received a check from R. Horne in payment of his note due today. The amount of the note was $450.

21   Sent an invoice to G. Crane for sale made today for $310. Terms: 2/10, n/30.

25   Received a check for $235 from T. Ross in full payment of his October 1 balance.

29   Received $350 from cash customers for miscellaneous sales of merchandise.

31   Received a check from G. Crane in payment of the invoice dated October 21.

After you have recorded the above transactions to the appropriate journals, prepare the summary entry for the sales and cash receipts journal.

EXERCISE 3   Set up the following accounts with balances as indicated:

GENERAL LEDGER

Acc. #	Account	Balance
1	Cash	$1,100 (dr.)
5	Accounts Receivable	770 (dr.)
7	Notes Receivable	750 (dr.)
40	Estelle Rafferty, Capital	8,000 (cr.)
50	Sales	—
51	Sales Discounts	—

ACCOUNTS RECEIVABLE LEDGER

R. Adams	$210
G. Crane	180
L. Marin	145
T. Ross	235

Based on the solution you prepared for Exercise 2, post from the sales and cash receipts journals to the accounts set up. Record the summary entries and prepare a schedule of accounts receivable to verify that the ledger agrees with the accounts receivable control account.

PURCHASES JOURNAL

Recording Transactions

We have learned that sales on credit and subsequent cash received, regardless of source, are recorded in the sales and cash receipts journals, respectively. Whenever a special journal is used, this will reduce the need for and the use made of the general journal. When the volume of transactions dealing with purchases an organization makes on credit is great, this calls for the introduction and use of the PURCHASES JOURNAL. Any kind of purchase that is made on credit is recorded in the purchases journal. This special journal is a multicolumn journal. The typical form of the purchases journal is presented on page 95.

Purchases Journal

Date		Account Credited	PR	A/P (Cr.)	Purchases (Dr.)	General Accounts Debited		
						Account Debited	PR	Amount
200-Jan.	1	Smith Co. (n/30)	S	200 00	200 00			
	12	Able Co. (n/30)	A	750 00		Equipment	30	750 00
	17	Rand Inc. (n/60)	R	175 00		Supplies	18	175 00
	28	Ace Freight Co.	A	35 00		Freight on Purchases	70	35 00
	30	Baker Co. (n/30)	B	300 00	300 00			
	31			1460 00	500 00			960 00
				(60)	(60)			(✓)

The use of the purchases journal is very similar to that of the sales journal, except that the purchases journal is used for the purchase of *anything* on credit. The purchase journal is a multicolumn journal that has special columns for recording recurring information. The use of the special purchase column is obvious. In practice a special column should be set up for any account that may be used frequently. If there were a large number of supplies bought on credit, a special column for supplies could be established. In the purchases journal illustrated, the supplies are shown as part of the general accounts debit columns; however, if the volume of supplies purchased on credit was significant, a special column for the supplies could be included in the purchases journal. Notice that this journal has provisions for two post-reference columns. Whenever the general accounts debit area is used, it is posted immediately to the general ledger and noted in the second post-reference column. When the purchases column is used, the posting will take place at the end of the month in summary, in a similar fashion to the summary of the sales column in the cash receipts journal.

Every purchase recorded in the purchases journal must be on credit in order to record it to this journal. Each transaction results in the establishment of a liability known as accounts payable. In practice it is important for businesses to know specifically to whom they owe money. In order to keep track of this information, it is necessary to set up an additional subsidiary ledger to accomplish this. The ACCOUNTS PAYABLE LEDGER is a subsidiary ledger in which separate accounts are maintained for all the creditors of a business organization. In the general ledger the ACCOUNTS PAYABLE CONTROL account is maintained to mirror the subsidiary ledger. Notice that the first post-reference column is to the immediate left of the accounts payable credit column. The purpose of this post-reference column is to post the obligations to the various creditor accounts on a daily basis to the subsidiary accounts payable ledger. The workings of the accounts payable control and subsidiary ledger is very similar to that of the accounts receivable control and accounts receivable subsidiary ledger. During the month the credit entries to the various creditor accounts are posted to the subsidiary ledger and page letter designations corresponding to the first letter of the last name are used to indicate that posting has taken place. It is necessary at the end of the month to see to it that whatever has been posted to the subsidiary accounts payable ledger is also reflected in the accounts payable control account in the general ledger.

The Summary Entry

The summary entry is made on the last day of the month as with the other special journals. Since the purchases journal is a multicolumn journal, it is first necessary to pencil-foot the money columns. The combined total of the debit columns must agree with the total credit to the accounts payable column. Once this has been determined, it is then appropriate to write the totals in ink and then double underscore the columns. The summary entry will indicate the appropriate accounts to be posted to, by number shown under the ruled column. The total of the accounts payable column would be posted in summary to the accounts payable account in the general ledger. The debit from the purchases column would be posted in summary to the merchandise purchases account in the general ledger. The general accounts debited column would be checked off, since no posting is necessary at the end of the month. (Remember that we post the general ledger accounts debited column amounts to the specific accounts during the month, thus no posting is necessary or appropriate at the end of the month.)

EXERCISE 4 Set up a purchases journal in a form similar to the one just illustrated. Record the following journal entries to the purchases journal:

200-
April 1 Purchased merchandise from the Bolden Co., amounting to $700. Terms: n/30.

5 Purchased office supplies from the Reliable Office Supply Co. for $125. Terms: n/15.

9 Bought office equipment consisting of a typewriter and table for $325. Terms: n/20 from A & B Equipment Co.

15 Purchased merchandise from the Caldwell Manufacturing Co. for $375. Terms: n/30.

After journalizing the previous four entries to the purchases journal, pencil-foot the journal, verify that total debits are equal to the accounts payable credit total, and rule the journal indicating the last day of the month.

Set up three-column general ledger accounts for office supplies, office equipment, merchandise purchases and accounts payable. Set up an accounts payable ledger account for the creditors listed in the purchases journal. Post the transactions from the purchases journal to the appropriate ledgers during the month and in summary at the end of the month.

Prepare a schedule of accounts payable to verify that the subsidiary ledger is in agreement with the accounts payable control account in the general ledger. The form of the schedule of accounts payable is similar to that of the schedule of accounts receivable that we have previously illustrated.

CASH PAYMENTS JOURNAL

Recording Transactions

Credit purchases, regardless of their nature or terms, eventually must be paid. This requirement is the basis for the cash payments journal. The CASH PAYMENTS JOURNAL is used any time that there is an outlay of cash, regardless of the reason. Cash payments will automatically call for the use of this multicolumn special journal. The form that the cash payments journal takes will basically be dependent upon the needs of the organization. The following form of the cash payments journal is typical, but is not the only form used:

Cash Payments Journal   Page CP = 1

Date	Account Debited	PR	General Accounts Dr.	Accounts Payable Dr.	Purchases Debit	Purchases Discount Cr.	Cash Cr.
200-							
Jan. 2	Purchases	✓			500 00		500 00
4	S. Allen	A		150 00			150 00
9	Jones Supply Co.	J		2000 00		40 00	1960 00
14	Rent Expense	45	200 00				200 00
19	Office Supplies	15	50 00				50 00
31			250 00	2150 00	500 00	40 00	2860 00
			(✓)	(60)	(66)	(67)	(1)

The multicolumn cash payments journal illustrated has special columns for accounts payable, purchases, purchases discounts, and cash. When recording in the last three account columns, no posting is made from these columns during the month. Since the nature of the entries to each individual column is the same, time and labor is saved in posting at the end of the month. The accounts payable column records the reduction in liabilities to individual creditor accounts. This column is posted daily to the subsidiary accounts payable ledger. Since the accounts payable account in the general ledger presents a summary of the postings to the subsidiary ledger accounts, it is necessary to post the total of the accounts payable column at the end of the month as part of the summary entry.

Where there are a substantial number of cash payments dealing with a specific item such as salaries, the accountant may choose to introduce another special column such as salaries expense. If this column is used, posting would be made in summary at the end of the month only. Where a special column does not exist (Jan. 14—Rent Expense) the debited account is named in the account debited column and the general accounts debited column records the amount. Since there are numerous different accounts recorded in this column, posting must be made on a daily basis.

The Summary Entry

The summary entry for the cash payments journal is prepared in a fashion similar to the preparation of the cash receipts journal. At the end of the month the columns are first pencil-footed. The total of the debit column totals must agree with the totals of the credit column totals. Once this has been determined, the figures are placed in ink and the columns are double underscored. The accounts payable column and all special columns are then posted in total to their respective accounts found in the general ledger with the appropriate posting reference numbers placed in brackets under the amounts. A check-mark is placed under the general accounts debit column to indicate that no summary posting of that column is to be made. The individual transactions to that column have been posted daily.

Bracket Entries

The use of subsidiary ledgers (accounts receivable ledger, accounts payable ledger) and the control accounts (accounts receivable, accounts payable) in the general ledger requires that both the general ledger and subsidiary ledger contain the same total information. The schedule of accounts receivable and accounts payable verifies the correctness of the control accounts. When the four special journals are used, the daily posting and summary entries assume that the control accounts agree with the schedules of the subsidiary ledger. On occasion it becomes necessary to record transactions in the general journal. When these transactions involve customer or creditor accounts, unique problems result. Both the control and subsidiary account must be posted. The use of a BRACKET ENTRY or a DOUBLE-POSTING ENTRY solves this problem. Whenever a general journal entry requires an entry to a customer or creditor account, a bracket entry is prepared.

EXAMPLE   A business received a thirty-day promissory note on March 10, 200-, from R. Friend for $3,000 in payment of her oral promise.

200-				
Mar. 10	Notes Receivable	8	3,000	
	[R. Friend	F		
	Accounts Receivable]	5		3,000
	30-day note, due 4/6.			

Notice that the requirements of double-entry accounting have been met in that the debits are equal to the credits; however, notice also that there are two accounts credited. The posting of R. Friend is made to the subsidiary ledger. Since there is no special column for the customer, there is a resulting need to post the credit to the control account. This posting is also done immediately. Transactions involving sales returns as well as purchases returns are handled in a similar fashion (if the returns are the result of previous credit transactions).

EXERCISE 5   Set up the following journals on appropriate accounting paper using the forms previously illustrated: Sales Journal, Cash Receipts Journal, Purchases Journal, Cash Payments Journal, and a two-column General Journal.

The following transactions took place during the month of March, 200-. Record these transactions in the appropriate journals.

200-
March   1 Issued a check for $150 to Landis Co. for the March rent.

3 Purchased merchandise from Harris Co. for $950. Terms: 2/10, n/30.

5 Cash sales for the week amounted to $1,000.

6 Received a credit memorandum from Harris Co. authorizing the return of $50 worth of merchandise purchased on 3/3.

200-
March   8 Sold merchandise to Adams Bros. for $1,200. Terms: 1/2 cash, balance in 30 days.

   9 Received a check from Adams Bros. in accordance with the terms of March 8 sale.

   11 Issued a $200 check to Brooklyn College to pay the tuition for Mr. Reynold's son (the owner of the business).

   13 Issued a check to Harris Co. to pay the invoice of March 3, less the return of March 6.

   16 Merchandise sold to Stone Bros. Terms: 1/10, n/30. The amount of the invoice was $800.

   17 Issued a check for $70 to Rapit Transit, Inc. for freight charges on the sale of March 16.

   19 Received a 60-day, $500 promissory note from Black Co. in settlement of their account.

   20 Issued a $20 check to the Ace Stationery Co. for the purchase of office supplies.

   23 Purchased $800 worth of merchandise from Young & Son. Terms: 30-day note.

   24 Issued our 30-day note to Young & Son as per terms of the purchase of March 23.

   25 Received a check from Stone Bros. as per terms of March 16 sale.

   26 Received a check for $900 from Carson Company in payment of their 30-day promissory note due today. The note included interest of $15.

   31 Paid the monthly payroll amounting to $3,450.

Summarize the journals and indicate which columns are to be posted at the end of the month. Any columns that are not to be posted at the end of the month should contain a checkmark.

OTHER SPECIAL JOURNALS

Special journals are introduced into the accounting system if they are required by the volume of transactions recorded or the need for a division of labor. Additional special journals are also used for analysis of data. Two special journals that will meet the criteria for use are the PURCHASES RETURNS AND ALLOWANCES JOURNAL and the SALES RETURNS AND ALLOWANCES JOURNAL. When these journals are used, the entries for sales returns and purchases returns are not recorded in the general journal as previously discussed, but rather in the special journal established.

The purchases returns and allowances journal may show that a large number of credit purchases are being returned by the buyer to the seller. A significant number of purchase returns would indicate that there is a problem that must be rectified. The intent of a buyer in purchasing merchandise is to resell the goods and recognize a profit from doing so. Goods returned to the seller are obviously not available for resale by the purchaser. If a pattern of continued returns is established with a supplier, this situation is readily seen in the purchases returns and allowances journal. This will probably result in the reduction or total elimination of any business dealings with that particular seller (creditor).

The purchases returns and allowances journal has an account debited column in order to record the reduction in the obligation to the creditor, as well as an explanation column and an amount column. The following purchases returns and allowances journal is a typical journal form used.

Purchases Returns and Allowances Journal   *Page PR-1*

Date		Account Debited	Explanation	PR		Amount
200- Jan.	3	R. Smith	Damaged Mdse.	S		75 00
	9	Alpine Co.	Wrong goods sent	A		45 00
	31			25/41		120 00

Daily postings are made to the creditor accounts in the subsidiary ledger. At the end of the month, the summary entry causes a debit to be posted to the accounts payable control account in the general ledger, and a corresponding credit to be posted to the purchases returns and allowances account in the general ledger.

The need for the sales returns and allowances journal arises when there are a large number of sales returns that were originally sales to customers on credit. A large volume of transactions justifies the use of the journal, but this journal may also help you analyze the reasons these sales returns are taking place. It is a basic assumption that the purchaser of the goods bought them in good faith with the intention of keeping them. Circumstances beyond the buyers' control caused them to request permission to return the goods to the seller. Sales returns may have resulted from incorrect goods being shipped, goods being received in damaged or soiled condition, goods being received not in a timely fashion as ordered, and numerous other reasons. It is important for the seller to recognize the reason he is sending a credit memorandum to buyer is to hopefully remedy the situation. The use of the sales returns and allowances journal will highlight various problems so that corrective action may be taken. The following sales returns and allowances journal is typically used by many organizations.

Sales Returns and Allowances Journal   *Page SR-1*

Date		Credit Memo #	Account Credited	Explanation	PR	Amount
200-						
Jan.	4	402	L. Breen	Soiled goods	B	65 00
	19	403	Restin Co.	Incorrect order	R	435 00
	26	404	Arnold Bros.	Soiled goods	A	10 00
	31				35/5	510 00

Posting is made to the individual customer accounts during the month. At the end of the month, the summary entry posts a debit to the sales returns and allowances account in the general ledger and a credit posting is made to the accounts receivable control account in the general ledger.

EXERCISE 6   The following business transactions occurred during an accounting period. Using the five primary journals discussed, indicate in the appropriate area which journal the transaction would be recorded in:

                              Journal

1. Sale of goods on account   _____
2. Sale of merchandise for cash   _____
3. Issued a credit memo to a customer   _____
4. Cash payment of a promissory note   _____
5. Sale of a service on credit   _____
6. Purchase of office furniture on credit   _____
7. Purchased merchandise for cash   _____
8. Received a credit memo from a creditor   _____
9. Adjusting entry to recognize accrued salaries   _____
10. Received a promissory note in place of an oral promise from a customer
11. Paid monthly rent   _____
12. Received a check from a customer in part payment of an oral promise
13. End of period adjusting entry for revenue   _____

EXERCISE 7   Rule "T" accounts for a general ledger, accounts receivable ledger, and an accounts payable ledger. In the general ledger the 100 series will be used for assets, the 200 series will be used for liabilities and account numbers, and 301 and 302 will be used for the proprietor's capital and drawing accounts. Account numbers 305 through 310 will be used for revenue accounts, and account numbers 311 through 330 will be used for expenses.

Rule the five special journals discussed in this chapter.

Elizabeth Sasoon began a retail beauty parlor business on March 10, 200-. You are to record the following business transactions in the appropriate journals and post to the correct ledger accounts on a daily basis. At the end of the month, summarize the journals and post the summary entries. Prepare a schedule of accounts receivable and accounts payable. If the schedules agree with the control accounts, prepare a trial balance dated March 31, 200-.

Elizabeth Sasoon began business on March 10, by investing the following assets in the business: Cash $5,000; Beauty Supplies $2,000; and Equipment $2,500. (Since the proprietor is beginning business on this date, this entry is traditionally recorded in the general journal, even though cash has been received. Record this compound entry in the general journal recognizing the assets and the proprietor's capital. This transaction is to be posted immediately to the various ledger accounts.)

200-
March 11   Sent a check for $300 to the Reliable Leasing Corp. in payment of the rent for the month of March.

12   Purchased beauty supplies from the Avon Supply Co. for $260. Terms 2/10, n/30.

13   Sent a check to the Drago Insurance Co. for the premium on an insurance policy on the premises for $180.

14   Cash sale for the week amounted to $2,600.

15   Sold beauty supplies to Estelle Evans, a customer for $200. Terms: 1/10, n/30.

16   Ms. Evans returned $50 of the beauty supplies and a credit memorandum was issued for the return.

17   Purchased a professional hair dryer for $300 from the Consolidated Equipment Co. Terms: 3/10, 1/20, n/30.

19   Sent a check to the Avon Supply Co. in payment of the invoice of March 12.

20   Received a credit memorandum from Consolidated Equipment Co. for $20. This allowance was for the repair of the dryer.

21   The proprietor withdrew $300 cash from the business for personal use.

24   Received a check from Ms. Evans for payment of the March 15 invoice less the return of March 16.

25   Cash sales from March 15 to today amounted to $5,300.

26   Sold beauty supplies on credit to Ruth Glasser for $350. Terms: 1/10, n/30.

27   Paid salaries for the three weeks ending today, amounting to $675.

28   Purchased store supplies from the Eveready Stationery Co. for $75 cash.

200-
March 29 Sent a check to the Consolidated Equipment Co. for balance due them.

30 Purchased beauty supplies from the Avon Supply Co. amounting to $350. Terms: 2/10, n/30.

31 Sold beauty supplies to Estelle Evans for $600. Terms: 30-day promissory note.

31 Received promissory note from Estelle Evans as per terms of sale made today.

EXERCISE 8 Test your knowledge of this chapter by answering the following statements as either *True* or *False*. If your answer is *False*, explain why.

1. The use of special journals and ledgers makes it possible for several bookkeepers to work on different accounting records at the same time.
2. If merchandise costing $500 is purchased with terms of 2/10, n/30, the amount due in 10 days is $500.
3. The cash receipts journal is used to record the collection of cash made by the business.
4. A sales discount represents a form of revenue to the seller.
5. Cash refunds to customers are recorded in the sales returns and allowances journal.
6. The purchases journal is used to record all purchases that are made on credit.
7. Transportation costs paid on the purchase of merchandise are recorded in the merchandise purchases account.
8. Purchases discounts represent a form of revenue to the buyer of goods.
9. The summary entry in the sales journal is a debit to the accounts receivable account and a credit to the sales account.
10. The accounts payable subsidiary ledger is posted to at the end of the month as part of the summary entry from the purchase and the cash payments journals.
11. Adjusting entries at the end of the accounting period are recorded in the general journal.
12. If a purchases returns and allowances journal is not used, any purchase returns would be recorded in the general journal, assuming that the obligation has not been paid yet.
13. A refund received from a creditor is recorded in the purchases returns and allowances journal, assuming that this journal is used by the business.
14. The general ledger columns found in the cash receipts and the cash payments journals are not posted as part of the month-end summary entries and checkmarks are placed under the columns.
15. When a promissory note is sent to a creditor in exchange for an oral promise, this transaction is recorded in the cash payments journal.

Summing Up

As the size of a business organization increases as measured by the volume of its business transactions, two factors must be recognized: (1) the need for a division of labor so that the necessary recordkeeping can take place in an efficient and accurate manner, and (2) the introduction of various special journals and ledgers to permit the division of labor and at the same time to reduce the amount of work of a repetitive nature done by those in charge of the financial records.

The special journals that have been discussed include the:

Sales Journal, which is used to record all credit sales of goods and/or services to customers.

Purchases Journal, which is used to record the purchases of all goods and/or services on credit.

Cash Receipts Journal, which is used to record the receipt of cash regardless of its source.

Cash Payments Journal, which is used to record the payment of cash regardless of the reason for the payment.

Sales Returns and Allowances Journal, which is used to record the issuance of a credit memorandum, which evidences the return of merchandise to the seller, giving the buyer credit for the return.

Purchases Returns and Allowances Journal, which is used by the buyer of goods to acknowledge the receipt of a credit memorandum from the seller authorizing the return of goods and the reduction or elimination of the buyer's obligation to the seller.

General Journal, which is used to record all business transactions that are not recorded in the special journals listed above. In the event that one or more of these special journals is not used, then the general journal will be pressed into service.

The use of the special journals requires that a subsidiary ledger be used in addition to the general ledger. In the general ledger the accounts receivable account and the accounts payable account are known as control accounts. The function of these accounts is to provide a summary of the transactions affecting various customers and creditors. The actual transactions with the individual customers and creditors are posted on a daily basis to the appropriate subsidiary ledger. The subsidiary ledgers consist of the accounts receivable ledger and the accounts payable ledger.

The subsidiary accounts receivable ledger is a separate ledger that contains individual customer accounts. These accounts are established for each customer for sales made to the customers on credit. The sale is initially recorded in the sales journal. The debit is then posted to the customer's account in the subsidiary ledger. When payment is received from the customer at a later date, the entry is first recorded in the cash receipts journal, and the credit is posted to the customer's account. The summary entry from the sales journal and the cash receipts journal is posted to the accounts receivable control account in the general ledger at the end of the month.

The subsidiary accounts payable ledger is a separate ledger that contains individual creditor accounts. These accounts are established for each creditor as a result of purchases made from these creditors on credit. The purchase is initially recorded in the purchases journal. The credit part of the entry is posted to the individual creditor account found in the subsidiary accounts payable ledger. When payment is made to the creditor at a later date, the entry is first recorded in the cash payments journal, and the debit to the creditor's account is posted to the debit column of the individual creditor's account in the accounts payable ledger. At the end of the month the total of the accounts payable column in both the purchases and the cash payments journal are posted to the accounts payable control account in the general ledger. Remember, the control account mirrors the activity of the subsidiary ledger.

The preparation of the schedules of accounts receivable and accounts payable will verify the correctness of the respective control accounts in the general ledger. If they fail to agree, the accountant must locate the discrepancy, make the necessary corrections, and then proceed to prepare a trial balance.

The summary entries from the special journals are made so that the special columns not posted during the month are posted to the appropriate ledger accounts in the general ledger at the end of the month. Remember, the accounts receivable and accounts payable columns in the special journals are posted daily to the specific subsidiary ledger accounts and at the end of the month to the respective control accounts in the general ledger.

Whenever an entry involving either an accounts receivable or an accounts payable is recorded in the general journal, it must be recorded as a bracket entry. The bracket entry enables a double posting to be made first to the control account in the general ledger and then to the individual account in the subsidiary ledger. The bracket entry causes two accounts to be listed (thus the double posting), but only one amount to be shown. If the sales returns and allowances journal or the purchases returns and allowances journal are not used, these credit returns must be recorded in the general journal and require bracket entries.

CHAPTER 7

ACCOUNTING FOR CASH— SPECIAL CONTROLS

Internal Control

A properly designed accounting system must meet the needs of the business organization that it is being created for. Provisions must be made for the accumulation, recording, and reporting of data. Chapter 6 dealt with special journals and addressed the basic organization of the books of account in use. Once these financial records are in place, it becomes necessary to see to it that the system design provides for:

1. Measurement of the various phases of the business's operations.
2. Assignment of authority and responsibility.
3. Implementation of a program for the prevention of errors and fraud.

The control of an organization's operations, regardless of the size of the firm, is generally known as INTERNAL CONTROL. In a small organization where the owner personally supervises the employees and directs the operation of the business, the degree of internal control is not as complex as a larger more decentralized organization. As the number of employees and the complex nature of the organization increases, it becomes virtually impossible for management to be involved in every phase of operations. As the firm expands, management must delegate authority and place greater reliance on the accounting systems in controlling the enterprise's operations.

Internal control must see to it that assets are safeguarded, appropriate accounting data is generated, management policies and procedures are followed, and that productivity and efficiency is achieved throughout the organization.

Special Controls to Safeguard Cash

The most liquid asset within any organization is cash. Because cash is easily transferable, it is the asset most susceptible to improper diversion and use by employees. Since there are numerous transactions that either directly or indirectly affect the receipt of cash and its payment, it is essential that cash be effectively safeguarded through the development and use of special controls.

Within most organizations there is usually no significant amounts of cash available. Any cash received is immediately or within a reasonable amount of time deposited in a bank account. Any payments made by the organization are done by check. Most businesses deposit all cash receipts in a checking account at a convenient commercial bank and make all payments by check drawn against that bank. The forms used by the depositor in working with the commercial bank are signature cards, deposit slips, checks, and bank statements.

When a checking account is first opened by a business concern, certain employees are given the responsibility of signing the checks that will be drawn on the business's checking account. The authority to sign the checks is given by the signature appearing on the SIGNATURE CARD. This puts the bank on notice that the signatories on the signature card are authorized to sign the check for the concern. Usually the organization will require that the signature on the check be a two-party signature. There may be numerous individuals who are authorized to sign the checks; however, there must at all times be two signatures on the check in order for it to be valid. The two-party check acts to reduce the possibility of misappropriation of funds, and also makes more than one individual aware of where funds are being spent.

In order for an organization to write checks on an account, there must be funds within the account to cover the checks written. In order to accomplish this, a DEPOSIT SLIP or DEPOSIT TICKET must be prepared. The deposit slip, which is usually prepared in duplicate, has a space for writing the amount of currency and coin being deposited as well as for listing the checks being deposited. The deposit slip will have a place to write in the checking account number on the slip, or if the deposit slip is preprinted, it will already contain the account number and the name of the business organization on the face of the form.

Once the checking account has been set up and there exists funds in the account, it is possible to make cash payments by writing checks on the account. A check by definition is said to take the place of cash. The CHECK is a written instrument that orders the bank it is written on to pay a specific sum of money to the party designated on the face of the check. There are three parties to a check; the bank on which the check is drawn, known as the drawee; the person to whom the check is being paid to (pay to the order of), the payee; and the person who signs the check, the drawer or payor. The check, or more specifically, the check stub or duplicate copy of the check, becomes the basis for the journal entry made in the cash payments journal. While the form of the individual checks issued by different banks may vary, basically the following information is found on the typical check: the name and address of the depositor; serial numbering in order to facilitate the depositor's internal control; a preprinted account number; and the name of the bank on which the check is written.

The records maintained by the business organization having the checking account are usually found in the checkbook, which contains the unwritten checks and the check stubs. The bank maintains a separate record of the activity within an individual checking account, and forwards to the checking account customer a bank statement, usually on a monthly basis. The BANK STATEMENT reflects the record that the bank maintains of activities affecting the customer's checking account for the month. Like any account that is maintained for a customer or a creditor, certain specific information is found in the bank statement. This account is treated by the bank as if the customer is actually a creditor, because the funds being safeguarded for the checking account customer, as far as the bank is concerned, represents a liability to the bank.

The bank statement contains the opening balance in the customer's account. Any increases to the account as a result of deposits are listed on the bank statement and are known as credits. Any checks the customer has written and the bank has paid during the month are shown as reductions on the bank statement, and thus are recorded as debits to the bank statement. Any charges that the bank has made, such as monthly service charges, appear on the bank statement and are shown as reductions from the balance in the account. When the bank has been asked to pay obligations for the customer, these payments are shown as debits to the account. In using the bank "debit card" the customer is authorizing the bank to reduce the checking account balance by the amount of the charge, as if the bank were paying a check that had been written by the customer. Where the bank has acted as a collection agent for the customer, these collections appear as credits on the bank statement. The final line on the bank statement represents the ending balance in the statement. This balance should agree with the balance on the check stub for the same date. This is usually not the case and will be explained shortly.

BANK RECONCILIATION STATEMENT

There are two records that are kept of the checking account. The records are basically maintained by the bank and the customer. The balance in a checking account can be found by referring to the balance as indicated on the last check stub or by referring to the cash balance in the general ledger plus the cash receipts, less the cash payments to date. If the bank statement were compared with the balance as per the customer's records (regardless of the record used), the accountant would usually find that the two records are not in agreement. Bringing these records into agreement is known as a BANK RECONCILIATION. A bank reconciliation is the process whereby the balance in the bank's records of a checking account and the balance in the depositor's records are brought into agreement. On a monthly basis a BANK RECONCILIATION STATEMENT is prepared that brings the checkbook balance in the customer's checkbook into agreement with the bank's balance as found on the bank statement.

The inequality that exists between the balance per the bank statement and the balance per the checkbook is due to a number of things. When a check is written by a business, the effect on the checkbook balance at that time is to reduce immediately the balance by the amount of the check written. The bank, however, would not reduce its record of the business's balance to the extent of the check written because at that time it has no knowledge of the check having been written. This kind of check is then known as an OUTSTANDING CHECK. An outstanding check is one that has been written but has not been paid by the bank because the bank has not yet received the check. The balance per the bank statement will show a higher balance than that of the checkbook because of the outstanding checks.

In some cases it is the bank that is aware of things that the customer only becomes aware of when the bank statement is received. The monthly bank service charge calculated by the bank is recorded on the bank statement as a debit memorandum. This, as well as other charges made by the bank, are not known to the customer until the receipt of the bank statement. At that time, it is necessary for the customer to adjust the business's books to reflect the information presented on the bank statement. When the bank is authorized to act as a collection agent for the customer or authorized to pay bills for the customer, this information as well is not usually known by the customer until the receipt of the monthly bank statement. In these situations it is necessary to adjust the checkbook balance to the extent of the information in the bank statement. Any adjustments made to the checkbook side of the bank reconciliation will not only affect the checkbook balance, but must also result in an adjusting entry being made to the books of account. If interest income has been earned and received or interest expense has been paid, these factors should be reflected on the checkbook side of the bank reconciliation. Error on the part of the customer or bank should also be shown. When the bank statement has a NSF (not sufficient funds) notice, this customer's check must generate a reduction in the checkbook balance on the reconciliation as well as an adjusting entry. Following the preparation of the bank reconciliation statement, the adjusting entries are recorded to the books of account.

Preparing the Statement

The bank reconciliation statement represents a comparison between the checkbook balance and the bank statement at a specific moment in time (usually at the end of the month). The form of the reconciliation statement will either represent the account or the report form. Regardless of the form, the headings will ask the same questions that all financial statements ask: who?, what?, and when? The end result of the bank reconciliation statement is to see to it that both records are in agreement. This agreement is not merely a mathematical activity, but represents a logical approach to what has taken place, what will take place, and how the books of account should reflect the changes. The following illustrates the form of the bank reconciliation statement. Each item listed will be explained following the presentation.

Anthony Raymond Co.
Bank Reconciliation Statement
August 1, 200-

Checkbook Balance	$3,000		Bank Balance		$4,000
Less: Bank Service			Less: Outstanding Checks		
Charge	5		Check # 203	$35	
Add: Notes Receivable	905		207	65	100
Adjusted Checkbook					
Balance	$3,900		Adjusted Bank Balance		$3,900

Notice that the bottom lines of the bank reconciliation statement illustrate the equality of the balances. Both final amounts are labeled "Adjusted Balance." The reason for this terminology is that in both cases there were changes shown to both sides that resulted in the change being recorded, thus affecting the balances on both sides. Note the changes that have affected each side of the statement.

Let's discuss the bank balance side first. The list of outstanding checks is made by comparing the checks written according to the check stubs with the checks paid according to the bank statement. Any checks that are not listed on the bank statement are considered to be outstanding and are listed on the bank side of the reconciliation statement. This is completed in this fashion because it is recognized that the checks written but not received by the bank will be received and paid within a few days. The accountant anticipates this happening and treats the checks as if received and thus paid by the bank. Any adjustment that the bank has no knowledge of would be recorded on the bank balance side of the reconciliation statement. A deposit in transit that has not yet been received by the bank (as evidence by the bank statement) would be added to the bank balance side as if the deposit had been received.

The adjustments recorded on the checkbook side of the bank reconciliation statement are those items that the bank usually knows about, but the customer does not until either a memorandum from the bank is received or the information appears on the bank statement. On the bank reconciliation illustrated above, it appears that the bank is charging its customer for the monthly bank service charge. The bank will automatically reduce its record of the customer's balance to the extent of the bank service charge. On the bank statement, a debit memorandum will appear in which the bank charges the customer for the service rendered. When the customer reviews the statement, the subtraction for the bank service charge is then shown on the bank reconciliation statement. If the bank is also charged with the responsibility of paying obligations for the customer, these payments are handled in the same manner. Payments by the bank would be noted on the bank statement and these payments would be recorded as reductions on the checkbook side of the bank reconciliation statement. Although not illustrated on the checkbook side of the bank reconciliation statement, any debit card transactions would also be listed on the checkbook side of the statement as a subtraction from the checkbook balance. These amounts may be listed in a separate section of the bank statement, and once the customer has verified that these transaction amounts agree with the debit card receipts, the amount of the debit card charge would be subtracted from the checkbook side of the statement. The addition of the notes receivable on the checkbook side of the bank reconciliation statement indicates that a customer has paid an obligation to Raymond Co. through the bank. The bank is acting as a collection agent. When the note is payed, the bank returns the note to the customer and credits Raymond Co.'s checking account with the value of the note collected. A credit memorandum is usually sent to the customer at the time of the settlement of the note, and this transaction will appear on the bank statement for the month. Since the bank may be called upon to act as a collecting agent for the customer, any time the bank receives funds in the name of the customer, it is the bank's responsibility to credit the customer's account. The credit memorandum appears on the bank statement and is recorded as an increase on the checkbook balance side of the bank reconciliation statement.

The Steps

The bank reconciliation statement is prepared using two documents: the bank's statement and the checkbook stub. The bank statement contains the beginning balance, deposits made during the month, checks paid during the month, debit memoranda resulting from charges made by the bank and activities causing a reduction on the customer's balance, credit memoranda resulting from collections made by the bank for the customer, and ending bank balance. The customer's checkbook stub contains the balance in the checking account as well as deposits and the information as to the checks written. In order to prepare the bank reconciliation statement, the following steps should be followed:

1. Compare the deposits found on the check stub with the deposits listed on the bank statement. Any deposits not shown on the statement are known as DEPOSITS IN TRANSIT. These deposits in transit represent deposits made but not yet credited to the customer's account by the bank. Deposits in transit are to be added to the bank balance side of the reconciliation statement as if received by the bank.
2. Compare the cancelled (paid) checks returned by the bank, as part of the bank statement, with the check stubs to determine which checks, if any, have been written but not yet paid by the bank. If there are any outstanding checks, they would be listed on the bank balance side of the reconciliation statement. The outstanding checks would be subtracted from the bank balance as if the checks had been paid by the bank.
3. Locate any debit and credit memoranda appearing on the bank statement. These charges and credits are recorded as adjustments to the checkbook side of the bank reconciliation statement.
4. Based on the above information, the bank reconciliation statement is prepared.
5. Prepare the necessary adjusting entries based on the information that has been recorded to the checkbook side of the bank reconciliation statement. Any adjustment to the checkbook side must result in the recording of an adjusting entry.

Recording Adjusting Entries

When the bank reconciliation has been completed, it becomes necessary to prepare adjusting entries to correct or reconcile the cash balance. The adjusting entries required will be based on the adjustments made to the checkbook balance side only.

If the bank service charge as recorded on the bank statement amounted to $5, the following adjusting entry would be made:

```
200-
Aug. 1   Bank Service Charge Expense              5
              Cash                                      5
         Monthly service charge.
```

If the bank acted as a collection agent and collected a note in the customer's favor, charging a nominal fee, the following entry would result:

200-			
Aug. 1	Cash	905	
	Bank Service Charge	15	
	Notes Receivable		920
	Collection of note.		

It is possible for another difference between the bank balance and the checkbook balance to result from an error in the customer's books. When such an error is discovered, its correction also requires an adjusting entry. For example, if a check was properly written for $75, but on the check stub it was recorded as $57, this transposition would result in a difference in balances of $18. The correcting entry for such an error would be:

200-			
Aug. 1	Accounts Payable/J. Jones	18	
	Cash		18
	To correct checkbook error.		

Adjusting entries are only made as a result of adjustments made to the checkbook side of the bank reconciliation statement.

EXERCISE 1 Prepare a bank reconciliation statement dated May 30, 200-, based on the following list representing receipts and payments that were made by the Reliable Retail Store:

MAY CASH RECEIPTS

Date	Receipts	Deposits
5/2	$100	$100
5/9	200	
5/9	100	300
5/16	400	400
5/23	200	200
5/30	300	300

MAY CASH DISBURSEMENTS

Date	Check No.	Amount
5/3	101	$50
5/10	102	150
5/10	103	20
5/10	104	10
5/17	105	200
5/24	106	560
5/24	107	30
5/31	108	20

From the company's checkbook records:
  Cash balance (in bank) May 1, 200- $300
  Cash balance (in bank) May 31, 200- $560

The May 31, 200-, bank statement for the Reliable Retail Store from the First City Bank appears as follows:

Account Of: Reliable Retail Store				FIRST CITY BANK
Date 200-	Check No.	Amount	Deposits	Balance
Apr. 30				300
May 4			100	400
6	101	50		350
11	102	150	300	490
	104	10		
18			400	890
19	105	200		690
25	107	30	200	860
		10 NSF		850
26	106	560		290
31		2 SC		288
May 31				288

Code Explanations: EC—Error Correction; NSF—Not Sufficient Funds (the bank charges a $10 fee for all NSF checks); Col—Collection Charge; SC—Service Charge.

After you have prepared the bank reconciliation statement for the Reliable Retail Store, prepare the necessary adjusting journal entries.

EXERCISE 2   The following data has been accumulated for use in preparing the bank reconciliation statement for Alice Reinholt and Co. for the month of September 200-

1. Balance per depositor's records on September 30—$4,239.35.
2. Balance per bank statement on September 30—$4,581.50.
3. Deposits in transit—$362.80.
4. Checks outstanding—$694.10.
5. A check for $57 in payment of a bill was erroneously recorded on the check stub as $75.
6. A bank debit memo for service charges amounted to $7.15.

PETTY CASH FUND

Most businesses need to have small amounts of money available for various expenditures for which writing a check would be inappropriate or impractical. Small amounts of cash might be needed to pay for transportation charges, postage fees, supplies, or coffee, as well as other small expenditures that occur on a regular basis. Because these small payments occur frequently and amount to a considerable sum of money, it is desirable to maintain close control over the payments. This can be accomplished through the establishment of a PETTY CASH FUND. The purpose of the petty cash fund is to have a small amount of cash on hand with which to make some minor expenditures. The person who is in charge of this fund is generally known as the petty cashier. The petty cashier is given a check written to his or her order for between $50 and $150 to establish the petty cash fund with. The initial establishment of the fund is recorded by the following journal entry:

```
200-
April 1   Petty Cash                        100
              Cash                                100
          To establish the fund.
```

The petty cashier then cashes the check and places the money into a petty cash box, which resembles the inside of a cash register drawer. The money is distributed by the petty cashier when requested by a signed petty cash voucher. The PETTY CASH VOUCHER is a piece of paper that states what the funds are to be used for, the date of the transaction, the voucher number, the account to be charged, the individual approving the voucher, and the fact that payment has been received. The petty cash voucher is then placed in the petty cash box. The combination of the cash in the box and the total amount of the vouchers should be equal at any time to the amount of the petty cash fund. The petty cashier also makes use of a record called the PETTY CASH BOOK. The purpose of the petty cash book is to keep track of the expenditures from the petty cash fund. It represents a form of a cash payments journal, except that expenditures are not evidenced by a check but rather by a petty cash voucher. During the course of a month, it may be necessary to REPLENISH THE FUND. When the amount of the disbursements from the fund begins to approach the amount of money established for the fund, it is necessary to replenish the fund. The replenishment of the fund is justified by the fact that expenditures were made from the fund and should be recognized. The following entry would be made in the cash payments journal, although illustrated in general journal form, to replenish the fund based on totals obtained from the petty cash book:

```
200-
April 25   Transportation on Purchases      62.50
           Office Supplies                    2.00
           Postage Expense                    3.00
              Cash                                 67.50
           To replenish the petty cash fund.
```

Petty Cash Book

Date		Vo #	Receipts		Payments		Postage Expense		Office Supplies		Store Supplies		Transp. on Purchase		Other	Amount
200-Apr.																
1	Check #302	—	100	00												
5	U.S. Post Office	101			2	00	2	00								
9	R & L Stationery	102			2	00			2	00						
11	Cosmo Freight	103			37	50							37	50		
14	U.S. Post Office	104			1	00	1	00								
24	Reliable Freight	105			25	00							25	00		
25			100	00	67	50	3	00	2	00			62	50	—	—
25	Total Payments		67	50												
25	Balance		32	50												
25	Check #367	—	67	50												
			100	00												

This replenishment will restore the balance in the petty cash box to $100 and enable the petty cashier to continue distributing small amounts of cash. The petty cash fund is usually replenished when the balance in the fund has gotten low. However, at the end of the accounting period, the fund should be replenished so that expenses for that accounting period can be properly recognized.

The only time an entry is made to petty cash is at the time the fund is established. The replenishment recognizes the expenses incurred. If the organization feels that the amount of the petty cash fund is either too great or too small, an entry can be made adjusting the balance in the petty cash account. The basic entry, however, usually only occurs when the fund is first established.

EXERCISE 3   The Spelvin Co. established a petty cash fund of $150 on January 1, 200-. On January 24, 200-, the fund was replenished for the payments made to date as shown by the following petty cash vouchers: Freight on Purchases, $9.50; Postage Expense, $46.00; Telephone Expense, $3.20; Repairs Expense, $31.70; Miscellaneous Expenses, $22.00. Prepare the necessary journal entries to record (1) the establishment of the fund on January 1, 200-, and (2) the replenishment of the fund on January 24, 200-.

VOUCHER SYSTEM

Just as it is important to control the expenditures of small amounts of cash through the petty cash fund, it is important to be able to control expenditures which take the form of checks. In every form of business a large number of expenditures must be made each month for goods and services. The handling of these kinds of transactions require that the following steps be taken:

1. The expenditures must be authorized, prior to payment, by a purchase order or some other document that evidences that the purchase was originally authorized.
2. The goods must be inspected upon receipt and verified as to the specifications of the order.
3. Invoices from suppliers must be examined for correctness of prices, extensions, shipping costs, and credit terms.
4. Checks must be issued for payment with the necessary signatures and approvals.

In a very small business the sole proprietor would probably be responsible for all the steps listed above. As the size of a business increases, it becomes inpractical for the owner of the business to be directly involved in the four steps listed above. A well-designed accounting system assigns certain employees to handle each step and to guard against waste and fraud. Since the safeguarding of cash, whether it is in the form of coins and currency or checks, is an important aspect of any business, the use of the voucher system will help to provide this needed safeguard.

The VOUCHER SYSTEM is a method of establishing control over the making of expenditures and the payment of liabilities. This system requires that every liability be recorded as soon as it is incurred, regardless of when it is payable, and payment is made only when an approved voucher is prepared. The voucher is a written authorization that is prepared prior to every expenditure, regardless of whether the expenditure covers services, merchandise for resale, or assets for use in the business. A simple entry, such as the payment of the monthly rent, will no longer involve a debit to rent expense and a corresponding credit to cash, but will now involve the establishment of a liability and then the subsequent payment. The following general journal entries illustrate the recognition and payment of the rent:

```
200-
Jan. 1   Rent Expense                            300
              Vouchers Payable                         300
         To recognize the expense.

         1          Vouchers Payable            300
              Cash                                     300
         To record the payment of the voucher.
```

The Voucher

A VOUCHER is merely a document that contains specific information regarding the recognition and subsequent payment of an obligation. When an invoice is received as a result of purchasing a product or service, the bill is attached to the voucher. The following voucher is used by the Reliable Service Co.:

Reliable Service Co.
Chicago, Ill.

Pay to _____   Voucher No. _____
       _____   Date   _____
       _____   Terms: _____

Date of Invoice _____   Gross Amount $_____
Invoice Number _____   Less: Cash Discount _____
                                       Net Amount $_____

Approval _____

Page 1

```
┌─────────────────────────────────────────────────────────────────────┐
│       Account Distribution                    Voucher No. _____      │
│   Debit                    Amount                                     │
│  Purchases                                          Payee             │
│  Supplies                                   _____ │
│  Delivery Expense                           _____ │
│  Misc. Selling Exp.                         _____ │
│  Misc. Gen'l Exp.                              Voucher Summary        │
│                                             Amount _____  │
│                                             Adjustment _____  │
│  Credit Vouchers Payable                    Discount _____  │
│                                             Net _____  │
│                                             Approved _____  │
│                                                Payment Summary        │
│                                             Date _____  │
│                                             Amount _____  │
│                                             Check No. _____  │
│  Page 2                                     Approved _____  │
└─────────────────────────────────────────────────────────────────────┘
```

The face of the voucher is completed, indicating the name and address of the creditor. A voucher number is assigned, and the date of the entry is noted along with the terms of the transaction. The date of the invoice is also recorded, as well as the gross amount of the bill. On page 2 of the voucher, the account distribution information is completed. The purchases invoice is then attached to the voucher and is placed in a file generally known as the UNPAID VOUCHER FILE. The unpaid voucher file is set up according to when the earliest date of payment should take place in order to take advantage of the terms of the purchase. A voucher is prepared for every transaction that will eventually require the payment of cash utilizing the checkbook. Transactions that are normally thought of as mere payments of cash, such as paying the business's monthly rent, are not treated in that manner when the voucher system is used. Each transaction must first be recorded as a credit transaction.

Effect of System on Books of Original Entry

The purchases journal, as we have developed it, is not used when the voucher system is in use. The purchases journal is replaced by another book of original entry that is known as the VOUCHER REGISTER, which is used to record all transactions that resulted in the preparation of a voucher. Prior to the filing of the voucher (and invoice attached) in the unpaid voucher file, the information is recorded in the voucher register. Each entry in the voucher register includes the assigned voucher number and all the information typically entered in a purchases journal. Instead of an accounts payable column appearing in the voucher register, it is usually replaced by a column called vouchers payable. Two additional information columns are also used to indicate the date the voucher is paid and the check number evidencing the payment.

The following represents the typical form of the voucher register:

Voucher Register

Date	Payee	Voucher No.	Date Paid	Check No.	Vouchers Payable Credit	Purchases Debit	Supplies Debit	Salaries Expense Debit	Advertising Expense Debit	General Accounts Debited	PR	Amount

The use of the voucher and voucher register also eliminates the need for the subsidiary accounts payable ledger. In place of this ledger is the unpaid voucher file. Also, a glance at the paid column (check no. and date) in the voucher register will indicate which vouchers are outstanding. If that area has been completed, it indicates that the obligation has been paid. If the area is blank, the obligation is still outstanding. The vouchers payable account replaces the accounts payable control account in the general ledger, but still shows the amount of the outstanding obligations, which you will need to know to prepare the trial balance.

Following the entry of the voucher in the voucher register, the voucher is filed in the unpaid voucher file. The voucher will remain in this file until it is paid. In order to be aware of and to take advantage of discounts offered as part of the terms of a purchase, proper filing of the voucher is essential. The amount due on each voucher represents the credit balance that in a traditional system would be comparable to a creditor account in a subsidiary ledger. Since the subsidiary ledger is not used in a voucher system, it is assumed that the business will avail itself, wherever possible, of the favorable credit terms offered. In order to do so the unpaid voucher is filed according to the earliest date that payment should take place to earn the discount. Since the file is set up in a fashion similar to a calendar, the individual in charge of the file will be able to determine readily which vouchers are due for payment on any given date. When a voucher is paid, it is removed from the unpaid voucher file and a check is usually prepared to pay the obligation. Information as to the date, check number, and payment are recorded on the voucher. If the checkbook provides for a duplicate check, this copy is usually attached to the voucher and then filed in the paid voucher file, which is organized in numerical order according to the voucher number assigned.

Recording Voucher Payment

All vouchers are paid by check. The traditional accounting system utilizes the cash payments journal to record the payment. When the voucher system is used, however, the cash payments journal is replaced by a book of original entry called the CHECK REGISTER. All vouchers paid by check are recorded in the check register according to the check number. Each check written is in payment of a voucher that has previously been entered as a vouchers payable in the voucher register. The effect of each entry in the check register is to cause a debit entry to be recorded to the vouchers payable account. The only additional columns needed in the check register are columns for cash credit to indicate payment, and columns to recognize a credit entry to discount on purchases. The following check register illustrated is commonly used by businesses using a voucher system:

Check Register

Date		Payee	Voucher No.	Check No.	Vouchers Payable—Dr.	Purchases Discounts—Cr.	Cash Cr.

Notice that the check register has no provision for a post-reference column. There is no need for a post-reference column because all of the columns are special columns that need only be posted once a month, at the end of the month, as part of the summary entry. Remember, the voucher system eliminates the need for a subsidiary accounts payable ledger. The check number and date that the payment is made as evidenced by the entry in the check register are also recorded in the voucher register. Remember, the paid area of the voucher register indicates that the obligation has been paid.

The introduction of a voucher system eliminates the need for a purchases journal, cash payments journal, and the subsidiary accounts payable ledger as we have used it. These account documents are replaced with the voucher register, check register, and the paid and unpaid voucher files. All documentation, from the original purchase to the final payment, is recorded on or attached to the voucher. The use of the voucher system ensures that expenditures are properly authorized and that payments made are in legitimate payment of an organization's obligations.

EXERCISE 4   The Renfield Co. uses a voucher system. Record the following business transactions in general journal form. Also indicate as an explanation the appropriate special journal that would be used for each transaction.

200-
Apr. 2   Voucher #245 was prepared for the purchase of office supplies at a cost of $85 from the Buyrite Stationery Co. The terms of the transaction are 2/10, n/30.

10   Check #333 was issued in payment of voucher #245.

14   Voucher #246 was prepared to establish a petty cash fund amounting to $50.

15   Check #334 written in payment of voucher #246.

16   Voucher #247 was prepared to replenish the petty cash fund, which contained receipts for: postage, $20.00; miscellaneous expenses, $15.00; delivery expenses, $4.50.

19   Issued check in payment of voucher #247.

EXERCISE 5   Set up a voucher register and check register for the Mansfield Co. Record the following transactions in the appropriate registers:

200-
Aug. 2   Received a bill from the Best Realty Co. for the month's rent amounting to $700. (Begin with voucher #201.)

5   Received an invoice from Spelvin Co. for a purchase of merchandise made today amounting to $2,457. Terms: 2/10, n/30.

7   Issued check #435 in payment of voucher #201.

13   Prepared a voucher payable to the Buyrite Stationery Co. for a purchase made today of office supplies amounting to $95. Terms: 2/10, 1/15, n/30.

14   Sent a check in payment of voucher #202.

18   Issued voucher #204 for $3,769.60 in favor of L. Sprang Co. for our note. Face value of note $3,720.00, interest on note $49.60.

26   Paid voucher #204 as per terms.

27   Prepared voucher to reimburse the petty cash fund.

The expenditures were as follows: Postage, $12.70; Transportation on Purchases, $43.10; Store Supplies, $13.80.
Pencil foot and rule both registers at the end of the month.

EXERCISE 6   Set up a petty cash book, voucher register, and check register. Record the following selected transactions, and total and rule the records at the end of the month as appropriate.

200-
Sept. 1   Purchased goods from Smith Inc. Terms: n/10, $500. Prepared voucher #916.

2   Issued voucher #917 to establish a petty cash fund amounting to $200. Issued check #371 in payment to R. Brown.

5   Advertising expenses amounted to $762. Received an invoice from Jantzen Co. and set up voucher.

7   Paid cash of $9 out of the petty cash fund for postage stamps. (Petty Cash Voucher #1.)

11   Paid voucher #918.

12   Received a freight bill from Hall Freight Inc. for $96 payable in twenty days. Issued a voucher.

15   Issued a check for $713 to Howard Co. in payment of voucher #912, which had been issued last month for office supplies.

18   Paid cash from the petty cash fund for transportation on purchases amounting to $12. (Paid A.B. Freight Inc.)

200-
Sept. 19   Purchased merchandise from Bell Co. paying $45 cash from the petty cash fund.

21   Purchased goods from Texas Originals for $950. Terms: 2/10, n/30.

29   Replenished the petty cash fund.

30   Issued a check in payment of the September 21 voucher to Texas Originals.

Summing Up

As we have seen, some of the important activities of management center around the planning and controlling of cash. This includes cash-flow planning, controlling cash receipts, controlling cash payments, the voucher system, monthly bank reconciliations and even the disbursement of small amounts of cash through the petty cash system.

The preparation of monthly bank reconciliation statements and the resulting adjusting entries are performed by every business organization regardless of its size (providing it has a checking account). The voucher system is appropriate for medium- to large-sized business operations only. Its objective is to control the incurring of liabilities and the making of expenditures. The cash payments journal and the purchases journal are replaced by the voucher register and the check register, while the subsidiary accounts payable ledger is replaced by the unpaid and paid voucher files.

CHAPTER 8

ACCOUNTING FOR RECEIVABLES AND PAYABLES

Selling Goods and Services

Goods and services may be sold by a business organization for cash or on credit. Most organizations, if they were given a choice, would probably prefer to sell their product or service for cash. Due to competition and other factors, many businesses, out of necessity, must offer their products and/or services to customers on credit. As we have learned in a previous chapter, when a sale is made to a customer on credit, the effect of the transaction is to establish an accounts receivable account on the books in the name of the customer. This account is classified as an asset. When the customer pays the obligation to the seller, the customer's account is credited and the cash account is debited as a result of the receipt of cash.

No business organization prefers to sell on credit, especially since it is possible the customer may prove to be unwilling or unable to pay his or her obligation when it becomes due. Most businesses will utilize a credit department or service to ascertain the creditworthiness of a customer. The credit department will investigate the debt-paying ability of each new customer and determine the maximum amount of credit to extend. A credit service such as Dun & Bradstreet, Inc., furnishes credit reports on prospective customers. Whether the customer is an individual or a business, some form of credit information is obtained prior to extending credit to the customer. The amount of credit extended depends on a number of factors. The credit terms offered by the seller may be modified for a new customer until the debt-paying ability of the customer can be determined firsthand. A seller who normally offers credit terms of n/30, may decide to offer terms initially of only n/10 to a new customer. Many sellers who have previously sold to buyers for cash may use this information as a means of extending credit to the customer. In smaller organizations, where competition is great, credit checks may not be made at all. A "seat of the pants" approach or a "gut feeling" approach may be used by smaller organizations.

Recognizing Bad Debts

When a sale is made without the immediate receipt of cash, a portion of these credit sales may prove to be uncollectible. Regardless of a credit department's efforts or the credit service used, a small portion of the outstanding accounts receivable may prove to be uncollectible. When this happens, a provision must be made to match costs and revenue by recognizing this receivable as a BAD DEBT. A bad debt is an expense recognized by a business that was caused by a customer failing to pay an obligation arising out of a prior credit sale. The recognition of this uncollectible account receivable may be handled in many ways depending on the nature of the business.

There are three methods used to recognize customer obligations that have proven to be uncollectible:

1. Direct Write-off Method.
2. Net Sales Method.
3. Aging of Accounts Receivable Method. } Allowance Methods

DIRECT WRITE-OFF METHOD

The DIRECT WRITE-OFF METHOD is used by businesses when it is possible to determine that an account will prove to be uncollectible within the same accounting period as the original sale took place. Although this method is not allowed on the business's books, when it sells most of its products or services for cash, the direct write-off method may be appropriate, since the amount of its credit sales will be very low. Since the credit period offered by the seller is probably rather short, any uncollectible accounts can be ascertained quickly and probably within the same accounting period. Given this information, the bad debt recognition is made when the debt proves to be uncollectible. The following information will illustrate the direct write-off method.

On August 10, 200-, a credit sale was made to John Reston for $300, terms: n/30. On November 8, 200-, it was determined that Mr. Reston would not pay his obligation, which at that point was two months past due. A decision was made to write off Mr. Reston's account as uncollectible.

200-			
Aug. 10	John Reston Accounts Receivable	300	
	Sales		300
	Terms: n/30.		
Nov. 8	Bad Debt Expense	300	
	John Reston Accounts Receivable		300
	To write off the uncollectible account.		

The entry on August 10 represents the credit sale made to Mr. Reston. The November 8 entry recognizes that the customer will not pay his obligation. This second entry recognizes the expense and eliminates the obligation that Mr. Reston has to the seller. By writing off the account as uncollectible in the same accounting period as the original sale, the accountant is able to more correctly match cost with revenue. The effect on the debit to bad debt expense directly offsets the revenue recognized in the credit sale of August 10. According to the Tax Reform Act of 1986 the direct write-off method is the only method allowed on a tax return.

Should a customer whose debt was previously written off pay his obligation, the following reversal entry would be recorded:

200-			
Nov. 25	{ John Reston ⎱ Accounts Receivable ⎰	300	
	Bad Debts Expense		300
	To restore obligation previously written off.		
25	Cash	300	
	{ John Reston ⎱ Accounts Receivable ⎰		300
	Payment received originally due on September 9, 200-		

If this reinstatement took place in the following accounting period, the bad debts expense account might temporarily have a credit balance. If this balance is not eliminated by additional write-offs in the new accounting period, the account with a credit balance would represent a form of revenue.

While the direct write-off method is an accurate means of writing off uncollectibles, it is less desirable than other methods because of its failure to match costs and revenue within the same accounting period.

EXERCISE 1   Record the following transactions using the two-column general journal.

200-
Mar. 6   Sold goods to Standish, Inc., for $840, terms: n/30

9   Sent a credit memorandum for $60 to Standish, Inc. for returning damaged merchandise.

Apr. 14   Received a check from Standish, Inc., for $300 in part payment of the March 6 invoice.

May 18   Determined that the balance Standish, Inc. owed us is uncollectible. Decided to write off the account.

26   Received a check from Standish, Inc. for $100. This represented partial restoration of the account previously written off.

NET SALES METHOD

In order for the direct write-off method to be effective, the volume of credit sales should be small and the write-off should take place during the same accounting period as the original sale. Since these requirements cannot be met by most businesses, the NET SALES METHOD would be more appropriate for them. We have stated that a bad debts expense results from credit sales to customers who later fail to pay their obligations. Since the accountant's primary concern is to match costs and revenue within an accounting period, an adjusting entry is made to recognize the anticipated uncollectible accounts. At the end of the accounting period, the net sales method is used to estimate the amount of net sales that will become uncollectible in subsequent accounting periods. This estimate is usually expressed as a percentage of net sales. Initially a business will rely on industry statistics, which will eventually be modified based on the firm's own experience. A company may decide that 1% of annual net sales of $150,000 may prove to be uncollectible. They would record an adjusting entry debiting bad debts expense for $1,500 ($150,000 × .01). Since the business would not know, at that time, which debts will actually prove to be uncollectible, a credit entry is recorded in an account entitled "Allowance for Bad Debts." This account is classified as a contra-asset account. It offsets the accounts receivable account in the general ledger. The resulting book value of the accounts receivable becomes known as the "realizable value" of the accounts receivable. This is the amount of the accounts receivable actually expected to be collected.

The adjusting entry using the net sales method to recognize the bad debts expense at the end of the accounting period would be:

```
2001
Dec. 31   Bad Debts Expense                      1,500
               Allowance for Bad Debts                   1,500
          1% of Net Sales.
```

On the balance sheet at the end of the accounting period, the accounts receivable section appears as follows:

```
Accounts Receivable                    $150,000
Less: Allowance for Bad Debts             1,500
Net Accounts Receivable                            148,500
```

During the next accounting period, as various debts prove to be uncollectible, these accounts are written off in the following manner:

```
2002
Jan. 13   Allowance for Bad Debts                    270
               John Reston
               Accounts Receivable                        270
          To write off uncollectible debt.
```

Note that the write-off causes a reduction in the balances in the customer's account (John Reston), the accounts receivable control account, and the allowance for bad debts account. The accounts receivable section of the balance sheet, if prepared following this entry, would appear as follows:

Accounts Receivable	$149,730	
Less: Allowance for Bad Debts	1,230	
Net Accounts Receivable		148,500

As additional customer accounts prove to be uncollectible, the same entry to write off the account would be recorded. At the end of the current accounting period, it is again necessary to prepare an adjusting entry to recognize the anticipated bad debt write-offs for the following year. If at the end of the year it is again determined that 1% of net sales is the expected rate of uncollectible debts, then an adjusting entry is once again prepared. Since it is virtually impossible to write off the exact amount of the estimate, there will be a remaining balance in the allowance for bad debts account. This balance is then changed as a result of the adjusting entry. The net sales approach to recognizing uncollectible debt expenses and the subsequent write-off is a widely used method. It is a simple method to use and provides a good means for charging bad debts expense to the period in which the related sales were made.

EXERCISE 2   The Ruth Allen Co. had these account balances at the end of the calendar year: accounts receivable, $541,300; allowance for bad debts, $10,912. Make entries in general journal form, and post to the Allowance for Bad Debts "T" account only, for the following transactions for the new year:

1. Sales made on credit amounted to $5,456,575.
2. Cash sales made during the year amounted to $121,214.
3. Collections of accounts during the year: actual cash collected, $5,381,642; sales discounts allowed, $130,004.
4. Wrote off uncollectible accounts amounting to $9,280.
5. Collected $2,340 for an account that had previously been written off.
6. Made the adjusting entry to recognize bad debts based on 1% of net credit sales for the year.

AGING OF ACCOUNTS RECEIVABLE METHOD

While the net sales method is certainly superior to the direct write-off method, it too has some limitations. If the balance in the allowance for bad debts always has a credit balance each year, prior to the adjusting entry, the balance in the account will continuously increase. No provision is usually made for this situation with the result that the bad debts expense recognized each year will tend to be overstated. In order to remedy this situation, another method can be used that will provide a greater degree of control over the recognition of the bad debts expense as well as providing for the proper amount to appear in the allowance for bad debts at the beginning of a new accounting period. The AGING OF ACCOUNTS RECEIVABLE METHOD provides for a more realistic presentation of the bad debts expense and the allowance for bad debts account. This allowance method is permitted for book purposes only.

The aging of accounts receivable method involves analyzing the accounts found in the accounts receivable ledger. Customer accounts are recorded in an analysis chart according to the due date of the receivables. Those accounts that are past due are listed according to the number of days they are past due, such as 1–30 days, 31–60 days, 61–90 days, and so on. A percentage based on past experience is then applied to the balance not due as well as the balances past due. The amount of the estimated uncollectibles is then determined and used as a basis for the adjusting entry. The adjusting entry is the same as that for the net sales method, except that the balance in the allowance for bad debts account is considered in arriving at the adjusting entry. The following example will illustrate how the aging method is used:

A business determines that $2,300 will be uncollectible according to the aging of accounts receivable method. The remaining balance in the allowance for bad debts account is a credit balance of $200. Since the purpose of this method is to consider the adjusting entry made in the prior period in arriving at the current adjusting entry, the following adjusting entry will be recorded:

200-
Dec. 31	Bad Debts Expense	2,100	
	Allowance for Bad Debts		2,100
	Using the Aging Method.		

While the anticipated amount of bad debts is $2,300, the adjusting entry only reflects $2,100 because the desired balance in the allowance account is to be $2,300. This method corrects the previously overstated expense by correcting it in the current adjusting entry.

If the balance in the allowance for bad debts account prior to adjustment had been a debit balance of $200, the amount of the adjusting entry would be $2,500. This would give a balance in the allowance account of $2,300, the actual estimated accounts to be written off.

EXERCISE 3   A company prepared an aging schedule of accounts receivable for the end of the year. The estimated adjusting entry for the uncollectible receivables amounted to $9,150. At the end of the year, before the adjusting entry, the allowance for bad debts had a credit balance of $350. Make the necessary adjusting entry at the end of the year.

EXERCISE 4   The aging of accounts receivable determines that write-offs for the coming year will amount to $2,445. The balance in the allowance for bad debts account, prior to the adjusting entry, shows a debit balance of $185. Record the adjusting entry under the aging of accounts receivable method.

Extending Credit

The extending of credit to customers is an important aspect of any business's operation. When credit is given, a receivable is set up on the books of the seller. As we have learned, this receivable is usually in the form of an "oral promise," known as an accounts receivable. A receivable represents claims against individuals, business organizations, or other debtors that will eventually be settled by the receipt of cash or any other asset accepted by the creditor. Where the creditworthiness or reliability of a customer is in doubt, the seller may decide to sell to the customer on credit with certain additional requirements. The seller may require the buyer to prepare a PROMISSORY NOTE as evidence of the buyer's obligation to the seller.

PROMISSORY NOTES

A promissory note is an unconditional written promise to pay a stated sum of money upon demand or at a future determinable date. This written promise is usually prepared by the debtor as a result of a request or requirement made by the creditor. The terms of a credit sale may read: 30-day, non-interest-bearing promissory note. Upon receipt of the invoice by the buyer, it is the buyer's obligation to prepare and deliver to the seller the promissory note within a reasonable time. The "maker" of the note (debtor) records the note in an account entitled "Notes Payable." If the original purchase had caused a credit to be recorded to the accounts payable control account and the individual creditor's account, then the issuance of the note would represent the payment of the oral promise with a corresponding credit to the notes payable account. Assume the following facts:

On April 23, 200-, Reliable Equipment Co. received an invoice from the Fireside Tire Co. for $650. Terms: 30-day, non-interest-bearing promissory note. The following entries were recorded in general journal from:

200-
Apr. 23   Trucking Supplies   650
                 [Fireside Tire Co.]
                 [Accounts Payable]   650
          Terms: 30-day note.

```
24   ⎡Fireside Tire Co. ⎤
     ⎣Accounts Payable ⎦                      650
        Notes Payable                                  650
     Issued 30-day note to Fireside Tire Co.
```

As a result of posting to the notes payable account, the following information appears in the account:

Notes Payable

	200- April 24	Fireside Tire Co. 30-day non-interest-bearing note	650

Since the notes payable account lists all the promissory notes that a company issues, it is necessary to indicate to whom the note is payable, the terms, and, where appropriate, the due date of the note. In the above account, the explanation should have also included the due date of the note. The note begins to run as of the date of the invoice, which was April 23. The due date of the note would be May 23, which is thirty days from April 23.

While the above transactions and ledger account are made by the Reliable Equipment Co., there are also entries to be made on the books of the Fireside Tire Co. The following general journal entries would be recorded on the books of the Fireside Tire Co.:

```
200-
April 23  ⎡Reliable Equipment Co.⎤
          ⎣Accounts Receivable    ⎦           650
             Sales                                     650
          30-day note

      25  Notes Receivable                     650
          ⎡Reliable Equipment Co.⎤
          ⎣Accounts Receivable    ⎦                   650
          From Reliable Equipment Co., due on
          May 23, 200-
```

Note that on the books of the seller, the original transaction was recorded according to the invoice date. The entry for the receipt of the note in payment of the oral promise is recorded on the day it is received. The due date of the note is shown as part of the explanation. The transaction of April 25 represents an exchange of assets. The oral promise (accounts receivable) is reduced as a result of the receipt of the written promise (notes receivable). Regardless of whether the promissory note is interest-bearing or non-interest-bearing, it is recorded at its face value in the notes receivable account. This account is handled in a fashion similar to that of the notes payable account in that the explanation must include the name of the company obligated to pay the note as well as the due date or terms of the note.

INTEREST-BEARING PROMISSORY NOTES

An interest-bearing promissory note is a written promise to pay a certain sum at a fixed and determinable future date along with an additional sum known as interest. This interest is calculated based on the holding period of the note, which is usually expressed in days, and the payment of a specific stated rate in interest, which is calculated on the face amount of the note. An interest-bearing note in the hands of the maker is known as a notes payable. The same interest-bearing note in the hands of the creditor is known as a notes receivable.

Determining Interest

The interest assigned to the promissory note is usually calculated based on three factors:

1. The face value of the note, known as the PRINCIPAL.
2. The amount of time the note is in the hands of the creditor before payment is made, known as the TIME.
3. The rate of interest being charged on the note, which is commonly referred to as the RATE.

The basic formula for calculating interest is:

$$\text{Principal} \times \text{Rate} \times \text{Time} = \text{Interest}$$

In using this formula there are certain assumptions that are made. In most cases the period of time for which money is borrowed as evidenced by a note is usually less than one year. In fact, it is not unusual for the terms of a note to call for payment within 30, 60, 90, or 120 days. Since this is the rule rather than the exception, an assumption is made that a year consists of 360 days. This is known as a "banking year." Using this rule, note the calculation of the interest on the following promissory note:

EXAMPLE   A note for $1,000 bearing a rate of interest of 6% for a period of time of 90 days. Using the formula $P \times R \times T = I$, find the amount of interest on the note.

$$\text{Principal} \times \text{Rate} \times \text{Time} = \text{Interest}$$
$$\$1,000 \times .06 \times 90/360 =$$
$$\$1,000 \times .06 \times 1/4 = \$15$$

EXERCISE 5   Determine the interest on the following notes using the formula just illustrated:

Face Amount	Number of Days	Interest Rate
1. $3,000	360	8%
2. 2,600	60	9%
3. 1,000	90	10%
4. 5,000	45	6%
5. 4,000	30	12%

Short Cut for Determining Interest

Since we have assumed that a year consists of 360 days (banking year), and that most promissory notes will be due and payable in 30, 60, 90, or 120 days, there is a shortcut method available for computing interest known as the 60-DAY METHOD OF DETERMINING INTEREST. This 60-day method is based on the fact that the interest on any amount of money borrowed at 6% interest for a period of 60 days will *always* equal 1% of the money borrowed.

Thus, an interest-bearing note for $1,000 due in 60 days and carrying a 6% rate of interest would accrue interest of $10. The following chart will assist in the analysis and solution of the above problem:

Problem	Principal	Rate	Time
	$ 1,000	.06	60 days
	$ 10		

The answer of $10 was arrived at by merely moving the decimal point two places to the left to calculate 1% of the principal. Regardless of the amount of money borrowed, if it is borrowed for 60 days at a 6% rate of interest, the cost of borrowing the money will always be 1% of the money borrowed.

Using the formula initially presented as a proof, the following will result:

$$\text{Principal} \times \text{Rate} \times \text{Time} = \text{Interest}$$
$$\$1,000 \times .06 \times 60/360 =$$
$$\$1,000 \times .06 \times 1/6 = \$10$$

While it is obvious that this formula works for any amount borrowed at 6% for 60 days, it is not as useful at today's lower rates of interest or for periods of time other than 60 days. This method may be modified, however, to take into consideration rates and time other than those used above.

Assume that the promissory note for $1,000 carried a rate of interest of 3% and was held for 60 days. The following represents the solution using the 60 day method:

Principal	Rate	Time	
$1,000	3%	60 days	(Problem Line)
10	6%	60 days	(known)
5	3%	60 days	(solution)

Picture an imaginary equals sign after the principal column and before the rate column. This equals sign would indicate that whatever is done to the right side of the equation must also be done to the left side of the equation to maintain the balance. Note that on line 3 when we show 3% on the right side (which is $1/2$ of 6%), we also show the value of the 3% (which is $1/2$ of $10) to the left side of the equation, thus maintaining the equality. Note the solution of the following problem:

$1,000	6%	90 days	(Problem Line)
$10.00	6%	60 days	(known)
+ $ 5.00		+ 30 days	
$15.00	6%	90 days	

In this situation it was not necessary to solve for the rate, but merely the number of days. Notice how a change on one side brings about a corresponding change on the other side. If both the rate and the time were other than the 60-day method, changes would have to be made to both. *However, only one variable can be changed at a time.* Note the following problem and subsequent solution:

$1,000.00	12%	90 days	(Problem Line)
$ 10.00	6%	60 days	(known)
+ $ 10.00	+ 6%		(solving for rate)
$ 20.00	12%	60 days	
+ $ 10.00		+ 30 days	(solving for time)
$ 30.00	12%	90 days	

Note that the cost of borrowing 1,000 for 90 days at 12% interest will cost the borrower $30 in interest. Remember, when using the 60-day method and solving for rates or times other than 6% and 60 days, the calculations must solve for each unknown separately.

EXERCISE 6   Using the 60-day method, determine the interest charges on the following notes:

Face Amount	Rate of Interest	Time
1. $600	6%	60 days
2. 600	9%	60 days
3. 600	6%	90 days
4. 600	2%	90 days
5. 600	3%	60 days
6. 600	6%	30 days
7. 600	3%	30 days
8. 600	2%	30 days
9. 600	3%	90 days
10. 600	2%	45 days

Recording Interest

The interest on a note is recorded at the time the note is paid. When the note is given by the buyer to the seller, it is recorded on the books as previously illustrated on pages 131 and 132. Notice that the explanations indicate the terms of the notes. In both instances the notes were 30-day notes that were non-interest-bearing by virtue of the fact that no interest was included in the terms. If those notes had been interest-bearing, then the explanation would have indicated that, and the following phrase might have appeared as an explanation: 30-day, 6% note.

The interest on a promissory note is recorded at the time the note matures. The following example illustrates the payment of an interest-bearing note by the person who originally issued the note.

On August 1, 200-, a promissory note was issued by the Able Trading Co. to the Reliable Manufacturing Co. for $1,000. The note was a 60-day, 6% note. The following general journal entry would be recorded upon payment of the note at maturity:

200-			
Aug. 31	Notes Payable	1,000	
	Interest Expense	10	
	Cash		1,010
	Paid 6%, 60-day note to		
	Reliable Manufacturing Co.		

On the books of the Reliable Manufacturing Co., the following entry would represent the receipt of the cash from Able Trading Co. in payment of their obligation:

200-			
Aug. 31	Cash	1,010	
	Notes Receivable		1,000
	Interest Income		10
	Payment of 6%, 60-day note		
	by Able Trading Co.		

Note that the interest paid on the note by the Able Trading Co. represents an expense (Interest Expense) to the company at the time that the payment is made on the note. The interest received by the Reliable Manufacturing Co. represents income (Interest Income) at the time that the notes receivable is paid.

If the note was payable in the next accounting period, then an adjusting entry would be recorded at the end of the accounting period to recognize the accrued interest expense on the books of the Able Trading Co., and accrued interest income at the end of the accounting period would be reflected in an adjusting entry on the books of the Reliable Manufacturing Co.

EXERCISE 7 A business organization issues a 60-day, 9% promissory note for $10,000 to a creditor in payment of an obligation. Present in general journal form entries to (1) record the issuance of the note, and (2) record the payment of the note, including appropriate interest.

EXERCISE 8 A promissory note dated December 1, 2002 bearing interest at a rate of 12% and due in 90 days, is sent to a creditor. The face value of the note is $900. Determine:

1. The due date of the note;
2. The total interest income that will be earned on the note;
3. Assuming the note is held for thirty days in the old accounting period (December 1–31, 2002), find the interest that would be earned on the note for that period (accrued interest income);

4. Prepare the general journal entry for the receipt of the note;
5. Record the adjusting entry on December 31, 2002 and any necessary reversal entries;
6. Record the entry for the payment of the note by the customer; and
7. Record entries 4, 5, and 6 on the books of the customer who issued the note.

Advantage of Note

If a seller of goods and/or services is given an option to sell for cash or on credit, the obvious preference is to receive cash at the time of the sale. As we have previously indicated, this is not usually a choice that the seller has due to the dictates of the industry or trade. However, in selling on credit, the seller has the choice of accepting an oral or a written promise. Having dealt with a particular customer on an ongoing basis, an oral promise from the customer may be adequate. Where your experience with a customer is limited, you might request a written promise when initially selling to the customer on credit. Should a dispute between the customer and the seller develop at a later date, the presence of a promissory note will assist the seller in having the dispute adjudicated in the seller's favor. The courts will accept written evidence over oral testimony in a litigation.

If a seller anticipates problems in collecting from a customer when the original sale is to be consummated, the seller should probably not sell to the customer on credit, whether or not the transaction is evidenced by a promissory note. But if a problem in collection should subsequently arise, the holding of a promissory note is advantageous. The primary benefit that a promissory note has over an oral promise is its negotiability. This is the ability to transfer the note in exchange for cash or other assets. Negotiability is not possible with an oral promise because of its lack of substance; however, it is quite common to transfer a promissory note.

Transferring and Discounting Notes

The receipt of a promissory note from a customer enables the business to sell that note prior to maturity for cash rather than to hold it until maturity. This process is known as DISCOUNTING THE NOTE. Discounting the note is the process of selling the promissory note to a bank or finance company. The note is endorsed, in a fashion similar to that of a check, and delivered to the bank. The bank deducts from the maturity value of the note (face value of the note plus interest) their discounting charges and provides the seller with the net proceeds (maturity value less discount). When the note becomes due, the lending institution that discounted the note expects to receive the maturity value of the note from its maker. The fact that the note has been discounted and turned over to the lending institution does not eliminate the seller's involvement with the note. The endorsement of the note expedites and enables the negotiation of the note, but at the same time it represents a guarantee on the part of the endorser that if the maker of the note fails to pay the bank, the seller will do so.

While this situation does not represent an actual liability, a contingent liability has developed. A CONTINGENT LIABILITY is the commitment of the endorser to pay the discounter the maturity value of the note in the event that the maker of the note defaults. The discounting of the note creates the contingent liability that continues in effect until the due date of the note. If the maker pays the appropriate amount at maturity, the contingent liability is eliminated without any action taken by the endorser. If the maker defaults, then the contingent liability becomes an actual liability. Note that the elimination of the contingent liability takes place on the due date regardless of the action or lack of action taken by the maker of the note. The following illustrates the entry for (1) the receipt of the promissory note, (2) the discounting of the note, and (3) the entry made on the due date of the note. Amounts have been intentionally omitted so that the flow of entries could be highlighted.

200-				
Apr.	1	Notes Receivable	xxxx	
		{Accounts Receivable}		
		{J. Jones}		xxxx
		Received 60-day note.		
May	1	Cash	xxxx	
		Notes Receivable Discounted		xxxx
		Discounted note at bank.		
	31	Notes Receivable Discounted	xxxx	
		Notes Receivable		xxxx
		Note honored by maker.		

When the note is discounted on May 1, the note is actually turned over to the lending institution. The contingent liability is recognized by crediting the notes receivable discounted account for the face value of the note. While it would be possible to credit notes receivable directly, it is not a preferred method because it is important that the contingent liability be recognized when the note is discounted.

If a balance sheet were to be prepared shortly after the transaction of May 1, the effects of this entry on the balance sheet would be as follows:

Notes Receivable	xxxx	
Less: Notes Receivable Discounted	xxxx	
Net Notes Receivable		xxxx

The reader of the balance sheet is immediately made aware of the fact that a contingent liability exists.

The entry of May 31 is made regardless of whether or not the maker of the note pays the maturity value to the lending institution. In the May 31 entry above, if the maker of the note had defaulted, the explanation would have stated that the note was dishonored by the maker. This entry eliminates the contingent liability and at the same time eliminates the balance in the notes receivable account to the extent of that particular note. If the maker of the note pays the obligation to the bank, the discounter of the note is relieved of any possible liability on the note that was discounted.

Should the maker of the note DEFAULT on the note, an actual liability will result and the contingent liability will be eliminated. This failure to pay the obligation when it becomes due (default) on the part of the maker causes the endorser (discounter) of the note to become primarily liable. The bank or financing company will then obtain the maturity value of the note from the discounter. If the endorser of the note has an account with the lending institution, which is usually the case, the bank will take the maturity value of the note out of the endorser's account and notify the endorser. This results in an entry reflecting payment out of the account of the endorser. The following entry is usually made:

```
200-
June 3   ⎧Accounts Receivable ⎫
         ⎩J. Jones            ⎭            xxxx
              Cash                                 xxxx
         Dishonored note and protest fee.
```

The bank will return the dishonored note to the endorser, but the note, having been dishonored, is no longer recognized on the books of the endorser. In its place an accounts receivable is established consisting of the maturity value of the note and any protest fee that the bank has charged to the endorser because of the dishonored note. This total amount is charged to the customer. No expense is recognized for the protest fee since it is the obligation of the defaulting customer. The initial recourse the endorser has against the maker of the note is to request payment of the obligation in full. If the maker of the note fails to pay, the endorser takes the note and other appropriate documentation to court in order to receive relief. The endorser may also be entitled to reasonable interest on the obligation from the due date to the final settlement date of the obligation. This will usually be determined by the court as part of the adjudication.

The following problem involves the discounting of a non-interest-bearing note and its subsequent payment:

Albert Co. received a non-interest-bearing, 90-day note from a customer on June 1, 200-. Thirty days later the note was discounted at the Fidelity Bank. The bank held the note for 60 days and charged a 6% rate for discounting the note, which had a face value of $1,000. The following entries reflect the receipt of the note, its discounting, and subsequent payment:

```
200-
June  1   Notes Receivable                          1,000
              ⎧Accounts Receivable ⎫
              ⎩A. Customer         ⎭                         1,000
          90-day note from A. Customer.

July  1   Cash                                         990
          Interest Expense                              10
              Notes Receivable Discounted                    1,000
          6%, 60 days at Fidelity Bank.

Aug. 30   Notes Receivable Discounted                1,000
              Notes Receivable                               1,000
          Note honored by maker.
```

Since the bank held the non-interest-bearing note for 60 days, they were entitled to interest calculated on the maturity value of the $1,000 note, which was the same as the face value because there was no interest to be earned on the note, at their discount rate of 6%. The calculation of the interest is as follows:

$$\$1,000 \times .06 \times 60/360 = \$10$$

When discounting the note, the bank will take the interest away from the maturity value of the note to determine the net proceeds of the note. The amount of cash received consisted of the maturity value of $1,000, less the bank's discount charge of $10. The credit part of the July 1 entry recognizes the contingent liability.

On August 30, the maturity date of the note, the contingent liability is eliminated. Remember, this entry is made whether or not the note is actually honored.

EXERCISE 9   On March 10, 200-, Arthur Cromwell received from the Bache Co., a customer, a 120-day, non-interest-bearing note for $1,500. The note was discounted at the Jackson National Bank on April 24, 200-. The Jackson National Bank charged Cromwell 6% for discounting the note. Answer the following questions based on the above information:

1. What is the due date of the note?
2. What is the maturity value of the note?
3. How many days did Cromwell hold the note?
4. How many days did the bank hold the note?
5. How much interest is the bank entitled to on the note?
6. What entry will Cromwell record for the receipt of the note?
7. What entry will Cromwell record for the discounting of the note?
8. What entry will Cromwell record on the due date of the note?
9. What entry will result if the note is dishonored on the due date by the maker, assuming a protest fee of $15?

Discounting Interest-Bearing Notes

The discounting of an interest-bearing promissory note is handled in the same manner as that of a non-interest-bearing note, except that the maturity value of the interest-bearing note will include the interest earned on the note by the discounter at the maturity date. The bank in discounting the note will discount it based on the maturity value, which is the amount of money the bank will receive at the maturity date. Thus, even though the face value of the note may be $1,000, if the maturity value is $1,010 ($1,000 + $10 interest), the bank will discount the note based on the maturity value as if the discounter had borrowed $1,010 from the bank originally.

EXAMPLE Assume that a 90-day, 6% note receivable for $1,000, dated August 5, is discounted at a bank on September 4 at a rate of 8%. The following calculations will result:

Face value of note dated August 5:	$1,000.00
Interest on note—6%, 90 days:	15.00
Maturity value of note on November 3:	1,015.00
Discount period—Sept. 4 to Nov. 3 (60 days):	
Discount on maturity value ($1,015 × .08 × 60/360):	13.53
Net Proceeds	$1,001.47

The entries recording receipt of the note and discounting the note would appear as follows:

```
200-
Aug. 5   Notes Receivable                         1,000.00
              Accounts Receivable                              1,000.00
         90-day, 6% note from XXXX.

Sept. 4  Cash                                      1,001.47
              Notes Receivable Discounted                      1,000.00
              Interest Income                                      1.47
         Discounted at 8% for 60 days.
```

If the discounter of the note had held it to maturity, the amount of interest earned on the note would be $15. Having discounted the note after 30 days caused the note to be in the hands of the bank for 60 days. The bank charged a discounting fee of 8% for the 60 days, which amounted to an interest expense to the discounter of $13.53. The excess of interest income earned ($15) over the interest expense charged by the bank ($13.53) resulted in a net interest income of $1.47 to be recorded. An alternate acceptable entry on September 4 could have been:

```
Sept. 4  Cash                                      1,001.47
         Interest Expense                             13.53
              Notes Receivable Discounted                      1,000.00
              Interest Income                                     15.00
         Discounted at 8% for 60 days.
```

While this second entry is acceptable, the first is preferred because it nets out the income and expense to reflect one amount. If the amount of the interest charged by the bank as a result of discounting the note had exceeded the interest income earned on the note, the first entry would have shown a debit to the interest expense account.

Whenever an interest-bearing note is discounted, the amount of the discount is always calculated on the maturity value.

EXERCISE 10

Arthur Andersen holds a 90-day, 7% note for $1,200 dated April 18 that had been received from a client on account. On May 28, the note is discounted to the Town Bank at a rate of 8%. Answer the following questions relating to the above information:

1. What is the maturity value of the note?
2. How long did Andersen hold the note?
3. How long did Town Bank hold the note?
4. What is the amount of the discount on the note?
5. What is the amount of the net proceeds as a result of discounting the note?
6. What is the general journal entry to be made on May 28 when the note is discounted?

EXERCISE 11

Epson Co. received the notes listed below during the last quarter of their calendar year:

Date	Face Amount	Terms	Interest Rate	Date Discounted	Discount Rate
(1) Oct. 8	$3,600	30 days	—	Oct. 18	9%
(2) Sept. 22	$8,000	60 days	6%	Oct. 1	7%
(3) Nov. 15	$3,000	90 days	7%	Nov. 20	8%
(4) Nov. 17	$900	30 days	8%	Dec. 7	7%
(5) Dec. 1	$2,000	60 days	6%	—	—

For each note find:

1. The due date;
2. The amount of the interest due at maturity;
3. The maturity value of the notes;
4. The discount period (where applicable);
5. The net proceeds of the discounted notes;
6. The interest expense or income on the individual notes;
7. The general journal entries for the discounting of notes (1)–(4); and
8. The adjusting entry necessary on December 31, the end of the accounting period, if note (5) is to be held until maturity.

Discounting a Company's Own Note

When a business wishes to borrow money from a lending institution, it may do so by issuing a promissory note payable to the bank. The bank in accepting the note will frequently discount the note. Discounting a notes payable will result in the firm receiving less cash than the face value of the note, to the extent of the interest charged by the bank for the privilege of borrowing the money. The discounting of the note is in actuality the process by which the bank lends money to the business.

EXAMPLE A business issues a 90-day, non-interest-bearing promissory note payable to a bank for $2,000. The bank's discount rate is 9%. The amount of the discount is $45 and the net proceeds are $1,995. This transaction would appear on the books of the borrower as follows:

```
200-
June 5   Cash                                    1,955
           Interest Expense                         45
             Notes Payable                                    2,000
           Issued 90-day note to XXXX Bank
           discounted at 9%.
```

Notice that the note was issued and recorded at face value, which is also the maturity value. The interest expense is recorded at the time the note is issued. When the note is paid in ninety days the following entry would be recorded:

```
200-
Sept. 3  Notes Payable                           2,000
             Cash                                             2,000
           90-day note previously discounted.
```

If the original intent of the borrower was to obtain the use of $2,000, it would be necessary to borrow an amount greater than $2,000 so that the net proceeds of discounting the note would amount to $2,000.

A bank in issuing a loan may choose not to discount the note, but rather require the business to issue a 90-day, 9% note to the bank. If this was the case, the following entries for the issuance and subsequent payment would be recorded on the buyer's books:

```
200-
June 5   Cash                                    2,000
             Notes Payable                                   2,000
           90-day, 9% note to XXXX Bank

Sept. 3  Notes Payable                           2,000
           Interest Expense                         45
             Cash                                             2,045
           Paid note plus interest.
```

EXERCISE 12

Renquist Co. issues a 30-day, non-interest-bearing note for $15,000 to the First National Trust Co., which the bank discounts at 6%. Record the necessary entries in general journal form to (1) issue the note and (2) pay the note at maturity. Assume that the note was written on January 3.

EXERCISE 13

You are given a choice by your bank as to the nature of the loan you are negotiating. You may (1) issue a $5,000, non-interest-bearing note that the bank will discount at a rate of 12% or (2) issue a $5,000 note bearing interest at a rate of 12% that will be accepted at face value.

Determine: (1) the amount of interest expense for each option, (2) the amount of the net proceeds for each option, and (3) indicate which option is most favorable to you and why.

Summing Up

When a choice is available, most organizations would prefer selling their goods and services for cash rather than on credit. When the nature of the industry dictates that credit must be extended, a provision should be made for uncollectible accounts receivable. There are basically three methods that can be utilized: (1) the direct write-off method, (2) the net sales method, and (3) the aging of accounts receivable method. The method selected will be determined by the amount of credit sales, the timeliness of determining the uncollectible accounts, and the degree of accuracy desired according to the concept of matching costs and revenue. Regardless of the method selected, the effect will be to recognize an expense entitled bad debts expense. This expense recognition will result in adjusting the income for the particular accounting period involved. When the net sales or aging methods are used, the expense is immediately recognized as an adjusting entry at the end of the accounting period, with subsequent write-offs being taken as the debts prove to be uncollectible.

Some business organizations, as a result of selling goods on credit, may require a promissory note from the buyer. The advantage of this commitment on the part of the buyer is that it provides written evidence of the transaction with the buyer's signature on it. Should a dispute subsequently develop, the seller will be in a better position to have the dispute adjudicated in his favor. Also, the possession of a promissory note enables the seller to convert this asset to cash, prior to the maturity of the note, though the process of discounting the note. The promissory notes receivable is an asset that may be interest-or non-interest-bearing in nature. An interest-bearing note will result in interest income being recognized on the note when it is paid at maturity. On the books of the issuer of the note, it represents a liability. An interest-bearing notes payable will recognize interest expense on the issuer's books when the note is paid. The maturity value of the note, whether on the books of the issuer or the recipient, is the face value of the note (principal) plus the interest.

CHAPTER 9

ACCOUNTING FOR LONG-LIFE AND INTANGIBLE ASSETS

Long-Life Assets

We have previously defined an asset as anything owned that has money value. Assets were further classified in terms of their useful life. An asset that can readily be expected to be consumed or converted to cash within a year or less was classified as a CURRENT ASSET. Any asset that has a useful life of more than one year is usually considered to be a LONG-LIFE ASSET. There are other terms used to describe long-life assets, including FIXED ASSETS or PROPERTY, PLANT, AND EQUIPMENT.

USING LONG-LIFE ASSETS

Long-life assets are acquired through purchase for use in the operation of the business and are not intended for resale. Assets included in this category are: equipment, tools, furniture, machinery, automotive equipment, buildings, and land. In order for the above-mentioned items to be classified as plant assets, they must be used in the business, though not necessarily used continuously, and have a minimum useful life of at least one year. The function of long-life assets is to assist in the generation of revenue, which is the primary activity of most business organizations. A fixed asset such as a delivery truck enables a firm to transport goods that have been sold to the organization's various customers. Thus, this long-life asset is an integral part of the consummation of the sale. Without this fixed asset the firm would have to incur the expense of hiring a delivery service to complete the transaction. While the cost of hiring the delivery service is an obvious expense, the use of the firm's delivery truck is also an expense that must be recognized over the assigned useful life of the truck. While this expense is not so apparent, it still must be recognized, which we will do shortly.

DETERMINING PLANT AND EQUIPMENT COSTS

The cost of plant and equipment includes all expenditures necessary to acquire and place the asset in use by the organization. Costs include the purchase price of the asset, plus any applicable sales taxes, the cost of transporting the equipment to its place of use, the installation costs and any other incidental costs necessary to make the asset operational for the organization. The justification for including all the costs indicated, rather than recording some as expenses, is that these costs are all an integral part of making the asset usable by the organization. The benefits derived from the cost assigned will be recognized over the useful life of the asset. The COST PRINCIPLE, previously discussed, states that all assets are set up on the books at their actual cost. This cost includes any specific or incidental costs necessary to place the asset in use by the firm. This principle is an integral part of the concept of matching costs and revenue.

A business wishes to acquire a machine that has a list price of $5,000. The seller offers a trade discount of 20%. There is a delivery charge of $175, and applicable sales taxes on the net purchase price amounting to 8%. In order to make the machine operational, a special cement pad must be constructed at a cost of $500. The installation charge amounts to $250. The following represents the determination of the total cost of the machine as it will appear on the buyer's books should the organization decide to acquire the asset:

List Price of Machine	$5,000
Less: Trade Discount (20%)	(1,000)
Net Purchase Price	4,000
Add: Sales Tax (8%)	320
Delivery Charge	175
Cement Pad	500
Installation Charge	250
Total cost of machine	$5,245

On the books of the buyer, the machine will be set up at a total cost of $5,245. Any subsequent costs, such as repairs, would be treated as expenses. This asset will remain on the books at the value assigned, unless the asset is sold or there is a subsequent CAPITAL EXPENDITURE. A capital expenditure is a material expenditure that usually increases the useful life of a fixed asset. For example, the replacement of a roof on a building is a capital expenditure that increases the cost of the building on the books and also increases the building's useful life. A repair to the roof, however, is considered an expense that does not increase the cost of the asset.

EXERCISE 1 A building with an assessed value of $70,000 for property tax purposes is offered for sale at $95,000. The building is acquired by a business firm for $32,000 cash and the balance in the form of a 2-year non-interest-bearing note. The real estate brokerage fee is 5% of the selling price. Legal fees for the contract and closing are $2,500. Determine the cost of the building to be recorded on the books of the purchaser.

Allocating Plant and Equipment Costs

A short-life (current) asset such as supplies is adjusted annually to reflect the fact that it has been used up. This conversion from an asset to an expense is accomplished by recording an adjusting entry. At the end of the accounting period, an inventory is taken of the actual supplies that are on hand. The difference between the book value of the supplies and the inventory tells the accountant the value of the supplies used up, and becomes the basis for the adjusting entry. Plant and equipment cannot be treated in the same fashion because there is no apparent change in the value of the asset that can be readily measured. However, the approximate useful life of a plant asset can be determined. This useful life, expressed in years or usage, becomes the basis for assigning a cost or expense for the asset periodically. The term used to describe the recognition of an annual expense for a plant asset is DEPRECIATION.

Depreciation is the recognition of a loss in value of a plant asset due to wear and tear over time. Thus, the recognition of depreciation causes a portion of the asset value to be converted to an expense the same way that the asset supplies was converted. In recognizing this annual expense, the accountant must still follow the dictates of the cost principle. The value assigned to the fixed asset on the books must remain the same unless the asset is sold or changed as a result of a capital improvement.

DEPRECIATION

The entry to record depreciation is an adjusting entry and is usually recorded at least once a year. Some organizations may choose to record depreciation monthly, quarterly, or semiannually. Regardless of when it is recorded, it still represents an adjusting entry similar to the conversion of the asset supplies to an expense. Since it is necessary to retain the original balance in the asset account for a plant asset, the adjusting entry first recognizes the expense by debiting an account entitled "Depreciation Expense." The corresponding credit is not made directly to the asset account, but rather to an account that is classified as a CONTRA-ASSET. A contra-asset is a negative account that will always represent a credit entry offsetting a specific plant asset. If the plant asset being depreciated is equipment, the contra-asset account would be entitled "Accumulated Depreciation—Equipment." If we were to recognize annual depreciation of the asset equipment amounting to $500, the following entry would be recorded in the general journal:

```
200-
Dec. 31   Depreciation Expense—Equipment            500
                Accumulated Depreciation—Equipment          500
            To recognize annual depreciation.
```

The depreciation expense account is handled in the same manner as any other expense. Shortly after the adjusting entry is recorded and posted at the end of the accounting period, it is closed to income summary and becomes a part of the income statement that is prepared.

The credit entry to accumulated depreciation—equipment is a contra-asset account and as such will not be closed but rather appear as a subtraction from the asset account on the balance sheet of the business when it is prepared. The following represents how the asset and related contra-asset will appear on the balance sheet of the business:

Equipment	$12,400
Less: Accumulated Depreciation	500
	$11,900

Depreciation may result from one of two major causes. Ideally, depreciation results from PHYSICAL DETERIORATION due to the plant asset being used. Some assets are depreciated based on the somewhat arbitrary useful life (in years) assigned to it, and other assets are depreciated based on their capacity to complete a number of specific functions. For example, a machine may be depreciated based on its ability to stamp out a specified number of items. The machine's output is used to determine the depreciation expense. Another cause resulting in the recognition of depreciation is obsolescence. OBSOLESCENCE is the process of becoming obsolete or out of date. A personal computer designed a mere two years ago may be considered obsolete today, even though it is operational, because a more sophisticated computer has been developed. Obsolescence may also happen when a plant asset cannot meet the needs of a rapidly growing business. Inadequacy of a plant asset may necessitate replacement with a larger unit, even though the asset is in good physical condition and is not obsolete.

CALCULATING DEPRECIATION

The method used to calculate depreciation will vary depending on a number of factors. The most obvious factor is the nature and use made of the plant and equipment. An asset that is used infrequently would probably not be depreciated based on useful life but rather actual usage. Another asset that is in continuous use may be appropriately depreciated based on useful life. The depreciation of another asset may be accelerated because of rapid changes in the value of the asset or other factors, such as anticipated repair costs. A business organization utilizes as many methods of recognizing depreciation as are suitable for the assets being depreciated. The four methods most commonly used to recognize depreciation are; STRAIGHT-LINE, UNITS OF PRODUCTION, DOUBLE-DECLINING BALANCE, and SUM-OF-THE-YEARS'-DIGITS.

The Straight-Line Method

The straight-line method is the simplest and most widely used method of recognizing depreciation. This method provides for the annual recognition of depreciation in equal amounts over the useful life of the asset. If the asset being depreciated is expected to lose value in a uniform manner year after year, then this method would probably be appropriate. The amount of the asset that is subject to depreciation is known as the DEPRECIABLE VALUE. The depreciable value is determined by subtracting from the total cost of the asset the salvage or scrap value of the asset. This residual value represents the value of the asset after it has been fully depreciated and also the minimum value of the asset when it is no longer of use to the business. The salvage value is usually an estimate and represents the amount that can be obtained for the asset when it is no longer of use to its owner. If a plant asset has a total cost of $10,000 and a residual value of $500, then the depreciable value would be determined as follows:

$$\text{Cost} - \text{Residual Value} = \text{Depreciable Value}$$

$$\$10,000 - \$500 = \$9,500$$

The useful life, usually expressed in years, is divided into the depreciable value to determine the annual depreciation expense to be recognized.

$$\frac{\text{Cost} - \text{Residual Value}}{\text{Useful life (in years)}} = \text{Annual Depreciation Expense}$$

If the above asset with a depreciable value of $9,500 had a useful life of ten years, then the annual depreciation would be calculated as follows:

$$\frac{\$9,500}{10 \text{ years}} = \$950 \text{ (Annual Depreciation)}$$

The annual depreciation can also be expressed as a rate. This is done by taking the useful life expressed in years and placing it in fractional form under 1. Thus, in the above situation, a useful life of 10 years would be expressed as the fraction $\frac{1}{10}$, which converted to a percentage would represent annual depreciation of 10% under the straight-line method.

This calculation would take the depreciable value ($9,500) and multiply it by the straight-line rate of 10%.

$$\$10,000 - \$500 = \$9,500 \times .10 = \$950$$

EXERCISE 2   An asset is acquired at the beginning of the accounting period at a total cost of $7,850. It is expected to have a useful life of 5 years and a scrap value of $350.
   Determine:

1. The annual rate of depreciation using the straight-line method;
2. The depreciable value of the asset;
3. The amount of annual depreciation expense to be recognized;
4. The total depreciation recognized after the third year;
5. The net asset value after recognizing three years of depreciation.

Recording Depreciation

In the previous illustration, the adjusting entry for the first full year's depreciation would be recorded as follows:

```
2001
Dec. 31   Depreciation Expense—Equipment              950
                 Accumulated Depreciation—Equipment          950
             To recognize first year's depreciation.
```

As a result of this entry being posted to the ledger accounts, the accounts would appear as follows:

Equipment

2002 Jan. 1 10,000	

Accumulated Depreciation—Equipment

	2002 Dec. 31 950

After the second year's depreciation expense is recognized, the equipment account would remain as illustrated above; however, the accumulated depreciation—equipment account would appear as follows:

Accumulated Depreciation—Equipment

	2001 Dec. 31 (After 1st Year) 950
	2002 Dec. 31 (After 2nd Year) 950

Notice that the accumulated depreciation account has increased from $950 at the end of the first year's depreciation recognition to $1,900 after the recognition of the second year's depreciation. The balance sheet after the second year would show the asset equipment as follows:

Equipment	$10,000
Less: Accumulated Depreciation	1,900
	$8,100

The resulting balance for the equipment account is known as its BOOK VALUE. The book value is the original cost of the asset as established on the books, less the accumulated depreciation. The book value for this asset at the end of the third year would be $7,150 ($10,000 − $950 − $950 − $950 = $7,150).

If the asset was to be fully depreciated over its useful life of ten years, the resulting book value would be its scrap value of $500 ($10,000 − $9,500 = $500). Remember that book value represents the original cost ($10,000), less accumulated depreciation ($9,500).

In the previous illustrations and discussion, we assumed that the plant asset was acquired at the beginning of the calendar year and depreciated for the entire year, as first-year depreciation. In practice as we will see, the first year's depreciation is calculated from the date the asset is put in service until the end of that business year. Since plant and equipment assets are acquired and placed in service as needed, this date will probably be other than the beginning of the calendar year. The calculation of the first year's depreciation will be as previously illustrated, but consideration is given to the fraction of the first year of service. A calendar year business placing an asset in service on March 2 will only recognize first year's depreciation from March 2 through December 31. The annual straight-line depreciation will then be multiplied by 10/12 to determine the appropriate first year's depreciation.

The depreciation expense account would be closed to income summary at the end of each accounting period.

EXERCISE 3   A mimeograph machine was acquired for use in the office on July 1 of the current year. The cost of the machine was $3,250. It has a useful life of 8 years and a salvage value estimated to be $50. Using the straight-line method, answer the following questions:

1. What is the annual rate of depreciation?
2. What is the depreciable value of the asset?
3. What is the amount of annual depreciation to be recognized?
4. What is the amount of depreciation to be recognized for the first year? (July 1–December 31)
5. What is the adjusting entry to be recorded for depreciation at the end of the first calendar year?
6. What is the balance in the accumulated depreciation account at the end of the second year after the appropriate adjusting entry?
7. When the asset has been fully depreciated, what is its book value?

THE UNITS-OF-PRODUCTION METHOD

The units-of-production method allocates the cost of a plant asset to the various accounting periods on the basis of the actual output by the asset. Thus, the useful life of the asset may be unlimited in terms of time, but limited as to the number of items that can be produced using the asset. As in the case of the straight-line method, the portion of the cost of the asset under this method subject to depreciation is known as the depreciable value. By dividing the depreciable value by the estimated productive capacity, the accountant can ascertain the depreciation expense charged against each unit produced by the machine.

$$\frac{\text{Depreciable Value}}{\textit{Productive } \text{Capacity}} = \text{Per-Unit Depreciation}$$

If the number of units produced for the accounting period is then multiplied by the per unit depreciation, the total adjusting entry for depreciation expense can be determined.

A lathe acquired at a total cost of $20,750, with a salvage value of $750, is to be depreciated using the units-of-production method. The estimated productive capacity of the lathe is 40,000 hours. The per-hour depreciation is determined as follows:

$$\frac{\$20,750\,(\text{Cost}) - \$750\,(\text{Salvage Value})}{40,000\,\text{Hours}\,(\text{Productive Capacity})} = \$0.50\,(\text{Per-Hour Depreciation})$$

If the lathe was used for 1,500 hours during an accounting period, the hours multiplied by the $0.50 rate of depreciation would mean a depreciation expense of $750 for the year.

When the amount of usage of a plant asset varies greatly from year to year, the units-of-production method would be more appropriate than the straight-line method. Certainly costs are more appropriately charged against revenue for the specific accounting period, as dictated by the matching of costs and revenue principle.

EXERCISE 4 A van is acquired by the Acme Delivery Service at a cost of $15,600. The expected salvage value is $600 and the useful life as expressed in mileage is estimated to be 150,000 miles. Using the units-of-production method answer the following questions:

1. What is the depreciable value of the van?
2. What is the rate of depreciation per mile?
3. What is the adjusting entry for the first year's depreciation if the van is driven 23,200 miles?
4. What is the balance in the accumulated depreciation account after the van has been driven for 65,400 miles?
5. What is the book value of the van given the information in question 4?

ACCELERATED DEPRECIATION

ACCELERATED DEPRECIATION is the recognition of greater amounts of depreciation in the early years of use of the plant asset and reduced amounts in later years. Accelerated depreciation is automatically recognized when the units-of-production method is used, since this method recognizes use that may be greater in the early years of the asset. Some assets may not be appropriately depreciated using the units-of-production method if a greater amount of depreciation should be recognized in the early years. An automobile used in business might normally be depreciated using the straight-line method, and yet this method may not adequately reflect the use made of the automobile. If the productivity of the automobile is greater in its earlier years of use, then a form of accelerated depreciation should be used. In the case of many plant assets, there is an increase in maintenance and repair costs the longer the asset is used. An automobile might not be subject to repair charges within the first two or three years of its use, but it can be expected to incur greater repair costs as the years progress. By recognizing accelerated depreciation in the earlier years and lower depreciation in the later years, the maintenance and repair costs tend to equalize the overall cost recognition for the asset being depreciated. This philosophy is consistent with the basic accounting concept of matching costs and revenue.

The Double-Declining Balance Method

This method is appropriate when the asset subject to depreciation contributes to the production of earnings to a greater extent in its early years of use than in its later life. This method modifies the straight-line method in that depreciation is taken at "double" the straight-line rate. Thus, an asset with a useful life of 10 years is depreciated under the straight-line method at a rate of 10% per year. Using the double-declining balance method the same asset is depreciated at a rate of 20% per year on the remaining balance or book value of the asset. When using this method, the residual value is not a part of the calculation. The formula used to calculate first-year depreciation under this method is:

Cost × Double-Declining Balance Rate = First-Year Depreciation

The plant asset costing $10,000, with a useful life of 10 years and salvage value of $500, would be depreciated under the double-declining balance method as follows:

$$\$10,000 \times .20 = \$2,000.$$

Note that the salvage value is ignored in this calculation. The depreciation recognition in subsequent years is based on the book value of the asset multiplied by the double-declining balance rate.

The depreciation of the above asset over its useful life would be calculated as follows:

Equipment Cost—$10,000; Salvage Value—$500 (ignored)

Useful Life—10 years; Straight-Line Rate 10% (1/10)

Double-Declining Balance Rate—20% (2/10)

YEAR	COMPUTATION (BOOK VALUE × RATE)			DEPRECIATION EXPENSE	ACCUMULATED DEPRECIATION	BOOK VALUE
1	$10,000.00	×	20%	$2,000.00	$2,000.00	$8,000.00
2	8,000.00	×	20%	1,600.00	3,600.00	6,400.00
3	6,400.00	×	20%	1,280.00	4,880.00	5,120.00
4	5,120.00	×	20%	1,024.00	5,904.00	4,096.00
5	4,096.00	×	20%	819.20	6,723.20	3,276.80
6	3,276.80	×	20%	655.36	7,378.56	2,621.44
7	2,621.44	×	20%	524.29	7,902.85	2,097.15
8	2,097.15	×	20%	419.43	8,322.28	1,677.72
9	1,677.72	×	20%	335.54	8,657.82	1,342.18
10	1,342.18	×	20%	268.44	8,926.26	1,073.74

The last amount shown in the book-value column following the calculation of the tenth year's depreciation represents the salvage value of the asset. Under the double-declining method, the asset, after being fully depreciated over its useful life, will have a residual value equal to the remaining book value of the asset. A comparison of this accelerated depreciation method with the straight-line method will graphically show the difference in the amount of depreciation recognized each year.

Following the determination of the first full year's depreciation, the calculation for the second and subsequent years is based on the book value (cost—accumulated depreciation) multiplied by the double-declining balance rate (straight-line rate × 2).

If the above asset had not been acquired at the beginning of the accounting period, which is usually the case, the amount of depreciation to be recognized will be a fraction of the year, based on that portion of the year the asset was used. Let us assume that the above asset was acquired on April 2 of the same year. The first year's depreciation would be calculated based on the asset's being used from April 2 through December 31, a period of nine months. The first year's double-declining balance depreciation for the nine months would be calculated as follows:

$$\$10,000 \times 20\% \times 9/12 = \$1,500$$

The book value of the asset after the above adjusting entry would be $8,500. This amount would be used to calculate the second full year's depreciation as follows:

$$\$8,500 \times 20\% = \$1,700$$

The book value of the asset after the second year's adjusting entry would be $6,800. This amount would be used to calculate the third full year's depreciation as follows:

$$\$6,800 \times 20\% = \$1,360$$

Regardless of when the asset is acquired, the amount of depreciation to be recognized for the first year is based on the amount of time the asset is in service for that first year. The fraction of the year for the recognition of the first year's depreciation is usually not calculated for periods of time less than one-half month. Thus, an asset acquired on May 10 will probably be depreciated from May 15 through December 31 for the calendar year (7 1/2 months). The fraction used in this case would be 15/24, which would be reduced to 5/8. Some businesses will depreciate the asset only on the basis of a full month; thus, an asset acquired on February 10 would be depreciated from February 1. An asset acquired on February 17 would be depreciated from March 1.

EXERCISE 5 On January 6 of the current year, the Halpern Service Co. acquired a plant asset at a cost of $5,000. The asset is expected to have a useful life of five years and a scrap value of $450. Using the double-declining balance method, determine the depreciation to be recognized on the asset over its useful life. Prepare a table similar to the one illustrated in this unit.

EXERCISE 6 On July 1 of the current fiscal year ending December 31, Balley and Co. acquired a plant asset at a total cost of $70,000. The asset has an expected useful life of four years and no salvage value is anticipated. Using the double-declining balance method, determine the depreciation over its useful life. Prepare a table similar to the one illustrated in this unit. Be careful to recognize the first fiscal year's depreciation only from July through December. Also, the last year's depreciation recognition will only be from January through June.

The Sum-of-the-Years'-Digits Method

Comparing the straight-line method with the double-declining balance method shows a substantial difference in the amount of depreciation recognized, especially during the early years of depreciation recognition. An accelerated form of depreciation may be desirable that provides a depreciation expense that is greater than under the straight-line method, but not as severe as with the double-declining method. An appropriate compromise can be accomplished using the sum-of-the-years'-digits method (SYD method).

The SYD method produces a depreciation expense in a form similar to, but not as extreme as, the double-declining balance method. The yearly depreciation declines steadily over the estimated useful life of the asset because a successively smaller fraction is applied each year to the original cost of the asset less the estimated salvage value. The fraction used to determine the SYD depreciation expense is determined by finding the sum of the years' digits. If an asset has a useful life of 5 years, the sum of the years' digits would be $5 + 4 + 3 + 2 + 1 = 15$. The number 15 becomes the value assigned to the denominator of the fraction to be used. The numerator of the fraction will change each year over the useful life of the asset. Since the earlier years should be charged greater depreciation under this accelerated approach, the first year's numerator will be the highest year (5), the second year's numerator will be the next highest year (4), and so forth. The first year's fraction will be 5/15, the second year's fraction will be 4/15, the third year's fraction will be 3/15, and so forth, Each year's depreciation is obtained by multiplying the appropriate fraction by the original cost, less the residual value. The plant asset illustrated above would be depreciated using the SYD method as follows:

YEAR	COST LESS RESIDUAL VALUE	× RATE	DEPRECIATION FOR YEAR	ACCUMULATED DEPRECIATION	BOOK VALUE AT YEAR END
1	$9,500.00	× 10/55	$1,727.27	$1,727.27	$8,272.73
2	9,500.00	× 9/55	1,554.55	3,281.82	6,718.18
3	9,500.00	× 8/55	1,381.82	4,663.64	5,336.36
4	9,500.00	× 7/55	1,209.09	5,872.73	4,127.27
5	9,500.00	× 6/55	1,036.37	6,909.10	3,090.90
6	9,500.00	× 5/55	863.64	7,772.74	2,227.26
7	9,500.00	× 4/55	690.91	8,463.65	1,536.35
8	9,500.00	× 3/55	518.18	8,981.83	1,018.17
9	9,500.00	× 2/55	345.45	9,327.28	672.72
10	9,500.00	× 1/55	172.72	9,500.00	500.00

After the asset has been fully depreciated, the remaining book value of the asset is its residual value. In order to obtain the denominator of the fraction for the SYD method it was necessary to add the sum of the digits $(10 + 9 + 8 + \ldots 1)$. The denominator can more easily be determined by using the following formula (S = sum of the digits; N = number of years of the estimated useful life):

$$S = N\left(\frac{N+1}{2}\right)$$

$$S = 10\left(\frac{10+1}{2}\right) = 55$$

Each year's depreciation expense is 1/55 less than the previous year's, multiplied by the original cost less the salvage value. The above illustration once again assumes that the asset was acquired at the beginning of the accounting period and will be depreciated for the entire first year. In practice, assets are acquired when needed, and the first year's depreciation must reflect the period of time for which the asset was used. If the above plant asset had been acquired on April 5, then the first year's depreciation expense would be calculated as follows:

$$\$9,500 \times 10/55 \times 9/12 = \$1,295.45$$

The 9/12 represents the fraction of the first year for which the asset was used. The second and subsequent year's depreciation using the SYD method would remain the same as previously illustrated. Remember that the asset will be fully depreciated after 10 years, which in this case means that 3 months' depreciation will be recognized at the beginning of the eleventh year. The calculation for the last three months (first 3 months of the eleventh year) would be:

$$\$9,500 \times 1/55 \times 3/12 = \$43.18$$

EXERCISE 7 Using the information provided in Exercise 5, determine the depreciation expense in tabular form using the SYD method.

EXERCISE 8 Referring to Exercise 6, determine the depreciation expense in tabular form using the SYD method.

EXERCISE 9 A factory is acquired on January 9 at a cost of $325,000 and has an estimated useful life of twenty-five years. Assuming that it has no residual value, determine the depreciation for each of the first two years by: (a) the straight-line method, (b) the double-declining balance method, and (c) the SYD method.

DISPOSAL OF PLANT ASSETS

Plant assets may be disposed of at any time. They may be disposed of because of obsolescence, sale, or deterioration prior to, at, or after being fully depreciated. The details as to the entries for disposal will vary, but in all cases it is necessary to remove the book value of the asset from the accounts. The two accounts always affected are the asset account and the accumulated depreciation account (contraasset account). The mere fact that an asset has been fully depreciated does not mean that it should be removed from the books. Many assets that have been fully depreciated and have a zero book value, are still in use and retained on the books until the asset is actually disposed of. An asset that has been fully depreciated and has no residual value and no further service to provide the business is discarded. When this occurs the following entry is made to record the disposal:

```
200-
Nov. 26   Accumulated Depreciation—Equipment     10,000
               Equipment                                      10,000
          To write off equipment discarded.
```

If this asset had been fully depreciated but still had a book value of $500 representing its residual value, and it was sold for its residual value, the following entry would be recorded:

```
200-
Nov. 26   Cash                                          500
          Accumulated Depreciation—Equipment        9,500
               Equipment.                                     10,000
```

When an asset is sold prior to its being fully depreciated, an adjusting entry is recorded at the time of sale to reflect the depreciation for the current accounting period up to the date of sale. Following the adjusting entry, an entry recording the disposal is made. The following illustration shows the recognition of depreciation to the date of sale and the disposal of the asset where the proceeds of the sale are less than the remaining book value of the asset:

```
200-
Jun 27   Depreciation Expense—Equipment          475
               Accumulated Depreciation—Equipment           475
         To record depreciation to the date of sale.

    27   Cash                                       900
         Accumulated Depreciation—Equipment       9,025
         Loss on Disposal of Equipment              75
               Equipment                                   10,000
         To write off equipment sold.
```

If the asset had been sold for $1,000, the following entry for its sale would be recorded:

```
200-
Jun 27   Cash                                     1,000
         Accumulated Depreciation—Equipment       9,025
               Gain on Sale of Equipment                      25
               Equipment                                   10,000
         To write off equipment sold.
```

Whenever assets are sold or disposed of and the cash received is in excess of the asset's book value, the resulting difference is recorded as a gain. When the cash received is less than the book value of the asset, the resulting difference is recorded as a loss. Both gains and losses on the disposal of plant assets are non-operating items and are reported on the income statement in the respective non-operating sections.

EXERCISE 10

A depreciable plant asset was sold for $22,000. At the end of the previous accounting period, the balance in the accumulated depreciation account was $90,000, and the original cost of the asset was $115,000. The adjusting entry on the date of sale (October 22) is $5,000. Record the adjusting entry to recognized depreciation on the date of sale and record the sale of the plant asset.

Trade-in of Plant Assets

Certain assets when they are no longer of use to the organization may be traded for similar or different assets. The treatment of a trade-in will be based on the kind of asset given as compared with the asset acquired.

When the asset being traded is *different* from the one being acquired, there is a recognition to the gain or loss as a result of the transaction. The TRADE-IN ALLOWANCE is the amount of credit the seller is willing to extend to the buyer for the asset being traded in. To determine whether a gain or loss is recognized, you compare the book value of the asset given with the trade-in allowance given by the seller on the old asset.

The following facts will be used to illustrate the entries required to record the trading in of different assets: (1) new asset cost—$9,400; (2) trade-in allowance on old asset—$1,675; and (3) book value of old asset after adjusting depreciation to the date of sale—$1,500 (original cost, $6,000).

A comparison of the trade-in allowance ($1,675) with the book value of the old asset ($1,500) indicates that the seller is giving the buyer an allowance of $175 in excess of the buyer's book value for the old asset. This excess represents the gain on the trade-in that is recognized by the buyer. The following general journal entry represents the trade-in:

200-			
Aug. 6	Furniture	9,400	
	Accumulated Depreciation—Furniture	4,500	
	Cash		7,725
	Equipment		6,000
	Gain on Trade-In of Equipment		175
	To record the trade-in of equipment for furniture.		

Had the asset furniture been purchased outright without a trade-in, the cost of the furniture would have been $9,400 in cash. The amount of cash paid in this case is $7,725. This was determined by taking the cost of the asset ($9,400) less the trade-in allowance given by the seller ($1,675).

Whenever one asset is traded in for another asset that is not similar in nature, the gain or loss resulting from the trade-in must be recognized. If the trade-in allowance is less than the book value of the asset being given, then the difference is a loss that is recorded in an account entitled "Loss on Trade-In of Plant Asset."

When one plant asset is traded in for a *similar* asset, the recognition of gain or loss on trade-in is *not* recognized. This method, which is frequently referred to as the INCOME TAX METHOD, permits the postponement of the recognition of the gain or loss so that the postponement is spread out over the useful life of the similar asset acquired. If the asset acquired in the above illustration had been similar to the one given, the gain of $175 would have reduced the cost of the new asset acquired. The new asset would have been recorded on the books at $9,225 rather than $9,400 as illustrated. The postponement of a loss on trade-in would cause the cost of the new asset acquired to be increased to the extent of the loss. If a loss in trade-in of $200 occurred, then the new asset would be set up on the books at $9,600, rather than at the purchase price of $9,400.

EXERCISE 11

A computer was purchased on January 1, for $75,000 cash. The useful life was estimated to be 6 years, with a salvage value of $10,000. The SYD method of depreciation was used. On July 1, four and one-half years later, the computer was traded in on another computer. The following information is available to us: (1) cost of the new computer— $100,000, and (2) trade-in allowance on the old computer—$20,000.

The company is on a calendar-year basis. Prepare the adjusting entries needed on July 1 to record the trade-in.

Depletion

Not all long-life assets are subject to depreciation. The land that the depreciable asset building is on is not subject to depreciation. The reason for this should be obvious: the land does not lose its value, even though the building does.

Other assets, because of their nature, may not be subject to depreciation, but may lose value which still has to be recognized. For example, a business may own land that it uses for purposes other than the placement of a building on it. Land may be used for farming or for the extraction of metal ores and other minerals. The business may not even actually own the land, but may merely lease the rights to use the land for a period of years. The cost of the lease or the cost of the land owned can be converted to an expense based on the fact that the use made of the land may cause its value to decrease. An oil company may estimate that there are 20,000 barrels of crude oil beneath the land they lease. If the leasehold on the land calls for a total payment of $20,000, then for every barrel of oil extracted from the land, a cost of $1 per barrel can be assigned to the cost of the oil. This form of depreciation that applies to land use is known as DEPLETION. Depletion is the pro-rate allocation of the cost of land (through direct ownership or by lease) to the units of natural resources removed from the land.

Calculating Depletion

The calculation of depletion is very similar to the units-of-production form of depreciation previously discussed. Since depletion represents the assignment of a cost to that which is extracted from land, two factors must be known: (1) the cost of the land (ownership or lease costs), and (2) the expected units to be extracted from the land.

Once these two factors are known, it is then possible to assign the depletion expense for a particular accounting period based on the rate of extraction from the land.

Assume that a company leases the rights to extract coal from a coal mine estimated to contain 2 million tons of coal. The cost of the lease is $1 million. The depletion charge per unit extracted is calculated by dividing the anticipated total units to be extracted (2 million tons) into the cost of the lease ($1 million). Each ton of coal extracted would carry an assigned cost of $.50. The adjusting entry to recognize the depletion based on extraction of 250,000 tons would be:

```
200-
Dec. 31   Depletion Expense                    125,000
              Accumulated Depletion—Coal
              To record extraction of 250,000 tons.        125,000
```

Notice that the entry for depletion is very similar to the entry for depreciation. In this case an accumulated depletion account is used in place of the accumulated depreciation. The book value of the lease or land owned is the cost of the investment (land, or lease), less the accumulated depletion.

When the land is leased for a specific period of time and the amount of the minerals that will be extracted cannot be readily determined, a straight-line approach similar to straight-line depreciation is used. Naturally, no residual value is recognized since at the end of the lease the land reverts back to the owner.

EXERCISE 12

Timber rights on a tract of land were purchased for $60,000. The amount of timber to be harvested is estimated at 600,000 board feet. During the current year, 45,000 feet of timber were cut. Record the entry to recognize the depletion expense for the fiscal year.

INTANGIBLE ASSETS

We have previously learned that an intangible asset is something that cannot readily be seen or touched; it has no physical substance. Examples of intangible assets include leaseholds, copyrights, franchises, licenses, trademarks, and goodwill. In order for these items to qualify as assets, they must be owned (or the rights of use must be owned) and must have a money value. A LEASEHOLD is the right of a tenant to use and occupy real property under a lease. COPYRIGHTS are exclusive rights applied for to the federal government and given to an individual or organization to use and control literary and artistic works. These rights currently extend for fifty years beyond the life of the creator. A FRANCHISE and a LICENSE (PATENT) are rights given by a company or governmental unit to conduct a certain type of business in a specific area. These rights are purchased. A TRADE-MARK is a symbol or design used to distinguish a film's product or service. Trademarks are issued by the United States Patent Office. The golden arches of McDonald's restaurants is an example of a trademark. GOODWILL is usually said to represent the reputation and manage-rial skill of a business. It represents the excess earnings of a particular business organization over the normal rate of return of other businesses in the same industry. Goodwill is usually only recorded when the buyer of a business pays a price that exceeds the fair market value of the acquired company's net identifiable assets.

Amortizing Intangible Assets

Unlike depreciation and deletion, which can be readily measured, the expense of intangible assets is determined in a somewhat arbitrary fashion. The systematic write-off of the cost of an intangible asset over the periods of its economic life is known as AMORTIZATION. The entry to record amortization of an intangible asset is a debit to amortization expense and a credit directly to the intangible asset ac-count. The period of time for which a particular intangible asset is to be written off is dependent upon the asset. Goodwill should not be written-off for a period of less than sixty months, and usually not more than forty years. A copyright is granted for seventy years beyond the life of its creator; however, this may be impractical from the stand-point of recognizing amortization. If the specific work covered by the copyright is expected to have a useful life of twenty-five years, then this would be an appropriate period to recognize amortization. A patent is recorded at the cost and legal fees to register and defend it. Patents have a legal life of twenty years.

Other intangible assets, such as organizational costs, may also be subject to amortization. Determining the useful life of these assets is usually left up to the discretion of the accountant. A general guide is that they should not be amortized over less than five years, unless it can be substantiated that their benefits will be for a lesser period of time. The fact that a useful life has been assigned to an intangible asset does not mean that it cannot be adjusted at a later date. If the holder of a franchise that has a useful life of ten years finds that the benefits of the franchise will not extend beyond the eighth year, an adjust-ment in amortization would be appropriate. If any intangible asset is no longer worth anything, it should be written off as an extraordinary loss.

EXAMPLE   A business is purchased for $300,000. The assets of the business totaled $265,000, and the balance represents goodwill. The buyer expects the goodwill to be of value for a period of seven years. The following entries represent the purchase and first full year's amortization of goodwill:

```
200-
Jan. 10   Assets (various)                265,000
          Goodwill                         35,000
              Cash                                    300,000
          For purchase of business.

Dec. 31   Amortization Expense—Goodwill    5,000
              Goodwill                                5,000
          To write off annual goodwill.
```

CAPITAL IMPROVEMENTS

We have seen that plant assets when acquired are set up at their actual cost, which includes any costs necessary to get the asset operational within the organization. Subsequent maintenance and repair costs are treated as current expenses and do not directly affect the accounting for the plant asset. As the asset is used on a continuous basis, there may come a time when major repairs or improvements are needed to keep the asset operational. When this situation arises, there may be a need for a CAPITAL IMPROVEMENT. Capital improvements are costs that add to the utility of a plant asset for more than one accounting period. Overhauling the engine of a delivery truck is an example of a capital improvement. Although the cost of the expenditure is relevant, the primary consideration in designating this work as a capital improvement or expenditure is that without this work the continued use of the asset may be impossible. Since this work is necessary and will probably extend the useful life of the asset, the expense is CAPITALIZED, meaning that the cost of this overhaul is added to the original cost of the asset. The following problem will illustrate how the accountant records this capital expenditure:

```
Original Cost of Truck                        $10,500
Salvage Value                                     500
Depreciation Method—Straight-Line
Useful Life—10 Years
Accumulated Depreciation                        7,000
Capital Expenditure after Seventh Year          2,400
```

Entry to record capital expenditure:

```
200-
Jan.  4   Delivery Truck                   2,400
              Cash                                  2,400
          To record capital expenditure
          & increase useful life by one year.

Dec. 31   Depreciation Expense—Delivery Truck  1,350
              Accumulated Depreciation                1,350
```

To recognize adjusted annual depreciation $\left(\dfrac{5,400}{4 \text{ YRS}}\right)$.

Note that the annual depreciation recognized has changed. This change was brought about because of the capital expenditure, which increased the original cost of the truck. The following calculations resulted in the new depreciation recognition as well as the extension of the useful life of the delivery truck:

Original Cost of Delivery Truck	$10,500
Salvage Value	500
Depreciable Value (10 years)	10,000
Accumulated Depreciation (after 7 years)	7,000
Book Value (after 7 years)	3,000
Capital Expenditure	2,400
New Book Value (extending life by 1 year)	5,400
New Annual Depreciation Rate ($5,400/4 years useful life)	1,350

In this illustration both the useful life and the depreciation to be recognized have changed. If the useful life of the truck had not been affected, then only the depreciation expense recognized would have been increased over the remaining three years to the extent of $800 per year.

EXERCISE 13

A factory with an original cost of $450,000 and an expected useful life of thirty years has been depreciated using the straight-line method for twenty years (no scrap value). The roof of the building is replaced at a cost of $45,000 after the twentieth year, and it is expected to extend the useful life of the structure by five years. Determine:

1. The annual depreciation recognized per year prior to the capital improvement.
2. The accumulated depreciation over the twenty years.
3. The entry to record the capital improvement.
4. The book value of the building prior to the capital improvement.
5. The book value of the building after the capital improvement.
6. The depreciation expense to be recognized annually as a result of the capital improvement. (Life extended five years.)

Summing Up

Accounting for long-life assets is quite different from the accounting for current assets. The cost principle requires that all long-life assets be set up on the books at their actual cost and that costs remain on the books until such time as the asset is sold, discarded, or adjusted as a result of a capital improvement. Since long-life assets in general lose value over time due to use, it is necessary to recognize this loss in value. Loss in value is recognized through depreciation, depletion, or amortization, depending on the nature of the asset.

Depreciation is the loss in value of a plant asset over time due to wear and tear. The methods used to recognize depreciation are:

straight-line; units of production; double-declining balance; and sum-of-the-years'-digits. The latter two methods are considered to be accelerated forms of depreciation that recognize greater depreciation in the earlier years of the asset's use.

Depletion is the loss in value of land resulting from the extraction of metal ores or other minerals. Depletion converts the cost of the land or the cost of the lease on the land to an expense based on that which is being taken from the land.

Amortization is the conversion of the cost of an intangible asset to an expense based on the benefits of the intangible asset being used up. The period of time used to take this write-off is dependent upon the period of time benefitted by the intangible asset.

Long-life and intangible assets are maintained on the books until such time as they are converted through sale, trade-in, or obsolescence. With the exception of intangibles that are written off directly through the recognition of amortization expense, all other assets are eliminated from the books at the time that they are sold, traded in, or discarded. Any cash received in excess of the book value of the asset is reported as a gain, and any amount received that is less than the book value of the asset is recognized as a loss. When like assets are traded in or exchanged, any gain or loss is postponed.

Capital improvements cause the value of an asset to be increased by the extent of the improvement. This will affect the remaining depreciation to be recognized regardless of whether it extends the useful life of the asset or not.

CHAPTER **10**

ACCOUNTING FOR INVENTORIES

What Is Merchandise Inventory?

In an earlier chapter you were introduced to a trading form of business organization in which the primary function of the business was the sale of a product. At the end of the accounting period for this form of business it was necessary to determine the value of the ending merchandise inventory. Expressing the value of the inventory on the balance sheet and the income statement was illustrated, with particular emphasis placed on the procedures used to determine the cost of goods available for sale and the cost of goods sold. MERCHANDISE INVENTORY was defined as the cost of the goods on hand as of the date the inventory was taken. We have previously illustrated the taking of the inventory at the end of the accounting period. The valuation of the inventory taken is based on its cost. Keep in mind that merchandise inventory represents only those assets that were acquired exclusively for the purpose of resale in the normal course of business. The taking of an inventory of supplies on the other hand was for the purpose of converting an asset on the books to an expense to the extent those supplies had been used up.

INVENTORIES AND THE TRADING BUSINESS

A multi-step income statement for a trading business highlights the fact that between 40% and 60% of revenue from sales is accounted for as the cost of goods sold. Cost of goods sold is found by taking the cost of goods available for sale (beginning merchandise inventory + net purchases), less the ending merchandise inventory. In a wholesale or retail trading business, merchandise held for resale in the normal course of business is the largest asset owned by the organization. For this reason it is vital that accurate up-to-date records be maintained when goods are acquired and inventories taken.

Merchandise inventory is listed under the current asset section of the balance sheet, which usually follows cash and accounts receivable. Due to its relatively large value and its appearance on both the balance sheet and the income statement, an error in calculating inventory can have a significant effect on the recognition of income and the financial position for the accounting period. Also, since the ending merchandise inventory for one accounting period becomes the beginning merchandise inventory for the next period, an erroneous merchandise inventory figure will affect future as well as the current accounting periods.

ERRORS IN VALUING MERCHANDISE INVENTORIES

The following income statement for the Classic Fabric Co. will illustrate the effects of incorrectly stating the ending merchandise inventory:

Classic Fabric Co.
Income Statement
For the Year Ended December 31, 2002

	Correct Ending Inventory	Overstated Inventory	Understated Inventory
Sales	$500,000	$500,000	$500,000
Cost of Goods Sold			
Merchandise Inv. 1/1/02	$150,000	$150,000	$150,000
Net Purchases	300,000	300,000	300,000
Cost of Goods Available for Sale	450,000	450,000	450,000
Less: Merchandise Inventory 12/31/02	150,000	180,000	120,000
Cost of Goods Sold	300,000	270,000	330,000
Gross Profit on Sales	200,000	230,000	170,000
Operating Expenses	150,000	150,000	150,000
Net Income	$ 50,000	$ 80,000	$ 20,000

First, note the differences reported for net income between the correctly and incorrectly stated inventories on the income statement. The overstatement of the ending merchandise inventory causes an understatement of the cost of goods sold to the extent of the error ($30,000) in the ending inventory. This causes the gross profit on sales to be overstated to the extent of the error in ending inventory. Not only are the gross and net income affected, but the error will also affect the value assigned to current assets on the balance sheet. Remember that the ending merchandise inventory is set up on the books at the end of the accounting period and will be shown as a current asset, thus an overstatement of the ending inventory will also cause a corresponding overstatement of the merchandise inventory on the balance sheet at the end of the accounting period. The overstatement of net income will also cause an overstatement of the proprietor's permanent capital, since profits not taken out of the business are transferred to the proprietor's capital account. Since the merchandise inventory account in the next accounting period is overstated, this will affect the determination of profit for that year. Assuming that the second year's ending inventory is properly stated, the overstatement of the beginning inventory for the second year will probably result in an overstatement of the cost of goods sold at the end of the second year.

If the ending merchandise inventory is understated, there will be a corresponding overstatement of the cost of goods sold, which results in an understatement of the gross profits and net income for the year. Since the ending inventory becomes the beginning inventory for the next accounting period, the balance sheet will show the current asset merchandise inventory to be understated. The net income at the end of the accounting period is understated by $30,000 and this will cause an understatement of the proprietor's capital account on the balance sheet. In the second year of operations, the understatement of merchandise inventory will cause an understatement of the cost of goods sold, thus inflating net income at the end of the second year.

The effect on net income, current assets, and proprietor's capital of incorrectly determining the ending merchandise inventory can be summarized as follows:

An *overstatement* of ending merchandise inventory causes:

1. Understatement of cost of goods sold;
2. Overstatement of net income;
3. Overstatement of current assets;
4. Overstatement of proprietor's capital.

An *understatement* of ending merchandise inventory causes:

1. Overstatement of cost of goods sold;
2. Understatement of net income;
3. Understatement of current assets;
4. Understatement of proprietor's capital.

Remember that an incorrectly stated ending inventory not only affects the current accounting period, but will also have an adverse effect on the next accounting period as to the statement of current assets, proprietor's capital, and the determination of net income.

TYPES OF INVENTORY SYSTEMS

The Periodic System

There are basically two inventory systems used in accounting: the periodic and the perpetual inventory systems. So far we have discussed only the former. When the PERIODIC INVENTORY SYSTEM is used, only the income from sales is recorded when sales are made. No entries are made in either the merchandise inventory or the purchases account to recognize the cost of the particular items sold. Periodically (at least once a year, usually at the end of the accounting period), a physical inventory is taken to determine the cost of the ending inventory. A comparison between the cost of goods available for sale (beginning merchandise inventory + net purchases) and the ending merchandise inventory enabled the accountant to determine the cost of goods sold. Most businesses use the periodic inventory system, especially if the goods sold consist of large quantities of diverse products. With the advent of high technology, this system may be modified somewhat by many trading organizations.

The Perpetual Inventory System

With the PERPETUAL INVENTORY SYSTEM, accounting records that continuously disclose the amount of inventory are maintained. A separate subsidiary ledger is maintained that contains separate accounts for each type of inventory item. Increases in the specific inventory item are debited directly to the specific account and corresponding decreases due to sales or returns are credited directly to the specific account. Thus, the balance in the individual subsidiary ledger account at any moment in time represents the actual amount of that particular product on hand. Since this method is time-consuming and expensive to maintain, it is primarily used by those organizations that sell relatively small numbers of items with high unit cost, such as automobile dealerships. While a perpetual inventory system may be used for the sale of automobiles, the parts department of the dealership will use a periodic inventory system.

To use the perpetual inventory system, the actual cost of the goods assigned to the various accounts in the subsidiary inventory ledger must be known. While the periodic system segregated cost and revenue items related to merchandise purchased into specific accounts, such as purchases returns and allowances, purchases discounts, and freight on purchases, this is not done under the perpetual system. The cost assigned to the various inventory accounts under the perpetual system is composed of the purchase price and all costs incurred in acquiring such merchandise, less savings from discounts and any subsequent authorized purchase returns. The most significant difference in using the perpetual system is the activity that takes place in the merchandise inventory account, which replaces the merchandise purchases account used in the periodic system.

The following general journal entries are typical entries relating to the acquisition and subsequent sale of goods, using a perpetual inventory system:

200-				
Feb.	3	Merchandise Inventory	5,000	
		Accounts Payable		5,000
		1,000 units at $5 per unit		
	10	Cash	2,700	
		Sales		2,700
		300 units at $9 per unit		
	10	Cost of Goods Sold	1,500	
		Merchandise Inventory		1,500
		300 units at $5 = $1,500		
	14	Merchandise Inventory	3,060	
		Cash		3,060
		600 units at $5.10 per unit		
	17	Cash	7,200	
		Sales		7,200
		800 units at $9 per unit		

200-
Feb. 17   Cost of Goods Sold   4,010
       Merchandise Inventory   4,010
       700 units at $5.00 per unit = $3,500
       100 units at $5.10   =   510
                        $4,010

    The entry of February 3 records the purchase of merchandise on credit. This entry and others that follow would normally be recorded to special journals; however, for ease of analysis they are recorded in simple two-column general journal form. Unlike the periodic system, which uses the merchandise purchases account, the perpetual system records purchases of merchandise directly in the inventory account. Each type of good acquired is posted to a specific subsidiary ledger account that contains an explanation similar to that of the journal entry. The actual subsidiary ledger account is also known as a STOCK RECORD CARD. The purpose of the stock record card is to list specific information pertaining to the goods acquired and subsequently sold. The following represents the typical form of the subsidiary ledger, stock record card:

Item Stock # -432A   Description: Hand Tool
Location: Bin 5E   Basis—FIFO

	Received			Issued			Balance		
Date	Units	Unit Cost	Total Cost	Units	Unit Cost	Total Cost	Unit	Unit Cost	Total Cost
200- Feb. 3	1,000	5.00	5,000				1,000	5.00	5,000
10				300	5.00	1,500	700	5.00	3,500
14	600	5.10	3,060				700	5.00	3,500
							600	5.10	3,060
									6,560
17				700	5.00	3,500			
				100	5.10	510	500	5.10	2,550

    Note that the stock record card contains the date of the transaction, and the number of units, unit cost, and total cost of goods received and issued, as well as a running balance. The posting of the February 3 entry to the stock record card records the receipt of goods and then extends the information to the balance column. As of February 3, the balance in this inventory account consisted of 1,000 units at a per unit cost of $5, making a total cost value of $5,000.
    The first general journal entry above for February 10 initially records the sale of the product as it would be recorded regardless of the inventory system in use. The second entry for the tenth, however, represents the recognition of the cost assigned to the product being sold. Because the accountant can specifically identify the cost of the goods being sold, this entry charges the cost to a new account entitled "Cost of Goods Sold." This account is used when the perpetual inventory system is employed by a trading organization.

The cost of goods sold account is classified as an expense that will offset net sales in order to determine the gross profit on sales. Gross profit on sales can thus be determined at any moment in time by simply comparing the net sales with the cost of goods sold account. The explanation to the entry indicates how the value was assigned to the transaction. Referring to the stock record card, note the entry and the extension to the balance column. As of February 10, the balance in this particular inventory account consists of 700 units at a unit cost of $5, for a total cost of $3,500.

The February 14 entry records the additional acquisition of 600 units at a unit cost of $5.10. The stock record card records the receipt as well as the extension. Notice that the extension utilizes three lines. This is necessary because there are different unit costs assigned to the goods in the inventory at this date. The first balance represents the February 10 balance still on hand as of February 14. The second line represents the additional inventory acquired at a per-unit cost of $5.10. The total value of the inventory as of February 14 (which is shown on the third line) amounts to $6,560.

The first entry on February 17 records the cash sale of 800 units at the selling price of $9 per unit. The second entry for that date represents the assignment of the cost of the goods sold in a similar fashion to the second entry of the tenth. The explanation for this entry differs from the one on the tenth in that the sale of the 800 units is taken from two separate inventory costs. This inventory method assumes that units will be sold in the order they were acquired; thus, the earliest cost is charged against the earliest sale. If you refer back to the stock record card for the balance on the fourteenth, you will notice that there are two separate inventory balances listed. First, 700 units at $5.00, and then 600 units at $5.10. The earliest acquisition has a remaining balance of 700 units, which is first charged against the 800 units sold. Since these units now have been exhausted, the accountant will take the remaining 100 units out of the 600 units remaining at a cost of $5.10 per unit. Note the entry on the stock record card for the issuance of February 17. The authorization for charging the cost against the units sold is obtained from the expression "FIFO," which appears after the word "Basis." FIFO means "first-in, first-out."

Five-hundred units remained after this transaction at a per-unit cost of $5.10. If we wished at this time to determine our gross profit on sales, we would subtract the cost of goods sold ($5,510) from our net sales ($9,900) to arrive at our gross profit on sales ($4,390).

Determining the Cost of Inventories

A major aspect of financial reporting is the determination of the cost of the ending merchandise inventory. Whether the periodic or perpetual inventory system is used, it is necessary to use a specific method for the assignment of costs to the ending inventory as well as to the goods sold account. Since goods are usually purchased at different costs during the accounting period, the assignment of costs can become a rather complex procedure.

The beginning point used in determining the value of the ending inventory and the cost assigned to the goods sold is the COST-FLOW

ASSUMPTION. This procedure permits the consistent recognition of costs assigned to the ending inventory as well as the goods sold account. There are three cost-flow assumptions generally used: FIFO (first in, first out); LIFO (last in, first out); and the WEIGHTED AVERAGE. Each method will generate a different outcome and is used according to an organization's needs.

THE FIFO METHOD

The basis for the assignment of inventory costs on the stock record card illustrated above was FIFO. This method dictates that the oldest cost assigned to the inventory is charged against the cost of goods sold. The cost assigned to the first goods in, is charged to the first sales made. Obviously, there must be a sufficient number of units at the earliest price in the inventory to absorb the units first sold. If this is not the case, then a part of the subsequent purchases will be used to meet the deficiency. Referring to the stock record card, the units sold on February 10 were taken from the inventory of February 3. However, the units sold on February 17 were first taken from the earliest remaining inventory of 700 units, with the balance of 100 units coming from the goods acquired later. If the unit cost of the merchandise acquired on February 3 and 14 had been the same, there would have been no need to differentiate between them. The cost assigned to the cost of goods sold through February 17 would be $5,510. The value assigned to the ending inventory under the FIFO basis would be $2,550 as of February 17. Notice that the per-unit cost assigned to the ending inventory represents the most recent unit cost of $5.10.

While business organizations are free to choose among a number of inventory methods, many will adopt FIFO simply because there is a tendency to dispose of goods in the order of their acquisition. While this method is not as accurate as one which would specifically identify the item being sold, it does closely approximate it. During a period of rising costs, this method will cause the value of the ending inventory to be high, which will more closely approximate the current replacement cost of the inventory and therefore allows a realistic cost to be assigned to the inventory. With the FIFO method, the same ending value results with either the periodic or perpetual system.

EXERCISE 1   The following transactions relating to the purchase and subsequent sale of merchandise took place during the month of May for the current year.

200-
May 3   Acquired 500 units of goods at $10.00 per unit.

5   Purchased 300 units of goods at $10.20 per unit.

9   Sold 150 units.

10   Sold 400 units.

15   Purchased 200 units of goods at $10.10 per unit.

24   Sold 300 units.

Rule a stock record card similar to the one illustrated previously. Record the above transactions on the card, determining the appropriate balances after each transaction.

Prepare general journal entries for the above transactions. Assume that the unit selling price of the items sold was $20 in each case. Further assume that the sales were cash sales and the purchases were paid for in cash.

THE LIFO METHOD

The LIFO method of assigning costs to inventory assumes that the most recent cost of merchandise acquired should be charged against the most recent sales. Thus, the assignment of a cost to the ending inventory would represent the cost of all earlier purchases, without regard to the order in which the goods are actually sold, since we can assume that the goods are all the same and readily interchangeable. The justification for using this method is that as goods are sold, more goods must be acquired to replenish the stock in inventory. The cost assigned to current sales should closely reflect the cost of replacing such goods sold. The concept of matching costs and revenue applies as well, under the theory that the current cost of merchandise should be matched against the current sales price. As the cost of purchasing merchandise increases, there is a tendency for this additional cost to be passed along to the consumer in the form of an increased selling price for the product. The following example will illustrate the use of the LIFO cost-flow assumption as evidenced by the completed stock record card:

Item Stock # -432A Location: Bin 5E							Description: Hand Tool Basis—LIFO		
	Received			Issued			Balance		
Date	Units	Unit Cost	Total Cost	Units	Unit Cost	Total Cost	Units	Unit Cost	Total Cost
200- Feb. 3	1,000	5.00	5,000				1,000	5.00	5,000
10				300	5.00	1,500	700	5.00	3,500
14	600	5.10	3,060				700 600	5.00 5.10	3,500 3,060 6,560
17				600 200	5.10 5.00	3,060 1,000	500	5.00	2,500

The information on the above stock record card is the same as on the previous card, except that the basis (LIFO) and the resulting cost flow assumptions as indicated in the body of the card are different. The general journal entries will also be the same as those previously illustrated, except for the amount assigned to the cost of goods sold on February 17. Note that for the entry of the seventeenth on the stock record card, the first units to be transferred to cost of goods sold were the last units acquired (600 units at $5.10). Once the most recent acquisition has been exhausted, the balance is obtained from the earlier inventory purchase. The final balance in the ending inventory under LIFO is $2,500 as compared with $2,550 under the FIFO method. Should additional goods be received prior to the next sale, the most current goods would be charged against the next sale.

EXERCISE 2   Referring to Exercise 1, complete that problem using the LIFO method of determining the cost of the merchandise inventory.

THE WEIGHTED AVERAGE METHOD

The WEIGHTED AVERAGE method determines the cost assigned to the ending inventory and the cost of goods sold by determining an average unit cost for all the goods that are available for sale during the accounting period. The total cost of goods available for sale is divided by the number of units available for sale. This provides an average cost per unit, which is then multiplied by the number of units remaining in the ending merchandise inventory. The resulting figure is the average unit cost of the inventory. This method is primarily used when the trading concern uses a periodic inventory system. It permits the taking of a physical inventory in units only, rather than specifically identifying the cost of each physical unit being counted.

EXAMPLE

Cost of goods available for sale:		$45,000
Number of units available for sale:		3,000
Average unit cost:	=	$ 15
Ending Merchandise Inventory (250 units × $15) =		$ 3,750

Average unit cost = Cost of goods available for sale/Number of units available for sale

Ending merchandise inventory = Number of units in the ending inventory × average unit cost

Since this method does not take into consideration the cost of the goods purchased at any specific time during the accounting period, it may not appropriately enable the proper matching of costs and revenue. This deficiency is offset, however, by its ease in calculation and other cost-saving benefits derived from its use.

EXERCISE 3   The following information was obtained from the Able Trading Co. during the current accounting period:

    Purchases—500 units at $6.50, 240 units at $5.90, 370 units at $6.10, and 320 units at $6.00.

    Ending Merchandise Inventory physical count—290 units.

    Determine: (1) The average cost per unit; (2) The cost assigned to the ending inventory; (3) The value of the cost of goods sold.

SIGNIFICANT CHANGES IN INVENTORY VALUE

The dollar value assigned to inventory, as well as other assets, is based on the actual cost of obtaining the inventory. Circumstances may cause this value assigned to differ significantly from the replacement cost of the inventory. For example, if handheld calculators were originally purchased by a firm for $10 each, but the same calculators can now be purchased for $4 each, this represents a significant and perhaps permanent change in the replacement cost of the asset. Or, if this same asset became obsolete before it could be sold, that would also be a significant change in the value of the asset. In either illustration, a permanent decline in the value of the asset must be recognized. Since it would be virtually impossible to sell the above asset at what would be considered its normal selling price of perhaps $20, it is necessary to recognize and adjust for the loss in value so that the asset could at least be sold at a competitive price. Since the utility of the asset has fallen below cost by reason of a decline in the price level or by obsolescence, an actual loss has occurred. This loss may appropriately be recognized as a loss in the current accounting period by reducing its cost to a level that approximates the replacement cost of the asset. This concept is known as the LOWER OF COST OR MARKET RULE. The lower of cost or market rule permits the recognition of a permanent reduction in the value of inventory due to physical deterioration of the asset, a permanent price decline in terms of the replacement cost, or obsolescence. Under the lower of cost or market rule, merchandise inventory is re-valued at cost or current replacement cost (market), whichever is lower.

    The entry to recognize this permanent reduction in value when the market value is less than the cost converts this difference to an expense:

```
200-
Dec. 31   Loss from Inventory Decline        2,150
              Merchandise Inventory                    2,150
          To recognize permanent decline.
```

    The effect of recognizing this loss in value of the inventory as an expense is to reduce the income recognized for the period. The expense could also be charged directly to the cost of goods sold account, causing the same effect.

    Should the replacement cost (market price) of this inventory increase in the next or subsequent accounting periods, an increase in the firm's profits would be recognized.

Estimating Inventory Value

THE GROSS PROFIT METHOD

There are two methods widely used to estimate inventory: (1) the GROSS PROFIT METHOD and (2) the RETAIL METHOD. The periodic inventory system requires that a physical inventory be taken at least once a year, usually at the end of the accounting period. For financial accounting purposes, inventory information may be needed more frequently. Because of the cost involved in taking physical inventories, the gross profit method can provide a viable alternative. The gross profit method is used to estimate the cost of goods sold and the ending inventory for an accounting period or for interim statement purposes.

The gross profit method utilizes information that is available from past accounting periods and applies it to the current period. The following formula is used:

Cost of goods sold for past period/Net sales for past period = The ratio of cost of goods sold to net sales

$$\$75,000/\$100,000 = 0.75 \text{ or } 75\%$$

This calculation determines that 75% of past period net sales actually represented the cost of goods sold. This percentage is then applied to the current net sales figure. If net sales for the current year amounted to $120,000, then by using the gross profit method, the cost of goods sold for the current period would be $90,000 ($120,000 × 75%). If we were then to subtract the cost of goods sold ($90,000) from the cost of goods available for sale, we would then have the value of the ending merchandise inventory for the current accounting period.

Using this formula we can also determine the gross profit percentage of net sales. If we know that net sales is equal to 100%, and we subtract the cost of goods sold percentage determined above (75%), the resulting percentage of 25% represents our gross profit percentage. Thus, for every dollar of sales, $.25 would be the company's gross profit. In the above illustration, the gross profit would be $30,000 ($120,000 × 25%).

The use of the gross profit method is usually based on the actual rate for the preceding year, adjusted for any known or anticipated changes during the current year. When interim statements are needed, this method is an invaluable tool for determining the value of the ending inventory, cost of goods sold, and gross profits on sales.

EXERCISE 4   The owner of the D&L Trading Co. wants to know the value of the company's ending inventory as of April 30, which is the end of the fourth month of the accounting period. The following information is known about the current year's operations to date:

Beginning Merchandise Inventory	$22,500
Net Purchases to date	15,750
Net Sales to date	30,000

During the previous year, the actual net sales amounted to $100,000 and the actual cost of goods sold amounted to $65,000. Use the gross profit method to determine:

1. The gross profit rate;
2. The value of the ending inventory;
3. The cost of goods sold to date;
4. The gross profit on sales to date.

THE RETAIL METHOD

The second method frequently used to estimate the ending merchandise inventory is the retail method. The retail method is widely used by retail businesses that use the periodic inventory system. Unlike the gross profits method, which relies on data obtained from prior accounting periods, the RETAIL METHOD uses a ratio based on actual information currently available to the business. The total cost of the goods available for sale is divided by the total selling prices of all the goods. The resulting ratio is the average cost of goods sold to be applied to each dollar of sales. The ratio is computed as follows:

Total cost of goods available for sale/Total selling price of all goods available for sale =
Ratio (or percentage) of cost of goods sold to net sales

EXAMPLE   The following information is available to the accountant:

	Cost	Retail
Merchandise Inventory, Jan. 1	$ 20,000	$ 40,000
Net Purchases for the Year:	230,000	410,000
Retail Method Ratio: $250,000/$450,000 = 55.6%	250,000	450,000
Net Sales for the Year		420,000
Merchandise Inventory, 12/31 at Retail		30,000
Estimated Merchandise Inventory, 12/31 at Cost		
($30,000 × 55.6% =)		16,680

It is important to recognize that each item sold did not cost the retailer 55.6% of net sales and that the actual gross profits did not amount to 44.4% of net sales. It is assumed that using the *average* of all sales will amount to the above percentages. When the markup on different products in the inventory varies substantially, it is advisable to develop separate ratios for each of the various goods. The retail method does not eliminate the need to take a physical inventory at the end of the year; however, it does provide valuable information, especially for interim statement purposes. Many retailers prepare interim statements on a monthly basis for analytical purposes. In addition to assisting in the frequent determinations of income, the retail method provides a business with the value of the inventory at retail as well as at cost, and acts as a means of disclosing the extent of inventory shortages.

EXERCISE 5   Based on the following information, determine the cost of the ending inventory using the retail method:

	Cost	Retail
Merchandise Inventory, January 1	$ 90,000	$160,000
Net purchases (January 1–June 30)	350,000	640,000
Net Sales (January 1–June 30)		730,000

Summing Up

The stock-in-trade of a retail business is its inventory. Between 40% and 60% of the revenues received by a retail business go to cover the cost of the goods that are sold. Thus, the maintenance of records relating to inventories is one of the most important aspects of the accounting function. An inadvertent overstatement of the ending merchandise inventory will cause an understatement of the cost of goods sold, an overstatement of gross profit, and an overstatement of the value assigned to the current assets and proprietor's capital on the balance sheet. If the ending inventory is understated, the opposite effects will result.

Inventory systems used by trading businesses may either be on a periodic basis (usually taken once a year) or on a perpetual basis (usually taken almost daily). The choice of which system to use will depend upon the kinds of products sold and the specific information needed. The use of a perpetual inventory system creates an account entitled "Cost of Goods Sold," which is charged with the cost of the goods sold in each transaction. This entry reduces the amount of the merchandise inventory account.

A merchandise purchases account is not maintained with a perpetual system, and is replaced by a merchandise inventory account, which is used to record all goods acquired for resale in the normal course of business. The stock record card is used as part of a subsidiary inventory ledger. Changes are posted to the stock record card as a result of goods being purchased, returned, and sold.

The costs to be assigned to the cost of goods sold account and the ending inventory are based on either the FIFO, LIFO, or weighted average methods. In accounting periods when costs remain relatively constant, the FIFO method is probably the most appropriate. If it is important that replacement costs relate as closely as possible to the cost of the goods sold, the LIFO method is more appropriate. The weighted average method is a third option that can be used, even though it doesn't necessarily bring about the matching of costs and revenue. Its simplicity may have a cost-saving effect.

When it is ascertained that there is a permanent change in the market value of the inventory, the lower of cost or market rule can be applied in assigning a value to the ending inventory. If the market price for the inventory is less than its cost, then the reduction in merchandise inventory causes a corresponding recognition of an expense.

The gross profit method and the retail method are used to estimate the value of the ending merchandise inventory. The gross profit method uses information from past years to approximate the value of the current ending inventory. The retail method compares the total cost of goods available at both cost and retail to ascertain the average percentage that cost is of selling price. This percentage is then applied to the ending physical inventory for the current year to assign a cost to it.

CHAPTER 11

ACCOUNTING FOR PAYROLL

What Is Payroll?

One of the largest expenses that most businesses incur on a regular, ongoing basis is payroll. PAYROLL represents the compensation that is regularly paid to the employees of a business organization. Labor costs and the related payroll taxes represent a large and constantly increasing portion of the total cost of operating most business organizations. Based on the dollar expenditures and the governmental regulations relating to payroll, it is one of the most important accounting activities. While one tends to think in terms of his or her payroll check at the end of the particular payroll period, there is more to payroll than just take-home pay.

All employees of a business organization receive compensation for the activities they perform within the organization. The compensation is known as salary, wages, or other more descriptive terms, such as commissions or piecework earnings. The number of employees is not as significant as the nature of the payroll system that is in use. The payroll system in use must be designed to perform the intricate computations required by the various governmental authorities, process the payroll data quickly, and assure the payment of the correct amount to each employee. The system should also provide for safeguards against payments to nonexistent employees or other misappropriations of funds.

PAYROLL DEDUCTIONS

The amount earned by an employee, whether paid on an hourly, weekly, semimonthly, monthly, piecework, or commission basis, is the employee's GROSS PAY. Gross pay is the total earnings of the employee for the particular payroll period. The amount of money the employee actually takes home is known as TAKE-HOME PAY or NET PAY. Net pay is arrived at by subtracting certain deductions from the gross pay. DEDUCTIONS consist of various taxes that the employer is required to withhold from the employee's pay on a regular basis that coincides with the payroll period in use.

Form W-4 (2003)

Purpose. Complete Form W-4 so that your employer can withhold the correct Federal income tax from your pay. Because your tax situation may change, you may want to refigure your withholding each year.

Exemption from withholding. If you are exempt, complete only lines 1, 2, 3, 4, and 7 and sign the form to validate it. Your exemption for 2003 expires February 16, 2004. See **Pub. 505,** Tax Withholding and Estimated Tax.

Note: *You cannot claim exemption from withholding if: (a) your income exceeds $750 and includes more than $250 of unearned income (e.g., interest and dividends) and (b) another person can claim you as a dependent on their tax return.*

Basic instructions. If you are not exempt, complete the **Personal Allowances Worksheet** below. The worksheets on page 2 adjust your withholding allowances based on itemized deductions, certain credits, adjustments to income, or two-earner/two-job situations. Complete all worksheets that apply. **However, you may claim fewer (or zero) allowances.**

Head of household. Generally, you may claim head of household filing status on your tax return only if you are unmarried and pay more than 50% of the costs of keeping up a home for yourself and your dependent(s) or other qualifying individuals. See line **E** below.

Tax credits. You can take projected tax credits into account in figuring your allowable number of withholding allowances. Credits for child or dependent care expenses and the child tax credit may be claimed using the **Personal Allowances Worksheet** below. See **Pub. 919,** How Do I Adjust My Tax Withholding? for information on converting your other credits into withholding allowances.

Nonwage income. If you have a large amount of nonwage income, such as interest or dividends, consider making estimated tax payments using

Form 1040-ES, Estimated Tax for Individuals. Otherwise, you may owe additional tax.

Two earners/two jobs. If you have a working spouse or more than one job, figure the total number of allowances you are entitled to claim on all jobs using worksheets from only one Form W-4. Your withholding usually will be most accurate when all allowances are claimed on the Form W-4 for the highest paying job and zero allowances are claimed on the others.

Nonresident alien. If you are a nonresident alien, see the **Instructions for Form 8233** before completing this Form W-4.

Check your withholding. After your Form W-4 takes effect, use Pub. 919 to see how the dollar amount you are having withheld compares to your projected total tax for 2003. See Pub. 919 especially if your earnings exceed $125,000 (Single) or $175,000 (Married).

Recent name change? If your name on line 1 differs from that shown on your social security card, call 1-800-772-1213 for a new social security card.

Personal Allowances Worksheet (Keep for your records.)

A Enter "1" for **yourself** if no one else can claim you as a dependent . . . . **A** _____

B Enter "1" if:
- You are single and have only one job; or
- You are married, have only one job, and your spouse does not work; or
- Your wages from a second job or your spouse's wages (or the total of both) are $1,000 or less.

. . **B** _____

C Enter "1" for your **spouse.** But, you may choose to enter "-0-" if you are married and have either a working spouse or more than one job. (Entering "-0-" may help you avoid having too little tax withheld.) . . . . **C** _____

D Enter number of **dependents** (other than your spouse or yourself) you will claim on your tax return . . . . . . **D** _____

E Enter "1" if you will file as **head of household** on your tax return (see conditions under **Head of household** above) . **E** _____

F Enter "1" if you have at least $1,500 of **child or dependent care expenses** for which you plan to claim a credit . . **F** _____
(**Note:** *Do not include child support payments. See Pub. 503, Child and Dependent Care Expenses, for details.*)

G **Child Tax Credit** (including additional child tax credit):
- If your total income will be between $15,000 and $42,000 ($20,000 and $65,000 if married), enter "1" for each eligible child plus **1 additional** if you have three to five eligible children or **2 additional** if you have six or more eligible children.
- If your total income will be between $42,000 and $80,000 ($65,000 and $115,000 if married), enter "1" if you have one or two eligible children, "2" if you have three eligible children, "3" if you have four eligible children, or "4" if you have five or more eligible children. **G** _____

H Add lines A through G and enter total here. **Note:** *This may be different from the number of exemptions you claim on your tax return.* ▶ **H** _____

For accuracy, complete all worksheets that apply.
- If you plan to **itemize or claim adjustments to income** and want to reduce your withholding, see the **Deductions and Adjustments Worksheet** on page 2.
- If you have **more than one job** or are **married and you and your spouse both work** and the combined earnings from all jobs exceed $35,000, see the **Two-Earner/Two-Job Worksheet** on page 2 to avoid having too little tax withheld.
- If **neither** of the above situations applies, **stop here** and enter the number from line H on line 5 of Form W-4 below.

- - - - - - - - - - Cut here and give Form W-4 to your employer. Keep the top part for your records. - - - - - - - - - -

| Form **W-4** Department of the Treasury Internal Revenue Service | **Employee's Withholding Allowance Certificate** ▶ **For Privacy Act and Paperwork Reduction Act Notice, see page 2.** | OMB No. 1545-0010 **2003** |

1 Type or print your first name and middle initial: *AARON*   Last name: *HERNANDEZ*   **2** Your social security number: *012 01 0011*

Home address (number and street or rural route): *465 MAIN STREET*

3 ☐ Single ☒ Married ☐ Married, but withhold at higher Single rate.
Note: *If married, but legally separated, or spouse is a nonresident alien, check the "Single" box.*

City or town, state, and ZIP code: *ANYTOWN, NY 10000*

4 If your last name differs from that shown on your social security card, check here. You must call 1-800-772-1213 for a new card. ▶ ☐

5 Total number of allowances you are claiming (from line **H** above **or** from the applicable worksheet on page 2) **5** *3*

6 Additional amount, if any, you want withheld from each paycheck . . . . **6** $

7 I claim exemption from withholding for 2003, and I certify that I meet **both** of the following conditions for exemption:
- Last year I had a right to a refund of **all** Federal income tax withheld because I had **no** tax liability **and**
- This year I expect a refund of **all** Federal income tax withheld because I expect to have **no** tax liability.

If you meet both conditions, write "Exempt" here . . . . ▶ **7**

Under penalties of perjury, I certify that I am entitled to the number of withholding allowances claimed on this certificate, or I am entitled to claim exempt status.

Employee's signature (Form is not valid unless you sign it.) ▶ *Aaron Hernandez*   Date ▶ *1/15/03*

8 Employer's name and address (Employer: Complete lines 8 and 10 only if sending to the IRS.) *A.B.C. TRADING 4289 Bdwy ANYTOWN, NY 10000*   **9** Office code (optional) *11*   **10** Employer identification number *403287*

Cat. No. 10220Q

Deductions and Adjustments Worksheet

te: *Use this worksheet **only** if you plan to itemize deductions, claim certain credits, or claim adjustments to income on your 2003 tax return.*

Enter an estimate of your 2003 itemized deductions. These include qualifying home mortgage interest, charitable contributions, state and local taxes, medical expenses in excess of 7.5% of your income, and miscellaneous deductions. (For 2003, you may have to reduce your itemized deductions if your income is over $139,500 ($69,750 if married filing separately). See **Worksheet 3** in Pub. 919 for details.) . . .	**1**	$ _____
Enter: { $7,950 if married filing jointly or qualifying widow(er) / $7,000 if head of household / $4,750 if single / $3,975 if married filing separately }	**2**	$ _____
Subtract line 2 from line 1. If line 2 is greater than line 1, enter "-0-".	**3**	$ _____
Enter an estimate of your 2003 adjustments to income, including alimony, deductible IRA contributions, and student loan interest	**4**	$ _____
Add lines 3 and 4 and enter the total. Include any amount for credits from **Worksheet 7** in Pub. 919 .	**5**	$ _____
Enter an estimate of your 2003 nonwage income (such as dividends or interest)	**6**	$ _____
Subtract line 6 from line 5. Enter the result, but not less than "-0-"	**7**	$ _____
Divide the amount on line 7 by $3,000 and enter the result here. Drop any fraction	**8**	_____
Enter the number from the **Personal Allowances Worksheet**, line H, page 1	**9**	_____
Add lines 8 and 9 and enter the total here. If you plan to use the **Two-Earner/Two-Job Worksheet,** also enter this total on line 1 below. Otherwise, **stop here** and enter this total on Form W-4, line 5, page 1 .	**10**	_____

Two-Earner/Two-Job Worksheet

te: *Use this worksheet **only** if the instructions under line H on page 1 direct you here.*

Enter the number from line H, page 1 (or from line 10 above if you used the **Deductions and Adjustments Worksheet**)	**1**	_____
Find the number in **Table 1** below that applies to the **lowest** paying job and enter it here	**2**	_____
If line 1 is **more than or equal to** line 2, subtract line 2 from line 1. Enter the result here (if zero, enter "-0-") and on Form W-4, line 5, page 1. **Do not** use the rest of this worksheet	**3**	_____

te: *If line 1 is **less than** line 2, enter "-0-" on Form W-4, line 5, page 1. Complete lines 4-9 below to calculate the additional withholding amount necessary to avoid a year-end tax bill.*

Enter the number from line 2 of this worksheet	**4**	_____
Enter the number from line 1 of this worksheet	**5**	_____
Subtract line 5 from line 4	**6**	_____
Find the amount in **Table 2** below that applies to the **highest** paying job and enter it here	**7**	$ _____
Multiply line 7 by line 6 and enter the result here. This is the additional annual withholding needed . .	**8**	$ _____
Divide line 8 by the number of pay periods remaining in 2003. For example, divide by 26 if you are paid every two weeks and you complete this form in December 2002. Enter the result here and on Form W-4, line 6, page 1. This is the additional amount to be withheld from each paycheck	**9**	$ _____

Table 1: Two-Earner/Two-Job Worksheet

Married Filing Jointly				All Others			
ages from **LOWEST** ng job are—	Enter on line 2 above	If wages from **LOWEST** paying job are—	Enter on line 2 above	If wages from **LOWEST** paying job are—	Enter on line 2 above	If wages from **LOWEST** paying job are—	Enter on line 2 above
$0 - $4,000 0		44,001 - 50,000 . . . 8		$0 - $6,000 . . . 0		75,001 - 100,000 . . . 8	
)01 - 9,000 1		50,001 - 60,000 . . . 9		6,001 - 11,000 . . . 1		100,001 - 110,000 . . . 9	
)01 - 15,000 2		60,001 - 70,000 . . . 10		11,001 - 18,000 . . . 2		110,001 and over . . . 10	
)01 - 20,000 3		70,001 - 90,000 . . . 11		18,001 - 25,000 . . . 3			
)01 - 25,000 4		90,001 - 100,000 . . . 12		25,001 - 29,000 . . . 4			
)01 - 33,000 5		100,001 - 115,000 . . . 13		29,001 - 40,000 . . . 5			
)01 - 38,000 6		115,001 - 125,000 . . . 14		40,001 - 55,000 . . . 6			
)01 - 44,000 7		125,001 and over . . . 15		55,001 - 75,000 . . . 7			

Table 2: Two-Earner/Two-Job Worksheet

Married Filing Jointly		All Others	
If wages from **HIGHEST** paying job are—	Enter on line 7 above	If wages from **HIGHEST** paying job are—	Enter on line 7 above
$0 - $50,000 . . . $450		$0 - $30,000 . . . $450	
50,001 - 100,000 . . . 800		30,001 - 70,000 . . . 800	
100,001 - 150,000 . . . 900		70,001 - 140,000 . . . 900	
150,001 - 270,000 . . . 1,050		140,001 - 300,000 . . . 1,050	
270,001 and over . . . 1,200		300,001 and over . . . 1,200	

In order for the employer to withhold taxes from the employee's paycheck, there are certain things the employer must know about the employee. This needed information is obtained through the employee's preparation of a W-4 Form, the EMPLOYEE'S WITHHOLDING ALLOWANCE CERTIFICATE, which is available from the Internal Revenue Service (IRS). This certificate asks for the employee's full name, social security number, home address, marital status, and the number of dependents that the person is claiming. The form is then signed and dated by the employee and used by the employer to determine the amounts of the various deductions to be taken from the employee's gross pay.

The typical deductions made by the employer from the employee's gross pay include:

1. Social Security Tax (FICA)
2. Medicare Tax
3. Federal Income Taxes Withheld
4. State and Local Income Taxes Withheld (where applicable)
5. State Disability Insurance (where applicable)
6. Other Voluntary Deductions

Social Security Taxes

The Social Security tax is the result of the Federal Insurance Contributions Act (FICA). This act provides for monthly pension benefits to be paid to retirees, for survivor benefits, and for disability benefits. The Social Security tax is levied on all employees, the funds received going to support the abovementioned programs. In addition, employers are required to match the employee's contribution, which is treated as an expense (FICA tax expense) by the employer. Beginning in calendar year 1991, the federal government separated Social Security tax into two components. While the combined rate was the same, the federal government calculated FICA tax and Medicare tax separately. Both taxes are known as NONPROGRESSIVE TAXES because each individual has withheld from his or her salary the same percentage, regardless of the amount of the earnings for the pay period. The FICA tax rate for 2003 is 6.2% of the gross pay of the employee. There is a ceiling on the amount of gross pay subject to FICA tax. The 2003 maximum gross earnings subject to FICA tax is $87,000. Any earnings in the 2003 calendar year in excess of $87,000 are not subject to FICA tax. The Medicare tax rate for 2003 is 1.45% of the gross pay of the employee. There is no ceiling (maximum earnings subject to the tax) on the Medicare tax. Over the last few years, the respective FICA and Medicare tax rates have remained constant; however, the ceiling for FICA taxes has increased each year (1994 FICA tax ceiling was $60,400). The following employees would have FICA and Medicare taxes withheld from their weekly salaries as follows (assuming they have not reached the FICA ceiling):

	Gross Pay	FICA Tax	Medicare Tax
A. Adams	$345.00	$21.39	$5.00
B. Brown	742.00	46.00	10.76
C. Campbell	905.30	56.13	13.13
D. Davis	630.00	39.06	9.14

As an employee's earnings approach the ceiling, the accountant must calculate the Social Security tax so as not to withhold the tax on income in excess of the ceiling ($87,000 for 2003). Assuming that the year is 2003, the following represents the FICA tax and Medicare tax based on current period earnings as compared with the cumulative earnings to date:

	Gross Pay	FICA Tax	Medicare Tax
E. Elman (cumulative earnings $86,500)	$1,450.00	$31.00	$21.03

Note that the FICA tax was withheld on only $500, which is the amount of earnings remaining necessary to reach the FICA tax ceiling of $87,000. The Medicare tax has no ceiling so that the entire gross pay of $1,450 was subject to the 1.45% rate.

The employer is required to withhold a matching amount of FICA and Medicare taxes in addition to the amounts withheld from the employee's salary, which is usually deposited on a monthly basis, or even more frequently, depending on the amount of the taxes being withheld. The employer's matching amount represents an expense to the employer.

For the calendar year 2003, the maximum earning subject to FICA tax is $87,000 based on a Social Security tax rate of 6.2%. The Medicare tax rate is 1.45% on total earnings for the calendar year, regardless of the total amount of the earnings.

EXERCISE 1

The following weekly wages were earned for the week ending November 7, 2003. Determine for each employee the amount of the Social Security tax and Medicare tax to be withheld from their earnings (wages) for the week.

Employee	Wages	Cumulative Earnings	FICA Tax	Medicare Tax
A. Albert	$ 685.30	$30,240.45	_____	_____
B. Blume	1,020.85	44,917.40	_____	_____
C. Carter	1,900.00	83,600.00	_____	_____
D. Delphine	2,180.00	93,825.00	_____	_____
E. Edwards	1,945.00	85,770.50	_____	_____

Federal Income Taxes

The federal income tax is a pay-as-you-go tax. The amount withheld from the employee's salary every pay period is not actually a tax, but rather income withheld in anticipation of the federal income tax. All employees (individuals) are considered to be calendar year taxpayers, which means that the calculation of their federal income tax is based on earnings from January 1 through December 31 of any calendar year. By the following April 15, each taxpayer is required to voluntarily prepare and submit an income tax return covering the preceding calendar year. The tax liability of the individual is determined based on the income tax return, and the funds withheld by the employer are used to satisfy the tax liability. If the amount withheld during the year is in excess of the actual tax liability, the taxpayer is entitled to a refund. If the tax liability is greater than the total federal income tax withheld, the taxpayer has a balance due, which must be sent in along with the income tax return.

The calculation of the payroll period federal income tax withheld will be based on three factors: (1) earnings for the pay period, (2) marital status, and (3) the number of exemptions claimed by the taxpayer.

Since the federal income tax is a progressive tax, the more money the taxpayer earns, the greater will be the percentage of his income paid in taxes. A single individual is said to have less expenses than a married person, thus the amount withheld from a single individual will be somewhat greater than from a married person. The more dependents a taxpayer claims as exemptions, the lower the amount withheld from the gross pay and the lower the eventual tax liability. These three factors are taken into consideration by the employer in withholding taxes for federal income tax purposes from the employee's gross pay. The following withholding tax tables provided by the federal government illustrate the amounts withheld from an employee based on (1) gross pay, (2) marital status, and (3) the number of exemptions claimed. The employer refers to the W-4 Form to determine the marital status and the number of exemptions claimed by the employee.

Note that in either of the two tables reproduced, as the amount of earnings increases, the amount of the withholding taxes increases within the same withholding allowance column. An individual who is single and earns $165 per week, claiming one withholding allowance, will have $6 withheld from his wages. If that same individual earned $175 a week, then $7 will be withheld, earnings of $185 will cause withholding of $8. As either table is read horizontally, the amount of withholding taxes decreases as a direct result of the increase in the number of withholding allowances claimed. A married individual, as illustrated on the third withholding table, earning $150 a week will have $3 withheld if "0" exemptions are claimed. The same earnings with "2" exemptions claimed will have $0 withheld. Recall that marital status will also affect the amount of withholding taxes. A single individual earning $150 and claiming "1" withholding allowance will have $4 withheld, as compared to $0 for his or her married counterpart. An individual wishing to have more money withheld may claim fewer exemptions than entitled to for federal income tax purposes. This will not adversely affect the preparation of the income tax return, but provide for greater withholding to offset the tax liability on April 15.

The employer is required to safeguard the federal income taxes withheld from an employee's gross earnings by turning the funds over to a federal depository, usually on a monthly basis, along with any Social Security taxes withheld and the employer's matching payments.

EXERCISE 2   The employees listed on page 189 had weekly earnings as indicated. Also, the status and number of exemptions claimed on the W-4 Form appear in brackets immediately following the weekly earnings. For each employee determine the amount of federal income tax to be withheld:

SINGLE Persons—WEEKLY Payroll Period

(For Wages Paid in 2003)

If the wages are—		And the number of withholding allowances claimed is—										
At least	But less than	0	1	2	3	4	5	6	7	8	9	10
		The amount of income tax to be withheld is—										
$0	$55	$0	$0	$0	$0	$0	$0	$0	$0	$0	$0	$0
55	60	1	0	0	0	0	0	0	0	0	0	0
60	65	1	0	0	0	0	0	0	0	0	0	0
65	70	2	0	0	0	0	0	0	0	0	0	0
70	75	2	0	0	0	0	0	0	0	0	0	0
75	80	3	0	0	0	0	0	0	0	0	0	0
80	85	3	0	0	0	0	0	0	0	0	0	0
85	90	4	0	0	0	0	0	0	0	0	0	0
90	95	4	0	0	0	0	0	0	0	0	0	0
95	100	5	0	0	0	0	0	0	0	0	0	0
100	105	5	0	0	0	0	0	0	0	0	0	0
105	110	6	0	0	0	0	0	0	0	0	0	0
110	115	6	0	0	0	0	0	0	0	0	0	0
115	120	7	1	0	0	0	0	0	0	0	0	0
120	125	7	1	0	0	0	0	0	0	0	0	0
125	130	8	2	0	0	0	0	0	0	0	0	0
130	135	8	2	0	0	0	0	0	0	0	0	0
135	140	9	3	0	0	0	0	0	0	0	0	0
140	145	9	3	0	0	0	0	0	0	0	0	0
145	150	10	4	0	0	0	0	0	0	0	0	0
150	155	10	4	0	0	0	0	0	0	0	0	0
155	160	11	5	0	0	0	0	0	0	0	0	0
160	165	11	5	0	0	0	0	0	0	0	0	0
165	170	12	6	0	0	0	0	0	0	0	0	0
170	175	13	6	0	0	0	0	0	0	0	0	0
175	180	13	7	1	0	0	0	0	0	0	0	0
180	185	14	7	1	0	0	0	0	0	0	0	0
185	190	15	8	2	0	0	0	0	0	0	0	0
190	195	16	8	2	0	0	0	0	0	0	0	0
195	200	16	9	3	0	0	0	0	0	0	0	0
200	210	17	10	4	0	0	0	0	0	0	0	0
210	220	19	11	5	0	0	0	0	0	0	0	0
220	230	20	12	6	0	0	0	0	0	0	0	0
230	240	22	13	7	1	0	0	0	0	0	0	0
240	250	23	15	8	2	0	0	0	0	0	0	0
250	260	25	16	9	3	0	0	0	0	0	0	0
260	270	26	18	10	4	0	0	0	0	0	0	0
270	280	28	19	11	5	0	0	0	0	0	0	0
280	290	29	21	12	6	0	0	0	0	0	0	0
290	300	31	22	13	7	1	0	0	0	0	0	0
300	310	32	24	15	8	2	0	0	0	0	0	0
310	320	34	25	16	9	3	0	0	0	0	0	0
320	330	35	27	18	10	4	0	0	0	0	0	0
330	340	37	28	19	11	5	0	0	0	0	0	0
340	350	38	30	21	12	6	0	0	0	0	0	0
350	360	40	31	22	14	7	1	0	0	0	0	0
360	370	41	33	24	15	8	2	0	0	0	0	0
370	380	43	34	25	17	9	3	0	0	0	0	0
380	390	44	36	27	18	10	4	0	0	0	0	0
390	400	46	37	28	20	11	5	0	0	0	0	0
400	410	47	39	30	21	12	6	0	0	0	0	0
410	420	49	40	31	23	14	7	1	0	0	0	0
420	430	50	42	33	24	15	8	2	0	0	0	0
430	440	52	43	34	26	17	9	3	0	0	0	0
440	450	53	45	36	27	18	10	4	0	0	0	0
450	460	55	46	37	29	20	11	5	0	0	0	0
460	470	56	48	39	30	21	12	6	0	0	0	0
470	480	58	49	40	32	23	14	7	1	0	0	0
480	490	59	51	42	33	24	15	8	2	0	0	0
490	500	61	52	43	35	26	17	9	3	0	0	0
500	510	62	54	45	36	27	18	10	4	0	0	0
510	520	64	55	46	38	29	20	11	5	0	0	0
520	530	65	57	48	39	30	21	13	6	0	0	0
530	540	67	58	49	41	32	23	14	7	1	0	0
540	550	68	60	51	42	33	24	16	8	2	0	0
550	560	70	61	52	44	35	26	17	9	3	0	0
560	570	71	63	54	45	36	27	19	10	4	0	0
570	580	73	64	55	47	38	29	20	11	5	0	0
580	590	75	66	57	48	39	30	22	13	6	1	0
590	600	78	67	58	50	41	32	23	14	7	2	0

SINGLE Persons—WEEKLY Payroll Period
(For Wages Paid in 2003)

If the wages are— At least	But less than	And the number of withholding allowances claimed is— 0	1	2	3	4	5	6	7	8	9	10
		The amount of income tax to be withheld is—										
$600	$610	$81	$69	$60	$51	$42	$33	$25	$16	$8	$3	
610	620	83	70	61	53	44	35	26	17	9	4	
620	630	86	72	63	54	45	36	28	19	10	5	
630	640	89	73	64	56	47	38	29	20	12	6	
640	650	91	76	66	57	48	39	31	22	13	7	
650	660	94	78	67	59	50	41	32	23	15	8	
660	670	97	81	69	60	51	42	34	25	16	9	
670	680	99	84	70	62	53	44	35	26	18	10	
680	690	102	86	72	63	54	45	37	28	19	11	
690	700	105	89	73	65	56	47	38	29	21	12	
700	710	108	92	76	66	57	48	40	31	22	13	
710	720	110	94	79	68	59	50	41	32	24	15	
720	730	113	97	81	69	60	51	43	34	25	16	
730	740	116	100	84	71	62	53	44	35	27	18	
740	750	118	103	87	72	63	54	46	37	28	19	
750	760	121	105	89	74	65	56	47	38	30	21	
760	770	124	108	92	76	66	57	49	40	31	22	
770	780	126	111	95	79	68	59	50	41	33	24	
780	790	129	113	97	82	69	60	52	43	34	25	
790	800	132	116	100	84	71	62	53	44	36	27	
800	810	135	119	103	87	72	63	55	46	37	28	
810	820	137	121	106	90	74	65	56	47	39	30	
820	830	140	124	108	92	77	66	58	49	40	31	
830	840	143	127	111	95	79	68	59	50	42	33	
840	850	145	130	114	98	82	69	61	52	43	34	
850	860	148	132	116	101	85	71	62	53	45	36	
860	870	151	135	119	103	87	72	64	55	46	37	
870	880	153	138	122	106	90	74	65	56	48	39	
880	890	156	140	124	109	93	77	67	58	49	40	
890	900	159	143	127	111	96	80	68	59	51	42	
900	910	162	146	130	114	98	82	70	61	52	43	
910	920	164	148	133	117	101	85	71	62	54	45	
920	930	167	151	135	119	104	88	73	64	55	46	
930	940	170	154	138	122	106	90	75	65	57	48	
940	950	172	157	141	125	109	93	77	67	58	49	
950	960	175	159	143	128	112	96	80	68	60	51	
960	970	178	162	146	130	114	99	83	70	61	52	
970	980	180	165	149	133	117	101	85	71	63	54	
980	990	183	167	151	136	120	104	88	73	64	55	
990	1,000	186	170	154	138	123	107	91	75	66	57	
1,000	1,010	189	173	157	141	125	109	94	78	67	58	
1,010	1,020	191	175	160	144	128	112	96	80	69	60	
1,020	1,030	194	178	162	146	131	115	99	83	70	61	
1,030	1,040	197	181	165	149	133	117	102	86	72	63	
1,040	1,050	199	184	168	152	136	120	104	89	73	64	
1,050	1,060	202	186	170	155	139	123	107	91	75	66	
1,060	1,070	205	189	173	157	141	126	110	94	78	67	
1,070	1,080	207	192	176	160	144	128	112	97	81	69	
1,080	1,090	210	194	178	163	147	131	115	99	83	70	
1,090	1,100	213	197	181	165	150	134	118	102	86	72	
1,100	1,110	216	200	184	168	152	136	121	105	89	73	
1,110	1,120	218	202	187	171	155	139	123	107	92	76	
1,120	1,130	221	205	189	173	158	142	126	110	94	78	
1,130	1,140	224	208	192	176	160	144	129	113	97	81	
1,140	1,150	226	211	195	179	163	147	131	116	100	84	
1,150	1,160	229	213	197	182	166	150	134	118	102	87	
1,160	1,170	232	216	200	184	168	153	137	121	105	89	
1,170	1,180	234	219	203	187	171	155	139	124	108	92	
1,180	1,190	237	221	205	190	174	158	142	126	110	95	
1,190	1,200	240	224	208	192	177	161	145	129	113	97	
1,200	1,210	243	227	211	195	179	163	148	132	116	100	
1,210	1,220	245	229	214	198	182	166	150	134	119	103	
1,220	1,230	248	232	216	200	185	169	153	137	121	105	
1,230	1,240	251	235	219	203	187	171	156	140	124	108	
1,240	1,250	253	238	222	206	190	174	158	143	127	111	

$1,250 and over   Use Table 1(a) for a **SINGLE person** on page 34. Also see the instructions on page 32.

MARRIED Persons—WEEKLY Payroll Period

(For Wages Paid in 2003)

If the wages are—		And the number of withholding allowances claimed is—										
At least	But less than	0	1	2	3	4	5	6	7	8	9	10
		The amount of income tax to be withheld is—										
$0	$130	$0	$0	$0	$0	$0	$0	$0	$0	$0	$0	$0
130	135	1	0	0	0	0	0	0	0	0	0	0
135	140	1	0	0	0	0	0	0	0	0	0	0
140	145	2	0	0	0	0	0	0	0	0	0	0
145	150	2	0	0	0	0	0	0	0	0	0	0
150	155	3	0	0	0	0	0	0	0	0	0	0
155	160	3	0	0	0	0	0	0	0	0	0	0
160	165	4	0	0	0	0	0	0	0	0	0	0
165	170	4	0	0	0	0	0	0	0	0	0	0
170	175	5	0	0	0	0	0	0	0	0	0	0
175	180	5	0	0	0	0	0	0	0	0	0	0
180	185	6	0	0	0	0	0	0	0	0	0	0
185	190	6	0	0	0	0	0	0	0	0	0	0
190	195	7	1	0	0	0	0	0	0	0	0	0
195	200	7	1	0	0	0	0	0	0	0	0	0
200	210	8	2	0	0	0	0	0	0	0	0	0
210	220	9	3	0	0	0	0	0	0	0	0	0
220	230	10	4	0	0	0	0	0	0	0	0	0
230	240	11	5	0	0	0	0	0	0	0	0	0
240	250	12	6	0	0	0	0	0	0	0	0	0
250	260	13	7	1	0	0	0	0	0	0	0	0
260	270	14	8	2	0	0	0	0	0	0	0	0
270	280	15	9	3	0	0	0	0	0	0	0	0
280	290	16	10	4	0	0	0	0	0	0	0	0
290	300	17	11	5	0	0	0	0	0	0	0	0
300	310	18	12	6	1	0	0	0	0	0	0	0
310	320	19	13	7	2	0	0	0	0	0	0	0
320	330	20	14	8	3	0	0	0	0	0	0	0
330	340	21	15	9	4	0	0	0	0	0	0	0
340	350	22	16	10	5	0	0	0	0	0	0	0
350	360	23	17	11	6	0	0	0	0	0	0	0
360	370	25	18	12	7	1	0	0	0	0	0	0
370	380	26	19	13	8	2	0	0	0	0	0	0
380	390	28	20	14	9	3	0	0	0	0	0	0
390	400	29	21	15	10	4	0	0	0	0	0	0
400	410	31	22	16	11	5	0	0	0	0	0	0
410	420	32	23	17	12	6	0	0	0	0	0	0
420	430	34	25	18	13	7	1	0	0	0	0	0
430	440	35	26	19	14	8	2	0	0	0	0	0
440	450	37	28	20	15	9	3	0	0	0	0	0
450	460	38	29	21	16	10	4	0	0	0	0	0
460	470	40	31	22	17	11	5	0	0	0	0	0
470	480	41	32	24	18	12	6	0	0	0	0	0
480	490	43	34	25	19	13	7	1	0	0	0	0
490	500	44	35	27	20	14	8	2	0	0	0	0
500	510	46	37	28	21	15	9	3	0	0	0	0
510	520	47	38	30	22	16	10	4	0	0	0	0
520	530	49	40	31	23	17	11	5	0	0	0	0
530	540	50	41	33	24	18	12	6	1	0	0	0
540	550	52	43	34	25	19	13	7	2	0	0	0
550	560	53	44	36	27	20	14	8	2	0	0	0
560	570	55	46	37	28	21	15	9	3	0	0	0
570	580	56	47	39	30	22	16	10	4	0	0	0
580	590	58	49	40	31	23	17	11	5	0	0	0
590	600	59	50	42	33	24	18	12	6	0	0	0
600	610	61	52	43	34	25	19	13	7	1	0	0
610	620	62	53	45	36	27	20	14	8	2	0	0
620	630	64	55	46	37	28	21	15	9	3	0	0
630	640	65	56	48	39	30	22	16	10	4	0	0
640	650	67	58	49	40	31	23	17	11	5	0	0
650	660	68	59	51	42	33	24	18	12	6	0	0
660	670	70	61	52	43	34	26	19	13	7	1	0
670	680	71	62	54	45	36	27	20	14	8	2	0
680	690	73	64	55	46	37	29	21	15	9	3	0
690	700	74	65	57	48	39	30	22	16	10	4	0
700	710	76	67	58	49	40	32	23	17	11	5	0
710	720	77	68	60	51	42	33	24	18	12	6	0
720	730	79	70	61	52	43	35	26	19	13	7	1
730	740	80	71	63	54	45	36	27	20	14	8	2
740	750	82	73	64	55	46	38	29	21	15	9	3

MARRIED Persons—WEEKLY Payroll Period
(For Wages Paid in 2003)

If the wages are—		And the number of withholding allowances claimed is—										
At least	But less than	0	1	2	3	4	5	6	7	8	9	10
		The amount of income tax to be withheld is—										
$750	$760	$83	$74	$66	$57	$48	$39	$30	$22	$16	$10	
760	770	85	76	67	58	49	41	32	23	17	11	
770	780	86	77	69	60	51	42	33	25	18	12	
780	790	88	79	70	61	52	44	35	26	19	13	
790	800	89	80	72	63	54	45	36	28	20	14	
800	810	91	82	73	64	55	47	38	29	21	15	
810	820	92	83	75	66	57	48	39	31	22	16	
820	830	94	85	76	67	58	50	41	32	23	17	
830	840	95	86	78	69	60	51	42	34	25	18	
840	850	97	88	79	70	61	53	44	35	26	19	
850	860	98	89	81	72	63	54	45	37	28	20	
860	870	100	91	82	73	64	56	47	38	29	21	
870	880	101	92	84	75	66	57	48	40	31	22	
880	890	103	94	85	76	67	59	50	41	32	23	
890	900	104	95	87	78	69	60	51	43	34	25	
900	910	106	97	88	79	70	62	53	44	35	26	
910	920	107	98	90	81	72	63	54	46	37	28	
920	930	109	100	91	82	73	65	56	47	38	29	
930	940	110	101	93	84	75	66	57	49	40	31	
940	950	112	103	94	85	76	68	59	50	41	32	
950	960	113	104	96	87	78	69	60	52	43	34	
960	970	115	106	97	88	79	71	62	53	44	35	
970	980	116	107	99	90	81	72	63	55	46	37	
980	990	118	109	100	91	82	74	65	56	47	38	
990	1,000	119	110	102	93	84	75	66	58	49	40	
1,000	1,010	121	112	103	94	85	77	68	59	50	41	
1,010	1,020	123	113	105	96	87	78	69	61	52	43	
1,020	1,030	126	115	106	97	88	80	71	62	53	44	
1,030	1,040	128	116	108	99	90	81	72	64	55	46	
1,040	1,050	131	118	109	100	91	83	74	65	56	47	
1,050	1,060	134	119	111	102	93	84	75	67	58	49	
1,060	1,070	137	121	112	103	94	86	77	68	59	50	
1,070	1,080	139	123	114	105	96	87	78	70	61	52	
1,080	1,090	142	126	115	106	97	89	80	71	62	53	
1,090	1,100	145	129	117	108	99	90	81	73	64	55	
1,100	1,110	147	132	118	109	100	92	83	74	65	56	
1,110	1,120	150	134	120	111	102	93	84	76	67	58	
1,120	1,130	153	137	121	112	103	95	86	77	68	59	
1,130	1,140	155	140	124	114	105	96	87	79	70	61	
1,140	1,150	158	142	127	115	106	98	89	80	71	62	
1,150	1,160	161	145	129	117	108	99	90	82	73	64	
1,160	1,170	164	148	132	118	109	101	92	83	74	65	
1,170	1,180	166	150	135	120	111	102	93	85	76	67	
1,180	1,190	169	153	137	121	112	104	95	86	77	68	
1,190	1,200	172	156	140	124	114	105	96	88	79	70	
1,200	1,210	174	159	143	127	115	107	98	89	80	71	
1,210	1,220	177	161	145	130	117	108	99	91	82	73	
1,220	1,230	180	164	148	132	118	110	101	92	83	74	
1,230	1,240	182	167	151	135	120	111	102	94	85	76	
1,240	1,250	185	169	154	138	122	113	104	95	86	77	
1,250	1,260	188	172	156	140	125	114	105	97	88	79	
1,260	1,270	191	175	159	143	127	116	107	98	89	80	
1,270	1,280	193	177	162	146	130	117	108	100	91	82	
1,280	1,290	196	180	164	148	133	119	110	101	92	83	
1,290	1,300	199	183	167	151	135	120	111	103	94	85	
1,300	1,310	201	186	170	154	138	122	113	104	95	86	
1,310	1,320	204	188	172	157	141	125	114	106	97	88	
1,320	1,330	207	191	175	159	143	128	116	107	98	89	
1,330	1,340	209	194	178	162	146	130	117	109	100	91	
1,340	1,350	212	196	181	165	149	133	119	110	101	92	
1,350	1,360	215	199	183	167	152	136	120	112	103	94	
1,360	1,370	218	202	186	170	154	138	123	113	104	95	
1,370	1,380	220	204	189	173	157	141	125	115	106	97	
1,380	1,390	223	207	191	175	160	144	128	116	107	98	
1,390	1,400	226	210	194	178	162	147	131	118	109	100	

$1,400 and over   Use Table 1(b) for a **MARRIED person** on page 34. Also see the instructions on page 32.

Employee	Gross Pay	Federal Withholding Taxes
G. Brown (S,1)	$ 146.50	_____
L. Albert (M,2)	875.00	_____
R. Talley (M,3)	1,240.00	_____
S. Russo (S,2)	745.75	_____
M. Santini (M,5)	1,320.00	_____

State and Local Taxes

A business may also be liable for state and local income taxes depending on where it is located. If the business is located in the City of New York, there is both a New York State and a New York City income tax. The rules for withholding taxes for these taxing authorities are similar to that of the federal government. These taxing authorities also publish withholding tax tables, which the employer uses to determine the amount of taxes to be withheld. These taxes are then turned over to the appropriate taxing authority, usually on a monthly basis. State and local income taxes are withheld by the employer according to directives received from the various taxing authorities. Some government entities also have taxes called nonresident taxes that are levied against employees who work within the taxing authority, but reside outside of that government's jurisdiction. These taxes are usually nominal in amount, but are still withheld by the employer and turned over to the taxing authority on a monthly basis. The following tables illustrate the income tax rates of the State of New York and the City of New York.

Disability Insurance Taxes

Many states also have STATE DISABILITY INSURANCE programs which require employees to contribute a nominal sum each week to fund the program. An amount such as $0.60 per week will be taken from the employee's gross pay to fund this program. Employees who become temporarily disabled then receive compensation from the state during their disability. In some industries this cost is absorbed by the employer, usually as a result of a collective bargaining agreement. Regardless of who actually pays for this program, the money collected is usually turned over to the state on a quarterly basis.

The New York State disability insurance program deducts a weekly payment equal to 0.5% of an employee's gross earnings up to maximum earnings of $120. Thus, if an employee earns $120 or more in any given week, the total disability insurance withheld from the employee's salary would be $0.60. An employee earning $80 per week would have $0.40 withheld for disability insurance.

EXERCISE 3   Based on the employee information obtained from Exercise 2, determine the amount of New York State and New York City withholding taxes to be taken out of each employee's gross pay.

Voluntary Deductions

The deductions discussed above are compulsory and must be made by the employer. If the employer fails to do so, the company can be held personally liable for the various deductions.

T - 2

Method I

Table I

NY STATE

Income Tax

SINGLE

WEEKLY

Payroll Period

WAGES		EXEMPTIONS CLAIMED										10 or more
At Least	But Less Than	0	1	2	3	4	5	6	7	8	9	
		TAX TO BE WITHHELD										
$0	$100	$0.00										
100	105	0.00										
105	110	0.00										
110	115	0.00	$0.00									
115	120	0.00	0.00									
120	125	0.00	0.00									
125	130	0.00	0.00									
130	135	0.00	0.00	$0.00								
135	140	0.10	0.00	0.00								
140	145	0.30	0.00	0.00								
145	150	0.50	0.00	0.00								
150	160	0.80	0.10	0.00	$0.00							
160	170	1.20	0.50	0.00	0.00							
170	180	1.60	0.90	0.10	0.00	$0.00						
180	190	2.00	1.30	0.50	0.00	0.00						
190	200	2.40	1.70	0.90	0.10	0.00	$0.00					
200	210	2.80	2.10	1.30	0.50	0.00	0.00					
210	220	3.20	2.50	1.70	0.90	0.20	0.00	$0.00				
220	230	3.60	2.90	2.10	1.30	0.60	0.00	0.00				
230	240	4.00	3.30	2.50	1.70	1.00	0.20	0.00	$0.00			
240	250	4.40	3.70	2.90	2.10	1.40	0.60	0.00	0.00	$0.00		
250	260	4.80	4.10	3.30	2.50	1.80	1.00	0.20	0.00	0.00		
260	270	5.20	4.50	3.70	2.90	2.20	1.40	0.60	0.00	0.00	$0.00	
270	280	5.60	4.90	4.10	3.30	2.60	1.80	1.00	0.30	0.00	0.00	
280	290	6.00	5.30	4.50	3.70	3.00	2.20	1.40	0.70	0.00	0.00	$0.00
290	300	6.50	5.70	4.90	4.10	3.40	2.60	1.80	1.10	0.30	0.00	0.00
300	310	6.90	6.10	5.30	4.50	3.80	3.00	2.20	1.50	0.70	0.00	0.00
310	320	7.40	6.50	5.70	4.90	4.20	3.40	2.60	1.90	1.10	0.30	0.00
320	330	7.80	7.00	6.10	5.30	4.60	3.80	3.00	2.30	1.50	0.70	0.00
330	340	8.30	7.40	6.50	5.70	5.00	4.20	3.40	2.70	1.90	1.10	0.30
340	350	8.70	7.90	7.00	6.10	5.40	4.60	3.80	3.00	2.30	1.50	0.70
350	360	9.20	8.30	7.40	6.60	5.80	5.00	4.20	3.50	2.70	1.90	1.10
360	370	9.80	8.80	7.90	7.00	6.20	5.40	4.60	3.90	3.10	2.30	1.50
370	380	10.30	9.30	8.30	7.50	6.60	5.80	5.00	4.30	3.50	2.70	1.90
380	390	10.80	9.80	8.80	7.90	7.10	6.20	5.40	4.70	3.90	3.10	2.30
390	400	11.40	10.30	9.30	8.40	7.50	6.60	5.80	5.10	4.30	3.50	2.70
400	410	12.00	10.90	9.80	8.80	8.00	7.10	6.20	5.50	4.70	3.90	3.10
410	420	12.60	11.50	10.40	9.40	8.40	7.50	6.70	5.80	5.10	4.30	3.50
420	430	13.20	12.00	10.90	9.90	8.90	8.00	7.10	6.30	5.50	4.70	3.90
430	440	13.80	12.60	11.50	10.40	9.40	8.40	7.60	6.70	5.90	5.10	4.30
440	450	14.40	13.20	12.10	11.00	9.90	8.90	8.00	7.20	6.30	5.50	4.70
450	460	15.00	13.80	12.70	11.50	10.50	9.40	8.50	7.60	6.70	5.90	5.10
460	470	15.50	14.40	13.30	12.10	11.00	10.00	9.00	8.10	7.20	6.30	5.50
470	480	16.10	15.00	13.90	12.70	11.60	10.50	9.50	8.50	7.60	6.80	5.90
480	490	16.70	15.60	14.50	13.30	12.20	11.00	10.00	9.00	8.10	7.20	6.40
490	500	17.30	16.20	15.00	13.90	12.80	11.60	10.50	9.50	8.50	7.70	6.80
500	510	17.90	16.80	15.60	14.50	13.40	12.20	11.10	10.00	9.00	8.10	7.30
510	520	18.50	17.40	16.20	15.10	14.00	12.80	11.70	10.60	9.60	8.60	7.70
520	530	19.10	17.90	16.80	15.70	14.50	13.40	12.30	11.10	10.10	9.10	8.20
530	540	19.80	18.50	17.40	16.30	15.10	14.00	12.90	11.70	10.60	9.60	8.60
540	550	20.50	19.20	18.00	16.90	15.70	14.60	13.50	12.30	11.20	10.10	9.10
550	560	21.20	19.90	18.60	17.40	16.30	15.20	14.00	12.90	11.80	10.70	9.60
560	570	21.90	20.60	19.20	18.00	16.90	15.80	14.60	13.50	12.40	11.20	10.20
570	580	22.60	21.20	19.90	18.60	17.50	16.40	15.20	14.10	13.00	11.80	10.70
580	590	23.20	21.90	20.60	19.30	18.10	16.90	15.80	14.70	13.50	12.40	11.30
590	600	23.90	22.60	21.30	20.00	18.70	17.50	16.40	15.30	14.10	13.00	11.90
600	610	24.60	23.30	22.00	20.70	19.40	18.10	17.00	15.90	14.70	13.60	12.50
610	620	25.30	24.00	22.70	21.40	20.00	18.70	17.60	16.40	15.30	14.20	13.00
620	630	26.00	24.70	23.40	22.00	20.70	19.40	18.20	17.00	15.90	14.80	13.60
630	640	26.70	25.40	24.00	22.70	21.40	20.10	18.80	17.60	16.50	15.40	14.20
640	650	27.40	26.00	24.70	23.40	22.10	20.80	19.50	18.20	17.10	15.90	14.80
650	1,730	6.85% (.0685) of the excess over $650 plus:										
		27.70	26.40	25.10	23.80	22.40	21.10	19.80	18.50	17.40	16.20	15.10
$1,730 & OVER		Use Method II, "Exact Calculation Method," on page T-13 of this booklet										

WAGES		EXEMPTIONS CLAIMED										10
At Least	But Less Than	0	1	2	3	4	5	6	7	8	9	or more
		TAX TO BE WITHHELD										
$0	$100	$0.00										
100	105	0.00										
105	110	0.00										
110	115	0.00	$0.00									
115	120	0.00	0.00									
120	125	0.00	0.00									
125	130	0.00	0.00									
130	135	0.00	0.00	$0.00								
135	140	0.00	0.00	0.00								
140	145	0.00	0.00	0.00								
145	150	0.20	0.00	0.00								
150	160	0.50	0.00	0.00	$0.00							
160	170	0.90	0.10	0.00	0.00							
170	180	1.30	0.50	0.00	0.00	$0.00						
180	190	1.70	0.90	0.10	0.00	0.00						
190	200	2.10	1.30	0.50	0.00	0.00	$0.00					
200	210	2.50	1.70	0.90	0.10	0.00	0.00					
210	220	2.90	2.10	1.30	0.50	0.00	0.00	$0.00				
220	230	3.30	2.50	1.70	0.90	0.20	0.00	0.00				
230	240	3.70	2.90	2.10	1.30	0.60	0.00	0.00	$0.00			
240	250	4.10	3.30	2.50	1.70	1.00	0.20	0.00	0.00	$0.00		
250	260	4.50	3.70	2.90	2.10	1.40	0.60	0.00	0.00	0.00		
260	270	4.90	4.10	3.30	2.50	1.80	1.00	0.20	0.00	0.00	$0.00	
270	280	5.30	4.50	3.70	2.90	2.20	1.40	0.60	0.00	0.00	0.00	
280	290	5.70	4.90	4.10	3.30	2.60	1.80	1.00	0.30	0.00	0.00	$0.00
290	300	6.10	5.30	4.50	3.70	3.00	2.20	1.40	0.70	0.00	0.00	0.00
300	310	6.50	5.70	4.90	4.10	3.40	2.60	1.80	1.10	0.30	0.00	0.00
310	320	6.90	6.10	5.30	4.50	3.80	3.00	2.20	1.50	0.70	0.00	0.00
320	330	7.40	6.50	5.70	4.90	4.20	3.40	2.60	1.90	1.10	0.30	0.00
330	340	7.80	7.00	6.10	5.30	4.60	3.80	3.00	2.30	1.50	0.70	0.00
340	350	8.30	7.40	6.60	5.70	5.00	4.20	3.40	2.70	1.90	1.10	0.40
350	360	8.70	7.90	7.00	6.10	5.40	4.60	3.80	3.10	2.30	1.50	0.80
360	370	9.30	8.30	7.50	6.60	5.80	5.00	4.20	3.50	2.70	1.90	1.20
370	380	9.80	8.80	7.90	7.00	6.20	5.40	4.60	3.90	3.10	2.30	1.60
380	390	10.30	9.30	8.40	7.50	6.60	5.80	5.00	4.30	3.50	2.70	2.00
390	400	10.80	9.80	8.80	7.90	7.10	6.20	5.40	4.70	3.90	3.10	2.40
400	410	11.40	10.40	9.30	8.40	7.50	6.70	5.80	5.10	4.30	3.50	2.80
410	420	12.00	10.90	9.90	8.90	8.00	7.10	6.20	5.50	4.70	3.90	3.20
420	430	12.60	11.50	10.40	9.40	8.40	7.60	6.70	5.90	5.10	4.30	3.60
430	440	13.20	12.10	10.90	9.90	8.90	8.00	7.10	6.30	5.50	4.70	4.00
440	450	13.80	12.70	11.50	10.40	9.40	8.50	7.60	6.70	5.90	5.10	4.40
450	460	14.40	13.20	12.10	11.00	9.90	8.90	8.00	7.20	6.30	5.50	4.80
460	470	15.00	13.80	12.70	11.60	10.50	9.50	8.50	7.60	6.80	5.90	5.20
470	480	15.60	14.40	13.30	12.20	11.00	10.00	9.00	8.10	7.20	6.30	5.60
480	490	16.20	15.00	13.90	12.70	11.60	10.50	9.50	8.50	7.70	6.80	6.00
490	500	16.70	15.60	14.50	13.30	12.20	11.10	10.00	9.00	8.10	7.20	6.40
500	510	17.30	16.20	15.10	13.90	12.80	11.70	10.60	9.50	8.60	7.70	6.80
510	520	17.90	16.80	15.70	14.50	13.40	12.20	11.10	10.10	9.10	8.10	7.30
520	530	18.50	17.40	16.20	15.10	14.00	12.80	11.70	10.60	9.60	8.60	7.70
530	540	19.20	18.00	16.80	15.70	14.60	13.40	12.30	11.20	10.10	9.10	8.20
540	550	19.90	18.60	17.40	16.30	15.20	14.00	12.90	11.80	10.60	9.60	8.60
550	560	20.50	19.20	18.00	16.90	15.70	14.60	13.50	12.30	11.20	10.10	9.10
560	570	21.20	19.90	18.60	17.50	16.30	15.20	14.10	12.90	11.80	10.70	9.70
570	580	21.90	20.60	19.30	18.10	16.90	15.80	14.70	13.50	12.40	11.30	10.20
580	590	22.60	21.30	20.00	18.60	17.50	16.40	15.20	14.10	13.00	11.80	10.70
590	600	23.30	22.00	20.60	19.30	18.10	17.00	15.80	14.70	13.60	12.40	11.30
600	610	24.00	22.60	21.30	20.00	18.70	17.60	16.40	15.30	14.20	13.00	11.90
610	620	24.60	23.30	22.00	20.70	19.40	18.10	17.00	15.90	14.70	13.60	12.50
620	630	25.30	24.00	22.70	21.40	20.10	18.70	17.60	16.50	15.30	14.20	13.10
630	640	26.00	24.70	23.40	22.10	20.70	19.40	18.20	17.10	15.90	14.80	13.70
640	650	26.70	25.40	24.10	22.70	21.40	20.10	18.80	17.70	16.50	15.40	14.20
650	1,730	6.85% (.0685) of the excess over $650 plus:										
		27.00	25.70	24.40	23.10	21.80	20.50	19.10	17.90	16.80	15.70	14.50
$1,730 & OVER		Use Method II, "Exact Calculation Method," on page T-14 of this booklet										

Method I

Table I

NY STATE

Income Tax

MARRIED

WEEKLY

Payroll Period

T-18

City of NEW YORK - RESIDENT TAX

SINGLE - WEEKLY

Payroll Period

Method I

WAGES At Least	But Less Than	0	1	2	3	4	5	6	7	8	9	10 or more
						TAX TO BE WITHHELD						
$0	$50	$0.00										
50	96	0.00										
96	100	0.05										
100	105	0.10										
105	110	0.20										
110	115	0.30										
115	120	0.40	$0.05									
120	125	0.50	0.15									
125	130	0.60	0.25									
130	135	0.70	0.35									
135	140	0.80	0.40	$0.05								
140	145	0.90	0.50	0.15								
145	150	1.00	0.60	0.25								
150	160	1.10	0.75	0.40								
160	170	1.30	0.95	0.60	$0.20							
170	180	1.50	1.15	0.75	0.40	$0.05						
180	190	1.70	1.30	0.95	0.60	0.25						
190	200	1.90	1.50	1.15	0.80	0.40	$0.05					
200	210	2.05	1.70	1.35	0.95	0.60	0.25					
210	220	2.25	1.90	1.55	1.15	0.80	0.45	$0.05				
220	230	2.45	2.10	1.70	1.35	1.00	0.60	0.25				
230	240	2.65	2.25	1.90	1.55	1.20	0.80	0.45	$0.10			
240	250	2.85	2.45	2.10	1.75	1.35	1.00	0.65	0.25			
250	260	3.05	2.65	2.30	1.90	1.55	1.20	0.85	0.45			
260	270	3.35	2.85	2.50	2.10	1.75	1.40	1.00	0.65	$0.10		
270	280	3.65	3.10	2.65	2.30	1.95	1.55	1.20	0.85	0.50		
280	290	3.95	3.35	2.85	2.50	2.15	1.75	1.40	1.05	0.65		
290	300	4.25	3.65	3.10	2.70	2.30	1.95	1.60	1.20	0.85	$0.10	
300	310	4.60	4.00	3.40	2.85	2.50	2.15	1.80	1.40	1.05	0.70	$0.10
310	320	4.90	4.30	3.70	3.10	2.70	2.35	1.95	1.60	1.25	0.85	0.30

Table I

City of NEW YORK - RESIDENT TAX — WEEKLY

Payroll Period

WAGES At Least	But Less Than	0	1	2	3	4	5	6	7	8	9	10 or more
							TAX TO BE WITHHELD					
$320	$330	$5.20	$4.60	$4.00	$3.40	$2.90	$2.50	$2.15	$1.80	$1.45	$1.05	$0.70
330	340	5.50	4.90	4.30	3.70	3.15	2.70	2.35	2.00	1.60	1.25	0.90
340	350	5.80	5.20	4.60	4.05	3.45	2.90	2.55	2.15	1.80	1.45	1.05
350	360	6.15	5.55	4.95	4.35	3.75	3.15	2.75	2.35	2.00	1.65	1.25
360	370	6.45	5.85	5.25	4.65	4.05	3.45	2.90	2.55	2.20	1.80	1.45
370	380	6.75	6.15	5.55	4.95	4.35	3.75	3.20	2.75	2.40	2.00	1.65
380	390	7.05	6.45	5.85	5.25	4.65	4.10	3.50	2.95	2.55	2.20	1.85
390	400	7.40	6.75	6.15	5.60	5.00	4.40	3.80	3.20	2.75	2.40	2.00
400	410	7.80	7.10	6.50	5.90	5.30	4.70	4.10	3.50	2.95	2.60	2.20
410	420	8.15	7.45	6.80	6.20	5.60	5.00	4.40	3.80	3.20	2.75	2.40
420	430	8.55	7.80	7.10	6.50	5.90	5.30	4.70	4.10	3.55	2.95	2.60
430	440	8.90	8.20	7.50	6.80	6.20	5.65	5.05	4.45	3.85	3.25	2.80
440	450	9.25	8.55	7.85	7.15	6.55	5.95	5.35	4.75	4.15	3.55	3.00
450	460	9.65	8.95	8.20	7.50	6.85	6.25	5.65	5.05	4.45	3.85	3.25
460	470	10.00	9.30	8.60	7.90	7.15	6.55	5.95	5.35	4.75	4.15	3.55
470	480	10.40	9.65	8.95	8.25	7.55	6.85	6.25	5.65	5.10	4.50	3.90
480	490	10.75	10.05	9.35	8.60	7.90	7.20	6.60	6.00	5.40	4.80	4.20
490	500	11.10	10.40	9.70	9.00	8.30	7.55	6.90	6.30	5.70	5.10	4.50
500	510	11.50	10.80	10.05	9.35	8.65	7.95	7.20	6.60	6.00	5.40	4.80
510	520	11.85	11.15	10.45	9.75	9.00	8.30	7.60	6.90	6.30	5.70	5.10
520	530	12.25	11.50	10.80	10.10	9.40	8.70	7.95	7.25	6.65	6.05	5.45
530	540	12.60	11.90	11.20	10.45	9.75	9.05	8.35	7.60	6.95	6.35	5.75
540	550	12.95	12.25	11.55	10.85	10.15	9.40	8.70	8.00	7.30	6.65	6.05
550	560	13.35	12.65	11.90	11.20	10.50	9.80	9.05	8.35	7.65	6.95	6.35
560	570	13.70	13.00	12.30	11.60	10.85	10.15	9.45	8.75	8.00	7.30	6.65
570	580	14.10	13.35	12.65	11.95	11.25	10.55	9.80	9.10	8.40	7.70	7.00
580	590	14.45	13.75	13.05	12.30	11.60	10.90	10.20	9.45	8.75	8.05	7.35
590	600	14.85	14.10	13.40	12.70	12.00	11.25	10.55	9.85	9.15	8.40	7.70
600	610	15.25	14.50	13.75	13.05	12.35	11.65	10.90	10.20	9.50	8.80	8.10
610	620	15.65	14.90	14.15	13.45	12.70	12.00	11.30	10.60	9.85	9.15	8.45
620	630	16.05	15.30	14.55	13.80	13.10	12.40	11.65	10.95	10.25	9.55	8.80
630	640	16.40	15.65	14.90	14.15	13.45	12.75	12.05	11.30	10.60	9.90	9.20
640	650	16.80	16.05	15.30	14.55	13.85	13.10	12.40	11.70	11.00	10.25	9.55
650	660	17.20	16.45	15.70	14.95	14.20	13.50	12.75	12.05	11.35	10.65	9.95
660	670	17.60	16.85	16.10	15.35	14.60	13.85	13.15	12.45	11.70	11.00	10.30
670	680	18.00	17.25	16.50	15.75	15.00	14.25	13.50	12.80	12.10	11.40	10.65
680	690	18.35	17.60	16.85	16.10	15.35	14.60	13.90	13.15	12.45	11.75	11.05
690	700	18.75	18.00	17.25	16.50	15.75	15.00	14.25	13.55	12.85	12.10	11.40

T-19

WAGES / EXEMPTIONS CLAIMED — TAX TO BE WITHHELD (Table I)

At Least	But Less Than	0	1	2	3	4	5	6	7	8	9	10 or more
$1,100	$1,110	$34.75	$34.00	$33.25	$32.50	$31.75	$31.00	$30.25	$29.50	$28.75	$28.00	$27.25
1,110	1,120	35.15	34.40	33.65	32.90	32.15	31.40	30.65	29.90	29.15	28.40	27.65
1,120	1,130	35.55	34.80	34.05	33.30	32.55	31.80	31.05	30.30	29.55	28.80	28.05
1,130	1,140	35.90	35.15	34.40	33.65	32.90	32.15	31.40	30.65	29.90	29.15	28.40
1,140	1,150	36.30	35.55	34.80	34.05	33.30	32.55	31.80	31.05	30.30	29.55	28.80
1,150	1,160	36.70	35.95	35.20	34.45	33.70	32.95	32.20	31.45	30.70	29.95	29.20
1,160	1,170	37.10	36.35	35.60	34.85	34.10	33.35	32.60	31.85	31.10	30.35	29.60
1,170	1,180	37.50	36.75	36.00	35.25	34.50	33.75	33.00	32.25	31.50	30.75	30.00
1,180	1,190	37.85	37.10	36.35	35.60	34.85	34.10	33.35	32.60	31.85	31.10	30.35
1,190	1,200	38.25	37.50	36.75	36.00	35.25	34.50	33.75	33.00	32.25	31.50	30.75
1,200	1,210	38.65	37.90	37.15	36.40	35.65	34.90	34.15	33.40	32.65	31.90	31.15
1,210	1,220	39.05	38.30	37.55	36.80	36.05	35.30	34.55	33.80	33.05	32.30	31.55
1,220	1,230	39.45	38.70	37.95	37.20	36.45	35.70	34.95	34.20	33.45	32.70	31.95
1,230	1,240	39.80	39.05	38.30	37.55	36.80	36.05	35.30	34.55	33.80	33.05	32.30
1,240	1,250	40.20	39.45	38.70	37.95	37.20	36.45	35.70	34.95	34.20	33.45	32.70
1,250	1,260	40.60	39.85	39.10	38.35	37.60	36.85	36.10	35.35	34.60	33.85	33.10
1,260	1,270	41.00	40.25	39.50	38.75	38.00	37.25	36.50	35.75	35.00	34.25	33.50
1,270	1,280	41.40	40.65	39.90	39.15	38.40	37.65	36.90	36.15	35.40	34.65	33.90
1,280	1,290	41.80	41.05	40.25	39.50	38.75	38.00	37.25	36.50	35.75	35.00	34.25
1,290	1,300	42.20	41.45	40.65	39.90	39.15	38.40	37.65	36.90	36.15	35.40	34.65
1,300	1,310	42.60	41.85	41.05	40.30	39.55	38.80	38.05	37.30	36.55	35.80	35.05
1,310	1,320	43.00	42.25	41.45	40.70	39.95	39.20	38.45	37.70	36.95	36.20	35.45
1,320	1,330	43.40	42.65	41.85	41.10	40.35	39.60	38.85	38.10	37.35	36.60	35.85
1,330	1,340	43.80	43.05	42.25	41.50	40.75	40.00	39.20	38.45	37.70	36.95	36.20
1,340	1,350	44.20	43.45	42.65	41.90	41.15	40.35	39.60	38.85	38.10	37.35	36.60
1,350	1,360	44.60	43.85	43.05	42.30	41.55	40.75	40.00	39.25	38.50	37.75	37.00
1,360	1,370	45.00	44.25	43.45	42.70	41.95	41.15	40.40	39.65	38.90	38.15	37.40
1,370	1,380	45.40	44.65	43.85	43.10	42.35	41.55	40.80	40.05	39.30	38.55	37.80
1,380	1,390	45.80	45.05	44.25	43.50	42.75	41.95	41.20	40.40	39.65	38.90	38.15
1,390	1,400	46.20	45.45	44.65	43.90	43.15	42.35	41.60	40.80	40.05	39.30	38.55
1,400	1,410	46.60	45.85	45.05	44.30	43.55	42.75	42.00	41.20	40.45	39.70	38.95
1,410	1,420	47.00	46.25	45.45	44.70	43.95	43.15	42.40	41.60	40.85	40.10	39.35
1,420	1,430	47.40	46.65	45.85	45.10	44.35	43.55	42.80	42.00	41.25	40.50	39.75
1,430	1,440	47.80	47.05	46.25	45.50	44.75	43.95	43.20	42.40	41.65	40.90	40.10
1,440	1,450	48.20	47.45	46.65	45.90	45.15	44.35	43.60	42.80	42.05	41.30	40.50
1,450	1,460	48.60	47.85	47.05	46.30	45.55	44.75	44.00	43.20	42.45	41.70	40.90
$1,460 & OVER		48.80	48.05	47.25	46.50	45.75	44.95	44.20	43.40	42.65	41.90	41.10

4.00% (.040) of the excess over $1,460 plus:

WAGES / EXEMPTIONS CLAIMED — TAX TO BE WITHHELD (Method I)

At Least	But Less Than	0	1	2	3	4	5	6	7	8	9	10 or more
$710	$720	$19.55	$18.80	$18.05	$17.30	$16.55	$15.80	$15.05	$14.30	$13.55	$12.85	$12.15
720	730	19.95	19.20	18.45	17.70	16.95	16.20	15.45	14.70	13.95	13.25	12.50
730	740	20.30	19.55	18.80	18.05	17.30	16.55	15.80	15.05	14.30	13.60	12.90
740	750	20.70	19.95	19.20	18.45	17.70	16.95	16.20	15.45	14.70	13.95	13.25
750	760	21.10	20.35	19.60	18.85	18.10	17.35	16.60	15.85	15.10	14.35	13.65
760	770	21.50	20.75	20.00	19.25	18.50	17.75	17.00	16.25	15.50	14.75	14.00
770	780	21.90	21.15	20.40	19.65	18.90	18.15	17.40	16.65	15.90	15.15	14.40
780	790	22.25	21.50	20.75	20.00	19.25	18.50	17.75	17.00	16.25	15.50	14.75
790	800	22.65	21.90	21.15	20.40	19.65	18.90	18.15	17.40	16.65	15.90	15.15
800	810	23.05	22.30	21.55	20.80	20.05	19.30	18.55	17.80	17.05	16.30	15.55
810	820	23.45	22.70	21.95	21.20	20.45	19.70	18.95	18.20	17.45	16.70	15.95
820	830	23.85	23.10	22.35	21.60	20.85	20.10	19.35	18.60	17.85	17.10	16.35
830	840	24.20	23.45	22.70	21.95	21.20	20.45	19.70	18.95	18.20	17.45	16.70
840	850	24.60	23.85	23.10	22.35	21.60	20.85	20.10	19.35	18.60	17.85	17.10
850	860	25.00	24.25	23.50	22.75	22.00	21.25	20.50	19.75	19.00	18.25	17.50
860	870	25.40	24.65	23.90	23.15	22.40	21.65	20.90	20.15	19.40	18.65	17.90
870	880	25.80	25.05	24.30	23.55	22.80	22.05	21.30	20.55	19.80	19.05	18.30
880	890	26.15	25.40	24.65	23.90	23.15	22.40	21.65	20.90	20.15	19.40	18.65
890	900	26.55	25.80	25.05	24.30	23.55	22.80	22.05	21.30	20.55	19.80	19.05
900	910	26.95	26.20	25.45	24.70	23.95	23.20	22.45	21.70	20.95	20.20	19.45
910	920	27.35	26.60	25.85	25.10	24.35	23.60	22.85	22.10	21.35	20.60	19.85
920	930	27.75	27.00	26.25	25.50	24.75	24.00	23.25	22.50	21.75	21.00	20.25
930	940	28.10	27.35	26.60	25.85	25.10	24.35	23.60	22.85	22.10	21.35	20.60
940	950	28.50	27.75	27.00	26.25	25.50	24.75	24.00	23.25	22.50	21.75	21.00
950	960	28.90	28.15	27.40	26.65	25.90	25.15	24.40	23.65	22.90	22.15	21.40
960	970	29.30	28.55	27.80	27.05	26.30	25.55	24.80	24.05	23.30	22.55	21.80
970	980	29.70	28.95	28.20	27.45	26.70	25.95	25.20	24.45	23.70	22.95	22.20
980	990	30.05	29.30	28.55	27.80	27.05	26.30	25.55	24.80	24.05	23.30	22.55
990	1,000	30.45	29.70	28.95	28.20	27.45	26.70	25.95	25.20	24.45	23.70	22.95
1,000	1,010	30.85	30.10	29.35	28.60	27.85	27.10	26.35	25.60	24.85	24.10	23.35
1,010	1,020	31.25	30.50	29.75	29.00	28.25	27.50	26.75	26.00	25.25	24.50	23.75
1,020	1,030	31.65	30.90	30.15	29.40	28.65	27.90	27.15	26.40	25.65	24.90	24.15
1,030	1,040	32.00	31.25	30.50	29.75	29.00	28.25	27.50	26.75	26.00	25.25	24.50
1,040	1,050	32.40	31.65	30.90	30.15	29.40	28.65	27.90	27.15	26.40	25.65	24.90
1,050	1,060	32.80	32.05	31.30	30.55	29.80	29.05	28.30	27.55	26.80	26.05	25.30
1,060	1,070	33.20	32.45	31.70	30.95	30.20	29.45	28.70	27.95	27.20	26.45	25.70
1,070	1,080	33.60	32.85	32.10	31.35	30.60	29.85	29.10	28.35	27.60	26.85	26.10
1,080	1,090	33.95	33.20	32.45	31.70	30.95	30.20	29.45	28.70	27.95	27.20	26.45
1,090	1,100	34.35	33.60	32.85	32.10	31.35	30.60	29.85	29.10	28.35	27.60	26.85

City of NEW YORK - RESIDENT TAX

SINGLE   -   WEEKLY

Payroll Period

Table I

Method I

City of NEW YORK - RESIDENT TAX
MARRIED   -   WEEKLY
Payroll Period

Method I

WAGES At Least	But Less Than	0	1	2	3	4	5	6	7	8	9	10 or more
					EXEMPTIONS CLAIMED — TAX TO BE WITHHELD							
$0	$50	$0.00										
50	98	0.00										
98	100	0.00										
100	105	0.00										
105	110	0.05										
110	115	0.15										
115	120	0.20										
120	125	0.30										
125	130	0.40	$0.05									
130	135	0.50	0.15									
135	140	0.60	0.25									
140	145	0.70	0.35									
145	150	0.80	0.45	$0.05								
150	160	0.95	0.55	0.20								
160	170	1.15	0.75	0.40	$0.05							
170	180	1.30	0.95	0.60	0.20							
180	190	1.50	1.15	0.75	0.40	$0.05						
190	200	1.70	1.35	0.95	0.60	0.20						
200	210	1.90	1.50	1.15	0.80	0.40	$0.05					
210	220	2.10	1.70	1.35	1.00	0.60	0.25					
220	230	2.25	1.90	1.55	1.15	0.80	0.45	$0.05				
230	240	2.45	2.10	1.70	1.35	1.00	0.66	0.25				
240	250	2.65	2.30	1.90	1.55	1.20	0.80	0.45	$0.10			
250	260	2.85	2.45	2.10	1.75	1.35	1.00	0.65	0.30			
260	270	3.05	2.65	2.30	1.95	1.55	1.20	0.85	0.45	$0.10		
270	280	3.35	2.85	2.50	2.10	1.75	1.40	1.00	0.65	0.30		
280	290	3.65	3.10	2.65	2.30	1.95	1.60	1.20	0.85	0.50	$0.10	
290	300	3.95	3.35	2.85	2.50	2.15	1.75	1.40	1.05	0.65	0.30	
300	310	4.30	3.70	3.10	2.70	2.30	1.95	1.60	1.25	0.85	0.50	$0.15
310	320	4.60	4.00	3.40	2.90	2.50	2.15	1.80	1.40	1.05	0.70	0.30

Table I

WAGES At Least	But Less Than	0	1	2	3	4	5	6	7	8	9	10 or more
					EXEMPTIONS CLAIMED — TAX TO BE WITHHELD							
$320	$330	$4.90	$4.30	$3.70	$3.15	$2.70	$2.35	$1.95	$1.60	$1.25	$0.90	$0.50
330	340	5.20	4.60	4.00	3.40	2.90	2.55	2.15	1.80	1.45	1.05	0.70
340	350	5.50	4.90	4.35	3.75	3.15	2.70	2.35	2.00	1.60	1.25	0.90
350	360	5.85	5.25	4.65	4.05	3.45	2.90	2.55	2.20	1.80	1.45	1.10
360	370	6.15	5.55	4.95	4.35	3.75	3.15	2.75	2.35	2.00	1.65	1.25
370	380	6.45	5.85	5.25	4.65	4.05	3.45	2.90	2.55	2.20	1.85	1.45
380	390	6.75	6.15	5.55	4.95	4.35	3.80	3.20	2.75	2.40	2.00	1.65
390	400	7.05	6.45	5.90	5.30	4.70	4.10	3.50	2.95	2.55	2.20	1.85
400	410	7.45	6.80	6.20	5.60	5.00	4.40	3.80	3.20	2.75	2.40	2.05
410	420	7.80	7.10	6.50	5.90	5.30	4.70	4.10	3.50	2.95	2.60	2.20
420	430	8.20	7.45	6.80	6.20	5.60	5.00	4.40	3.85	3.25	2.80	2.40
430	440	8.55	7.85	7.10	6.50	5.90	5.35	4.75	4.15	3.55	3.00	2.60
440	450	8.90	8.20	7.50	6.85	6.25	5.65	5.05	4.45	3.85	3.25	2.80
450	460	9.30	8.60	7.85	7.15	6.55	5.95	5.35	4.75	4.15	3.55	3.00
460	470	9.65	8.95	8.25	7.50	6.85	6.25	5.65	5.05	4.45	3.85	3.25
470	480	10.05	9.30	8.60	7.90	7.20	6.55	5.95	5.40	4.80	4.20	3.60
480	490	10.40	9.70	8.95	8.25	7.55	6.90	6.30	5.70	5.10	4.50	3.90
490	500	10.75	10.05	9.35	8.65	7.90	7.20	6.60	6.00	5.40	4.80	4.20
500	510	11.15	10.45	9.70	9.00	8.30	7.60	6.90	6.30	5.70	5.10	4.50
510	520	11.50	10.80	10.10	9.35	8.65	7.95	7.25	6.60	6.00	5.40	4.85
520	530	11.90	11.15	10.45	9.75	9.05	8.30	7.60	6.95	6.35	5.75	5.15
530	540	12.25	11.55	10.80	10.10	9.40	8.70	8.00	7.25	6.65	6.05	5.45
540	550	12.60	11.90	11.20	10.50	9.75	9.05	8.35	7.65	6.95	6.35	5.75
550	560	13.00	12.30	11.55	10.85	10.15	9.45	8.70	8.00	7.30	6.65	6.05
560	570	13.35	12.65	11.95	11.20	10.50	9.80	9.10	8.40	7.65	6.95	6.40
570	580	13.75	13.00	12.30	11.60	10.90	10.15	9.45	8.75	8.05	7.30	6.70
580	590	14.10	13.40	12.65	11.95	11.25	10.55	9.85	9.10	8.40	7.70	7.00
590	600	14.50	13.75	13.05	12.35	11.60	10.90	10.20	9.50	8.75	8.05	7.35
600	610	14.85	14.15	13.40	12.70	12.00	11.30	10.55	9.85	9.15	8.45	7.70
610	620	15.25	14.50	13.80	13.05	12.35	11.65	10.95	10.25	9.50	8.80	8.10
620	630	15.65	14.90	14.15	13.45	12.75	12.00	11.30	10.60	9.90	9.15	8.45
630	640	16.05	15.30	14.55	13.80	13.10	12.40	11.70	10.95	10.25	9.55	8.85
640	650	16.45	15.70	14.95	14.20	13.45	12.75	12.05	11.35	10.60	9.90	9.20
650	660	16.80	16.05	15.30	14.55	13.85	13.15	12.40	11.70	11.00	10.30	9.55
660	670	17.20	16.45	15.70	14.95	14.20	13.50	12.80	12.10	11.35	10.65	9.95
670	680	17.60	16.85	16.10	15.35	14.60	13.85	13.15	12.45	11.75	11.00	10.30
680	690	18.00	17.25	16.50	15.75	15.00	14.25	13.55	12.80	12.10	11.40	10.70
690	700	18.40	17.65	16.90	16.15	15.40	14.65	13.90	13.20	12.45	11.75	11.05
700	710	18.75	18.00	17.25	16.50	15.75	15.00	14.25	13.55	12.85	12.15	11.40

WAGES		EXEMPTIONS CLAIMED										
At Least	But Less Than	0	1	2	3	4	5	6	7	8	9	10 or more
		TAX TO BE WITHHELD										
$710	$720	$19.15	$18.40	$17.65	$16.90	$16.15	$15.40	$14.65	$13.95	$13.20	$12.50	$11.80
720	730	19.55	18.80	18.05	17.30	16.55	15.80	15.05	14.30	13.60	12.85	12.15
730	740	19.95	19.20	18.45	17.70	16.95	16.20	15.45	14.70	13.95	13.25	12.55
740	750	20.35	19.60	18.85	18.10	17.35	16.60	15.85	15.10	14.35	13.60	12.90
750	760	20.70	19.95	19.20	18.45	17.70	16.95	16.20	15.45	14.70	14.00	13.25
760	770	21.10	20.35	19.60	18.85	18.10	17.35	16.60	15.85	15.10	14.35	13.65
770	780	21.50	20.75	20.00	19.25	18.50	17.75	17.00	16.25	15.50	14.75	14.00
780	790	21.90	21.15	20.40	19.65	18.90	18.15	17.40	16.65	15.90	15.15	14.40
790	800	22.30	21.55	20.80	20.05	19.30	18.55	17.80	17.05	16.30	15.55	14.80
800	810	22.65	21.90	21.15	20.40	19.65	18.90	18.15	17.40	16.65	15.90	15.15
810	820	23.05	22.30	21.55	20.80	20.05	19.30	18.55	17.80	17.05	16.30	15.55
820	830	23.45	22.70	21.95	21.20	20.45	19.70	18.95	18.20	17.45	16.70	15.95
830	840	23.85	23.10	22.35	21.60	20.85	20.10	19.35	18.60	17.85	17.10	16.35
840	850	24.25	23.50	22.75	22.00	21.25	20.50	19.75	19.00	18.25	17.50	16.75
850	860	24.60	23.85	23.10	22.35	21.60	20.85	20.10	19.35	18.60	17.85	17.10
860	870	25.00	24.25	23.50	22.75	22.00	21.25	20.50	19.75	19.00	18.25	17.50
870	880	25.40	24.65	23.90	23.15	22.40	21.65	20.90	20.15	19.40	18.65	17.90
880	890	25.80	25.05	24.30	23.55	22.80	22.05	21.30	20.55	19.80	19.05	18.30
890	900	26.20	25.45	24.70	23.95	23.20	22.45	21.70	20.95	20.20	19.45	18.70
900	910	26.55	25.80	25.05	24.30	23.55	22.80	22.05	21.30	20.55	19.80	19.05
910	920	26.95	26.20	25.45	24.70	23.95	23.20	22.45	21.70	20.95	20.20	19.45
920	930	27.35	26.60	25.85	25.10	24.35	23.60	22.85	22.10	21.35	20.60	19.85
930	940	27.75	27.00	26.25	25.50	24.75	24.00	23.25	22.50	21.75	21.00	20.25
940	950	28.15	27.40	26.65	25.90	25.15	24.40	23.65	22.90	22.15	21.40	20.65
950	960	28.50	27.75	27.00	26.25	25.50	24.75	24.00	23.25	22.50	21.75	21.00
960	970	28.90	28.15	27.40	26.65	25.90	25.15	24.40	23.65	22.90	22.15	21.40
970	980	29.30	28.55	27.80	27.05	26.30	25.55	24.80	24.05	23.30	22.55	21.80
980	990	29.70	28.95	28.20	27.45	26.70	25.95	25.20	24.45	23.70	22.95	22.20
990	1,000	30.10	29.35	28.60	27.85	27.10	26.35	25.60	24.85	24.10	23.35	22.60
1,000	1,010	30.45	29.70	28.95	28.20	27.45	26.70	25.95	25.20	24.45	23.70	22.95
1,010	1,020	30.85	30.10	29.35	28.60	27.85	27.10	26.35	25.60	24.85	24.10	23.35
1,020	1,030	31.25	30.50	29.75	29.00	28.25	27.50	26.75	26.00	25.25	24.50	23.75
1,030	1,040	31.65	30.90	30.15	29.40	28.65	27.90	27.15	26.40	25.65	24.90	24.15
1,040	1,050	32.05	31.30	30.55	29.80	29.05	28.30	27.55	26.80	26.05	25.30	24.55
1,050	1,060	32.40	31.65	30.90	30.15	29.40	28.65	27.90	27.15	26.40	25.65	24.90
1,060	1,070	32.80	32.05	31.30	30.55	29.80	29.05	28.30	27.55	26.80	26.05	25.30
1,070	1,080	33.20	32.45	31.70	30.95	30.20	29.45	28.70	27.95	27.20	26.45	25.70
1,080	1,090	33.60	32.85	32.10	31.35	30.60	29.85	29.10	28.35	27.60	26.85	26.10
1,090	1,100	34.00	33.25	32.50	31.75	31.00	30.25	29.50	28.75	28.00	27.25	26.50

WAGES		EXEMPTIONS CLAIMED										
At Least	But Less Than	0	1	2	3	4	5	6	7	8	9	10 or more
		TAX TO BE WITHHELD										
$1,100	$1,110	$34.35	$33.60	$32.85	$32.10	$31.35	$30.60	$29.85	$29.10	$28.35	$27.60	$26.85
1,110	1,120	34.75	34.00	33.25	32.50	31.75	31.00	30.25	29.50	28.75	28.00	27.25
1,120	1,130	35.15	34.40	33.65	32.90	32.15	31.40	30.65	29.90	29.15	28.40	27.65
1,130	1,140	35.55	34.80	34.05	33.30	32.55	31.80	31.05	30.30	29.55	28.80	28.05
1,140	1,150	35.95	35.20	34.45	33.70	32.95	32.20	31.45	30.70	29.95	29.20	28.45
1,150	1,160	36.30	35.55	34.80	34.05	33.30	32.55	31.80	31.05	30.30	29.55	28.80
1,160	1,170	36.70	35.95	35.20	34.45	33.70	32.95	32.20	31.45	30.70	29.95	29.20
1,170	1,180	37.10	36.35	35.60	34.85	34.10	33.35	32.60	31.85	31.10	30.35	29.60
1,180	1,190	37.50	36.75	36.00	35.25	34.50	33.75	33.00	32.25	31.50	30.75	30.00
1,190	1,200	37.90	37.15	36.40	35.65	34.90	34.15	33.40	32.65	31.90	31.15	30.40
1,200	1,210	38.25	37.50	36.75	36.00	35.25	34.50	33.75	33.00	32.25	31.50	30.75
1,210	1,220	38.65	37.90	37.15	36.40	35.65	34.90	34.15	33.40	32.65	31.90	31.15
1,220	1,230	39.05	38.30	37.55	36.80	36.05	35.30	34.55	33.80	33.05	32.30	31.55
1,230	1,240	39.45	38.70	37.95	37.20	36.45	35.70	34.95	34.20	33.45	32.70	31.95
1,240	1,250	39.85	39.10	38.35	37.60	36.85	36.10	35.35	34.60	33.85	33.10	32.35
1,250	1,260	40.20	39.45	38.70	37.95	37.20	36.45	35.70	34.95	34.20	33.45	32.70
1,260	1,270	40.60	39.85	39.10	38.35	37.60	36.85	36.10	35.35	34.60	33.85	33.10
1,270	1,280	41.00	40.25	39.50	38.75	38.00	37.25	36.50	35.75	35.00	34.25	33.50
1,280	1,290	41.40	40.65	39.90	39.15	38.40	37.65	36.90	36.15	35.40	34.65	33.90
1,290	1,300	41.80	41.05	40.30	39.55	38.80	38.05	37.30	36.55	35.80	35.05	34.30
1,300	1,310	42.20	41.45	40.70	39.90	39.15	38.40	37.65	36.90	36.15	35.40	34.65
1,310	1,320	42.60	41.85	41.10	40.30	39.55	38.80	38.05	37.30	36.55	35.80	35.05
1,320	1,330	43.00	42.25	41.50	40.70	39.95	39.20	38.45	37.70	36.95	36.20	35.45
1,330	1,340	43.40	42.65	41.90	41.10	40.35	39.60	38.85	38.10	37.35	36.60	35.85
1,340	1,350	43.80	43.05	42.30	41.50	40.75	40.00	39.25	38.50	37.75	37.00	36.25
1,350	1,360	44.20	43.45	42.70	41.90	41.15	40.35	39.60	38.85	38.10	37.35	36.60
1,360	1,370	44.60	43.85	43.10	42.30	41.55	40.75	40.00	39.25	38.50	37.75	37.00
1,370	1,380	45.00	44.25	43.50	42.70	41.95	41.15	40.40	39.65	38.90	38.15	37.40
1,380	1,390	45.40	44.65	43.90	43.10	42.35	41.55	40.80	40.05	39.30	38.55	37.80
1,390	1,400	45.60	45.05	44.30	43.50	42.75	41.95	41.20	40.45	39.70	38.95	38.20
1,400	1,410	46.20	45.45	44.70	43.90	43.15	42.35	41.60	40.85	40.05	39.30	38.55
1,410	1,420	46.60	45.85	45.10	44.30	43.55	42.75	42.00	41.25	40.45	39.70	38.95
1,420	1,430	47.00	46.25	45.50	44.70	43.95	43.15	42.40	41.65	40.85	40.10	39.35
1,430	1,440	47.40	46.65	45.90	45.10	44.35	43.55	42.80	42.05	41.25	40.50	39.75
1,440	1,450	47.80	47.05	46.30	45.50	44.75	43.95	43.20	42.45	41.65	40.90	40.15
1,450	1,460	48.20	47.45	46.70	45.90	45.15	44.35	43.60	42.85	42.05	41.30	40.55
$1,460 & OVER		48.40	47.65	46.90	46.10	45.35	44.55	43.80	43.05	42.25	41.50	40.75

4.00% (.040) of the excess over $1,460 plus:

City of NEW YORK - RESIDENT TAX
MARRIED - WEEKLY
Payroll Period

Table I

Method I

T-21

In addition to these compulsory deductions, there may be many other VOLUNTARY DEDUCTIONS taken from the employee's salary that are authorized by the employee. These voluntary deductions include union dues, insurance premiums, payroll savings plans, charitable contributions, and supplementary pension plans. These deductions are provided as a service by the employer to the employee. The employer is responsible for turning these withheld funds over to the appropriate agency.

THE PAYROLL REGISTER

We will assume that the payroll period we are working with is a weekly payroll, but the same procedures are followed regardless of the payroll period used by the firm. A PAYROLL BOOK (REGISTER) is used to record the total employees that worked in a given payroll period. This book contains the employees' names and lists their total earnings and the various deductions that have been taken from their gross pay, arriving at their net pay. At this point we will not be concerned with how the individual employee's gross pay was determined, but rather how the individual deductions were arrived at, and thus the net pay.

The following completed payroll register illustrates the solutions to Exercises 2 and 3. In addition to the Social Security tax, the New York State disability tax and other deductions are included in the register. Note that the register has special columns for the various mandatory deductions as well as an "other deductions" column for those items we have called voluntary deductions. A column is provided for total deductions and net pay as well. The register is summarized as illustrated and double underscored once it has been determined that the sum of the individual deductions agrees with the total of the total deductions column, and the total deductions subtracted from the total gross pay column agrees with the sum of the net pay column.

The summary of the payroll register becomes the basis for the required entry in the cash payments journal for the payment of the weekly wages. An expanded form of the cash payments journal would probably be used. This journal contains special columns for the various liability accounts as well as a column to record the salaries expense. The general journal form of this payroll entry is illustrated as follows:

```
2003
April 4   Salaries Expense                      4,327.25
              FICA Taxes Payable                            268.29
              Medicare Taxes Payable                         62.74
              FWT Payable                                   441.00
              NYSWT Payable                                 174.86
              NYCWT Payable                                 109.15
              NYS Disability Ben. Payable                     3.00
              Union Dues Payable                             12.00
              Pension Payable                               124.00
              U.S. Bonds Payable                             12.50
              Payroll Payable                             3,119.71
          To record the payroll for the
          week ending April 4, 2003
```

Santini Stationery Co.
Payroll Register – Week Ending April 4, 2003

Name	Status, Exempt	Gross Pay	FICA Tax	Medicare Tax	Federal Withholding Tax	NYS Withholding Tax	NYC Withholding Tax	NYS Dis. Ben. Tax	Other Deductions Item	Other Deductions Amount	Total Deductions	Net Pay
Brown, G.	S,1	14650	908	212	400	00	60	60	Union Dues	1200	2840	11810
Albert, L.	M,2	87500	5425	1269	8400	13330	2390	60			18874	68626
Talley, R.	M,3	124000	7688	1798	138800	6352	3760	60	Pension	12400	45858	78142
Russo, S.	S,2	74575	4624	1081	8700	3164	785	60			18414	56161
Santini, M.	M,5	132000	8184	1914	128800	6640	3920	60	U.S. Bonds	1250	34768	97232
		432725	26829	6274	44100	17486	10915	300		14850	120754	311971

Notice that the entry recognized a credit to an account entitled Payroll Payable. This account would be correctly credited if the accountant did not use an expanded cash payments journal. The follow-up entry would be the payment of the liability which would cause a debit to payroll payable for 3,119.71 and a corresponding credit to cash.

EXERCISE 4 Prepare a payroll register similar to the one previously illustrated. Complete the register for the week ending August 22, 2003, from the following information. Use the various tax tables provided in this chapter:

Alan Gain (M,5)	585.40
Jerry Hand (M,4)	748.75
George Kurl (M,4)	877.00
Steven Feld (S,2)	615.50
Allan Finney (S,1)	1,025.75

Following the completion of the payroll register, make a general journal entry to record the payment of the payroll for the week ending August 22, 2003.

THE EMPLOYEE EARNINGS RECORD

In addition to the maintenance of the payroll register, individual CUMULATIVE EMPLOYEE EARNINGS RECORDS are maintained for each employee. The purpose of these records is to accumulate the weekly earnings of each employee. This record is usually summarized on a quarterly basis. It permits the employer to determine the cumulative earnings of an employee for Social Security tax ceiling purposes and also maintains data required by the various taxing authorities at the end of the calendar year. The form of the cumulative earnings record is similar to the payroll register in that the column headings are the same. (See the accompanying cumulative earnings record entitled "Individual Payroll Record.") Instead of listing the earnings of various employees, only the earnings of a single employee appear on the individual cumulative earnings record, along with the date the wages were earned. The heading of the record includes the employee's name, address, social security number, rate of pay, date service began, and the marital status and number of exemptions claimed as they appear on the W-4 Form. At the end of the calendar year, the quarterly summary entries are combined to provide the information as to total employee earnings, deductions, and net pay. We will shortly see another use that is made of the cumulative earnings record by the employer.

EMPLOYEE'S RECORD

Year _____

Name _____
Address _____
Soc. Sec. No. _____
Status (M, S) _____   Exemptions _____

Phone _____   Date Employed _____   Date Released _____

YEARLY SUMMARY BY QUARTERS

Qtr.	Total Earnings	FICA	Medicare	FWT	SWT	CWT	Other Deductions	Total Deductions	Net Payment
1									
2									
3									
4									
TOTALS									

FIRST QUARTER

Payroll Period	Total Earnings	FICA	Medicare	FWT	SWT	CWT	Other Deductions	Total Deductions	Net Pay
TOTAL									

SECOND QUARTER

Payroll Period	Total Earnings	FICA	Medicare	FWT	SWT	CWT	Other Deductions	Total Deductions	Net Pay
TOTAL									

THIRD QUARTER

Payroll Period	Total Earnings	FICA	Medicare	FWT	SWT	CWT	Other Deductions	Total Deductions	Net Pay
TOTAL									

FOURTH QUARTER

Payroll Period	Total Earnings	FICA	Medicare	FWT	SWT	CWT	Other Deductions	Total Deductions	Net Pay
TOTAL									

Payroll and Government Regulations

We have previously learned that the employer is required to turn over to the various government taxing authorities the monies collected, usually on a monthly basis. In addition, there is a responsibility to match some taxes such as the Social Security tax. Using the payroll record illustrated and the general journal just presented, the following entry would be made at the end of the month, or a few days into the next month, to turn over the taxes withheld to the proper agency. For simplicity, let us assume that the only payroll period for the month of April was the one illustrated for April 4, 2003. By the tenth day of the next month, the following entry is recorded to send the federal withholding tax and the Social Security taxes to the federal depository:

2003			
May 10	FICA Tax Expense	268.29	
	Medicare Tax Expense	62.74	
	FICA Taxes Payable		268.29
	Medicare Tax Payable		62.74
	FWT Payable		441.00
	Cash		1,103.06
	To recognize FICA Tax and		
	Medicare Expenses and		
	send tax obligation to the		
	federal depository.		

The entry to send the required monthly New York State and City withholding taxes to the state would be made so that the payment is received by the fifteenth day of the next month.

2003			
May 15	NYSWT Payable	174.86	
	NYCWT Payable	109.15	
	Cash		284.01
	To remit monthly withholding taxes		
	to New York State.		

The New York State disability benefits tax is usually remitted on a quarterly basis by the end of the following month. The entry would cause a debit to the liability account and a corresponding credit to cash. If by agreement with a union this tax is an expense of the employer, the entry would represent a debit to an expense account such as New York State disability benefits expense, and a credit to cash when payment is remitted. In the latter case, no liability column would be established in the payroll register, since it is an expense of the employer and not to be withheld from the employee's salary.

EXERCISE 5   Referring back to Exercise 4, prepare the necessary general journal entries to remit the appropriate taxes to the various taxing authorities at the end of the month.

UNEMPLOYMENT COMPENSATION TAXES

Not all taxes are the responsibility of the employee, such as the matching Social Security tax we previously discussed. UNEMPLOYMENT COMPENSATION TAXES are taxes that are levied upon employers by the federal and state governments. This tax provides temporary relief to those employees who become unemployed, usually as a result of economic factors beyond their control. The present level of earnings subject to this unemployment tax is $7,000. The first $7,000 of earnings is subject to this tax by the federal government at a rate of 3.5% for the current calendar year. Generally, the employer is able to take a 2.7% credit for the amount of unemployment taxes turned over to the state government. Thus, if the state unemployment tax rate is 2.7% or greater, this amount can be taken as a credit and the actual rate to the federal government becomes .8%. The state unemployment tax rate varies, depending upon the EXPERIENCE RATING of the employer. This experience rating is determined by the turnover of employees within the organization. The experience rating, as established by the state, is then multiplied by the first $7,000 in earnings to determine the employer's tax liability for each employee. Both federal unemployment and state unemployment taxes are calculated quarterly, with payments remitted the month following the quarter. Since both taxes are the obligation of the employer, the entry for the payment recognizes an expense such as federal unemployment tax expense and state unemployment tax expense. The cumulative earnings record previously discussed is used to determine when the first $7,000 of earnings subject to these unemployment taxes has been earned. Assuming that the majority of the employees are employed from the beginning of the calendar year, the greater unemployment expense will be recognized in the first and second quarters of the calendar year.

EXERCISE 6 The following employees had cumulative earnings for the first quarter of 200- as shown on their individual cumulative earnings reports. The state experience rating for this company for unemployment insurance purposes is 4.2%. Determine the federal and state unemployment tax that must be remitted to the respective taxing authorities at the end of the quarter.

Employee	Cumulative Earnings	FU Tax	SU Tax
A. Taylor	$5,465.00		
S. Stern	7,543.00		
A. Rothstein	3,565.40		
J. Shapiro	9,400.00		
S. Bailey	6,550.90		

CALCULATING EMPLOYEE EARNINGS

Individuals who work directly for a business organization are generally considered to be employees of that firm. On the other hand, an INDEPENDENT CONTRACTOR is an individual or a business that is not directly employed by the firm, but is used by the business only to do specific activities. Examples of independent contractors are public accountants, lawyers, and maintenance contractors. A fee is usually paid an independent contractor that does not have the various deductions discussed above made from the payment.

Earnings received by an employee are usually dependent upon the nature of the work performed and the job description. An individual who is paid based on the completion of a specific task is said to be paid on a PIECEWORK BASIS. This individual will receive remuneration at a specific dollar amount times the number of tasks completed. If the individual is given a piecework rate of $0.30 per unit completed, and completes 765 units, the earnings would be $229.50. Other employees may be paid on a COMMISSION BASIS, in which a certain predetermined percentage is given to an employee for the sale of a product or a service. A travel agent may receive a certain predetermined percentage of the value of the travel package sold. If the vacation package cost the customer $3,500 and the agent is entitled to a commission rate of 7%, then the agent will have earned $245.

Individuals may be employed based on an annual salary that for payment purposes is broken down into weekly, semimonthly, or monthly payments. A combination of salary and commission earnings are also common in many kinds of selling occupations. All forms of employee earnings are subject to the various deductions previously mentioned.

The vast majority of employees are paid for their services based on an hourly basis. An hourly employee is one who is paid a specific amount of money for each hour worked. There are specific laws that govern the amount of hours that this kind of employee can work as well as the added compensation that must be paid for excessive hours worked. The amount of money received per hour is known as the hourly rate. This individual's gross pay will be determined by taking the hours worked in a given week and multiplying it by the hourly rate. An employee who has worked 36 hours in a week and is paid at an hourly rate of $3.65 would earn a gross pay for the week of $131.40.

Overtime Earnings

A normal five-day workweek usually consists of 40 hours. In those industries that call for a six-day workweek, the usual hours worked are 48 hours. Government regulations require that additional compensation known as OVERTIME be paid for any hours worked in excess of the employee's normal workweek. Overtime is calculated at $1\frac{1}{2}$ times the regular rate of pay for each hour worked beyond the normal workweek. We will assume that a normal workweek consists of five days and a total of 40 hours. Thus any hours worked beyond 40 hours will be calculated at the OVERTIME RATE. The overtime rate is the hourly amount of money that will be paid for each hour worked beyond 40 hours in a five-day workweek. OVERTIME EARNINGS represent the remuneration received for the overtime hours worked.

EXAMPLE   An employee worked a total of 43 hours in a given workweek and is paid an hourly rate of $6.00. The following calculations represent the determination of the regular earnings, overtime earnings, and the resulting gross pay:

$$
\begin{array}{lr}
40 \text{ hours} \times \$6.00 & = \$240 \\
3 \text{ overtime hours} \times (1\frac{1}{2} \times \$6) & = \underline{27} \\
\text{Gross Pay} & \$267
\end{array}
$$

The first 40 hours worked were calculated based on the hourly rate of $6.00. The overtime rate was calculated by multiplying 1 1/2 times the regular rate of pay to arrive at an overtime rate of $9. This overtime rate multiplied by the overtime hours results in overtime earnings of $27.

Overtime is calculate based on the hours worked beyond the normal 40-hour workweek. If an individual normally works a 35-hour workweek, the fact that in a given week he works a total of 37 hours will not entitle that individual to overtime earnings under the minimum requirements established by the Department of Labor. This does not prevent the payment of overtime in such a situation or a payment at a rate twice the regular hourly rate for overtime can be made by union contract or merely by employer-employee agreement. Thus, individuals who are required to work on holidays may be entitled to double-time for that day, even though the total hours worked for the week don't call for this payment.

EXERCISE 7

Calculate the gross pay for the following employees based on the hours worked and their hourly rate. Distinguish between regular and overtime earnings.

Employee	Total Hours	Hourly Rate	Regular Earnings	Overtime Earnings	Gross Pay
Albert (S,2)	42	$5.35			
Baker (M,4)	39	9.10			
Cox (S,3)	45	6.20			
Daley (S,1)	47	8.50			
Evans (M,2)	41	5.15			
Fall (M,5)	44	9.80			

EXERCISE 8

Based on the gross pay determined for the employees in Exercise 7, prepare a payroll register. After completing the register, record in general journal form the entries needed to pay the payroll and remit the various taxes to the taxing authorities. Use the various tax tables presented in this chapter.

THE W-2 FORM

The employer prepares the payroll register reflecting the payroll periods of the organization. We have learned that this information is transferred to the cumulative earnings record maintained for each employee. This second record is used to assist in determining the maximum earnings subject to the Social Security tax and unemployment insurance tax. At the end of the calendar year, the totals from the individual earnings report is used for the preparation of the FORM W-2 WAGE AND TAX STATEMENT. This statement is prepared at the beginning of the following calendar year and must be given to the employee by January 31. The employer must also submit this form to the Social Security Administration by the end of February. The purpose of the W-2 Form is to provide the employee with information as to his or her total earnings for the year. This document will be used and included with the income tax return that the employee must send to the government by April 15 following the close of the calendar year covering the return.

The heading of the wage and tax statement contains the employer's name, address, and federal identification number. Each form indicates the employee's name, address, and Social Security number, which the employer obtains from the W-4 Form or other payroll records maintained on the employee. The federal income tax withheld for the calendar year is listed on the form along with the total wages earned, total FICA wages (to the maximum wages earned subject to FICA Tax), FICA withholding tax, state withholding taxes, and local withholding taxes, if applicable. The original copy of the form is sent to the Social Security Administration, a copy is sent to the state taxing authority, with the remaining three copies going to the employee.

Summing Up

The maintenance of payroll records within a business is one of the most important financial activities of an organization. Not only is payroll a substantial expense for the business, but the various governmental taxing authorities make the firm a collecting agent for the various taxes withheld from the employee's salary, as well as the taxes that are the obligation of the employer.

The end result of the payroll calculations is the net pay, or take-home pay, that the employee receives. This is calculated by taking the employee's gross pay (wages earned) and deducting from it FICA tax, Medicare tax, federal withholding tax, state and city withholding taxes (if applicable), disability benefits tax, and various voluntary deductions. The employer is provided with the necessary withholding tax tables from the various governmental taxing authorities, which permit the calculation of the appropriate deductions from the employee's salary. The FICA and Medicare taxes are nonprogressive taxes that are deducted from the employee's salary at respective rates of 6.2% and 1.45%. The ceiling for FICA taxes for year 2003 is earnings up to $87,000. There is no ceiling on earnings subject to Medicare taxes.

Taxes withheld for federal, state, and local purposes are progressive in nature and based on three factors: salary, marital status, and exemptions claimed by the employee. The preparation of the W-4 Form provides the employer with this necessary information.

The employer is responsible for the remittance of the withholding taxes to the appropriate taxing authorities. In addition, the employer must match the FICA and Medicare taxes withheld from the employee, which represents an expense to the employer. Unemployment compensation taxes levied by the federal and state governments represent expenses that are paid on a quarterly basis.

Payroll records maintained by the employer include the payroll register, which lists the wages paid to all employees for each payroll period. This book provides for the calculation of gross pay, a listing of the various deductions, and the determination of the net pay. The information from the payroll register is transferred to individual cumulative earnings records that are maintained for each employee. This record is used to calculate the maximum FICA tax to be withheld and unemployment compensation taxes, and is necessary for the completion of the employee's annual wage and tax statement at the end of the calendar year.

There are several criteria for determining the gross pay of employees. Employees may be paid on a number of bases—piecework, commission, annual salary paid at various intervals, actual hours worked, or a combination of these methods. Labor laws require that hourly employees who work more than 40 hours in a five-day workweek be compensated at an overtime rate of 1 1/2 times the regular hourly rate for each hour worked beyond 40 hours. Union contracts may establish overtime at higher rates and for specific days worked, regardless of the total hours an employee works (holiday and weekend overtime compensation).

CHAPTER 12

PARTNERSHIP ACCOUNTING

The Partnership Business Organization

DISADVANTAGES OF SOLE PROPRIETORSHIP

Throughout the entire book to this point, we have presented numerous accounting concepts and principles using the form of business organization known as the sole proprietorship. A SOLE PROPRIETORSHIP is a business organization owned by one individual. Any profits earned or losses incurred are the sole responsibility of the owner. Concentrating on this form of business organization gave continuity to the information presented. While there are other forms of business organizations, the sole proprietorship is the most prevalent form of ownership in the United States, and its similarity to other forms of business organizations permits it to be used as a role model. The major distinctions between a sole proprietorship and other forms of business organizations is primarily in the area of owner's equity.

There are obvious benefits to the sole proprietorship form of business. For instance, any profits earned by the business belong exclusively to the owner. But there are also numerous disadvantages to this form of ownership that may actually prevent the organization of the business or cause the life of the business to be short-lived. Obviously, if the owner dies or becomes permanently disabled, this will result in the dissolution of the business.

When an individual contemplates going into business, one of the primary considerations is the investment needed to do so. A lack of adequate capital investment will probably prevent the beginning of the business. A lack of the necessary expertise may also prevent the formation of the business. Even if these problems are overcome, the day-to-day operation of the business may prove to be more than a sole proprietor can handle, so that the business may fail or need to be reorganized. Obviously, since the predominant form of business in the United States is the sole proprietorship, in more cases than not the above-mentioned disadvantages have been overcome.

ADVANTAGES OF PARTNERSHIP

The disadvantages that we have mentioned in the sole proprietorship form of business may be overcome through the partnership form of business. A PARTNERSHIP is a joining of two or more individuals as co-owners of a business for profit. When funds are needed to organize the business, the partnership will enable the capital needed to be raised through the contributions of each partner to the partnership. An individual with money to invest who lacks expertise in a particular area of a proposed business may join forces with an individual having the necessary expertise. As the size of a business increases, the ability of a sole proprietor to oversee all aspects of the business diminishes. The reorganization of the company into a partnership may enable all aspects of the business to be properly managed.

Partnerships in general consist of relatively small businesses. There are certain professions, due to their nature, that are restricted from forming as corporations in many states. Many professions, such as accounting, law, and medicine, use the partnership form of business organization for this reason. Such partnerships may consist of as few as two partners or as many as hundreds of partners with offices located throughout the world.

CHARACTERISTICS OF THE PARTNERSHIP

The basic accounting procedures for a partnership are very similar to those for a sole proprietorship. There are distinctions, however, that should be recognized because they are unique to the partnership form of business. The characteristics of a partnership are:

Formation requirements

Agency relationship

Co-ownership of assets

Limited life

Unlimited liability

Participation in profits and losses

Articles of partnership

Formation Requirements

A partnership's FORMATION REQUIREMENTS are satisfied when two or more parties agree to join forces for the common purpose of earning a profit within a business environment. The parties to a partnership must simply agree to enter into a partnership. If, at a later date, the partners should decide not to continue the relationship, they can just as easily terminate the association.

Agency Relationship

It is most important that the selection of partners in a partnership be made with great care. Each partner has the power and right to act as an agent of the partnership. All parties dealing with a partner have the right to assume that this AGENCY RELATIONSHIP exists, and they can rely on its existence. The partnership is bound by the acts of its partners within the scope of their normal authority. If a reasonable person would assume that a partner has a particular power, then a court will usually assume so as well. In the event of a dispute, this authority is assumed, even though it may not have been actually given or intended to be given.

Co-ownership of Assets

Assets are contributed to the partnership by the individual partners. Once contributed, the asset is said to be owned by the partnership, and the value of the asset given is reflected in the capital account of the contributing partner. Once the asset is contributed, it no longer belongs to the person who gave it. The partner's right is only to the value of the capital resulting from the contribution. This is known as the CO-OWNERSHIP OF ASSETS. In the event of a discontinuance of the partnership, individual partners have no rights to the specific assets they previously contributed, but merely to the dollar value of their investment in the business as evidenced by their capital balance.

Limited Life

In a sole proprietorship, if the owner becomes disabled or dies, the organization comes to an end. In a partnership, one of two possible changes may occur to the partnership. A DISSOLUTION is said to occur as a result of any change in the composition of a partnership, and a LIQUIDATION takes place if the partnership is terminated. Either event is an example of the partnership's LIMITED LIFE. A partnership may dissolve upon the death of a partner, the withdrawal of a partner, the incapacity of a partner, partnership bankruptcy, or even the admission of a new partner. Dissolution only extends to a liquidation in the case of bankruptcy. The other changes do not necessarily result in liquidation, but the mere dissolution will require a reorganization of the existing partnership.

Unlimited Liability

The profits or losses of a sole proprietorship are the sole pleasure or burden of the owner. In the case of a partnership, the same is true. The concept of UNLIMITED LIABILITY applies equally to both forms of businesses, but it may have a more serious effect on the partners of a partnership. The creditors who are owed money by a partnership are not concerned with who pays the obligation; they are primarily concerned with being paid. The individual partner is said to be held liable for the debts of the partnership both collectively (jointly) and severally (individually). If the other partners are unable to contribute toward the liquidation of the debt, it becomes the obligation of the solvent partner to pay the entire obligation. The remaining partners are liable to the solvent partner, but this is often of little consolation.

Participating in Profits and Losses

Participation in profits and losses comes about through a partnership agreement, and if there is no agreement, then any profits recognized or losses incurred are distributed equally. If an agreement exists that states how profits are to be distributed, but is silent as to losses, these losses, should they occur, are divided in the same manner as the agreed-upon profit distribution. Participation agreements as to profits and losses are recognized by the courts, assuming there was no undue influence or illegality in the making of the agreement.

The distribution of profits or losses is usually determined according to what is known as the PROFIT AND LOSS SHARING RATIO. This ratio is assumed to be equal unless there is an agreement as to the distribution. If there is an agreement, that is the sole criterion for the determination of participation in profits or losses by the individual partners. Partner A may willingly accept 40% of the profits and 60% of the losses. As long as A agrees to this arrangement, it is perfectly valid.

Articles of Partnership

Participation in the profits or losses is determined by a court if there is no evidence of an agreement. It should be obvious that the rights and responsibilities of the partners in a partnership should be in written form. This will serve to eliminate any disputes that may arise from an oral agreement. Such a written agreement is a contract and is referred to as the ARTICLES OF PARTNERSHIP. While there is no legal or governmental requirement that a partnership agreement be in written form, the existence of such a document outlines the obligations of the partners, their specific duties, and the effect on the partnership of such occurrences as the death of a partner. Other provisions that should be made a part of the articles are the amount of the investment by each partner, the limitations on the withdrawal of funds, the policy with regard to the admission or withdrawal of partners, and any other contingencies that can be anticipated at the time that the articles are prepared. Amendment of the articles should take place from time to time to recognize changes in the operation of the organization.

The Partnership Finances

PARTNERSHIP INVESTMENTS

The basis for the partners' investment is by agreement. A separate entry is made for each partner's investment. The value assigned to all assets (except cash) is determined by agreement between the partners. An asset such as equipment may appear on the books of a partner at $5,000, less accumulated depreciation of $2,000. For the partnership to acquire a comparable asset, the market price might be $4,000. Through negotiation an agreement is reached whereby the partnership will accept the equipment at a value of $3,700. Even though the book value of the asset on the partner's books was $3,000, the partnership is accepting the asset and giving the incoming partner capital recognition of $3,700. The useful life is recalculated and a new method for recognizing depreciation is adopted. Assuming that this partner is also required to contribute cash amounting to $5,000, the following general journal entry would be recorded to recognize the investment by the partner:

```
200-
Jan. 15   Cash                                       5,000
              Equipment                              3,700
                  Alice Faye, Capital                          8,700
              To record the investment.
```

Had the partnership wished to recognize the original cost of the asset on the partnership's books, it could have recorded a debit to equipment for $5,000 and recognized accumulated depreciation of $1,300, which would reflect the same value for the asset on the books ($3,700) as the entry above. If Alice Faye had obligations to creditors amounting to $1,000, and the partnership agreed to accept these liabilities, there would be a credit recorded for accounts payable and the new capital balance would have been listed at $7,700.

EXERCISE 1   Cain and Able entered into a partnership. The agreement called for Cain to contribute the following assets: cash, $2,000; accounts receivable having a balance in Cain's books of $5,500; and an allowance for bad debts of $750. The partnership agreement called for recognition of accounts receivable for $5,200 and a new allowance account with a credit balance of $1,600. Record the general journal entry necessary for the admission of Cain into the partnership.

DISTRIBUTING INCOME AND LOSSES

The articles of partnership should state the profit and loss sharing ratio. In the absence of this statement, the profit and loss is shared equally among all the partners. Prior to the actual distribution of the net income or loss it is necessary to recognize other commitments made as part of the articles of partnership. Many agreements call for the recognition of time devoted to a business or other special expertise that one or more partners may have. By agreement a SALARY ALLOWANCE may be provided for. This may represent a weekly amount that a partner is automatically entitled to and the cost of this allowance is taken from the net income, prior to its distribution to the partners.

There may be provisions for the payment of interest on the original investment. This will also be paid out of net income prior to distribution to the partners. Whether or not the individual partners withdraw the interest or salary allowance is immaterial, they are automatically entitled to both, and their respective accounts must be credited for any amounts earned but not withdrawn. Let us assume that the partnership of Cain and Able earned a net income of $40,000 for the current year. The following additional information was also available about the partners:

1. Cain: capital balance, $35,000; salary allowance of $6,000 and an interest allowance of 6% on the capital balance.
2. Able: capital balance, $50,000; salary allowance of $10,000 and an interest allowance of 6% on the capital balance.
3. The articles of partnership was silent as to the distribution of profits and losses.

The following distribution would be made:

	Cain	Able	Total
Net Income			$40,000
Division of Net Income:			
Salary Allowance	$ 6,000	$10,000	(16,000)
Interest Allowance	2,100	3,000	(5,100)
Balance remaining to be distributed as per P&L Ratio			18,900
Net Income	9,450	9,450	(18,900)
Distribution (equal shares)			
Total Distribution	$17,550	$22,450	$40,000

The recognition of the individual interest allowances was based upon 6% of the respective capital balances. ($35,000 × 6% = $2,100; $50,000 × 6% = $3,000). The total obligations prior to using the profit and loss sharing ratio amounted to $21,100. The remaining balance of $18,900 was then distributed equally between the two partners because no specific ratio was mentioned in the agreement. It is possible for the total distribution of the salary allowance and the interest allowance to collectively exceed the net income. When this occurs there is a deficit. Let us assume the same information as above, except that the actual net income is only $20,000. The following calculations illustrate how this is analyzed:

	Cain	Able	Total
Net Income			$20,000
Salary and Interest Allowance	$8,100	$13,000	21,100
Excess of Allowances over Income			
			1,100
Deficit Distribution	(550)	(550)	(1,100)

While the deficit is not a loss in the sense that expenses have exceeded revenue, the effect on the partners' capital is basically the same. The lack of adequate net income to meet the obligations to the partners, as per the articles of partnership, requires that the deficit come from some other source. The appropriate source is the capital account of each of the partners, according to their profit and loss sharing ratio.

Assuming that there were no distributions of funds to the partners in anticipation of profits, the following entry will illustrate how the net income of $20,000 is distributed at the end of the year to the partners:

200-
Dec. 31	Income Summary	20,000	
	Cain, Capital		7,550
	Able, Capital		12,450
	To distribute according to P&L		
	ratio after allowances.		

The capital accounts characterizing a sole proprietorship are also found in a partnership. In fact, for each partner in a partnership there is an individual capital account and a drawing account. The capital statement of a partnership reflects the income distributed to each partner as shown by the drawing account. The new capital balances are determined when the partnership's capital statement is prepared.

EXERCISE 2   Able, Baker, and Crawford are partners in a partnership in which they have capital balances of $25,000, $35,000, and $45,000 respectively. Their profit and loss sharing ratio is 25 : 25 : 50. At the end of the current accounting period, the partnership earned total income amounting to $50,000. The articles of partnership called for interest on the partners' respective capital balances of 8% and individual salary allowances based on time contributed to the business: $12,000 for Able; $15,000 for Baker; and $3,000 for Crawford.

Using a chart similar to the one just illustrated, determine the distribution of the net income to each partner. Prepare the journal entry to transfer the net profit to the individual partner's capital accounts. Assume that during the year the following amounts were withdrawn from the respective partners' capital accounts: Able, $10,000; Baker, $17,000; and Crawford, $2,500. Prepare a capital statement dated December 31 for the partnership. Each partner's change in capital should be shown next to the others.

RECORDING CHANGES IN THE PARTNERSHIP

Admission of a Partner

A change in partnership composition results in a dissolution. In fact, any substantial change causes a dissolution. We have indicated that a liquidation will not necessarily follow a dissolution, although there must be a reorganization of the partnership. One common cause for a dissolution is the admission of a partner. An incoming partner may be admitted through the contribution of assets to the partnership. The value of the assets to the partnership will be determined by agreement, the incoming partner receiving capital recognition for his investment. An incoming partner may also purchase an interest from one or more of the existing partners. In this case, the purchase price may exceed the capital recognition it is given on the books. This profit recognized by the existing partners has no effect on the partnership books. The following example illustrates how this purchase of an existing partner's interest is recorded.

EXAMPLE   Davis and Graff, members of a partnership, have capital balances of $75,000 and $55,000 respectively. Arden is joining the partnership by purchasing a 10% interest from each of the existing partners at a cost to Arden of $15,000. The entry to recognize the admission of Arden is as follows:

```
200-
Nov. 22   Davis, Capital                      7,500
          Graff, Capital                       5,500
              Arden, Capital                              13,000
          To record purchase of existing
          partners' interest in the partnership
          by Arden.
```

The cost to Arden was $15,000, but on the books of the partnership the only entry is to recognize the portion of the capital that Arden is getting from the existing partners. The difference of $2,000 is the profit that the existing partners receive. After the admission of Arden, the total capital remains the same, but the balances of the existing partners' capital have been reduced and replaced by the entering partner's capital.

With the admission of a new partner, the existing partners may wish to recognize goodwill. GOODWILL is an intangible asset that places a value on a business's reputation, the owners' managerial skills, or other inherent factors that generate a greater return than other firms in a similar industry obtain. Since goodwill is only attributable to the existing partners, their respective capital accounts are increased to the extent of the goodwill recognized.

The adjustment to recognize goodwill comes about by comparing the net value of the old partnership's assets ($130,000) to the current replacement costs of the existing assets. If we assume, continuing with the above illustration, that the adjusted value of the net assets is $140,000, the old partnership may wish to recognize goodwill to the extent of $10,000 ($140,000–$130,000). The entry to recognize this goodwill as a result of the admission of a new partner would be:

```
200-
Nov. 22   Goodwill                            10,000
              Davis, Capital                             5,000
              Graff, Capital                             5,000
          To recognize goodwill.
```

If the admission of the new partner has a substantial impact on the earning capacity of the existing partnership, and the existing partners are anxious for the new partner to come on board, they may agree to recognize the goodwill of the incoming partner. If this is the case, goodwill is debited for an agreed-upon amount, and a corresponding credit is made to the incoming partner's capital account. This entry is part of the compound entry that recognizes the incoming partner's contributions to the partnership.

Withdrawal of a Partner

The withdrawal of a partner will also bring about a dissolution. Whether this withdrawal is a result of retirement or some other reason, the interest of the outgoing partner may be purchased by one or more of the remaining partners. The only effect of this action is that the capital of the outgoing partner is transferred to the partner(s) who have purchased the interest. Any profit or loss recognition is considered by the partners as individuals and has no effect on the partnership books. If the business (partnership) buys out the retiring partner, then the entire settlement would be reflected on the partnership books.

The untimely death of a partner will have the same effect the withdrawal had. Any profits earned by the deceased partner up to his death are credited to his capital account. Assuming that the partnership is to continue with the remaining partners, negotiations will take place with the decedent's estate to settle the capital balance of the deceased as if he or she had withdrawn from the partnership. It is advisable to include in the articles of partnership a provision for handling the distribution in the event of the death of a partner. In general, the surviving spouse or relatives have no right to step into the shoes of the deceased, unless it is specifically provided for in the articles of partnership.

LIQUIDATION OF A PARTNERSHIP

The term LIQUIDATION specifically refers to the payment of liabilities. In dealing with a partnership it refers to the process of winding up the activities of the business, including:

1. The conversion of all assets to cash.
2. The distribution of any gains or losses to the partners resulting from the conversion of the assets.
3. The payment of all liabilities.
4. The distribution of the remaining cash to the individual partners based on their respective capital balances.

The conversion through sale of all the noncash assets is generally referred to as a REALIZATION. An account entitled "Loss and Gain on Realization" is established on the books to recognize the difference between the book value of the asset sold and the amount of cash received from its sale. If a current asset such as supplies, with a book value of $250, was sold for $219, the following entry would reflect this liquidation and realization:

200-			
Oct. 3	Cash	219	
	Loss and Gain on Realization	31	
	Supplies		250

If the plant asset equipment was sold for $9,500, the following entry would be made based on an original cost of $30,000, with accumulated depreciation of $22,000 (as of 12/31):

200-

Oct. 3	Depreciation Expense—Equipment	750	
	Accumulated Depreciation—		
	Equipment		750
	To recognize depreciation up to the date of sale.		
3	Cash	9,500	
	Accumulated Depreciation—Equipment	22,750	
	Loss and Gain on Realization		2,250
	Equipment		30,000
	To recognize gain on realization.		

Note that the depreciation expense is recognized from the beginning of the year until the date of disposal. Since the cash received from the sale of the plant asset exceeded the book value of the asset, the loss and gain on realization account was credited.

After all noncash assets are sold and their gain or loss recorded to the loss and gain on realization account, this account is then closed to the respective partner's capital accounts *based on their profit and loss sharing ratios.*

From the above illustrations, the balance in the loss and gain on realization account is a credit balance of $2,219. This balance represents a gain or profit that is added to the respective partner's capital balances. The following entry closes the loss and gain on realization account to the partners' capital accounts (assuming equal distribution according to their profit and loss sharing ratio):

200-

Oct. 3	Loss and Gain on Realization	2,219.00	
	Albert, Capital		1,109.50
	Brown, Capital		1,109.50
	To close to capital accounts.		

If the resulting balance had been a debit balance to the loss and gain on realization account (which is usually the case) the partners' capital accounts would have been debited for their share of the loss.

Following the conversion of all the noncash assets to cash and the distribution of the gain or loss to the respective partnership capital accounts, the remaining cash available is first used to pay all outstanding liabilities of the partnership. Assuming that there is adequate cash available to pay the creditors, any excess cash then goes to liquidate the capital balances of the various partners.

Liquidating Partnership Deficits

The above illustrations and narrative have assumed that there was adequate capital balances in each of the partner's accounts to absorb any loss resulting from the conversion of the assets. There may be situations where the capital balance of a partner is inadequate to absorb his or her share of the loss. When this occurs, a deficit occurs that must be paid by the remaining partners. The other partners share in the deficit according to their profit and loss sharing ratio to each other. Thus, if three partners share profits equally (33 1/3% each), and two of the partners must absorb the third partner's deficit, the ratio of the solvent partners would be 33 1/3 to 33 1/3 or equally. The following example illustrates how one partner's deficit is absorbed by the remaining partners:

EXAMPLE Lane, Montz, and Nurko have the following capital balances respectively: $25,000; $15,000; and $5,000. The assets are in the following form: cash, $15,000; noncash assets, $35,000; and liabilities, $5,000. Their respective profit and loss sharing ratio is 40% : 30% : 30%. All the noncash assets are sold and the cash received from the sale amounts to $12,000.

The conversion of the noncash assets resulted in a loss on realization of $23,000 ($35,000–$12,000). The distribution of this loss to the respective partner's capital balances is as follows:

	Lane	Montz	Nurko
Capital Balance	$25,000	$15,000	$5,000
Loss Distribution	9,200	6,900	6,900
Resulting Balances	15,800	8,100	−1,900

Nurko's deficiency will have to be absorbed by Lane and Montz according to their profit and loss sharing ratio to each other. The ratio is 40% : 30% or 4/7 of the deficiency would be absorbed by Lane and 3/7 of the deficiency would be absorbed by Montz. Lane's capital will be reduced by $1,085.71 ($1,900 × 4/7). Montz's capital will be reduced by $814.29 ($1,900 × 3/7). The remaining cash is first used to pay the obligations to creditors and the balance in cash is then used to liquidate the Lane and Montz capital balances. The following entries are recorded for the liquidation and realization:

200-

Sept. 25	Cash	12,000.00	
	Loss and Gain on Realization	23,000.00	
	Non-Cash Assets		35,000.00
	To record sale of non-cash assets.		
25	Lane, Capital	9,200.00	
	Montz, Capital	6,900.00	
	Nurko, Capital	6,900.00	
	Loss and Gain on Realization		23,000.00
	To distribute loss on disposal.		
25	Lane, Capital	1,085.71	
	Montz, Capital	814.29	
	Nurko, Capital		1,900.00
	For Nurko's deficiency.		
25	Accounts Payable	5,000.00	
	Cash		5,000.00
	To pay creditors.		

200-

Sept. 25	Lane, Capital	14,714.29	
	Montz, Capital	7,285.71	
	Cash		22,000.00
	To liquidate capital balance.		

Note the Lane and Montz paid Nurko's deficit. Nurko now is obligated to Lane and Montz to the extent of the deficiency that each absorbed. If Nurko was to pay his deficit of $1,900.00, Lane would be entitled to $1,085.71 and Montz would get $814.29.

EXERCISE 3 The partnership of Roth, Stern, and Tom has respective capital balances of $20,000, $25,000, and $24,000. The assets of the partnership as of June 15 are: cash, $12,000; other assets, $60,000; and accounts payable, $3,000. All noncash assets are sold for $15,000. The profit and loss ratio is 2 : 1 : 1. Record the necessary general journal entries for the liquidation and realization as follows:

1. Recognize the sale of the noncash assets.
2. Distribute the loss or gain on realization to the partners' respective capital accounts.
3. Pay the creditors.
4. Distribute the remaining cash to the partners. (If there is a capital deficit, it must be shared by the remaining partners before the distribution of cash.)

EXERCISE 4 Evan, Felding, and Glickson share profits and losses in the ratio of 3 : 3 : 4. Their respective capital balances at the date of liquidation are: $12,000, $15,000, and $18,000. The firm's liabilities amount to $20,000. The cash in the firm's checking account is $44,000 and noncash assets amount to $21,000. The sale of the noncash assets generates cash of $11,000. Record the necessary transactions for the liquidation and realization.

THE PARTNERSHIP DRAWING ACCOUNT

The drawing account, whether in a sole proprietorship or a partnership, is merely an account that the individual borrows from in anticipation of profit. As such, the amount of cash and other assets in the drawing account will not necessarily have any relationship to the eventual profit earned by the individual. If the balance in the drawing account at the end of the accounting period is a debit balance of $10,000, but the profits recognized by the partner are only $8,000, then the excess withdrawn by the partner results in a reduction in that partner's capital balance. If the profits earned exceed the drawing, then the excess will be added to the capital account of the partner. When the articles of partnership make provisions for salary allowances and interest on the partners' capital balances, these amounts, whether or not withdrawn by the respective partners, represent earnings to them that are subtracted from the net income before the distribution of the income takes place.

The following example highlights the use of the partners' drawing account and the distribution of net income according to the profit and loss sharing ratio.

EXAMPLE   The partnership of Christen, Roth, and Zimmerman share in the partnership profits in the following ratio: 2:2:3. Their respective capital balances are $20,000, $20,000, and $40,000. Each is entitled to interest on their capital balances equal to 5%, and their respective salary allowances are: $10,000, $6,000, and $6,000. The net income earned by the partnership amounts to $30,000. During the year each partner withdrew from the business the following amounts respectively: $13,000, $5,500, and $9,500. First, we determine the total earnings that each partner is entitled to:

Christen: Salary Allowance =	$10,000	
Interest on Capital Balance =	1,000	$11,000
Roth: Salary Allowance =	$6,000	
Interest on Capital Balance =	1,000	7,000
Zimmerman: Salary Allowance =	$6,000	
Interest on Capital Balance =	2,000	8,000
Total prior to distribution according to profit and loss sharing ratio		$26,000

Distribution According to P&L Sharing Ratio

Net Income	$30,000
Prior Distribution as per Articles	(26,000)
Distribution According to P&L Sharing Ratio	$ 4,000
Christen: 2/7 × $4,000 = $1,142.86	
Roth: 2/7 × $4,000 = 1,142.86	
Zimmerman: 3/7 × $4,000 = 1,714.28	

Total Profit Earned by Each Partner	Drawing
Christen: $11,000 + $1,142.86 = $12,142.86	$13,000.00
Roth: $ 7,000 + $1,142.86 = $ 8,142.86	$ 5,500.00
Zimmerman: $ 8,000 + $1,714.28 = $ 9,714.28	$ 9,500.00

The entry to transfer the income earned to the respective partner's capital accounts would be as follows:

200-

Dec. 31	Income Summary	30,000.00	
	Christen, Capital		12,142.86
	Roth, Capital		8,142.86
	Zimmerman, Capital		9,714.28
	To transfer profit to capital.		

The entries to close the respective drawing accounts to capital would be as follows:

200-
Dec. 31   Christen, Capital   13,000.00
          Roth, Capital   5,500.00
          Zimmerman, Capital   9,500.00
                Christen, Drawing   13,000.00
                Roth, Drawing   5,500.00
                Zimmerman, Drawing   9,500.00
          To close drawing to capital.

As a result of closing the drawing account and the income summary accounts to capital, the following new capital balances appear for each partner:

Christen, Capital $19,142.86
Roth, Capital   22,642.86
Zimmerman, Capital   40,214.28

Since Christen's drawing exceeded the share of income, the net result was a reduction in the capital balance from $20,000 to $19,142.86. In the case of Roth and Zimmerman, their respective income exceeded their drawing so that their new capital balances reflected the increase in capital.

EXERCISE 5   The capital balances of Tinker and Chance are $32,500 and $50,000, respectively, at the beginning of the accounting period. During the year Tinker invests an additional $5,000, and the partners withdraw $9,500 and $15,200, respectively. The profit and loss sharing ratio is 3:2. The income earned by the partnership amounts to $30,000. Record in general journal form the entries:

1. The additional investment by Tinker.
2. The distribution of the net income to the partners.
3. The closing of the respective drawing accounts.

Find the new balances in the individual partner's accounts.

Financial Statements for a Partnership

The three financial statements discussed in Chapter 2 apply not only to a sole proprietorship form of business organization, but to a partnership as well.

The income statement for a partnership is prepared in the same manner as those illustrated for a sole proprietorship in Chapter 2 and Chapter 5 and will not be illustrated here.

While the statement of capital is also similar, the accountant must show changes in capital for each partner of the partnership. The following statement of capital represents the example presented on page 218.

Christen, Roth, and Zimmerman
Statement of Capital
For the Year Ended December 31, 200-

	Christen	Roth	Zimmerman
Partnership Capital, Jan. 1, 200-	$20,000.00	$20,000.00	$40,000.00
Net Income for the Year	12,142.86	8,142.86	9,714.28
Less: Partner's Drawing	13,000.00	5,500.00	9,500.00
Net Increase (Decrease) in Capital	(857.14)	2,642.86	214.28
Partnership Capital, Dec. 31, 200-	$19,142.86	$22,642.86	$40,214.28

The balance sheet for a partnership would contain the capital balances for each partner as determined on the statement of capital. The partnership balance sheet is identical to those previously illustrated for the sole proprietorship except for the inclusion of the individual partner's capital balances. The partnership balance sheet for Christen, Roth, and Zimmerman follows:

Christen, Roth, and Zimmerman
Balance Sheet
December 31, 200-

Assets			**Liabilities and Capital**		
Cash		$31,000.00	Accounts Payable		$15,000.00
Accounts Receivable		13,250.00	Christen, Capital	$19,142.86	
Delivery Equipment	$42,000.00		Roth, Capital	22,642.86	
Less: Accum. Depr.	18,750.00	21,250.00	Zimmerman, Capital	40,214.28	
Plant Equipment	35,000.00		Total Capital		81,999.00
Less: Accum. Depr.	3,501.00	31,499.00	Total Liabilities		
Total Assets		$96,999.00	and Capital		$96,999.00

Summing Up

The form of business organization in which two or more persons operate as co-owners for profit is a PARTNERSHIP. The advantages of this form of business are as follows:

1. More investment capital is available through the formation of the partnership.
2. The various skills of the partners are available to the organization.
3. The partnership is more easily formed than a corporate form of business.

While the partnership agreement may be written or oral, a written form, known as the articles of partnership, is preferred. The articles of partnership should include:

1. The date of formation and the names of the partners.
2. A statement of the kind of business that is being operated by the partnership.

3. The investment made by each partner and their respective capital balances, as well as their share in the profits and losses in the business.
4. The duties and responsibilities of each partner and any limitations on their activities.
5. The provisions made for salary allowances and interest on the partners' respective investments.
6. Provisions in the event of a dissolution caused by the death, withdrawal, or admission of a partner.

The formation of a partnership requires the contribution of assets to the business by the various partners. The value assigned to the assets contributed is based on negotiation among the partners. The assets become the property of the partnership, and each contributing partner has a claim based on the value of the capital balance, and not against the specific assets contributed. Each partner, in addition to having a capital account, is also provided with a drawing account that is handled in a similar fashion to that of the sole proprietor's. During the accounting period, funds and other assets taken by the individual partners are charged to the drawing account. At the end of the year, when the partners' share of the business's profits are determined, their respective capital accounts are credited (debited in the case of a loss distribution), and the individual drawing accounts are closed to their capital accounts. If the total drawing exceeds a partner's share of the partnership's profits, the resulting difference causes a decrease in that partner's capital balance. An excess of income over drawing will cause an increase in the partner's capital balance. The partnership does not file an income tax return, but merely an information return that indicates the share of profits distributed to each partner. As in the case of a sole proprietorship, the profits of the partnership are the income of the individual partners, which is subject to income tax whether or not the total income was withdrawn from the business.

A dissolution of a partnership may also result in a winding-up of the partnership. This process is known as a liquidation and realization. The procedures for winding up the partnership are as follows:

1. The assets are sold.
2. Any gains or losses resulting from the sale of the assets are reflected in the respective capital accounts according to the profit and loss sharing ratio.
3. Liabilities owed to creditors are paid.
4. The remaining cash is distributed to the partners according to their respective capital balances.

A capital deficiency by one partner has to be absorbed by the remaining partners based on their profit and loss sharing ratio to each other. This deficit becomes a liability of the deficient partner to the partners that picked up the deficit.

CHAPTER 13

CORPORATE ACCOUNTING

The Corporate Business Organization

Throughout this book financial accounting has been presented primarily from the view of a sole proprietorship. We have seen how a partnership form of business organization differs from the sole proprietorship, that difference being in the area of capital recognition and distribution of earnings. A third form of business organization is the corporation. A CORPORATION has been defined as "an artificial being, invisible, intangible, and existing only in contemplation of the law." Prior discussions have referred to the fact that certain forms of "personal service" businesses are prohibited from adopting the corporate form of organization and thus organize as either a sole proprietorship or a partnership. The reason for this prohibition relates to the fact that there are limitations placed on the liability of the owners of a corporation. This aspect will be discussed in greater detail shortly.

A corporation is a legal entity separate from its owners. A sole proprietorship and a partnership are relatively unstable, and a partnership has a limited life due to the dissolution that results from the death or retirement of a partner or the change in composition of the partnership.

The primary difference in accounting for a corporation is in the area of the capital of the organization. The capital section on the balance sheet of a corporation is known as STOCKHOLDERS' EQUITY. Stockholders' equity represents the ownership of the assets of the corporation as evidenced by transferable shares of stock. The owners of the corporation are called STOCKHOLDERS or SHAREHOLDERS. A corporation is said to have an UNLIMITED LIFE due to the fact that the ownership in the corporation is in the form of shares of stock, which are easily transferable; thus, the death of a stockholder has no effect on the continuance of the business organization. While the stockholders are the owners of the corporation, they have no direct duties or responsibilities in the running of the organization. This activity is the responsibility of a BOARD OF DIRECTORS who are elected to their positions by the stockholders. The directors then select a president and other corporate officers to carry on active management of the business.

With the exception of "personal service" businesses, practically any form of business may choose to organize as a corporation. Corporations may be classified as PROFIT CORPORATIONS or NOT-

FOR-PROFIT CORPORATIONS. A profit corporation engages in business activities and depends upon profitable operations in order to continue in existence. A not-for-profit corporation includes charitable, governmental, philanthropic, educational, and recreational organizations that depend upon contributions from their members or upon gifts or grants from public and private sources.

Profit corporations may be further classified as public corporations or close corporations. A PUBLIC CORPORATION is a profit corporation whose ownership is widely held by the public, such as the American Telephone and Telegraph corporation. A CLOSE CORPORATION is a profit corporation in which the stock is held by relatively few individuals, such as the immediate family of an individual or group of individuals who organized and operate the corporation. With the exceptions previously noted, corporations may consist of service businesses, retail businesses, manufacturing businesses, and wholesale businesses. Practically any form of business may organize as a corporation. Regardless of the nature or purpose of the corporations, they are created in accordance with state statutes.

ADVANTAGES OF THE CORPORATE FORM

There are a number of advantages offered by the corporate form of organization that are not available to other business forms. These advantages are as follows:

1. CAPITAL ACCUMULATION is virtually unlimited based on the ability to sell shares of ownership in the business. Some corporations may have more than a million stockholders. By selling stock to the general public, the necessary capital can be raised to organize and subsequently operate the business. This permits small and large investors to participate in the ownership of a business enterprise and earn income in the form of dividends.
2. A corporation is said to have a SEPARATE LEGAL EXISTENCE. This separate legal existence permits the corporation to acquire, own, and dispose of assets in its corporate name. It may also incur liabilities and enter into contracts in its own name.
3. The shareholders have a LIMITED LIABILITY in the corporation. Stockholders can only be held liable for the debts of the corporation to the extent of their investment in the shares of stock of the corporation. Creditors of a corporation may look to the corporation to settle these obligations, but not to the stockholders beyond the extent of their investment. If employees of the corporation are owed wages, however, these wage payments are the responsibility of the shareholders and they can be assessed a pro-rata share of this obligation. As we will shortly discuss, if a stockholder has purchased shares of stock at a cost less than their stated value, the stockholder's liability may extend to the stated value nevertheless.
4. NEGOTIABILITY OF STOCK enables the stock to be easily transferred by sale. Thus, an individual who wishes to invest or divest himself of stock may readily do so. This process in no way interferes with the operation of the corporation.

5. Since a corporation is a separate legal entity and does not rely on its owners for its management or operation, it is said to have a CONTINUOUS EXISTENCE. A corporation is not obligated to buy back stock previously sold to shareholders. This stock may be traded among investors, but this will have no effect on the existence of the corporation.

6. The ORGANIZATIONAL STRUCTURE of the corporation controls the operation of the organization. The day-to-day activities of the business are run by the president, officers, and employees of the corporation. The board of directors oversees this operation, and there is no direct input into the functioning of the business by the stockholders. The shareholders' only input comes as a result of the exercise of their voting rights in the election of the board.

7. A PROFESSIONAL MANAGEMENT STAFF is used to run the corporation. This staff is comprised of those individuals who are best suited to carry out the functions of management, without considering their ownership in the corporation as a criterion for selection.

DISADVANTAGES OF THE CORPORATE FORM

There are a number of disadvantages to the corporate form of business organization, which may either prevent its formation or cause its untimely demise. The disadvantages of a corporate form of organization are as follows:

1. The difficulty in organizing a corporation may prevent the use of this form of business. The corporation, an artificial being, must obtain permission from the state to incorporate. It must also comply with guidelines established by various federal agencies. The mere nature of the planned business (certain service businesses) may prevent its organization as a corporation. The cost of organizing is also prohibitive. Many smaller businesses choose to form as sole proprietorships or partnerships to avoid the high cost and difficulties of organizing as a corporation.

2. Governmental regulations are a part of the creation and subsequent operation of the corporation. State and federal laws regulate corporate activities. Large corporations are generally required to disclose financial statements on an annual basis. Corporate annual reports are prepared and distributed to shareholders and other interested parties. Restrictions may exist as to the ownership of certain assets such as real estate, a corporation's retention of earnings, and its ability to purchase its own stock.

3. The separation of ownership from management was previously listed as an advantage; however, separation of ownership and control can also be a disadvantage if management chooses to operate the corporation for its exclusive benefit, to the detriment of the stockholders. The separation of the board from the executives of a corporation may prevent this from occurring; however, if it does occur, the stockholders' only recourse is to bring pressure against the board by exercising their voting rights.

4. A corporation usually pays a high rate of taxation on its income. Income distributed in the form of a dividend to the corporate stockholder comes from after-tax dollars and results in a situation known as DOUBLE TAXATION. Double taxation results from the practice of first taxing corporate income to the corporation and then taxing shareholders on any dividends they receive from the corporation. Federal legislation in 2003 is considering the elimination of taxation of dividends to shareholders.

Forming the Corporation

An application signed by at least three INCORPORATORS is submitted to the state's Secretary of State (or other designated state official). The application includes the ARTICLES OF INCORPORATION. The articles become the company CHARTER, under which the corporation is empowered to conduct business in that particular state, as well as any other states. A business need not be incorporated within the state in which it actually does business, but it must comply with the guidelines for incorporation in the state that issues its charter. The incorporators are those individuals who organize and bring the corporation into existence. They also become the initial and, in most cases, the primary stockholders in the newly formed corporation. As stockholders, they elect the directors of the corporation, who in turn appoint the corporate officers. Stock certificates are issued to the incorporators and other investors, completing the formation of the corporation.

One disadvantage to the formation of the corporation is the ORGANIZATIONAL COSTS. Organizational costs include the incorporation fee to the state, attorneys' fees for preparing the articles of incorporation, and various other fees necessary to bring the organization into existence. These costs are set up on the books of the corporation as an intangible asset, and are amortized over a period of not less than five years.

RIGHTS OF THE STOCKHOLDERS

The rights that stockholders have may vary according to the class of stock they own. The ownership of stock usually carries the following rights:

1. To vote for the directors of the corporation, and to approve major changes in the corporation that are beyond the express authority given the directors in the corporate charter.
2. To maintain their percentage ownership in the corporation, which are known as PREEMPTIVE RIGHTS. When additional stock is sold by a corporation, existing stockholders have the first right to purchase shares so that their percentage ownership of the corporation remains the same. If a shareholder fails to exercise this right, it is lost. This does not prevent the stockholder from buying shares in excess of his preemptive rights.

3. To share in the corporation's distribution of income (dividends). DIVIDENDS are a distribution of profits to the stockholders as a result of their declaration by the board of directors.
4. In the event of a liquidation, the stockholders are entitled to share in the distribution of assets. The winding-up process first results in the payment of all obligations to creditors. Any assets remaining are distributed on a pro-rata basis to the various classes of stockholders.

Unlike the previous form of business discussed, owners of a corporation do not participate in the running of the firm. Their activity is limited to attending stockholders's meetings, usually held annually, and voting for directors. Shareholders do not have direct claims against either the earnings or the assets of a corporation. The issuance of dividends is solely at the discretion of the board of directors. There are additional rights given to stockholders of certain classes of stock, which will be discussed below.

CORPORATE DIRECTORS AND OFFICERS

The board of directors oversees the operation of the corporation. Two main concerns are the welfare of the corporation and the protection of the interests of the stockholders. The general policy of larger corporations is that board members are prohibited from becoming officers of the corporation while they are on the board. By preventing a board member from "wearing two hats," the possibility of a conflict of interest is minimized. The extent of board participation in corporate activities varies greatly from one firm to another. Greater participation may be encouraged by some firms because board members have a view of the organization of that of active management.

The responsibilities of the corporate officers vary based on their specific job functions. Corporate officers consist of the president (also known as the corporate executive officer [CEO]), a controller (sometimes known as the corporate financial officer [CFO]), a treasurer, and a secretary. Another title may exist such as chief corporate counsel. There may be additional descriptive titles indicating their actual functions within the organization, such as vice president for sales or research or production or personnel. A typical organizational chart looks somewhat like a pyramid. At the very top are the stockholders followed by the board of directors, then the CEO, CFO, the other officers, and, lastly, the employees.

Corporate Capital

STOCKHOLDERS' EQUITY

The primary source of corporate capital is through the issuance of stock. The incorporators subscribe to shares of stock in the corporation. The articles of incorporation state the nature and quantities of stock to be sold by the corporation. Sufficient stock is sold to permit the business to operate. The shares of stock that the corporation is permitted to sell at the time of its incorporation and at future dates are known as AUTHORIZED shares. This is the maximum quantity of stock, of various classes, that the charter permits to be sold.

Successful operations of the business should generate profits. The profits, or income remaining, after the payment of corporate income taxes, may be retained in the business as an additional source of capital. We have stated that a corporation pays dividends out of after-tax dollars. These dividends that are paid will reduce the amount of the earnings retained in the business. Since a corporation is not obligated to pay dividends, all of the after-tax earnings can be retained by the business as a source of capital.

The capital section of the balance sheet is generally known as the stockholders' equity. This section is quite different from that of a sole proprietorship or a partnership. All income not taken out of the other forms of businesses are transferred to the respective capital accounts. In a corporation, a distinction is made between the investment made by the stockholders and the income retained by the corporation. The following stockholders' equity section of a balance sheet of a corporation illustrates the difference:

Stockholders' Equity

Capital Stock		
Common Stock	$180,000	
Retained Earnings	40,000	
Total Stockholders' Equity		$220,000

The CAPITAL STOCK section represents the investment made by the shareholders as a result of purchasing stock. The RETAINED EARNINGS section represents the income, after corporate income tax, that was retained in the business. This retained earnings balance will continuously increase as each year's profits are retained in the business. If the corporation should sustain a loss, this loss would cause a reduction in the balance of the retained earnings account. The stockholders' equity section illustrated is in its simplest form. The Capital Stock section would have to be expanded if various classes of stock were sold or if other factors relating to the price stockholders pay for the stocks were considered.

TYPES OF STOCK

The articles of incorporation stipulate the quantity and kind of capital stock that will be sold by the firm. There are principally two kinds of stock that may be issued: (1) common stock and (2) preferred stock.

When more than one class of stock is issued, one kind is usually called COMMON STOCK. Common stock gives the stockholders the rights previously mentioned. The term "common" refers to the fact that the stock traditionally is sold at a price that can be afforded by practically all investors. It initially is sold by the corporation at a relatively low price when it is first issued. ISSUED STOCK refers to stock that is sold by the corporation and is in the hands of the shareholders. When common stock is traded on the open market, the price of the stock will vary based on supply and demand and other factors, such as the successful operation of the corporation. Common stock, as well as other classes of stock, are usually assigned an arbitrary money value that is known as PAR VALUE. This par value is printed on the stock certificate, but does not necessarily represent the price that the stock was sold for by the corporation. The actual selling price of the stock may be higher or lower than the par value. Stocks may also be issued without par, in which case it is known as NO-PAR stock. Some states require that no-par stock be assigned a STATED VALUE by the board of directors. The effect of this action is to cause a stated value stock to be similar to a par value stock in its treatment.

The second class of stock that a corporation may issue is generally known as PREFERRED STOCK. The term "preferred" indicates that there are certain advantages to owning this class of stock as compared to common. The cost to the stockholder of preferred stock is usually considerably more than the purchase price of common stock. Preferred stock also has a par or stated value assigned to it. The difference in cost between common stock and preferred stock can be seen in its par value. A corporation may assign a par value to common stock of $10 per share, while the same firm may assign a $50 par value to its preferred stock. While stockholders will not necessarily pay the par value in either case, this example indicates the substantial difference in anticipated selling prices of both kinds of stock. A corporation may offer different categories of preference stock based on the benefits that each class provides to stockholders.

ADVANTAGES OF PREFERRED STOCK

The higher cost of preferred stock is justified by its distinct advantages compared to common stock. The following advantages and characteristics should be noted when deciding which class of stock to invest in:

1. Dividends are stated as a percentage on the face of the preferred stock certificate. Dividends are distributed to all classes of preferred stock prior to distributions to common stock. If the preferred certificate indicates that it is CUMULATIVE preferred stock, this means that the corporation is obligated to pay dividends to preferred stockholders for past years prior to a distribution to common stockholders. If in past years a corporation has been unable to pay dividends, or has merely decided not to, then the arrearage for those past years, as well as current dividends, must be paid to the preferred stockholder first before a distribution can be made on common stock for the current year's dividends. If the certificate indicates that it is NONCUMULATIVE, then any dividends not paid at the end of a given year are lost. In a year in which dividends are paid there still exists preference rights for the preferred stock. The cumulative rights will obviously cause this form of preferred stock to be more costly to the investor than the noncumulative stock. Many corporations refrain from offering noncumulative stock because of the disadvantage in the possible loss of dividends.

2. A preferred stock may also have a provision for PARTICIPATION in the dividend distribution beyond the stated dividend percentage on the certificate. Participation is in the dividend to be paid to the common stock. A participating preferred stock participates dollar-for-dollar with the common stock in any dividend paid in excess of the stated rate on the preferred stock. Generally, when there are adequate funds available to pay both preferred and common dividends, the common dividend will be paid at the same rate as preferred. Any additional distribution will be shared by the common and preferred stockholders based on a ratio of the number of shares of each class of stock.

EXAMPLE   A corporation with both preferred stock and common stock declares a dividend amounting to $70,000. The preferred stock is participating and is entitled to an 8% dividend based on its par value of $100. There are 2,000 shares of preferred stock, and 5,000 shares of common stock, eligible for dividends. The distribution of dividends would be as follows:

	Preferred Dividend	Common Dividend	Total Dividend
Preferred (2,000 × $8)	$16,000	—	$16,000
Common (5,000 × $8)	—	$40,000	40,000
Pro-rata Distribution (7,000)	4,000	10,000	14,000
Total	$20,000	$50,000	$70,000
Dividends per Share	$10	$10	

The initial dividend obligation to participating preferred stock was 8% of $100 par or $8 per share. This accounted for the initial total dividend on preferred stock of $16,000. The common stock then receives a comparable distribution totaling $40,000. The balance of the dividend distribution amounted to $14,000. Total eligible preferred and common stock amounted to 7,000 shares (2,000 + 5,000). The 7,000 shares were divided into the remaining amount to be distributed ($14,000) to obtain the second distribution, amounting to $2 per share. Each class of stock then receives $2 per share times the eligible number of shares. Preferred receives $4,000 ($2 × 2,000) and common receives $10,000 ($2 × 5,000).

If, in this example, the total dividend declared had amounted to only $20,000 the preferred would have received $16,000 in dividends with the balance going to common stock, amounting to $4,000. Even though this is preferred participating stock, the preferred stock would not participate because common has not received their pro-rata share of the dividend, and so there was inadequate cash remaining for preferred and common to share. Preferred stock may be NONPARTICIPATING, in which case there is no additional dividend paid to the preferred stockholders.

3. Most preferred stock has what is known as a CALLABLE PROVISION. At the option of the issuing corporation, the preferred stock may be bought back by the corporation at a stated price,

usually above the original purchase price. The callable provision will be stated on the stock certificate. A corporation (usually when organizing) issues callable preferred stock in addition to other classes of stock. The intention in issuing the callable stock is to be able eventually to buy the stock back when profits are adequate to do so. The callable provision is exercised at the discretion of the corporation.

4. In the event of a liquidation of the corporation, the preferred stockholders are entitled to receive a distribution of the assets of the corporation following the settlement of all outstanding obligations to creditors. The preferred stockholder "stands" behind the creditors, but in front of the common stockholders in the distribution on liquidation. Preferred stockholders are entitled to payment in full of the par value of their stock, or even a higher stated liquidation value, before any payment is made to the common stockholders. Also, if the stock is cumulative preferred, any arrearage must be paid as well before paying the common stockholders.

5. Preferred stock, regardless of its class, lacks voting rights. The advantage to the corporation in issuing preferred stock is that capital can be raised without granting preferred stockholders control of the corporation through the election of the board of directors. Common stock is the only class of stock with voting rights.

6. A provision less commonly found in a preferred stock indenture is a CONVERSION CLAUSE, which permits the preferred stockholder to convert this stock into common stock. This provision makes the stock more attractive to future investors. The stock certificate indicates the conversion ratio. Should the company prosper and the value of the common stock increase, the holder of preferred stock may exercise this conversion privilege and benefit from the increased value in the company's common stock.

EXERCISE 1 The Albert Corporation has two classes of stock. Common stock of 10,000 shares with a par value of $50, and 1,000 shares of cumulative, participating 8% preferred stock, with a par value of $100. The board of directors has voted to distribute the following dividends during the next file years: year 1, $6,000; year 2, $3,500; year 3, $12,000; year 4, $30,000; and year 5, $36,000.

For each of these years, calculate the dividend distribution that the preferred stockholders and the common stockholders are entitled to. Use a chart similar to the one illustrated on page 229 for each year's distribution. Remember that the preferred stock is both participating and cumulative.

RECORDING STOCK TRANSACTIONS

The articles of incorporation set the number and classes of stock that a corporation may sell. The number of shares of stock that the charter permits to be sold are called the authorized shares. When all or part of the authorized shares are sold, these shares are said to be issued. The number of shares remaining in the hands of the stockholders are known as the OUTSTANDING shares. From time to time a corporation may, in addition to selling shares, go into the open market and buy back its own previously issued shares. When a corporation buys back its own shares, these become known as TREASURY STOCK. The difference between the number of shares issued and those outstanding represents treasury stock. When a corporation buys back its own stock, the stock loses certain rights that the traditional stockholder has. Treasury stock does not share in dividend distributions and, if the treasury stock is common, voting rights are lost as well.

Entries on the corporate books are made only when the following kinds of stock transactions take place:

1. Corporate sale of authorized stock.
2. Corporate purchase of its own stock in the open market.
3. Corporate sale of treasury stock.

Corporate Sale of Stock

When a corporation sells its authorized stock, this stock, regardless of its class, may be sold at par (stated value), above par, or below par value. Stock is sold at par when the selling price of the stock is identical with the par value.

EXAMPLE A corporation is authorized to sell 10,000 shares of $10 par common stock. It issues 1,500 shares at par. The following entry illustrates this sale:

200-
May 4   Cash   15,000
                Common Stock   15,000
            Sold 1,500 shares at par.

Even though the par or stated value of stock is an arbitrary value, new issues of stock would probably sell for these values. The price at which stock is sold is influenced by many factors, including financial conditions, potential earning power, the availability of money in the economy for investment purposes, and the general business and economic conditions. A successful corporation wishing to raise additional capital for expansion purposes may find it easier to sell additional authorized shares at a PREMIUM. When shares are sold at a premium, the amount of cash generated from the sale is in excess of the par or stated value of the stock. When this situation occurs, the following entry is recorded:

200-
May 16 Cash   115,000
                Preferred Stock (8%)   100,000
                Premium on Preferred Stock   15,000
            Sold 2,000 $50 par 8% preferred
            stock at a premium.

The excess over the par value of $15,000 would be shown on the balance sheet as an account called "Additional Paid-in Capital." The additional paid-in capital section of a balance sheet represents the excess proceeds of a stock issue over the par value of the stock.

A number of factors influence whether the stock is sold at par, above par, or below par. If the demand for the stock is not great, the corporation may be forced to offer the stock for sale at a price lower than par. When this occurs the stock is said to be sold at a DISCOUNT. In other words, when the issued price is less than the par value of the stock, it is sold at a discount. The entry to recognize this is as follows:

```
200-
May 10   Cash                                90,000
           Discount on Preferred Stock        10,000
             Preferred Stock                            100,000
           Issued 1,000 shares of 6% preferred
           stock at a discount.
```

The amount of cash generated from the sale of the shares of preferred stock is $10,000 less than the par value of the stock, thus a discount is recognized. On the capital section of the balance sheet, the preferred stock will be shown at par value ($100,000) and the discount on preferred stock will be a reduction in additional paid-in capital.

The stockholder's equity section of the balance sheet would appear as follows based on the illustrations just presented:

Stockholder's Equity

Capital Stock:

Preferred 8% stock, $50 par value, 5,000 shares authorized, and 2,000 shares issued and outstanding	$100,000	
Preferred 6% stock, $100 par value, 4,000 shares authorized, and 2,000 shares issued and outstanding	100,000	
Common stock, $10 par value, 10,000 shares authorized, and 1,500 shares issued and outstanding	15,000	$215,000

Additional Paid-in Capital:

Premium on 8% preferred stock	15,000	
Discount on 6% preferred stock	⟨10,000⟩	
Total additional paid-in capital		5,000
Total Capital Stock		220,000
Retained Earnings		45,000
Total Stockholders' Equity		$265,000

Note that the discount on preferred stock is shown as a reduction in the additional paid-in-capital section of the balance sheet, while the premium on the 8% preferred stock is shown as an addition. Subsequent sales of the various classes of stock will result in changes to this additional paid-in-capital account.

Also note that the discount on preferred stock may be shown as a reduction from shares sold at par to arrive at the book value of this class of stock. The premium received on the 8% preferred stock may be shown as an addition to arrive at the paid-in capital. Subsequent sales of the various classes of stock will result in changes to the premium and discount accounts. When this approach is used, the capital stock section is known as "Paid-in Capital" and the book value of each class of stock is readily seen.

Stockholders' Equity

Paid-in Capital:

Preferred 8% stock, $50 par (5,000 shares authorized, 2,000 shares issued)	$100,000	
Premium on preferred stock:	15,000	$115,000
Preferred 6% stock, $100 par (4,000 shares authorized, 1,000 shares issued)	$100,000	
Less discount on preferred stock	10,000	90,000
Common Stock, $10 par (10,000 shares authorized, 1,500 shares issued)		15,000
Total paid-in capital		$220,000
Retained Earnings		45,000
Total Stockholders' Equity		$265,000

EXERCISE 2   On April 3 of the current year, the Alice Walden Co. was organized. The corporate charter authorized the sale of 20,000 shares of cumulative preferred 8% stock, $100 par, and 50,000 shares of $10 par common stock. Record the following transactions in general journal form:

200-

Apr. 5   Sold 3,000 shares of common stock at par for cash.

10   Sold 2,000 shares of preferred stock at $105 per share for cash.

Aug. 4   Sold 5,000 shares of preferred stock at $99 per share for cash.

Oct. 6   Sold 2,500 shares of common stock at $12 per share for cash.

Corporate Purchase of Its Own Stock

From time to time a corporation may go into the open market and purchase its stock. The stock so acquired is known as TREASURY STOCK. Treasury stock must have been originally issued by the corporation, paid for, subsequently reacquired by the corporation, and not canceled or reissued. Treasury stock is not entitled to participate in dividend distributions, nor does it have any voting rights. Since treasury stock is not an asset in the usual sense, it is treated as a subtraction from the stockholders' equity section of the balance sheet. The entry to record the purchase of the treasury stock would be as follows:

200-
Jun. 10 Treasury Stock   7,500
                Cash   7,500
         Purchased 500 shares of common stock
         ($10 par).

The price paid for the treasury stock is set up on the books regardless of the par value. No gain or loss is recognized when the stock is purchased.

Sale of Treasury Stock

If 200 shares of treasury stock were subsequently sold, the difference between the selling price and the purchase price would be shown in an account called paid-in-capital from treasury stock. The balance in this account would either represent an increase or a decrease in the paid-in capital section of the stockholders' equity section of the balance sheet. The following entry illustrates the sale of the 200 shares of treasury stock:

200-
Sept. 5 Cash   3,400
              Paid-In Capital from
                 Treasury Stock   400
              Treasury Stock   3,000
         Sold 200 shares of treasury stock.

Each share of treasury stock had a cost assigned to it of $15. The stock was sold at $17 per share, thus, a total gain of $400 was recognized from its sale.

Corporations are not in the business of dealing or speculating in their own stock. The stock might have initially been repurchased for the purpose of distribution to the employees as part of a profit-sharing plan or some other arrangement. Remember that the benefits available to other stockholders are not available to holders of treasury stock.

Occasionally, a corporation may purchase assets and pay for them through the issuance of stock. When this sale of stock takes place, the assets are set up on the books at their cash value. If the value of the stock given is greater than the assets acquired, a discount is recorded. The same procedure is followed in recognizing a premium. The assets acquired simply take the place of the cash that would have otherwise been received as a result of a traditional sale of stock.

EXERCISE 3   Record the following transactions in general journal form:

200-
Jan. 23   Issued 3,000 shares of common stock, par value $50, for $52 per share.

      29   Sold 5,000 shares of $100 par cumulative preferred stock for $95 per share.

200-

Jan. 30 Purchased land, building, and equipment from L. Tweed. The appraised values were:

Land	$300,000
Building	125,000
Equipment	25,000

Issued 7,200 shares of common stock (with a market value of $52 per share) for the assets. Signed a 12%, 10-year note for the balance.

Remember, a premium or discount is recognized based on the market value of the stock as compared to its par value.

EXERCISE 4 A newly formed corporation, issued 10,000 shares of its common stock on August 10 of the current year for cash of $80,000 and for building and equipment with a fair market value of $40,000 and $20,000, respectively. Record the issuance of the stock in general journal form, assuming the following conditions:

1. The stock had a par value of $10 per share.
2. The stock had a par value of $15 per share.
3. The stock had a stated value of $12 per share.

EXERCISE 5 The Dismal Recreation Corporation's articles of incorporation authorizes the company to issue 500,000 shares of $5 par value common stock and 100,000 shares of $100 par value, 6% cumulative preferred stock. The company completed the following transactions on the dates indicated:

200-

Apr. 3 Sold 10,000 shares of common stock, receiving cash amounting to $60,000.

12 Issued 100,000 shares of its common stock for land which had a fair market value of $510,000.

16 Issued 1,000 shares of common stock for accounting and legal services amounting to $5,500 as organizational costs.

May 4 Sold 4,000 shares of preferred stock, receiving cash amounting to $375,000.

Record the above business transactions in general journal form providing an adequate explanation for each transaction.

EXERCISE 6 A corporation has the following classes of stock outstanding:

1. Preferred stock—$50 par value, 4% cumulative, participating, 10,000 shares authorized, issued, and outstanding.

2. Common stock—$5 par value, 150,000 shares authorized, issued, and outstanding.
3. The corporation paid dividends in each of four years as follows:
   Year 1—$15,000
   Year 2— 15,000
   Year 3— 47,000
   Year 4— 65,000

Determine the dividend distribution to each class of stock for each year. Use a form similar to that illustrated above.

Financial Statements for a Corporation

All forms of business organizations prepare financial statements at least once a year. These statements are required by the various governments (federal, state and city) for income tax purposes. Business firms, as well as other interested parties, utilize the information provided by these statements.

The income statement for a corporation is identical to that of a sole proprietorship and a partnership.

Since the ownership of a corporation is in the form of shares of stock, there is no statement of capital prepared, as previously illustrated. Income earned by a corporation and dividends paid are reflected in an account entitled "Retained Earnings." It becomes necessary for a corporation to prepare a retained earnings statement, which shows the changes in retained earnings from the beginning of the accounting period to the end of the accounting period. The following statement of retained earnings is based in part on the example on page 229. Note that the balance of retained earnings may be adjusted as a result of possible prior error corrections that may have been made to the beginning balance of retained earnings.

Typical Corporation
Statement of Retained Earnings
For the Year Ended December 31, 200-

Retained Earnings, January 1, 200-		$135,000
Net Income for 200-	$93,500	
Less: Dividends Paid for 200-	70,000	
Net Increase in Retained Earnings		23,500
Retained Earnings, December 31, 200-		$158,500

The balance sheet for a corporation contains a stockholders' equity section rather than a capital section as a sole proprietorship and partnership balance sheet. This section consists of basically two subdivisions, "Capital Stock" and "Retained Earnings." The following represents an expanded corporate balance sheet, including the stockholders' equity section as found on page 227.

Illustrative Corporation
Balance Sheet
December 31, 200-

Assets			Liabilities and Stockholder's Equity		
Cash		$70,000	Liabilities		
Accounts Receivable		35,000	Accounts Payable	$12,000	
Merchandise Inventory		50,000	Notes Payable	38,000	
Equipment	$120,000		Total Liabilities		$50,000
Less: Accum.			Stockholders' Equity		
Depreciation	15,000	105,000	Common Stock	$180,000	
Intangible Assets		10,000	Retained Earnings	40,000	
			Total Stockholders' Equity		220,000
Total Assets		$270,000	Total Liabilities and Stockholders' Equity		$270,000

A more detailed stockholders' equity section of the balance sheet could also be included on the corporate balance sheet as illustrated on pages 232 and 233.

In order for the corporate accountant to be able to prepare the balance sheet, the statement of retained earnings must first be prepared to obtain the end of year retained earnings balance. The preparation of the retained earnings statement relied on information as to net income or loss from the income statement.

Summing Up

A corporation is an artificial being existing only in contemplation of the law. As such there are numerous advantages to this form of business organization, including a virtually unlimited ability to raise necessary capital, a separate legal existence that permits the acquisition and disposal of assets in the corporate name, limited liability for the stockholders to the extent of their investments in the organization, negotiability of stock, unlimited life that is not affected by changes in corporate ownership, and a professional management staff separate from the owners.

The disadvantages of this form of business organization include: the cost and difficulty of organizing the corporation; governmental regulation of the creation of the corporation, issuance of stock, and operations of the organization; the separation of ownership and control of the firm; and the higher rate of taxation on the corporation.

The formation of the corporation requires the incorporators to file articles of incorporation with the state where it's located. The articles of incorporation stipulate the nature of the business and the number and kinds of shares of stock to be sold.

At the top of the organizational structure of the corporation are the stockholders, who elect the board of directors to oversee the operations of the organization. The board, in turn, appoints a president and other executive officers, who are responsible for the day-to-day operations of the corporation.

Stockholders have certain rights that are unique to this form of business organization. Their rights include voting rights, preemptive rights, the right to receive a distribution of earnings of the corporation in the form of dividends, and a right to receive a pro-rata share of the assets in the event of a liquidation.

Capital is raised through the sale of the various classes of stock that the corporation is authorized to sell. Regardless of the class of stock sold, any funds received from their sale in excess of the par or stated value is recognized as a premium and is recorded as an addition to the paid-in capital section of the balance sheet. If the stock is sold for less than the par or stated value, the deficiency is recorded as a discount, which is a reduction in paid-in capital. The number of shares of a particular class of stock that may be sold is said to be "authorized," and stock that is actually sold is said to be "issued." Treasury stock acquired by the corporation is reduced from the stock originally issued and the net stock remaining in the hands of the stockholders is said to be "outstanding."

There are generally two classes of stock that a corporation may issue: common stock and preferred stock. The arbitrary par value assigned to the two classes of stock is usually considerably higher for preferred stock because of the preference features of the stock. While preferred stock does not have voting rights, it may be participating and cumulative with regard to dividends. Also, the stock certificate indicates the dividend obligation of the corporation on its face. This obligation may be expressed as a dollar amount per share or a percentage of par or stated value. In the event of a corporate liquidation, the preferred stockholders are entitled to any dividend in arrears, and to a return of their investments before common stockholders are paid. Preferred stockholders receive these distributions after all creditors have been paid, but before any distributions are made to the common stockholders. Of the two classes of stock, the common stock has a considerably greater number of shares authorized. This is due to the fact that the common stock reaches a greater market of investors because of its relatively low par value as compared to the preferred stock.

The accounting records maintained for a corporate form of business organization are primarily the same as those for a sole proprietorship and a partnership, except for the capital accounts. The accountant must maintain accurate, detailed records as to the various classes of stock, each stockholder's number of shares, the total shares issued, reacquired treasury stock, and any other factors affecting the stockholders' equity section of the balance sheet.

EXERCISE SOLUTIONS

CHAPTER 1

Exercise 1

Item	Yes	No
Cash	X	
Automobile	X	
Rented Apartment		X
Checks	X	
Computer	X	
Library Book On Loan		X
Clothing	X	
Postage Stamps	X	
Grocery List		X
Food	X	

The rented apartment and the library book on loan are not assets because the requirement of ownership is lacking. The grocery list is not an asset because the requirement of money value is lacking.

Exercise 2

Personal assets may include: cash, coins, currency, checks, money orders, clothing, jewelry, real estate (land and/or building), obligations owed to you (accounts and notes receivable), supplies (stationery, writing instruments, cleaning supplies, and toiletries), equipment, automobile, tools, and other personal assets.

Exercise 3

Business assets may include: cash, coins, currency, checks, money orders, accounts receivable, investments, marketable securities, notes receivable, land, building, patents, goodwill (intangibles), equipment, office supplies, delivery equipment, store supplies, machinery, furniture and fixtures, and leased property.

Exercise 4

Cash	Office Supplies	Furniture and Fixtures	Office Equipment	Delivery Equipment
traveler's checks	pencils	tables	typewriter	truck
coins	software programs	lamp	adding machines	automobiles
money in bank	stationery	chairs	computer	
currency	wrapping paper	desk	computer printer	
	toner cartridge	showcases		
	light bulbs			
	pens			

1. Supplies represent assets that are expected to be used up within a relatively short period of time (less than one year). Equipment usually has a useful life in excess of one year.
2. As a supply, a toner cartridge is expected to be used up in less than one year.
3. No, a typewriter ribbon is a supply and as such it has a relatively short useful life. The extent of its use determines how quickly it will be replaced. The typewriter is classified as equipment, and its useful life far exceeds that of the typewriter ribbon.
4. A short-life asset that is expected to be used up or converted to cash in less than a year.
5. A typewriter is a long-life asset with an expected useful life in excess of one year.

Exercise 5

Current Assets	Investments	Plant Assets	Intangible Assets
cash in bank	First National City bonds	office equipment	patents
accounts receivable	mortgaged notes receivable	building	goodwill
office supplies		office machines	
notes receivable		furniture & fixtures	
petty cash		store equipment	
factory supplies			
merchandise			

Exercise 6

1. The cost assigned to the asset is $35,831. This cost is determined based on the "cost principle." The cost assigned to an asset includes the purchase price, transportation costs, and installation costs, as well as any other costs necessary to place the asset in use.
2. The new automobile is recorded at the cost of $35,831 regardless of the offer made for it.
3. Although the business is owned by the proprietor, his rights to the assets only extend to the dollar value of his investment. The asset automobile belongs to the business; it is not the proprietor's personal asset.

Exercise 7

The cost principle still applies. The asset is recorded on the books of his business at $150,000.

Exercise 8

1. The value of the assets contributed by Ms. Taylor is equal to the capital, that is, $6,075.

2. Her ownership is $6,075.

Exercise 9

	Assets					=	Capital
No.	Cash	+	Supplies	+	Equipment	=	Capital
1	+ $5,000						+ $5,000
2					+ $250		+ 250
3	− 200						− 200
4	− 75		+75				
5	− 50				+ 50		
	$4,675	+	$75	+	$300	=	$5,050

Exercise 10

No.	Cash	+	Accounts Receivable	+	Store Supplies	+	Office Supplies	+	Furniture & Fixtures	+	Equipment	=	Capital
1	+ $20,000												+ $20,000
2	− 1,200								+ $1,200				
3	− 170				+ $170								
4	− 1,500										+ $1,500		
5	− 750		+ $750										
6							+ $60						+ 60
7	+ 300		− 300										
8	− 900								− 100				− 1,000
9	+ 175										− 175		
10	− 65						+ 65						
	$15,890	+	$450	+	$170	+	$125	+	$1,100	+	$1,325	=	$19,060

Exercise 11

No.	Assets	=	Liabilities	+	Capital
1					$4,000
2			$3,200		
3	$8,150				
4					$10,065
5			0		

Exercise 12

	Cash	+	Accounts Receivable	+	Supplies	+	Equipment	=	Accounts Payable	+	A. L. Brandon, Capital
Jan. 1 Balance	$2,000	+	$400	+	$500	+	$6,000	=	$ 900	+	$8,000
1	− 300								− 300		
	1,700	+	400	+	500	+	6,000	=	600	+	8,000
2	+ 100		− 100								
	1,800	+	300	+	500	+	6,000	=	600	+	8,000
3					+ 250				+ 250		
	1,800	+	300	+	750	+	6,000	=	850	+	8,000
4	+ 1,200						− 1,200				
	3,000	+	300	+	750	+	4,800	=	850	+	8,000
5	+ 1,000								+ 1,000		
	4,000	+	300	+	750	+	4,800	=	1,850	+	8,000
6	− 200								− 200		
	3,800	+	300	+	750	+	4,800	=	1,650	+	8,000
7	− 200						+ 800		+ 600		
	3,600	+	300	+	750	+	5,600	=	2,250	+	8,000
8	− 65				+ 65						
	3,535	+	300	+	815	+	5,600	=	2,250	+	8,000
9	+ 250		− 250								
	$3,785	+	$ 50	+	$815	+	$5,600	=	$2,250	+	$8,000

Exercise 13

No.	Cash	+	Accounts Receivable	+	Office Supplies	+	Law Library	=	Accounts Payable	+	C. Goldstein, Capital	−	C. Goldstein Drawing	+	Income from Services	−	Rent Expense	−	Utilities Expense
1	+ $3,000										+ $3,000								
2	− 1,200						+ $1,200	=											
	1,800						1,200				3,000								
3	+ 500							=							+ $ 500				
	2,300						1,200				3,000				500				
4					+ $150			=	+ $150										
	2,300				150		1,200		150		3,000				500				
5	− 300							=									− $300		
	2,000				150		1,200		150		3,000				500		− 300		
6			+ $1,100					=							+ 1,100				
	2,000		1,100		150		1,200		150		3,000				1,600		− 300		
7	− 50							=	− 50										
	1,950		1,100		150		1,200		100		3,000				1,600		− 300		
8	+ 200		− 200					=											
	2,150		900		150		1,200		100		3,000				1,600		− 300		
9	− 60							=											− $60
	2,090		900		150		1,200	=	100		3,000				1,600		− 300		− 60
10	− 200												− $200						
	$1,890	+	$ 900		$150	+	$1,200		$100	+	$3,000		− $200	+	$1,600		− $300		− $60

CHAPTER 2 SOLUTIONS   243

CHAPTER 2

Exercise 1

1. For the year ended Dec. 31 200-. This means the statements reflect Jan. 1–Dec. 31 of that year.
2. The source of the revenue is from limousine rentals.
3. The total revenue is $24,000.
4. The total expense is $19,850 consisting of:

Repairs expense	$ 2,350
Salaries expense	$14,500
Gas and oil expense	$ 3,000

5. A net income results when total revenues ($24,000) are greater than total expenses ($19,850). The excess of revenue over expenses ($4,150) is the net income.
6. This statement is *not* an interim statement because it covers an entire accounting period. If it was for a period of less than one year, it would then be considered an interim statement.
7. The net income belongs to Regal. We have been assuming a sole proprietorship form of business. Thus, the income of the business belongs to the owner.

Exercise 2

New Wave Beauty Parlor
Income Statement
For the Month Ended January 31, 200-

Revenue:		
Revenue from Sales	$1,350	
Service Revenue	4,580	
Total Revenue		$5,930
Expenses:		
Rent Expense	$ 175	
Salaries Expense	500	
Supplies Expense	300	
Advertising Expense	850	
Total Expenses		1,825
Net Income		$4,105

Exercise 3

New Wave Beauty Parlor
Statement of Capital
For the Month Ended January 31, 200-

Bambi Sands, (Beginning) Capital, January 200-		$14,500
Plus: Net Income for the Month	$4,105	
Less: Bambi Sands, Drawing	1,600	
Net Increase in Capital		2,505
Bambi Sands, (Ending) Capital, January 31, 200-		$17,005

Exercise 4

Bradley Cleaning Service
Statement of Capital
For the Year Ended December 31, 200-

Albert Bradley, (Beginning) Capital, January 1, 200-		$20,500
Add: Additional Investment, March 23, 200-	$ 5,000	
Net Income for the Year	18,300	
	23,300	
Less: Albert Bradley, Drawing	$15,600	
Net Increase in Capital		7,700
Albert Bradley, (Ending) Capital, December 31, 200-		$28,200

Exercise 5

1. December 31, 200-.
2. The balance sheet date represents a moment in time when the statement was prepared. The other financial statements (income statement, statement of capital) represent a period of time reflecting changes that took place during the period indicated. A balance sheet prepared on another date would probably not have the same values as the one illustrated. This would be due to changes in values as a result of business transactions.
3. No. The business only has $16,000 cash available.
4. The total equity consists of total liabilities and proprietor's capital. The combined amount equals $57,700.
5. $24,150. This represents the extent of his ownership as evidenced by proprietor's capital.
6. $33,550. They consist of accounts payable of $3,200 and notes payable of $30,350.
7. This information cannot be obtained from the balance sheet. Refer back to page 14 where the income statement appears. The income statement indicates net income of $4,150.
8. This information cannot be obtained from the balance sheet. Referring back to the statement of capital on page 15 will answer this question. The January 1, 200- capital balance was $23,200.
9. The income statement and statement of capital had to be prepared prior to preparing the balance sheet. This is necessary in order to determine the new capital balance, which reflects changes enumerated on page 17.
10. The difference is only in the manner in which the information is listed on the reports. The appearance of an equality is more evident using the account form, which follows more closely the accounting equation form.

Exercise 6

New Wave Beauty Parlor
Balance Sheet
January 31, 200-

Assets		**Liabilities and Capital**	
Cash	$ 2,380	Accounts Payable	$ 300
Accounts Receivable	1,400	Notes Payable	2,275
Beauty Supplies	800	Total Liabilities	2,575
Beauty Equipment	15,000	Bambi Sands, Capital	17,005
Total Assets	$19,580	Total Liabilities & Capital	$19,580

Accounting Equation:

$$\underline{ASSETS} = \underline{LIABILITIES} + \underline{CAPITAL}$$
$$\$19,580 \quad = \qquad \$2,575 \qquad + \qquad ?$$

OR

$$\underline{ASSETS} - \underline{LIABILITIES} + \underline{CAPITAL}$$
$$\$19,580 \quad - \qquad \$2,575 \qquad + \qquad ?$$

Exercise 7

Citywide Tax Service
Income Statement
For the Year Ended April 30, 200-

Revenue:		
Revenue from Income Tax Preparation		$21,300
Revenue from Monthly Clients		43,800
Total Revenue		$65,100
Expenses:		
Salaries Expense	$12,500	
Advertising Expense	900	
Rent Expense	6,000	
Automobile Expense	1,300	
General Office Expenses	7,500	
Total Expenses		$28,200
Net Income:		$36,900

Exercise 7 continued

Citywide Tax Service
Statement of Capital
For the Year Ended April 30, 200-

Betty Brody, (Beginning) Capital, May 1, 200-		$32,000
Net Income for the Year	$36,900	
Less: Betty Brody, Drawing	18,600	
Net Increase in Capital		18,300
Betty Brody, (Ending) Capital, April 30, 200-		$50,300

Citywide Tax Service
Balance Sheet
April 30, 200-

Assets

Cash	$12,500
Accounts Receivable	3,700
Office Furniture & Fixtures	11,300
Office Machines & Computers	15,000
Automobile	9,500
Total Assets	$52,000

Liabilities and Capital

Accounts Payable	$ 1,700
Betty Brody, Capital	50,300
Total Liabilities & Capital	$52,000

Exercise 8

1. Income statement, statement of capital, and balance sheet.
2. Income statement, statement of capital, and balance sheet. The statement of capital relies on the results of the preparation of the income statement to determine the change in capital. The balance sheet relies on the statement of capital for its new capital balance.
3. The income statement.
4. Revenue (income) and expenses.
5. Net income.
6. The statement of capital.
7. Net income and drawing.
8. Proprietor's withdrawals.
9. Revenue and expenses.
10. Proprietor's withdrawals.
11. Assets, liabilities and capital.
12. The account form.

Exercise 9

North Shore Realty Co.
Balance Sheet
December 31, 200-

Assets

CURRENT ASSETS

Cash	$2,960	
Accounts Receivable	125	
Insurance	30	
Office Supplies	75	
Total Current Assets		$3,190

PLANT ASSETS

Office Equipment	2,005
Automobile	2,030
Total Plant Assets	4,035
Total Assets	$7,225

Liabilities

CURRENT LIABILITIES

Accounts Payable	$ 65	
Office Salaries Payable	60	
Total Current Liabilities		125

LONG-TERM LIABILITIES

Mortgage Payable	200
Total Liabilities	325
Samuel Fields, Capital	6,900
Total Liabilities and Capital	$7,225

CHAPTER 3

Exercise 1

1. In the account.
2. The ledger.
3. Date, explanation, and amount.
4. Debit.
5. Credit.
6. Debit (left side).
7. Debit. Increases in assets are shown on the same side as the beginning balance.
8. Credit (right side).
9. Credit. Increases in liability and/or permanent capital are added on the same side as the beginning balances.
10. Decreases are shown on the side opposite the beginning balances. Thus, a decrease in an asset would be credited. To show a decrease in a liability or permanent capital, the account is debited.

Exercise 1 continued

11. A balance in an account represents the dollar value of that particular account at a specific moment in time.
12. Every business transaction involves a minimum of two changes. This system is known as double-entry accounting.
13. The account form of the balance sheet indicates the positioning of the various accounts' beginning balances.
14. Total the debit and credit money columns. If the totals are the same, the account is said to be in balance. If the totals are not the same, then the balance is the excess of the two totals. The normal account balances follow their location on the balance sheet.

Exercise 2

Cash	
200-	
Jan. 1 4000	

Accounts Payable	
	200-
	Jan. 1 2000

Service Supplies	
200-	
Jan. 1 2000	

Jill Baxter, Capital	
	200-
	Jan. 1 11,000

Furniture and Fixtures	
200-	
Jan. 1 7000	

Exercise 3

Cash			
200-		200-	
Jan. 1 9000 4000		Jan. 8	600
4 −650 5000		31	50
8350 9000			650

Accounts Payable			
200-		200-	
Jan. 8	600	Jan. 1 2200 2000	
		26 −600 200	
		1600 2200	

Service Supplies	
200-	
Jan. 1 2000	
26 200	
31 50	
2250	

Jill Baxter, Capital	
	200-
	Jan. 1 11,000
	14 1,500
	12,500

Furniture and Fixtures	
200-	200-
Jan. 1 8500 7000	Jan. 4 5000
14 −5000 1500	
3500 8500	

Exercise 3 continued

Jill Baxter
Balance Sheet
January 31, 200-

ASSETS
Cash	$ 8,350
Service Supplies	2,250
Furniture and Fixtures	3,500
Total Assets	$14,100

LIABILITIES AND CAPITAL
Accounts Payable	$ 1,600
Jill Baxter, Capital	12,500
Total Liabilities and Capital	$14,100

Exercise 4

The setting up of the ledger account, even though you have used the "T" account form, still requires the inclusion of specific information. Note how this specific information is presented.

Cash

200-		
Dec. 31 Balance	16,000	

Accounts Payable

	200-	
	Dec. 31 Balance	3,200

A. Regal, Capital

	200-	
	Dec. 31 Balance	12,800

Exercise 5

Cash

200-		200-	
July 1	3,000	July 2	1,200
3	500	5	300
8	200	7	50
		9	60
		10	200

C. Goldstein, Capital

	200-	
	July 1	3,000

Law Library

200-		
July 2	1,200	

Imcome from Services

	200-	
	July 3	500
	6	1,100

Exercise 5 continued

Office Supplies

200- July 4	150	

Rent Expense

200- July 5	300	

Utilities Expense

200- July 9	60	

Accounts Payable

200- July 7	50	200- July 4	150

Accounts Receivable

200- July 6	1,100	200- July 8	200

C. Goldstein, Drawing

200- July 10	200	

Exercise 6

Cash

Date		Explanation	Debit	Credit	Balance
200- Oct.	1		12000 00		12000 00
	3		3000 00		15000 00
	8			500 00	14500 00
	15			250 00	14250 00
	19		1200 00		15450 00
	25			50 00	15400 00
	30			450 00	14950 00

Delivery Equipment

Date		Explanation	Debit	Credit	Balance
200- Oct.	1		8000 00		8000 00
	5		2500 00		10500 00

Exercise 6 continued

John Graves, Capital

Date		Explanation	Debit	Credit	Balance
200- Oct.	1			20000 00	20000 00
	5			3000 00	23000 00

Delivery Service Income

Date		Explanation	Debit	Credit	Balance
200- Oct.	3			3000 00	3000 00
	19			1200 00	4200 00

Warrehouse Supplies

Date		Explanation	Debit	Credit	Balance
200- Oct.	5		500 00		500 00

Rent Expense

Date		Explanation	Debit	Credit	Balance
200- Oct.	8		500 00		500 00

Exercise 6 continued

Repairs & Gasoline Expense

Date		Explanation	Debit	Credit	Balance
200-Oct.	15		250 00		250 00

Utilities Expense

Date		Explanation	Debit	Credit	Balance
200-Oct.	25		50 00		50 00

Salaries Expense

Date		Explanation	Debit	Credit	Balance
200-Oct.	30		450 00		450 00

ACCOUNT LISTING

	BALANCES	
	Debit	Credit
Cash	$14,950	
Delivery Equipment	10,500	
John Graves, Capital		$23,000
Delivery Service Income		4,200
Warehouse Supplies	500	
Rent Expense	500	
Repairs & Gasoline Expense	250	
Utilities Expense	50	
Salaries Expense	450	
	$27,200	$27,200

Exercise 7

Albert Kranz
General Journal   *Page 1*

Date		Account & Explanation	PR	Debit	Credit
200- Aug.	1	Delivery Equipment		2300 00	
		Cash			2300 00
		From A-l Used Truck Co.			
	4	Cash		900 00	
		Income from Services			900 00
		From Stevens Department Store			
	6	Albert Kranz, Drawing		200 00	
		Cash			200 00
		For personal use			
	9	Advertising Expenses		300 00	
		Cash			300 00
		Paid Radio Station WPBB for the week			
	10	Accounts Payable		230 00	
		Cash			230 00
		Paid Ready Repair Shop			
	16	Salaries Expense		370 00	
		Cash			370 00
		For two weeks ending today			
	19	Accounts Receivable		340 00	
		Income from Services			340 00
		Sent bill to May's Department Store			

Exercise 7 continued

Albert Kranz
General Journal   Page 2

Date		Account and Explanation	PR	Debit	Credit
200- Aug.	23	Gasoline & Oil Expense		120 00	
		Cash			120 00
		For three weeks ending this date			
	27	Albert Kranz, Drawing		150 00	
		Cash			150 00
		For personal use			
	29	Salaries Expense		385 00	
		Cash			385 00
		For two weeks ending today			
	31	Cash		340 00	
		Accounts Receivable			340 00
		Payment from May's Department Store			

Exercise 8

Ralph Speedy
Trial Balance
June 1, 200-

	DEBIT	CREDIT
Cash	2,000	
Accounts Receivable	1,500	
Supplies	300	
Car Wash Equipment	5,000	
Accounts Payable		500
Ralph Speedy, Capital		8,300
	8,800	8,800

Exercise 8 continued

Date		Account and Explanation	PR	DR	CR
200- June	3	Rent Expense	521	200 00	
		Cash	101		200 00
		To Ajax Realty Co. for June			
	5	Cash	101	500 00	
		Accounts Receivable	102		500 00
		From Adams Bros. part payment			
	8	Cash	101	1000 00	
		Car Wash Revenue	410		1000 00
		For week ending today			
	9	Salaries Expense	520	480 00	
		Cash	101		480 00
		For two weeks ending today			
	14	Accounts Payable	201	300 00	
		Cash	101		300 00
		To Randolph Supply Co. due today			
	15	Ralph Speedy, Drawing	302	500 00	
		Cash	101		500 00
		For personal use			
	22	Accounts Receivable	102	200 00	
		Car Wash Revenue	410		200 00
		To Granger Trucking Co.			

Exercise 8 continued

Date			Account and Explanation	PR	DR	CR
200- June	26		Utilities Expense	623	85 00	
			Cash	101		85 00
			Paid monthly water bill			
	27		Laundry Expense	522	60 00	
			Cash	101		60 00
			To Clean Towel Co.			
	29		Car Wash Equipment	115	1200 00	
			Accounts Payable	201		1200 00
			From Car Wash Equipment Co., payable in 30 days			
	30		Supplies	110	120 00	
			Cash	101		120 00
			For soap powder and liquid wax			(Cont'd)

Exercise 8 continued

General Ledger

Cash   #101

Date			PR	DR	CR	Balance
200- June	1	Balance	✓			2000 00
	3		J-1		200 00	1800 00
	5		J-1	500 00		2300 00
	8		J-1	1000 00		3300 00
	9		J-1		480 00	2820 00
	14		J-1		300 00	2520 00
	15		J-1		500 00	2020 00
	26		J-1		85 00	1935 00
	27		J-1		60 00	1875 00
	30		J-2		120 00	1755 00

Accounts Receivable   #102

Date			PR	DR	CR	Balance
200- June	1	Balance	✓			1500 00
	5	From Adams Bros.	J-1		500 00	1000 00
	22	To Granger Trucking Co.	J-1	200 00		1200 00

Supplies   #110

Date			PR	DR	CR	Balance
200- June	1	Balance	✓			300 00
	30		J-2	120 00		420 00

Car Wash Equpment   #115

Date			PR	DR	CR	Balance
200- June	1	Balance	✓			5000 00
	29		J-2	1200 00		6200 00

Exercise 8 continued

General Ledger (continued)

Accounts Payable #201

200-June				Debit	Credit	Balance
June	1	Balance	✓			500 00
	14	Randolph Supply Co.	J-1	300 00		200 00
	29	Car Wash Equipment Co.	J-2		1200 00	1400 00

Ralph Speedy, Capital #301

200-June				Debit	Credit	Balance
June	1	Balance	✓			8300 00

Ralph Speedy, Drawing #302

200-June				Debit	Credit	Balance
June	15		J-1	500 00		500 00

Car Wash Revenue #410

200-June				Debit	Credit	Balance
June	8		J-1		1000 00	1000 00
	22		J-1		200 00	200 00

Salaries Expense #520

200-June				Debit	Credit	Balance
June	9		J-1	480 00		480 00

Rent Expense #521

200-June				Debit	Credit	Balance
June	3		J-1	200 00		200 00

Exercise 8 continued

General Ledger (continued)

Laundry Expense					#522	
200- June	27		J-1	60 00		60 00

Utilities Expense					#523	
200- June	26		J-1	85 00		85 00

Ralph Speedy
Trial Balance
June 30, 200-

	DEBIT	CREDIT
Cash	1,755	
Accounts Receivable	1,200	
Supplies	420	
Car Wash Equipment	6,200	
Accounts Payable		1,400
Ralph Speedy, Capital		8,300
Ralph Speedy, Drawing	500	
Car Wash Revenue		1,200
Salaries Expense	480	
Rent Expense	200	
Laundry Expense	60	
Utilities Expense	85	
	10,900	10,900

CHAPTER 4

Exercise 1

	Date		Account & Explanation	PR	Debit	Credit
1.	2002 Dec.	31	Office Supplies Expense		25000	
			Office Supplies			25000
			To adjust for supplies used up			
2.		31	Rent Expense		80000	
			Rent Payable			80000
			To recognize Nov. and Dec. rent			
3.		31	Advertising Expense		20000	
			Advertising Payable			20000
			For second week of Nov.			
4.		31	Interest Expense		833	
			Interest Payable			833
			To recognize accrued interest expense			
5.		31	Insurance Expense		30000	
			Prepaid Insurance			30000
			To recognize insurance expense from			
			July 1 through Dec. 31			
6.		31	Salaries Expense		300000	
			Salaries Payable			300000
			To recognize accrued salaries for last			
			3 days of accounting period			

Exercise 2

	Date		Account & Explanation	PR	Debit	Credit
1.	200- Dec.	31	Interest Receivable		7500	
			Interest Income			7500
			To recognize accrued interest			
			income from Nov. 2 to date			
2.		31	Income from Commissions		32000	
			Unearned Comm. Income			32000
			To defer income previously received			
			but not earned			
3.		31	Office Supplies Expense		73000	
			Office Supplies			73000
			To recognize supplies used up			
4.		31	Salaries Expense		150000	
			Salaries Payable			150000
			Accrued salaries for last 3 days of			
			accounting period			
5.		31	Insurance Expense		124500	
			Prepaid Insurance			124500
			To recognize expired insurance			
6.		31	Interest Expense		9000	
			Interest Payable			9000
			($6,000 × .12 × 45/360)			
			To recognize interest expense			
			incurred for 45 days but not payable			
			at the end of the accounting period			

Exercise 3

1. Amount subject to depreciation: $3,000.

ORIGINAL COST – SCRAP VALUE = DEPRECIABLE VALUE
$3,400 – $400 = $3,000

2. $500.

$3,000 ÷ 6 yrs. = ANNUAL DEPRECIATION

3. Dec. 31 Depreciation Expense $500
                Accumulated Depreciation $500
            To record adjustment for annual
            depreciation

4. $2,900.

ORIGINAL COST – ACCUMULATED DEPRECIATION =
BOOK VALUE
$3,400 – $500 = $2,900

5. $400. (Annual depreciation of $500 × 6 years = $3,000 accumulated depreciation. Original cost – accumulated depreciation = book value. 3,400 – 3,000 = 400.)

6. The book value is reduced by the annual depreciation recognized. The loss in value is recognized in the contra-asset accumulated depreciation.

7. The cost principle requires that plant assets are shown on the books at their actual cost.

Exercise 4

	Date		Account & Explanation	PR	Debit	Credit
(a)	200- Dec.	31	Depreciation Expense		50000	
			Accumulated Depreciation			50000
			For the year			
(b)		31	Salaries Expense		52000	
			Salaries Payable			52000
			For last 4 days of accounting period			
(c)		31	Rental Income		120000	
			Unearned Rental Income			120000
			To recognize unearned income			
(d)		31	Prepaid Supplies		60000	
			Supplies Expense			60000
			To recognize unused supplies expense			

Exercise 5

Beldon Service Co.
Worksheet
For the Year Ended December 31, 200-

Account Title	Trial Balance Debit	Trial Balance Credit	Adjustments Debit	Adjustments Credit	Income Statement Debit	Income Statement Credit	Balance Sheet Debit	Balance Sheet Credit
Cash	16900 00						16900 00	
Accounts Receivable	2000 00						2000 00	
Prepaid Insurance	600 00			(a) 200 00			400 00	
Supplies	300 00			(b) 175 00			125 00	
Furniture	13500 00						13500 00	
Accumulated Depreciation		500 00		(c) 500 00				1000 00
Accounts Payable		1500 00						1500 00
Notes Payable		8000 00						8000 00
L. Beldon, Capital		12000 00						12000 00
L. Beldon, Drawing	4000 00						4000 00	
Service Revenue		21000 00	(d) 400 00			20600 00		
Rental Revenue		160 00				160 00		
Salaries Expense	5000 00		(e) 300 00		5300 00			
Rent Expense	1400 00				1400 00			
Utilities Expense	900 00				900 00			
	44600 00	44600 00						
Insurance Expense			(a) 200 00		200 00			
Supplies Expense			(b) 175 00		175 00			
Depreciation Expense			(c) 500 00		500 00			
Unearned Service Revenue				(d) 400 00				400 00
Salaries Payable				(e) 300 00				300 00
Interest Expense			(f) 40 00		40 00			
Interest Payable				(f) 40 00				40 00
			1615 00	1615 00	8515 00	22200 00	36925 00	23240 00
Net Income					13685 00			13685 00
					22200 00	22200 00	36925 00	36925 00

Exercise 5 continued

Beldon Service Co.
Income Statement
For the Year Ended December 31, 200-

Revenue:		
Service Revenue	$20,600	
Rental Revenue	1,600	
Total Revenue		$22,200
Expenses:		
Salaries Expenses	5,300	
Rent Expense	1,400	
Utilities Expense	900	
Insurance Expense	200	
Supplies Expense	175	
Depreciation Expense	500	
Interest Expense	40	
Total Expenses		8,515
Net Income		$13,685

Beldon Service Co.
Statement of Capital
For the Year Ended December 31, 200-

L. Beldon, (Beginning)* Capital, January 1, 200-		$12,000
Plus: Net Income	$13,685	
Less: L. Beldon, Drawing	4,000	
Net Increase in Capital		9,685
L. Beldon, (Ending)* Capital, December 31, 200-		$21,685

*In practice the words "beginning" and "ending" are omitted when recording the capital balances. These terms are understood from the data of the proprietor's capital.

Beldon Service Co.
Balance Sheet
December 31, 200-

Assets

Cash		$16,900
Accounts Receivable		2,000
Prepaid Insurance		400
Supplies		125
Furniture	$13,500	
Less: Accumulated Depreciation	1,000	12,500
Total Assets		$31,925

Liabilities and Capital

Accounts Payable	1,500	
Unearned Service Revenue	400	
Interest Payable	40	
Salaries Payable	300	
Notes Payable	8,000	
Total Liabilities		$10,240
L. Beldon, Capital		21,685
Total Liabilities and Capital		$31,925

Exercise 6

Adjusting Journal Entries (explanation omitted):

	Date		Account & Explanation	PR	Debit	Credit
a.	200- Dec.	31	Insurance Expense		200 00	
			Prepaid Insurance			200 00
b.		31	Supplies Expense		175 00	
			Supplies			175 00
c.		31	Depreciation Expense		500 00	
			Accumulated Depreciation			500 00
d.		31	Service Revenue		400 00	
			Unearned Service Revenue			400 00
e.		31	Salaries Expense		300 00	
			Salaries Payable			300 00
f.		31	Interest Expense		40 00	
			Interest Payable			40 00

Exercise 6 continued

Closing Journal Entries (explanations omitted):

Date		Account & Explanation	PR	Debit	Credit
200- Dec.	31	Service Revenue		20600 00	
		Rental Revenue		1600 00	
		Income Summary			22200 00
	31	Income Summary		8515 00	
		Salaries Expense			5300 00
		Rent Expense			1400 00
		Utilities Expense			900 00
		Insurance Expense			200 00
		Supplies Expense			175 00
		Depreciation Expense			500 00
		Interest Expense			40 00
	31	Income Summary		4000 00	
		L. Beldon, Drawing			4000 00
	31	Income Summary		9685 00	
		L. Beldon, Capital			9685 00

Exercise 7

Beldon Service Co.
Post-Closing Trial Balance
December 31, 200-

	DEBIT	CREDIT
Cash	$16,900	
Accounts Receivable	2,000	
Prepaid Insurance	400	
Supplies	125	
Furniture	13,500	
Accumulated Depreciation		$1,000
Accounts Payable		1,500
Unearned Service Revenue		400
Salaries Payable		300
Interest Payable		40
Notes Payable		8,000
L. Beldon, Capital		$21,685
	$32,925	$32,925

Exercise 8

Adjusting Entries:

			Adjusting Entries		
	200-				
1.	*Dec.*	*31*	Salaries Expense	70000	
			Salaries Payable		70000
			To recognize accrued salaries for one day		
2.		*31*	Office Supplies Expense	37000	
			Office Supplies		37000
			To recognize supplies used up		
3.		*31*	Prepaid Insurance	45000	
			Insurance Expense		45000
			To recognize expense not used up		
4.		*31*	Rental Income	40000	
			Unearned Rental Income		40000
			To recognize 4mo. income received in		
			advance but unearned at the end of the		
			Accounting Period		

Exercise 8 continued

Reversing Entries:

			Reversal Entries				
1.	200- Jan.	1	Salaries Payable		70000		
			Salaries Expense				70000
			To recognize expense for new year				
3.		1	Insurance Expense		45000		
			Prepaid Insurance				45000
			To record reversal				
4.		1	Unearned Rental Income		40000		
			Rental Income				40000
			To recognize income for new year				

Note that the second adjusting entry does not need a reversing entry since the office supplies expense account, created as a result of the adjusting process, was eliminated as part of the closing process. All other accounts created through the adjusting process required reversing entries.

CHAPTER 5

Exercise 1

1. Accounts Receivable   2,400
          Sales   2,400
          To Spencer Dept. Store 2/10, n/30.
2. Cash   2,352
      Sales Discount   48
          Accounts Receivable   2,400
      From Spencer Dept. Store, less discount.

On the books of the seller, the discount taken by the buyer represents an expense. On the buyer's books, the $48 represents a purchases discount, which is a form of income. On either books, the amount of the respective accounts receivable and accounts payable is eliminated in full when the obligation is paid.

Exercise 2

Since 14 days have elapsed between the date of the sale and the date of payment, the discount that the buyer is entitled to take is 1%. Since the total obligation is $12,000, the amount of the purchases discount that the buyer is entitled to take is $120. The amount of cash received by the seller on March 20 is $11,880 ($12,000 − $120). The entry to record the receipt of the payment is:

200-			
Mar. 20	Cash	11,880	
	Sales Discount	120	
	Accounts Receivable		12,000
	From customer, less 1% discount.		

Exercise 3

	Net Purchases	
1.	Purchases	$ 97,500
	Add: Freight on Purchases	2,260
		99,760
	Less: Purchases Returns and Allow.	2,500
	Net Purchases	97,260
2.	Cost of Goods Available for Sale	
	Merchandise Inventory, Jan. 1, 2002	52,390
	Add: Net Purchases	97,260
	Cost of Goods Available for Sale	149,650
3.	Cost of Goods Sold	
	Cost of Goods Available for Sale	149,650
	Less: Merchandise Inv. 12/31/02	46,200
	Cost of Goods Sold	103,450
4.	Gross Profit on Sales	
	Sales	219,180
	Less: Cost of Goods Sold	103,450
	Gross Profit on Sales	$115,730

Exercise 4

Trading Business
Income Statement
For the Year Ended December 31, 2002

Income:			
Sales			$172,200
Less: Sales Returns and Allowances			3,430
Net Sales			168,770
Cost of Goods Sold:			
Merchandise Inventory, January 1, 2002		$28,650	
Purchases	$138,900		
Freight on Purchases	2,300		
Less:	141,200		
Purchases Discount	$1,300		
Purch. Ret. & Allow.	1,820	3,120	
Net Purchases:		138,080	
Cost of Goods Available for Sale		166,730	
Less: Merchandise Inventory, 12/31/02		31,200	
Cost of Goods Sold			135,530
Gross Profit on Sales			$33,240

Exercise 5

Xavier Co.
Worksheet
For the Year Ended June 30, 2003

Account Title	Trial Balance Debit	Trial Balance Credit	Adjustments Debit	Adjustments Credit	Income Statement Debit	Income Statement Credit	Balance Sheet Debit	Balance Sheet Credit
Cash	650000						650000	
Merchandise Inventory, 7/1/02	300000		(a1) 395000	(a) 300000			395000	
Notes Receivable	150000						150000	
Accounts Receivable	220000						220000	
Office Supplies	50000			(b) 6000			44000	
Equipment	185000						185000	
Accounts Payable		155000						155000
Notes Payable		25000						25000
Sales		1264000				1264000		
Sales Returns and Allowances	15000				15000			
Merchandise Purchases	802500				802500			
Purchases Returns and Allowances		15000				15000		
Discount on Purchases		34000				34000		
Discount on Sales	11000				11000			
Freight on Purchases	4500				4500			
Rent Expense	60000				60000			
Interest Income		2500		(e) 7500		10000		
A. Xavier, Capital		1000000						1000000
A. Xavier, Drawing	47500						47500	
	2495500	2495500						
Income Summary			(a) 300000	(a1) 395000	300000	395000		
Office Supplies Expense			(b) 6000		6000			
Depreciation Expense			(c) 17500		17500			
Accumulated Depreciation				(c) 17500				17500
Interest Expense			(d) 1100		1100			
Interest Payable				(d) 1100				1100
Interest Receivable			(e) 7500				7500	
			727100	727100	1217600	1718000	1699000	1198600
Net Income					500400			500400
					1718000	1718000	1699000	1699000

Exercise 5 continued

Adjusting Journal Entries:

2003

June 30 (a)		Income Summary	3,000	
		Merchandise Inventory		3,000
		To close old inventory to income summary.		
(a1)	30	Merchandise Inventory	3,950	
		Income Summary		3,950
		To set up new inventory.		
(b)	30	Office Supplies Expense	60	
		Office Supplies		60
(c)	30	Depreciation Expense	175	
		Accumulated Depreciation		175
(d)	30	Interest Expense	11	
		Interest Payable		11
(e)	30	Interest Receivable	75	
		Interest Income		75
		To recognize interest income accrued but not received.		

Closing Journal Entries:

2003

June 30	Sales	12,640	
	Purchases Returns and Allowances	150	
	Discount on Purchases	340	
	Interest Income	100	
	Income Summary		13,230
	To close revenue items to Income Summary.		
30	Income Summary	9,176	
	Sales Returns and Allowances		150
	Merchandise Purchases		8,025
	Discount on Sales		110
	Freight on Purchases		45
	Rent Expense		600
	Office Supplies Expense		60
	Depreciation Expense		175
	Interest Expense		11
	To close expense items to Income Summary.		
30	Income Summary	475	
	A. Xavier, Drawing		475
	To close drawing to Income Summary		
30	Income Summary	4,529	
	A. Xavier, Capital		4,529
	To Close Income Summary to proprietor's capital		

Exercise 5 continued

Income Statement:

Xavier Co.

Income Statement

For the Year Ended June 30, 2003

Income:				
Sales			$12,640	
Less: Sales Returns and				
Allowances		$150		
Discount on Sales		110	260	
Net Sales				$12,380
Cost of Goods Sold:				
Merchandise Inventory, 7/1/02			$3,000	
Merchandise Purchases		$8,025		
Add: Freight on Purchases		45		
		8,070		
Less: Discount on Purchases	$340			
Purchases Returns and Allowance	150	490		
Net Purchases			7,580	
Cost of Goods Available for Sale			10,580	
Less: Merchandise Inventory, 6/30/03			3,950	
Cost of Goods Sold				6,630
Gross Profit on Sales:				5,750
Operating Expenses				
Rent Expense			$600	
Office Supplies Expense			60	
Depreciation Expense			175	
Interest Expense			11	
Total Operating Expenses				846
Net Income From Operations				4,904
Other Income				
Interest Income				100
Net Income				$ 5,004

Statement of Capital:

Xavier Co.

Statement of Capital

For the Year Ended June 30, 2003

A. Xavier, (Beginning) Capital, July 1, 2002		$10,000
Add Net Income	$5,004	
A. Xavier, Drawing	475	
Net increase in capital		4,529
A. Xavier, (Ending) Capital, June 30, 2003		$14,529

Exercise 5 continued

Balance Sheet:

Xavier Co.
Balance Sheet
June 30, 2003

Assets			**Liabilities and Capital**	
Cash		$ 6,500	Accounts Payable	$ 1,550
Merchandise Inventory		3,950	Interest Payable	11
Accounts Receivable		2,200	Notes Payable	250
Notes Receivable		1,500	Total Liabilities	1,811
Interest Receivable		75	A. Xavier, Capital	14,529
Office Supplies		440		
Equipment	$1,850			
Less: Accumulated				
Depreciation	175	1,675	Total Liabilities &	
Total Assets		$16,340	Capital	$16,340

Exercise 6

Items	Expense Category
(1)	General
(2)	Selling
(3)	Other
(4)	Selling
(5)	Selling
(6)	General
(7)	Selling
(8)	Other

Some of the items listed above may be appropriately listed in more than one expense category. The above responses represent placement within the category where the item most commonly is found.

Exercise 7

Adjusting Entries (Explanations omitted)

2002

1.	Dec. 31	Income Summary		35,700.00	
			Merchandise Inventory		35,700.00
1a.	31	Merchandise Inventory		36,500.00	
			Income Summary		36,500.00
2.	31	Salaries Expense		2,700.00	
			Salaries Payable		2,700.00
3.	31	Insurance Expense		596.00	
			Prepaid Insurance		596.00
4.	31	Interest Income		22.50	
			Unearned Interest Income		22.50

Exercise 7 continued

The closing entries are recorded to eliminate all the temporary capital accounts resulting from daily business transactions and from the adjusting entries recorded at the end of the accounting period. The reversal entry necessary for this exercise would be the fourth entry only. That reversal is as follows:

```
2003
Jan. 1   Salaries Payable                    2,700.00
              Salaries Expense                            2,700.00
         To recognize expense to
         be paid in new year, while
         incurred in previous year.

Jan. 1   Unearned Interest Income              22.50
              Interest Income
         To recognize interest income                      22.50
         to be earned in new year.
```

CHAPTER 6

Exercise 1

Sales Journal   *Page S-1*

Date		Account Debited	Terms	Inv. #	PR	Amount
200- Feb.	3	Clearview Mfg. Co.	n/30		B	680 00
	8	Data Word Associates	n/30		D	89 00
	17	HAL Corp.	n/30		H	700 00
	28	Clearview Mfg. Co.	n/30		B	180 00
	28	Dr. Accounts Receivable, Cr. Sales			5/40	1649 00

General Ledger

Accounts Receivable   *Page 5*

Date			PR	Debit	Credit	Balance Debit	Credit
200- Feb.	28		S-1	1649 00		1649 00	

Exercise 1 continued

Sales   *Page 40*

Date		PR	Debit	Credit	Balance Debit	Balance Credit
200- Feb.	28	S-1		1649 00		1649 00

Accounts Receivable Ledger

Clearview Mfg. Co.   *Page B*

Date		PR	Debit	Credit	Debit Balance
200- Feb.	3	S-1	680 00		680 00
	28	S-1	180 00		860 00

Data Word Associates   *Page D*

Date		PR	Debit	Credit	Debit Balance
200- Feb.	8	S-1	89 00		89 00

HAL Corp.   *Page H*

Date		PR	Debit	Credit	Debit Balance
200- Feb.	17	S-1	700 00		700 00

Anderson Stationery Co.
Schedule of Accounts Receivable
February 28, 200-

Clearview Mfg. Co.	$ 860.00
Data Word Associates	89.00
HAL Corp.	700.00
Total Accounts Receivable	$1,649.00

Exercise 2

Sales Journal

Date		Account Debited	Terms	Inv. #	PR	Amount
200- Oct.	5	T. Ross	2/10, n/30	201		100 00
	13	R. Adams	n/30	202		220 00
	21	G. Crane	2/10, n/30	203		310 00
	31	Dr. Accounts Receivable, Cr. Sales				630 00

Cash Receipts Journal

Date		Account Credited	PR	General Acct. Cr.	Sales Cr.	Accounts Receivable Cr.	Sales Discount Dr.	Cash Dr.
200- Oct.	1	L. Marin				100 00		100 00
	9	E. Rafferty, Capital		1500 00				1500 00
	15	T. Ross				100 00	2 00	98 00
	17	Notes Receivable (R. Horne)		450 00				450 00
	25	T. Ross (Oct. 1 Bal.)				235 00		235 00
	29	Sales			350 00			350 00
	31	G. Crane				310 00	6 20	303 80
	31			1950 00	350 00	745 00	8 20	3036 80

Exercise 3

Sales Journal

Date		Account Debited	Terms	Inv. #	PR	Amount
200- Oct.	5	T. Ross	2/10, n/30	201	R	100 00
	13	R. Adams	n/30	202	A	220 00
	21	G. Crane	2/10, n/30	203	C	310 00
	31	Dr. Accounts Receivable, Cr. Sales			5/50	630 00

Exercise 3 continued

Cash Receipts Journal

Date		Account Credited	PR	General Acct. Cr.	Sales Cr.	Accounts Receivable Cr.	Sales Discount Dr.	Cash Dr.
200- Oct.	1	L. Marin	M			100 00		100 00
	9	E. Rafferty, Capital	40	1500 00				1500 00
	15	T. Ross	R			100 00	2 00	98 00
	17	Notes Receivable (R. Horne)	7	450 00				450 00
	25	T. Ross (Oct. 1 Bal.)	R			235 00		235 00
	29	Sales	✓		350 00			350 00
	31	G. Crane	C			310 00	6 20	303 80
	31			1950 00	350 00	745 00	8 20	3036 80
				(✓)	(50)	(5)	(51)	(1)

General Ledger:

Cash   *Account #1*

Date			PR	Debit	Credit	Debit Balance
200- Oct.	1	Balance	✓			1100 00
			CR-1	3036 80		4136 80

Accounts Receivable   *Account #5*

Date			PR	Debit	Credit	Debit Balance
200- Oct.	1	Balance	✓			770 00
	31		S-1	630 00		1400 00
	31		CR-1		745 00	645 00

Exercise 3 continued

Notes Receivable   Account #7

Date			PR	Debit	Credit	Debit Balance
200- Oct.	1	Balance	✓			750 00
	17		CR-1		450 00	300 00

E. Rafferty, Capital   Account #40

Date			PR	Debit	Credit	Credit Balance
200- Oct.	1	Balance	✓			8000 00
	9		CR-1		1500 00	9500 00

Sales   Account #50

Date			PR	Debit	Credit	Credit Balance
200- Oct.	31		S-1		630 00	630 00
	31		CR-1		350 00	990 00

Sales Discounts   Account #51

Date			PR	Debit	Credit	Debit Balance
200- Oct.	31		CR-1	8 20		8 20

Exercise 3 continued

Accounts Receivable Ledger:

R. Adams   Page A

Date			PR	Debit	Credit	Debit Balance
200-						
Oct.	1	Balance	✓			210 00
	13		S-1	220 00		430 00

G. Crane   Page C

Date			PR	Debit	Credit	Debit Balance
200-						
Oct.	1	Balance	✓			180 00
	21		S-1	310 00		490 00
	31		CR-1		310 00	180 00

L. Marin   Page M

Date			PR	Debit	Credit	Debit Balance
200-						
Oct.	1	Balance	✓			145 00
	1		CR-1		100 00	45 00

Exercise 3 continued

L. Ross   Page R

Date			PR	Debit	Credit	Debit Balance
200- Oct.	1	Balance	✓			235 00
	5		S-1	100 00		335 00
	15		CR-1		100 00	235 00
	25		CR-1		235 00	0

E. Rafferty
Schedule of Accounts Receivable
October 31, 200-

R. Adams	$430
G. Crane	180
L. Marin	45
Total	$655

Exercise 4

Purchases Journal   Page P-23

Date		Account Credited	PR	A/P (Cr.)	Purchases (Dr.)	General Accounts Debited		
						Account Debited	PR	Amount
200- Apr.	1	Bolden Co. (n/30)	B	70000	70000			
	5	Reliable Office Supply Co. (n/15)	R	12500		Office Supplies	8	12500
	9	A & B Equipment Co. (n/20)	A	32500		Office Equipment	10	32500
	15	Caldwell Manufacturing Co. (n/30)	C	37500	37500			
	30			152500	107500			45000
				(20)	(40)			(✓)

Exercise 4 continued

General Ledger:

Office Supplies   *Page 8*

Date			PR	Debit	Credit	Debit Balance
200- Apr.	1		P-23	125 00		125 00

Office Equipment   *Page 10*

Date			PR	Debit	Credit	Debit Balance
200- Apr.	5		P-23	325 00		325 00

Accounts Payable   *Page 20*

Date			PR	Debit	Credit	Credit Balance
200- Apr.	30		P-23		1525 00	1525 00

Purchases   *Page 40*

Date			PR	Debit	Credit	Debit Balance
200- Apr.	30		P-23	1075 00		1075 00

Accounts Payable Ledger:

Bolden Co.   *Page B*

Date			PR	Debit	Credit	Credit Balance
200- Apr.	1		P-23		700 00	700 00

Exercise 4 continued

Reliable Office Supply Co. Page R

Date			PR	Debit	Credit	Credit Balance
200- Apr.	5		P-23		125 00	125 00

A & B Equipment Co. Page B

Date			PR	Debit	Credit	Credit Balance
200- Apr.	9		P-23		325 00	325 00

Caldwell Manufacturing Co. Page C

Date			PR	Debit	Credit	Credit Balance
200- Apr.	15		P-23		375 00	375 00

XXXX Company
Schedule of Accounts Payable
April 30, 200-

Bolden Co.	$ 700
Reliable Office Supply Co.	125
A&B Equipment Co.	325
Caldwell Manufacturing Co.	375
	$1,525

Exercise 5

Sales Journal

Date		Account Debited	Terms	Inv. #	PR	Amount
200- Mar.	8	Adams Bros.	1/2 cash, bal. n/30	201		1200 00
	16	Stone Bros.	1/10, n/30	202		800 00
	31	Dr. Accounts Receivable, Cr. Sales			( )/( )	2000 00

Purchases Journal

Date		Account Credited	PR	A/P (Cr.)	Purchases (Dr.)	General Accounts Debited		
						Account Debited	PR	Amount
200- Mar.	3	Harris Co. (2/10, n/30)		950 00	950 00			
	23	Young & Son (30-day note)		800 00	800 00			
	31			1750 00	1750 00			—0—
				( )	( )			(✔)

Cash Receipts Journal

Date		Account Credited	PR	General Acct. Cr.	Sales Cr.	Accounts Rec. Cr.	Sales Dis. Dr.	Cash Dr.
200- Mar.	5	Sales	✔		1000 00			1000 00
	9	Adams Bros.				600 00		600 00
	25	Stone Bros.				800 00	8 00	792 00
	26	{Interest Income}		15 00				
		{Notes Receivable}		885 00				900 00
	31			900 00	1000 00	1400 00	8 00	3292 00
				(✔)	( )	( )	( )	( )

Exercise 5 continued

Cash Payments Journal

Date		Account Debited	PR	General Accounts Dr.	Accounts Payable Dr.	Purchases Debit	Purchases Discount Cr.	Cash Cr.
200- Mar.	1	Rent Expense		150 00				150 00
	11	Mr. Reynolds, Drawing		200 00				200 00
	13	Harris Co.			900 00		18 00	882 00
	17	Freight on Sales		70 00				70 00
	20	Office Supplies		20 00				20 00
	31	Salaries Expense		3450 00				3450 00
	31			3890 00	900 00	—0—	18 00	4772 00
				(✓)	( )	(✓)	( )	( )

Journal

Date		Description	PR	Debit	Credit
200- Mar.	6	Harris Co./Accounts Payable		5000	
		Purchases Returns & Allowances			5000
		For purchase of 3/3.			
	19	Notes Receivable		50000	
		Blake Co./Accounts Receivable			50000
		Received 60-day Note from Blake.			
	24	Young & Son/Accounts Payable		80000	
		Notes Payable			80000
		Sent 30-day Note.			

Exercise 6

1. Sales Journal
2. Cash Receipts Journal
3. General Journal
4. Cash Payments Journal
5. Sales Journal
6. Purchases Journal
7. Cash Payments Journal
8. General Journal
9. General Journal
10. General Journal
11. Cash Payments Journal
12. Cash Receipts Journal
13. General Journal

Exercise 7

Purchases Journal   P-1

Date		Account Credited	PR	A/P (Cr.)	Purchases (Dr.)	Supplies (Dr.)	Account Debited	PR	Amount
200-							*General Accounts Debited*		
Mar.	12	Avon Supply Co., 2/10, n/30	A	260 00		260 00			
	17	Consolidated Equip. Co. 3/10, 1/20, n/30	C	300 00			Equipment	102	300 00
	30	Avon Supply Co., 2/10, n/30	A	350 00		350 00			
	31			910 00		610 00			300 00
				(200)	(✓)	(101)			(✓)

Sales Journal   S-1

Date		Account Debited	Inv. #	Terms	PR	Amount
200-						
Mar.	15	Estelle Evans	105	1/10, n/30	E	200 00
	26	Ruth Glasser	123	1/10, n/30	G	350 00
	31	Estelle Evans	167	30-day note	E	600 00
	31	Dr. Accounts Receivable, Cr. Sales			103/305	1150 00

Exercise 7 continued

Cash Receipts Journal   CR-1

Date		Account Credited	PR	General Acct. Cr.	Sales Cr.	Accounts Receivable Cr.	Sales Discount Dr.	Cash Dr.
200- Mar.	14	Sales	✓		2600 00			2600 00
	24	Estelle Evans	E			150 00	1 50	148 50
	25	Sales 3/15–3/25	✓		5300 00			5300 00
	31			–0–	7900 00	150 00	1 50	8048 50
				(✓)	(305)	(103)	(316)	(100)

Cash Payments Journal   CP-1

Date		Account Debited	PR	General Accounts Dr.	Accounts Payable Dr.	Purchases Debit	Purchases Discount Cr.	Cash Cr.
200- Mar.	11	Rent Expense	311	300 00				300 00
	13	Insurance Expense	312	180 00				180 00
	19	Avon Supply Co.	A		260 00		5 20	254 80
	21	E. Sason, Drawing	302	300 00				300 00
	27	Salaries Expense	315	675 00				675 00
	28	Supplies	101	75 00				75 00
	29	Consolidated Equip. Co.	C		280 00		2 80	277 20
	31			1530 00	540 00	–0–	8 00	2062 00
				(✓)	(200)	(✓)	(307)	(100)

Exercise 7 continued

General Journal   J-1

Date		Description	PR	Debit	Credit
200- Mar.	10	On March 10, Elizabeth Sasoon			
		began a retail beauty parlor			
		with the following:			
		Cash	100	500000	
		Supplies	101	200000	
		Equipment	102	250000	
		E. Sasoon, Capital	301		950000
	16	Sale Returns & Allowances	306	5000	
		Estelle Evans/Accounts Receivable	E/103		5000
		Issued Credit Memo #100.			
	20	Consolidated Equipment Co./ Accounts Payable	C/200	2000	
		Equipment	102		2000
		Received C.M. Toward Repair.			
	31	Notes Receivable	104	60000	
		Estelle Evans/Accounts Receivable	E/103		60000
		Received 30-day Note			
		from E. Evans.			

Cash   100

200- Mar. 10 31	13,048.50 − 2,062.00 10,986.50	5,000.00 8,048.50 13,048.50	200- Mar. 30	2,062.00

Exercise 7 coutinued

	Supplies			101
200-				
Mar. 10		2,000.00		
28		75.00		
31		610.00		
		2,685.00		

	Equipment			102
200-			200-	
Mar. 10	2,800.00	2,500.00	Mar. 20	20.00
17	− 20.00	300.00		
	2,780.00	2,800.00		

	Accounts Receivable			103
200-			200-	
Mar. 31	1,150.00	1,150.00	Mar. 16	50.00
	− 800.00		31	600.00
	350.00		31	150.00

	Notes Receivable		104
200-			
Mar. 31	E. Evans, 30 days	600.00	

	Accounts Payable			201
200-			200-	
Mar. 20	C. M.	20.00	Mar. 31	910.00 910.00
31		540.00		−560.00
		560.00		350.00

	E. Sasoon, Capital		301
		200-	
		Mar. 10	9,500.00

	E. Sasoon, Drawing		302
200-			
Mar. 21	300.00		

Exercise 7 continued

		Sales		303
		200-		
		Mar. 31		1,150.00
		31		7,900.00
				9,050.00

		Sales Returns and Allowances		104
200-				
Mar. 16	E. Evans	50.00		

	Rent Expense		311
200-			
Mar. 11	300.00		

	Insurance Expense		312
200-			
Mar. 13	180.00		

	Merchandise Purchases		313

	Purchases Returns and Allowances		314

	Salaries Expense		315
200-			
Mar. 27	675.00		

	Sales Discount		316
200-			
Mar. 31	1.50		

	Purchases Discount		307
	200-		
	Mar. 31		8.00

Exercise 7 continued

Accounts Receivable Ledger

Estelle Evans   Page E

Date			PR	Debit	Credit	Debit Balance
200- Mar.	15	1/10, n/30	S-1	200 00		200 00
	16	Credit Memo #100	J-1		50 00	150 00
	24	Bal. less 1% discount	CR-1		150 00	—0—
	31	30-day Note	S-1	600 00		600 00
	31	Received Note	J-1		600 00	—0—
				800 00	800 00	—0—

Ruth Glasser   Page G

Date			PR	Debit	Credit	Debit Balance
200- Mar.	26	1/10, n/30	S-1	350 00		350 00
				350 00		

Elizabeth Sasoon
Schedule of Accounts Receivable
March 31, 200-

Ruth Glasser	$350
Total	$350

Accounts Payable Ledger

Avon Supply Co.   Page A

Date			PR	Debit	Credit	Balance
200- Mar.	12	2/10, n/30	P-1		260 00	260 00
	19	Less 2%	CR-1	260 00		—0—
	30	2/10, n/30	P-1		350 00	350 00
				260 00	610 00	350 00

Exercise 7 continued

Consolidated Equipment Co.   Page C

Date			PR	Debit	Credit	Balance
200- Mar.	17	3/10, 1/20, n/30	P-1		300 00	300 00
	20	C. M. Received	J-1	20 00		280 00
	29	Less 1% discount	CP-1	280 00		—0—
				300 00	300 00	—0—

Elizabeth Sasoon
Schedule of Accounts Payable
March 31, 200-

Avon Supply Co.	$350
Total	$350

Elizabeth Sasoon
Trial Balance
March 31, 200-

ACCOUNT NO.	ACCOUNT TITLE	DEBIT	CREDIT
100	Cash	10,986.50	
101	Supplies	2,685.00	
102	Equipment	2,780.00	
103	Accounts Receivable	350.00	
104	Notes Receivable	600.00	
200	Accounts Payable		350.00
301	Elizabeth Sasoon, Capital		9,500.00
302	Elizabeth Sasoon, Drawing	300.00	
305	Sales		9,050.00
306	Sales Returns and Allowances	50.00	
311	Rent Expense	300.00	
312	Insurance Expense	180.00	
315	Salaries Expense	675.00	
316	Sales Discount	1.50	
307	Purchases Discount		8.00
		$18,908.00	$18,908.00

Exercise 8

1. True.
2. False. If the obligation is paid in 10 days, the buyer is entitled to take a purchases discount of 2% of the purchase price. This discount amounts to $10, thus the amount to be paid in 10 days is $490 ($500–$10).
3. True.
4. False. To the seller the sales discount is an expense. On the buyer's books the discount taken is known as a purchases discount, which to the buyer represents a form of revenue.
5. False. A cash refund given to a customer is recorded in the cash payments journal. If the seller had issued a credit memo, then this transaction would appropriately be placed in the sales returns and allowances journal. If no such journal was in use, then the entry for the credit memo is recorded in the general journal.
6. True.
7. False. A separate account entitled freight on purchases, or freight-in or freight inward, would be used to recognize this freight expense. The title of the above account also indicates the direction of the transportation charges. An account such as freight expense or transportation expense would not be an appropriate account title. The merchandise purchases account is debited only for the cost of the actual merchandise purchased.
8. True.
9. True.
10. True.
11. True.
12. True.
13. False. The purchases returns and allowances journal is used to record the receipt of a credit memo from the seller that authorizes the return of goods by the buyer. A refund is recorded on the purchaser's books in the cash receipts journal.
14. True.
15. False. This transaction is recorded in the general journal, since the transaction has no affect on either the receipt or the payment of cash.

CHAPTER 7

Exercise 1

Reliable Retail Store
Bank Reconciliation Statement
May 30, 200-

Checkbook Balance	$560	Bank Balance		$288
Less: Service Charge & N.S.F. Charge	12	Less: Outstanding Checks		
		Check #103	$20	
		108	20	
		Total Outstanding Checks		40
				248
		Add: Deposits in Transit		300
Adjusted Checkbook Balance	$548	Adjusted Bank Balance		$548

Exercise 2

Alice Reinholt and Co.
Bank Reconciliation Statement
September 30, 200-

Checkbook Balance	$4239.35	Bank Balance	$4581.50
Add: Error in Check	18.00	Add: Deposits in Transit	362.80
	4257.35		4944.30
Less: Service Charge	7.15	Less: Outstanding Checks	694.10
Adjusted Checkbook Balance	$4250.20	Adjusted Bank Balance	$4250.20

Exercise 3

200-				
Jan.	1	Petty Cash	150.00	
		Cash		150.00
		To establish the Petty Cash Fund.		
	24	Freight on Purchases	9.50	
		Postage Expense	46.00	
		Telephone Expense	3.20	
		Repairs Expense	31.70	
		Miscellaneous Expense	22.00	
		Cash		112.40
		To replenish the fund.		

If special journals are used by the organization, both entries are recorded in the cash payments journal.

Exercise 4

200-
Apr. 2 Office Supplies   85.00
            Vouchers Payable   85.00
        Voucher #245 for Purchase from Buyrite
        Stationery Co. Terms: 2/10, n/30. (Voucher register)

    10 Vouchers Payable   85.00
            Cash   83.30
            Purchases Discount   1.70
        Paid Voucher #245 less 2% discount. (Check register)

    14 Petty Cash   50.00
            Vouchers Payable   50.00
        To establish fund by preparing voucher #246.
        (Voucher register)

    15 Vouchers Payable   50.00
            Cash   50.00
        Paid voucher #246 to establish fund. (Check register)

    16 Postage Expense   20.00
        Miscellaneous Expense   15.00
        Delivery Expense   4.50
            Vouchers Payable   39.50
        Issued voucher #247 to replenish the petty
        cash fund. (Voucher register)

    19 Vouchers Payable   39.50
            Cash   39.50
        Issued check in payment of voucher #247.
        (Check register)

Each entry setting up a voucher is initially recorded in the voucher register. Subsequent payments are recorded in the check register. Vouchers prepared but not yet paid are filed in the unpaid voucher file according to the due date of the voucher. Once the voucher has been paid, it is refiled in the paid voucher file, which is usually organized in alphabetical order.

Exercise 5

Voucher Register   P. 3

Date		Payee	PR	Voucher No.	Date Paid	Check No.	Vouchers Payable Credit	Purchases Debit	General Accounts Account	Debit
200-Aug.	2	Best Realty Co.		201	8/7	435	700 00		Rent Expense	700 00
	5	Spelvin Co.		202	8/14	436	2457 00	2457 00		
	13	Buyrite Stationery Co.		203			95 00		Office Supplies	95 00
	18	L. Sprang Co.		204	8/26	437	3769 00		Notes Payable	3720 00
									Interest Expense	49 60
	27	Petty Cashier		205			69 60		Postage	12 70
									Transportation	43 10
									Store Supplies	13 80
	31						7091 20	2457 00		4634 20

Check Register

Date		Payee	Voucher No.	Check No.	Vouchers Payable—Dr.	Purchases Discounts—Cr.	Cash Cr.
200-Aug.	7	Best Realty Co.	201	435	700 00		700 00
	14	Spelvin Co.	202	436	2457 00	49 14	2407 86
	26	L. Sprang Co.	204	437	3769 60		3769 60
	31				6926 60	49 14	6877 46

Exercise 6

Petty Cash Book

Date	Vo #	Payee	Receipts	Payments	Postage Expense	Office Supplies	Store Supplies	Purchases	Other	Amount
200- Sept. 2	—	Check #371	200 00							
7	1	U.S. Post Office		9 00	9 00					
18	2	A.B. Freight Inc.		12 00					Freight on Purchases	12 00
19	3	Bell Co.		45 00				45 00		
			200 00	66 00	9 00	-0-	-0-	45 00		12 00
		Total Payment	66 00							
		Balance	134 00							
29	—	Check #374	66 00							
			200 00							

Voucher Register

Date	Voucher No.	Payee	Explanation	Date Paid	Check No.	Vouchers Payable Credit	Purchases Debit	Office Supplies Debit	General Accounts Account	PR	Debit
200- Sept. 1	916	Smith Inc.	n/10			50000	50000				
2	917	R. Brown	Petty Cashier	9/2	371	20000			Petty Cash		20000
5	918	Jantzen Co.	—	9/11	372	76200			Advertising Expense		76200
12	919	Hall Freight Inc.	Freight Bill n/20			9600			Freight on Purchases		9600
29	921	Petty Cash	Replenish Fund	9/29	374	6600	4500		Postage Expense		900
30	920	Texas Originals	2/10, n/30	9/30	375	95000	95000		Freight on Purchases		1200
30						257400	149500	-0-			107900

Exercise 6 continued

Check Register

Date		Payee	Voucher No.	Check No.	Vouchers Payable—Dr.	Purchases Discounts—Cr.	Cash Cr.
200- Sept.	2	R. Brown	917	371	200 00		200 00
	11	Jantzen Co.	918	372	762 00		762 00
	15	Howard Co.	912	373	713 00		713 00
	29	R. Brown	921	374	66 00		66 00
	30	Texas Originals	920	375	950 00	19 00	931 00
	30				2691 00	19 00	2672 00

CHAPTER 8

Exercise 1

200-
Mar. 6   Standish Inc. (Accounts Receivable)   840
         Sales   840
         Terms: n/30.

     9   Sales Returns and Allowances   60
         Standish Inc. (Accounts Receivable)   60
         Credit memo for damaged merchandise.

Apr. 14   Cash   300
         Standish Inc. (Accounts Receivable)   300
         Part payment

May 18   Bad Debts Expense   480
         Standish Inc. (Accounts Receivable)   480
         Write-off of uncollectible account.

    26   Standish Inc. (Accounts Receivable)   100
         Bad Debts Expense   100
         To restore part of account previously written off.

         Cash   100
         Standish Inc. (Accounts Receivable)   100
         For part payment received of account previously written off.

Exercise 2

1. Accounts Receivable   5,456,575
    Sales   5,456,575
Total credit sales for the year.

2. Cash   121,214
    Sales   121,214
Total cash sales for the year.

3. Cash   5,381,642
Sales Discount   130,004
    Accounts Receivable   5,511,646
Total collections for the year.

4. Allowance for Bad Debts   9,280
    Accounts Receivable   9,280
Wrote off uncollectibles.

5. Accounts Receivable   2,340
    Allowance for Bad Debts   2,340
To restore an account previously written off.

Cash   2,340
    Accounts Receivable   2,340
Collection from an account previously written off

6. Bad Debts Expense   54,565.75
    Allowance for Bad Debts   54,565.75
Adjusting entry based on 1% of net credit sales.

Allowance for Bad Debts

(4)	9,280.00	Bal.		10,912.00
		(5)	3,972.00	2,340.00
		(6)	58,537.75	54,565.75
				67,817.75

Exercise 3

200-

Dec. 31	Bad Debts Expense	8,800	
	Allowance for Bad Debts		8,800

Adjusting entry to recognize uncollectible account expense for the year.
*(Estimated uncollectibles: $9,150 − $350 = Credit ($9,150 estimated uncollectibles—$350 credit balance in allowance account = $8,800 bad debt expense to be recognized.)

Exercise 4

200-

Dec. 31 Bad Debts Expense   2,630

          Allowance for Bad Debts   2,630

Adjusting entry to recognize uncollectible
account expense for the year.
($2,445 estimated uncollectibles + $185 debit balance in
allowance account = $2,630 bad debt expense to be recognized.)

*Under the aging of accounts receivable method, the remaining
balance in the allowance account is considered in preparing the year-
end adjusting entry. Thus, if the allowance account has a credit balance
at the end of the year, the adjusting entry subtracts that balance from
the anticipated bad debts to arrive at the appropriate year-end adjusting entry. If the allowance account had a debit balance, this balance is
added to the anticipated bad debts to arrive at the appropriate year-end
adjusting entry.

Exercise 5

Problem	Interest
(1)	$240 ($3,000 × 8% × 1)
(2)	39 ($2,600 × 9% × 60/360)
(3)	25 ($1,000 × 10% × 90/360)
(4)	37.50 ($5,000 × 6% × 45/360)
(5)	40 ($4,000 × 12% × 30/360)

Exercise 6

Problem	Interest
(1)	$6
(2)	9
(3)	9
(4)	3
(5)	3
(6)	3
(7)	1.50
(8)	1
(9)	4.50
(10)	1.50

Exercise 7

1. Accounts Payable   10,000

         Notes Payable   10,000

Issued 60-day, 9% note this day.

2. Notes Payable   10,000

Interest Expense   150

         Cash   10,150

Paid interest-bearing note today.

Exercise 8

1. The due date of the note is 90 days from the date the note was issued. In this case it was issued on December 1, 2002. The due date is March 1, 2003.

2. The interest income on the note is $27.

3. The interest income that had accrued by December 31, 2002, was $9.

4. 2002

Dec.	1	Notes Receivable	900	
		Accounts Receivable		900
		For 12%, 90-day note		
		received.		

5. 2002

Dec.	31	Interest Receivable	9	
		Interest Income		9
		Accrued interest on note.		

2003

Jan.	1	Interest Income	9	
		Interest Receivable		9
		Reversal entry.		

6. 2003

Mar.	1	Cash	927	
		Interest Income		27
		Notes Receivable		900
		Received maturity value of note.		

7. 2002

Dec.	1	Accounts Payable	900	
		Notes Payable		900
		Issued 90-day, 12% note.		
	31	Interest Expense	9	
		Interest Payable		9
		To recognize accrued interest on note.		

2003

Jan.	1	Interest Payable	9	
		Interest Expense		9
		Reversal entry.		
Mar.	1	Notes Payable	900	
		Interest Expense	27	
		Cash		927
		Paid note plus interest.		

Exercise 9

1. The due date of the note is July 8.
2. The maturity value of the non-interest-bearing note is $1,500.
3. 45 days.
4. 75 days.
5. $1,500 \times 6\% \times 75/360 = \$18.75$.

Exercise 9 continued

6. 200-

Mar. 10	Notes Receivable	1,500.00	
	{Accounts Receivable}		
	{Bache Co.}		1,500.00
	Received 120 day, non-interest-		
	bearing note.		

7. Apr. 24

	Cash	1,481.25	
	Interest Expense	18.75	
	Notes Receivable Discounted		1,500.00
	Discounted at 6%.		

8. July 8

	Notes Receivable Discounted	1,500.00	
	Notes Receivable		1,500.00
	Note is dishonored today.		

9. 8

	{Accounts Receivable}		
	{Bache Co.}	1,515.00	
	Cash		1,515.00
	For dishonored note and protest fee.		

Exercise 10

1. The maturity value of the note is $1,221.
2. Andersen held the note for forty days.
3. Town Bank held the note for fifty days.
4. The amount of the discount on the note is $13.57 calculated as follows:
   Interest on Note at Maturity = $1,200 \times 7\% \times 90$ days = 21
   Principle + Interest = Maturity Value = 1,221
   Maturity Value of Note $\times$ time $\times$ Discount Rate = discount
   $1,221 \times 50$ days $\times 8\% = \$13.57$
5. Maturity Value of Note − Discount = Net Proceeds
   $\$1,221 - \$13.57 = \$1,207.43$
6. 200-

May 28	Cash	1,207.43	
	Interest Income		7.43
	Notes Receivable Discounted		1,200.00

   Discounted 90 day 7% note at a
   discount rate of 8% for 50 days at
   Town Bank.

Exercise 11

	1. Due Date	**2.** Interest Due at Maturity	**3.** Maturity Value	**4.** Discount Period	**5.** Net Proceeds	**6.** Interest Expense (Interest Income)
(1)	Nov. 7	–0–	$3,600.00	20 days	$3,582.00	$18.00
(2)	Nov. 21	$80.00	8,080.00	51 days	7,999.87	.13
(3)	Feb. 13	52.50	3,052.50	85 days	2,994.84	5.16
(4)	Dec. 17	6.00	906.00	10 days	904.24	(4.24)
(5)	Jan. 30	20.00	2,020.00	—	—	(20.00)

Exercise 11 continued

(2) Calculating the cost of discounting this interest-bearing note:

Maturity Value	×	Rate	×	Time
8,080.		7%		51 days
80.80		6%		60 days
+ 13.47		+ 1%		
94.27		7%		60 days
− 14.14				− 9 days
80.13		7%		51 days

Interest Income ($80.) − Interest Expense ($80.13) = Net Interest Expense (.13)

7. Entries for Discounting Each Note:

1. Cash   3,582.00
    Interest Expense   18.00
        Notes Receivable Discounted   3,600.00

2. Cash   7,999.87
    Interest Expense   .13
        Notes Receivable Discounted   8,000.00

3. Cash   2,994.84
    Interest Expense   5.16
        Notes Receivable Discounted   3,000.00

4. Cash   904.24
        Interest Income   4.24
        Notes Receivable Discounted   900.00

8. Adjusting Entries:

200-
Dec. 31   Interest Receivable   10.00
          Interest Income   10.00
      To recognize accrued interest income.

Exercise 12

1. 200-
   Jan. 3   Cash   14,925.00
        Interest Expense   75.00
          Notes Payable   15,000.00
        Discounted our note at First
        National Trust Co. at 6%.

2. Feb. 2   Notes Payable   15,000.00
          Cash   15,000.00
        Paid discounted note due today.

Exercise 13

1. The interest expense under each option is identical.
2. The net proceeds cannot readily be determined since the holding period was not given. However, let us assume a holding period by the bank of 60 days. Under the first option, the net proceeds are $4,900 ($5,000 × 12% × 60/360). The net proceeds under the second option are $5,000.
3. The second option is more favorable since under this option the amount of money available is $5,000, rather than $4,900 if the note is discounted. Most lending institutions will opt to give customers a loan based on discounting the obligation. Thus, if you wanted to borrow $5,000 and the bank required you to discount the loan, you would actually have to borrow a sum greater than $5,000 to obtain net proceeds of $5,000. In this case you would have to borrow approximately $5,110 in order to obtain net proceeds of $5,000.

CHAPTER 9

Exercise 1

Cost of Building
Purchase Price	$95,000
Real Estate Broker's Fee	4,750
Legal Fees	2,500
Total Costs	$102,250

Exercise 2

1. Since the useful life of the asset is five years, each year's depreciation recognized under the straight-line method will be 1/5 of the total depreciation, or 20%.
2. Subtracting the scrap value of the asset from its total cost gives the depreciable value of the asset. Thus, the depreciable value would be calculated as follows: $7,850 − $350 = $7,500.
3. Depreciable value × Straight-line rate = Annual depreciation ($7,500 × 20% = $1,500).
4. Annual depreciation × 3 years = Total depreciation for the period ($1,500 × 3 = $4,500).
5.
Total Asset Value	$7,850
Less 3 Year's Depreciation	4,500
Net Asset Value	3,350

Exercise 3

1. The annual depreciation rate is 1/8 or 12.5%.
2. The Depreciable value is $3,200.
3. Annual depreciation recognized is $3,200 × 12.5% = $400.
4. Depreciation for six months of the first year is $200.
5.

200-
Dec. 31   Depreciation Expense   200
          Accumulated Depreciation   200
     For 6 months depreciation.

Exercise 3 continued

6. $600 ($200 first year + $400 second year).

7. The book value of a fully depreciated asset under the straight-line method is equal to its scrap value, which in this case is $50.

Exercise 4

1. The depreciable value is $15,600 − $600 = $15,000.

2. $15,000/150,000 miles = $.10 per mile.

3.

200-

Dec. 31	Depreciation Expense		2,320	
	Accumulated Depreciation			2,320
	(23,200 miles × $.10)			

4. A credit balance of $6,540.

5. Assuming the total mileage driven was 65,400 miles, the book value of the asset would be:

Original Cost	$15,600
Less Accumulated Depreciation	6,540
Book Value	$9,060

Exercise 5

Original Cost of Asset: $5,000.
Scrap Value: $450.
Useful Life: 5 Years.
Method used: Double-Declining Balance.
DDBM Rate = Straight-Line Rate × 2 (20% × 2 = 40%).

YEAR	COMPUTATION (BV* × RATE)	DEPRECIATION EXPENSE	ACCUMULATED DEPRECIATION	BOOK VALUE
1	$5,000 × 40%	$2,000.00	$2,000.00	$3,000.00
2	3,000 × 40%	1,200.00	3,200.00	1,800.00
3	1,800 × 40%	720.00	3,920.00	1,080.00
4	1,080 × 40%	432.00	4,352.00	648.00
5	648 × 40%	259.20	4,611.20	388.80

*Book Value

Remember: scrap value is ignored when using the double-declining balance method of calculating depreciation. The remaining book value of $338.80 represents the scrap value of this particular asset.

Exercise 6

Original Cost Asset: $70,000
Scrap Value: 0
Useful Life: 4 years.
Method used: Double-Declining Balance.
DDBM Rate = Straight-Line Rate × 2 (25% × 2 = 50%).

Exercise 6 continued

YEAR	COMPUTATION (BV × RATE)	DEPRECIATION EXPENSE	ACCUMULATED DEPRECIATION	BOOK VALUE
1	$70,000 × 50% × 1/2 (6 mo.)	$17,500.00	$17,500.00	$52,500.00
2	52,500 × 50%	26,250.00	43,750.00	26,250.00
3	26,250 × 50%	13,125.00	56,875.00	13,125.00
4	13,125 × 50%	6,562.50	63,437.50	6,562.50
5	6,562.50 × 50% × 1/2 (6 mo.)	1,640.63	65,078.13	4,921.87

Note that in this problem the asset was acquired six months into the year. Thus, the first year's depreciation was only calculated for half a year. The fifth year's depreciation calculation is for the six-month period from January through June, which is the last six months' depreciation on the asset.

Exercise 7

Original Cost of Asset: $5,000.
Scrap Value: $450.
Useful Life: 5 years.
Method used: Sum-of-the-years'-digits.

YEAR	COST LESS RESIDUAL VALUE × RATE	DEPRECIATION FOR YEAR	ACCUMULATED DEPRECIATION	BOOK VALUE END OF YEAR
1	$4,550 × 5/15	$1,516.67	$1,516.67	$3,483.33
2	4,550 × 4/15	1,213.33	2,730.00	2,270.00
3	4,550 × 3/15	910.00	3,640.00	1,360.00
4	4,550 × 2/15	606.67	4,246.67	753.33
5	4,550 × 1/15	303.33	4,550.00	450.00

Exercise 8

Original Cost of Asset: $70,000 (asset acquired on July 1).
Scrap Value: 0.
Useful Life: 4 years.
Method used: Sum-of-the-years'-digits.

YEAR	COST LESS RESIDUAL VALUE × RATE	DEPRECIATION FOR YEAR	ACCUMULATED DEPRECIATION	BOOK VALUE
1	$70,000 × 4/10 × 1/2 (6 mo.)	$14,000.00	$14,000.00	$56,000.00
2	70,000 × 4/10 × 1/2 + 70,000 × 3/10 × 1/2	24,500.00	38,500.00	31,500.00
3	70,000 × 3/10 × 1/2 + 70,000 × 2/10 × 1/2	17,500.00	56,000.00	14,000.00
4	70,000 × 2/10 × 1/2 + 70,000 × 1/10 × 1/2	10,500.00	66,500.00	3,500.00
5	70,000 × 1/10 × 1/2 (final 6 mo. depreciation)	3,500.00	70,000.00	–0–

Exercise 8 continued

Since the asset was acquired on July 1, after, the first six month's depreciation is taken, each subsequent year's depreciation is made up of the second half of the first year's and the first half of the second year's depreciation calculation. The fifth year's depreciation is the last half of the fourth year's depreciation. In this problem, there was no scrap value so that the book value at the end of the four year's depreciation is zero.

Exercise 9

Original Cost of Asset: $325,000.
Scrap Value: 0
Useful Life: 25 Years.
Methods used: **a.** Straight-line method;
                b. Double-declining balance method;
                c. Sum-of-the-years'-digits method.
a. Annual straight-line depreciation is $325,000/25 Years = $13,000. Using this method each of the two years' depreciation would amount to $13,000.
b. The straight-line rate is 4% (1/25) per year. The double-declining balance rate would then be 8% each year on the book value of the asset.
1st year's depreciation = $325,000 × 8% = $26,000.
2nd year's depreciation = $299,000 × 8% = $23,920.
c. The sum-of-the-years'-digits fraction is determined as follows:
S = N × (N + 1)/2 (325 = 25 × (25 + 1)/2).
1st year's depreciation = $325,000 × 25/325 = $25,000.
2nd year's depreciation = $325,000 × 24/325 = $24,000.

Exercise 10

200-			
Oct. 22	Depreciation Expense	5,000.00	
	Accumulated Depreciation		5,000.00
	To recognize depreciation to the date on disposal of the asset.		
22	Cash	22,000.00	
	Accumulated Depreciation	95,000.00	
	Depreciable Asset		115,000.00
	Gain on Sale of Asset		2,000.00
	Sale of depreciable asset.		

Exercise 11

200-			
July 1	Depreciation Expense	3,095.24	
	Accumulated Depreciation		3,095.24
	To recognize 6 months' depreciation.		
1	Computer (New)	96,190.48	
	Accumulated Depreciation	58,809.52	
	Computer (old)		75,000.00
	Cash		80,000.00

Exercise 11 continued

To record trade in of like assets.

Trade-in Allowance:		$20,000.00
Original Cost	$75,000.00	
Accumulated Depreciation	58,809.52	
Book Value of Old Asset:		16,190.48
Gain on Trade-in to be Postponed:		$ 3,809.52
Assigning Cost of New Asset on the Books:		
Original cost	$100,000.00	
Less: Gain to be Postponed	3,809.52	
Value Assigned to New Asset on the Books:		$96,190.48

Exercise 12

Depletion is based on the relationship between the units to be taken from the land in relation to the cost of the rights to use the land. Thus, $60,000/600,000 board feet will give us the amount per board foot of $.10. If 45,000 feet of timber were cut, the depletion recognized would be calculated as follows: 45,000 feet × $.10 = $4,500.

```
200-
Dec. 31   Depletion Expense              4,500
              Accumulated Depletion              4,500
```

Exercise 13

1. Annual straight-line depreciation $450,000/30 = $15,000.
2. Annual depreciation × 20 years = $15,000 × 20 = $300,000.
3.
```
200-
Jan. 1   Building                        45,000
             Cash                                45,000
```
        To recognize capital improvement that will
        extend the useful life by 5 years.
4. Original cost ($450,000) − Accumulated Depreciation ($300,000) = Book Value ($150,000).
5. $150,000 + Capital improvement $45,000 = $195,000.
6. $195,000/15 years = $13,000 annual depreciation after the capital improvement. The old life remaining was 10 years; the capital improvement extended the life by 5 years.

CHAPTER 10

Exercise 1

		| Received			| Issued			| Balance		
Date		Units	Unit Cost	Total Cost	Units	Unit Cost	Total Cost	Units	Unit Cost	Total Cost
200- May	3	500	10.00	5,000.00				500	10.00	5,000.00
	5	300	10.20	3,060.00				500 300	10.00 10.20	5,000.00 3,060.00
	9				150	10.00	1,500.00	350 300	10.00 10.20	3,500.00 3,060.00
	10				350 50	10.00 10.20	3,500.00 510.00	250	10.20	2,550.00
	15	200	10.10	2,020.00				250 200	10.20 10.10	2,550.00 2,020.00
	24				250 50	10.20 10.10	2,550.00 505.00	150	10.10	1,515.00

Table title: Basis—FIFO

```
200-
May   3   Merchandise Inventory            5,000
              Cash                                    5,000
          Acquired 500 units @ $10.00
          per unit

      5   Merchandise Inventory            3,060
              Cash                                    3,060
          Bought 300 units @ $10.20
          per unit

      9   Cash                             3,000
              Sales                                   3,000
          150 units at $20 per unit.

          Cost of Goods Sold               1,500
              Merchandise Inventory                   1,500
          150 units at $10 = $1,500.

     10   Cash                             8,000
              Sales                                   8,000
          Sold 400 units at $20 per unit.

          Cost of Goods Sold               4,010
              Merchandise Inventory                   4,010
          350 units at $10   = $3,500.
          50 units at $10.20 =    510.
                                 $4,010.
```

Exercise 1 continued

15	Merchandise Inventory	2,020	
	Cash		2,020
	Bought 200 units @ $10.10 per unit		
24	Cash	6,000	
	Sales		6,000
	Sold 300 units at $20 each.		
	Cost of Goods Sold	3,055	
	Merchandise Inventory		3,055

250 units at $10.20 = $2,550.
50 units at $10.10 =   505.
                     $3,055.

Exercise 2

					Basis—FIFO						
		Received			**Issued**			**Balance**			
Date		Units	Unit Cost	Total Cost	Units	Unit Cost	Total Cost	Units	Unit Cost	Total Cost	
200- May	3	500	10.00	5,000.00				500	10.00	5,000.00	
	5	300	10.20	3,060.00				500	10.00	5,000.00	
								300	10.20	3,060.00	
	9				150	10.20	1,530.00	500	10.00	5,000.00	
								150	10.20	1,530.00	
	10				150	10.20	1,530.00				
					250	10.00	2,500.00	250	10.00	2,500.00	
	15	200	10.10	2,020.00				250	10.00	2,500.00	
								200	10.10	2,020.00	
	24				200	10.10	2,020.00				
					100	10.00	1,000.00	150	10.00	1,500.00	

200- May	3	Merchandise Inventory	5,000	
		Cash		5,000
		Bought 500 units @ $10.00 per unit		
	5	Merchandise Inventory	3,060	
		Cash		3,060
		Bought 300 units @ $10.20 per unit		

Exercise 2 continued

200- May	9	Cash		3,000	
		Sales			3,000
		Sold 150 units at $20 each.			
		Cost of Goods Sold		1,530	
		Merchandise Inventory			1,530
		150 units at $10.20 = $1,530.			
	10	Cash		8,000	
		Sales			8,000
		Sold 400 units at $20 each			
		Cost of Goods Sold		4,030	
		Merchandise Inventory			4,030
		150 units at $10.20 = $1,530.			
		250 units at $10.00 = 2,500.			
		$4,030.			
	15	Merchandise Inventory		2,020	
		Cash			2,020
		Purchased 200 units @ $10.10			
		per unit			
	24	Cash		6,000	
		Sales			6,000
		Sold 300 units at $20 per unit.			
		Cost of Goods Sold		3,020	
		Merchandise Inventory			3,020
		200 units at $10.10 = $2,020.			
		100 units at $10.00 = 1,000.			
		$3,020.			

Exercise 3

1.   500 units at $6.50 = $3,250
      240 units at $5.90 = 1,416
      370 units at $6.10 = 2,257
      320 units at $6.00 = 1,920
    1,430   8,843
    Average Cost per Unit: $8,843/1,430 = $6.18.
2. $6.18 × 290 = $1,792.20.
3. Cost of Goods Available for Sale: $8,843.00
    Ending Merchandise Inventory: 1,792.20
    Cost of Goods Sold: $7,050.80

Exercise 4

Gross Profit Method: Cost of goods sold/Net sales = $65,000/$100,000
= 65% (Last Year).

Exercise 4 continued

1. 100% − 65% = 35% (Gross Profit Rate).
2. Beginning Inventory: $22,500
   Net Purchases: 15,750
   Cost of Goods Available: $38,250
   —Cost of Goods Sold: 19,500 ($30,000 × 65% = $19,500)
   Ending Inventory Value: $18,750

3. Cost of Goods Sold = $30,000 × 65% = $19,500.
4. Gross Profit on Sales = $30,000 × 35% = $10,500.

Exercise 5

Retail Method = Total Cost Available/Total Retail Available = $440,000/$800,000 = 55%.

Total Cost of Goods Available for Sale: $440,000
Cost of Goods Sold ($730,000 × 55%):   −401,500
Ending Inventory at Cost: $ 38,500

CHAPTER 11

Exercise 1

The income ceiling on Social Security taxes for 2003 is $87,000 with a social security tax rate of 6.2%. The Medicare tax rate is 1.45%

Employee	Wages	Cumulative Earnings	FICA Tax	Medicare Tax
A. Albert	$ 685.30	$30,240.45	$ 42.49	$ 9.94
B. Blume	1,020.85	44,917.40	63.29	14.80
C. Carter	1,900.00	83,600.00	117.80	27.55
D. Delphine	2,180.00	93,825.00	−0−	31.61
E. Edwards	1,945.00	85,770.50	76.23	28.20

Exercise 2

Employee	Gross Pay	Federal Withholding Taxes
G. Brown (S,1)	$ 146.50	$ 4.00
L. Albert (M,2)	875.00	84.00
R. Talley (M,3)	1,240.00	138.00
S. Russo (S,2)	745.75	87.00
M. Santini (M,5)	1,320.00	128.00

Exercise 3

Employee	NYS Withholding Tax	NYC Withholding Tax
G. Brown (S,1)	$ .00	$ .60
L. Albert (M,2)	13.30	23.90
R. Talley (M,3)	63.52	37.60
S. Russo (S,2)	31.64	7.85
M. Santini (M,5)	66.40	39.20

Exercise 4

Payroll Register—Week Ending August 22, 2003

Name	Status Exempt	Gross Pay	FICA Tax	Medicare Tax	Federal Withholding Tax	NYS Withholding Tax	NYC Withholding Tax	NYS Dis. Ben. Tax	Other Deductions		Total Deductions	Net Pay
									Item	Amount		
Alan Gain	M,5	585 40	36 29	8 49	17 00	16 40	10 55	0 60			89 33	496 07
Jerry Hand	M,4	748 75	46 42	10 86	46 00	28 56	17 35	0 60			149 79	598 96
George Kurl	M,4	877 00	54 37	12 72	66 00	37 35	22 40	0 60			193 44	683 56
Steven Feld	S,2	615 50	38 16	8 92	61 00	22 70	14 15	0 60			145 54	469 96
Allan Finney	S,1	1025 75	63 60	14 87	178 00	52 14	30 90	0 60			340 11	685 64
		3852 40	238 85	55 86	368 00	157 15	95 35	3 00			918 21	2934 19

Exercise 4 continued

2003

Aug. 22	Salary Expense		3,852.40	
		FICA Taxes Payable		238.85
		Medicare Taxes Payable		55.86
		FWT Payable		368.00
		NYSWT Payable		157.15
		NYCWT Payable		95.35
		NYS Disability Benefits Payable		3.00
		Cash		2,934.19
	Payroll for week ending 8/19.			

Exercise 5

2003

Sept. 6	FWT Payable	368.00	
	FICA Payable	238.85	
	Medicare Taxes Payable	55.86	
	FICA Tax Expense	238.85	
	Medicare Taxes Expense	55.86	
	Cash		957.42

To remit payroll taxes to
federal depository.

6	NYSWT Payable	157.15	
	NYCWT Payable	95.35	
	Cash		252.50

To remit payroll taxes to state.

6	NYS Dis. Ben. Payable	3.00	
	Cash		3.00

To remit disability benefits
tax to state.

Exercise 6

	Federal Unemployment	State Unemployment
A. Taylor	$43.72	$229.53
S. Stern	56.00	294.00
A. Rothstein	28.52	149.75
J. Shapiro	56.00	294.00
S. Bailey	52.41	275.14

Exercises 7 and 8

Payroll Register—Week Ending _____

Name	Status Exempt	Total Regular (Hours)	Overtime (Hours)	Hourly Rate	Earnings Regular	Earnings Overtime	Earnings Total	FICA Tax	Medicare Tax	Federal Withholding Tax	NYS Withholding Tax	NYC Withholding Tax	NYS Dis. Ben. Tax	Total Deductions	Net Pay
Albert	S,2	40	2	5 35	214 00	16 05	230 05	14 26	3 34	7 00	2 50	1 55	0 60	29 25	200 80
Baker	M,4	39	0	9 10	354 00	0 00	354 90	22 00	5 15	0 00	5 40	3 45	0 60	36 60	318 30
Cox	S,3	40	5	6 20	248 00	46 50	294 50	18 26	4 27	7 00	4 10	2 70	0 60	36 93	257 57
Daly	S,1	40	7	8 50	340 00	89 25	429 25	26 61	6 22	42 00	12 00	7 80	0 60	95 24	334 01
Evans	M,2	40	1	5 15	206 00	7 73	213 73	13 25	3 10	0 00	1 30	1 35	0 60	19 60	194 13
Fall	M,5	40	4	9 80	392 00	58 80	450 80	27 95	6 54	4 00	8 90	5 95	0 60	53 94	396 86
		239	19		1754 90	218 33	1973 23	122 33	28 62	60 00	34 20	22 80	3 60	271 56	1701 67

Exercises 7 and 8 continued

Salaries Expense	1,973.23	
FICA Taxes Payable		122.33
Medicare Taxes Payable		28.62
FWT Payable		60.00
NYSWT Payable		34.20
NYCWT Payable		22.80
NYS Disability Benefits Payable		3.60
Cash		1,701.6
FICA Tax Expense	122.33	
FICA Taxes Payable	122.33	
Medicare Taxes Expense	28.62	
Medicare Taxes Payable	28.62	
FWT Payable	60.00	
Cash		361.92
NYSWT Payable	34.20	
NYCWT Payable	22.80	
Cash		69.00
NYS Dis. Ben. Payable	3.60	
Cash		3.60

CHAPTER 12

Exercise 1

Cash	2,000	
Accounts Receivable	5,200	
Allowance for Bad Debts		1,600
Cain, Capital		5,600
To record contributions of Cain.		

Exercise 2

	Able	Baker	Crawford	Total
Net Income				$50,000
Salary Allowance	$12,000	$15,000	$ 3,000	(30,000)
Interest on Capital	2,000	2,800	3,600	(8,400)
Balance to be distributed as per				11,600
P&L ratio distribution	2,900	2,900	5,800	(11,600)
Total Distribution	$16,900	$20,700	$12,400	$50,000

200-			
Dec. 31	Able, Capital	10,000	
	Baker, Capital	17,000	
	Crawford, Capital	2,500	
	Able, Drawing		10,000
	Baker, Drawing		17,000
	Crawford, Drawing		2,500
	To close drawing to respective capital accounts.		

Exercise 2 continued

```
200-
Dec 31   Income Summary                          50,000
               Able, Capital                                16,900
               Baker, Capital                               20,700
               Crawford, Capital                            12,400
          To transfer income earned to
          respective partners' capital accounts.
```

Able, Baker, Crawford Partnership
Statement of Capital
For the Year Ended December 31, 200-

	Able	Baker	Crawford
Capital Balances, Jan. 1, 200-	$25,000	$35,000	$45,000
Net Income	16,900	20,700	12,400
Less: Partners' Drawing	(10,000)	(17,000)	(2,500)
Net Increase in Capital	$ 6,900	$ 2,300	$ 9,900
Capital Balances, Dec. 31, 200-	$31,900	$37,300	$54,900

Exercise 3

	Cash	+	Other Assets	=	Accounts Payable	+	Roth (2)	Capital Balances Stern (1)	Tom (1)
(1,2)	$12,000 15,000		$60,000 – 60,000		$3,000		$20,000 – 22,500	$25,000 – 11,250	$24,000 – 11,250
(3)	$27,000 – 3,000		–0–		3,000 – 3,000		– $2,500	$13,750	$12,750
(4)	$24,000		–0–		–0–		– $2,500 + 2,500	$13,750 – 1,250	$12,750 – 1,250
							–0–	$12,500 – 12,500	$11,500 – 11,500
	– 24,000								
	–0–		–0–		–0–		–0–	–0–	–0–

```
200-
June 15   Cash                                    15,000
          Loss and Gain on Realization             45,000
               Other Assets                                60,000
          Sale of noncash assets.

     15   Roth, Capital                            22,500
          Stern, Capital                           11,250
          Tom, Capital                             11,250
               Loss and Gain on Realization                45,000
          To distribute loss to partners
          according to their profit-and-loss
          sharing ratio (2:1:1).
```

Exercise 3 continued

200-

June 15	Accounts Payable	3,000	
	Cash		3,000
	Payment of outstanding creditors.		
15	Stern, Capital	12,500	
	Tom, Capital	11,500	
	Cash		24,000
	Distribution of the remaining cash according to the partners' remaining capital balances.		

Note that the chart reflects the deficit of Roth, which is shared by Stern and Tom in their ratio to each other (1 : 1). No entry is recorded on the books to reflect their reduction in capital as a result of the deficit. The respective capital balances after liquidation would be: Roth, $2,500; Stern, $1,250; Tom, $1,250.

Exercise 4

Cash	11,000	
Loss and Gain on Realization	10,000	
Other Assets		21,000
Sale of noncash assets.		
Evan, Capital	3,000	
Felding, Capital	3,000	
Glickson, Capital	4,000	
Loss and Gain on Realization		10,000
To distribute loss according to the partners' profit-and-loss-sharing ratio (3 : 3 : 4).		
Accounts Payable	20,000	
Cash		20,000
To pay outstanding obligations to creditors.		
Evan, Capital	9,000	
Felding, Capital	12,000	
Glickson, Capital	14,000	
Cash		35,000
To distribute remaining cash according to partners' capital balances.		

Exercise 5

1.	Cash	5,000	
	Tinker, Capital		5,000
	For additional investment by partner.		
2.	Income Summary	30,000	
	Tinker, Capital		18,000
	Chance, Capital		12,000
	To distribute partnership profit according to their respective profit-and-loss sharing ratio of 3 : 2.		

Exercise 5 continued

3. Tinker, Capital   9,500
    Chance, Capital   15,200
        Tinker, Drawing   9,500
        Chance, Drawing   15,200
    To close respective drawing accounts to the
    individual capital accounts.

The new balances in the partnership capital accounts are calculated as follows:

	Tinker	Chance
Beginning Capital Balances:	$32,500	$50,000
Additional Investment:	5,000	—
	37,500	50,000
Net Income Distribution:	18,000	12,000
Less: Drawing	(9,500)	(15,200)
Net Chance in Capital:	8,500	(3,200)
Ending Capital Balances:	$46,000	$46,800

CHAPTER 13

Exercise 1

Year	Preferred Dividend	Common Dividend	Total Dividend
1			
Preferred	$ 6,000	–0–	$ 6,000
(Arrears owed to preferred stockholders amount to $2,000.)			
2			
Preferred	$ 3,500	–0–	$ 3,500
(Arrears owed to preferred stockholders amount to $6,500.)			
3			
Preferred	$12,000	–0–	$12,000
(Arrears owed to preferred stockholders amount to $2,500.)			
4			
Preferred	$10,500	—	$10,500
Common		$19,500	$19,500
Total			$30,000
5			
Preferred	$ 8,000	—	$ 8,000
Common	—	$28,000	28,000
Total			$36,000

Exercise 2

200-

Apr. 5	Cash	30,000	
	Common Stock		30,000
10	Cash	210,000	
	Premium on Preferred Stock		10,000
	Preferred Stock		200,000
Aug. 4	Cash	495,000	
	Discount on Preferred Stock	5,000	
	Preferred Stock		500,000
Oct. 6	Cash	30,000	
	Premium on Common Stock		5,000
	Common Stock		25,000

Exercise 3

200-

Jan. 23	Cash	156,000	
	Premium on Common Stock		6,000
	Common Stock		150,000
29	Cash	475,000	
	Discount on Preferred Stock	25,000	
	Preferred Stock		500,000

200-

Jan. 30	Land	300,000	
	Building	125,000	
	Equipment	25,000	
	Premium on Common Stock		14,400
	Common Stock		360,000
	Notes Payable		75,600

Exercise 4

1.	Aug. 10	Cash	80,000	
		Building	40,000	
		Equipment	20,000	
		Premium on Common Stock		40,000
		Common Stock		100,000
2.	Aug. 10	Cash	80,000	
		Building	40,000	
		Equipment	20,000	
		Discount on Common Stock	10,000	
		Common Stock		150,000
3.	Aug. 10	Cash	80,000	
		Building	40,000	
		Equipment	20,000	
		Common Stock		120,000

Exercise 5

200-			
Apr. 3	Cash	60,000	
	Premium on Common Stock		10,000
	Common Stock		50,000
	Sold 10,000 shares of common.		
12	Land	510,000	
	Premium on Common Stock		10,000
	Common Stock		500,000
	Issued 1,000 shares of common.		
16	Organizational Costs	5,500	
	Premium on Common Stock		500
	Common Stock		5,000
	Issued 1,000 shares of common.		
May 4	Cash	375,000	
	Discount on Preferred Stock	25,000	
	Preferred Stock		400,000
	Sold 4,000 shares of preferred at a discount.		

Exercise 6

Year	Preferred Dividend	Common Dividend	Total Dividend
1			
Preferred	$15,000	–0–	$15,000
(Arrears owed to preferred stockholders amount to $5,000.)			
2			
Preferred	$15,000	–0–	$15,000
(Arrears owed to preferred stockholders amount to $10,000.)			
3			
Preferred	$30,000	—	$30,000
Common	—	$17,000	17,000
Total			$47,000
4			
Preferred	$20,000	—	$20,000
Common	—	$30,000	30,000
Additional Distribution	6,000	9,000	15,000
Totals	$26,000	$39,000	$65,000

After the preferred and common stocks have received their initial dividend distributions, the balance of $15,000 to be distributed is done so based on each class of stock's ratio. Thus, the ratio is $500,000 : $750,000 or 2 : 3. (2/5 × $15,000 = $6,000 and 3/5 × $15,000 = $9,000.)

Exercise 6 continued

Note that in years 1 and 2, no dividend distribution was made to the common stockholders. In year 3, the extent of the distribution to common stockholders was limited to $17,000 due to the fact that the arrearage owed to preferred stockholders from years 1 and 2 had to be made up first. The high dividend distribution in the fourth year enabled both the preferred and common stockholders to share in the extra distribution of $15,000 according to their total capital ratio. If the preferred stock had been non-participative, then the entire distribution in excess of the obligation to the preferred stockholders ($20,000) would have been distributed to the common stockholders. This distribution to the common stockholders would have amounted to $45,000. Both the issuing corporation and the future investor must take the preference rights of the preferred stockholder into consideration because of their obvious effect on the distribution of dividends.

SUPPLEMENTARY EXERCISES

The first supplementary exercise for each chapter consists of general questions about accounting theory. The order of the questions follows closely the order in which the topics are presented in the chapter. Answers to these questions will be found readily within the chapter.

The remaining supplementary exercises mirror the exercises presented throughout the chapter. These exercises provide additional practice and reinforcement of the concepts presented. Use these additional exercises as necessary.

An "answer key" at the end of the supplementary exercises provides key figures (primary or most significant answers) to the exercises where appropriate and possible. Refer to the exercises illustrated in the chapter or the detailed solutions to the chapter exercises for further explanations as needed.

Chapter 1 The Accounting Equation

EXERCISE 1-1

1. What organizations, institutions, and individuals make use of accounting information?
2. What is a business transaction, and how does the accountant deal with it?
3. What are the three elements of the accounting equation? What is the accounting equation?
4. What are the four categories that assets are divided into? How are these categories defined?
5. What is the ownership of the assets of the business known as? What other classification of items might this definition pertain to?
6. If a service-oriented company has revenue of $3,500, and total expenses of $1,900, for a particular period, what is the difference between these amounts and what does the accountant call this difference?
7. When the owner of a business borrows assets for the business, what does the business acquire in addition to the assets, and how does it affect the ownership of the assets by the proprietor?
8. Define and give examples of "temporary" capital accounts. What is an example of a "permanent" capital account?

EXERCISE 1-2

The form of the **Accounting Equation** appears below. For each item listed place a plus (+) sign in the column in which the item belongs: asset, liability, or capital.

No.	Item Name	Asset	Liability	Capital
Ex.	Check	+		
1.	Equipment			
2.	Supplies			
3.	Accounts Payable			
4.	Bills and Coins			
5.	Investment			
6.	Due from R. Jones			
7.	Customer			
8.	Typewriters			
9.	Due to A. Brown			
10.	Owner's Equity			

EXERCISE 1-3

Refer to the directions and form illustrated in Exercise 1-2. Duplicate the form and classify the following items:

1. Cash
2. IOU
3. Due from Bluebel Co.
4. Microcomputer
5. Proprietor's Equity
6. Accounts Payable
7. Creditor
8. Desk
9. Due from Customer
10. Wrote a Check

EXERCISE 1-4

Based on the information provided below, fill in the missing amount for each element to get the **Accounting Equation** to balance.

	ASSETS	=	LIABILITIES	+	CAPITAL
1.	$5,000.00		?		$ 3,500.00
2.	?		$1,500.00		$ 6,250.00
3.	$6,550.00		$1,550.00		?
4.	$9,800.00		$2,700.00		?
5.	?		$4,153.00		$10,347.00

***EXERCISE
1-5***

Refer to instructions to Exercise 1-4.

	ASSETS	=	LIABILITIES	+	CAPITAL
1.	?		$1,330.00		$ 3,450.00
2.	$ 5,000.00		?		$ 4,200.00
3.	$ 6,990.00		$3,285.00		?
4.	?		$2,350.00		$ 8,946.00
5.	$12,440.00		?		$11,300.00

***EXERCISE
1-6***

Complete the form that appears below. Classify the assets listed, placing a plus (+) sign under the appropriate title that each of the ten assets would correctly belong under.

No.	Name of Asset	Cash	Accounts Receivable	Office Equipment	Furniture & Fixtures	Delivery Equipment
Ex.	Coins	+				
1.	Bills					
2.	Due from B. Brown					
3.	Typewriter					
4.	Desk					
5.	Automobile					
6.	Check					
7.	Customer					
8.	Filing Cabinet					
9.	Cash in Bank					
10.	Computer					

***EXERCISE
1-7***

Complete the form that appears below. Classify the assets listed, placing a plus (+) sign under the appropriate title that each of the ten assets would correctly belong under.

No.	Name of Asset	Cash	Accounts Receivable	Office Equipment	Furniture & Fixtures	Delivery Equipment
Ex.	Coins	+				
1.	Money Order					
2.	Adding Machine					
3.	Chair					
4.	Delivery Van					
5.	Due from Jones					
6.	Paper Cutter					
7.	Desk Lamp					
8.	Checks					
9.	Customer					
10.	Printer					

Chapter 2 Financial Statements

**EXERCISE
2-1**

1. What are the three basic reports prepared by the accountant? In what order are these statements prepared? How do the dates on the reports differ?
2. What information appears in the heading of the income statement? What are the two main parts of the income statement body? What are the two possible results that the income statement will provide?
3. What kinds of accounts appear on the income statement? How does the accountant classify these accounts?
4. What financial statement relies on the income statement for its preparation? What accounts are an integral part of the preparation of this statement?
5. What financial statement relies on the preparation of the statement of capital for its preparation?
6. When and for what period of time is the balance sheet prepared? What kind of accounts are found on the balance sheet?
7. What is the difference in appearance between the account form and the report form of the balance sheet?
8. What is the difference between a current liability and a long-term liability?

**EXERCISE
2-2**

Adam Brown is the owner of a beauty parlor business. From the information presented below, prepare an income statement for the month ending June 30 of the current year.

Revenue From Permanents	$4,375	Supplies Expense	$655
Haircut Revenue	5,080	Maintenance Expense	95
Rent Expense	400	Advertising Expense	800
Salaries Expense	950		

**EXERCISE
2-3**

Prepare an income statement for Sarah Fland, for the month ending September 30 of the current year. Ms. Fland is the owner of a car wash business.

Income From Services	$6,250	Rent Expense	$ 900
Car Wash Supplies Expense	1,380	Salaries Expense	1,250
Electricity Expense	765	Maintenance Expense	290
Water Tax Expense	1,200	Insurance Expense	355

**EXERCISE
2-4**

The January 1 capital balance for Robert Rockwell's business was $12,565. During the current year Mr. Rockwell withdrew $8,575, from the business in anticipation of profits. The income statement prepared for the current year ending December 31 indicated a net income of $11,300.

Prepare a Statement of Capital for Mr. Rockwell for the year ending December 31.

EXERCISE 2-5

Emanuel Rodriguez is the proprietor of the All-Hours Messenger Service. At the beginning of the current calendar year (January 1), his capital balance was $22,890. During the current year, he made an additional investment of $8,000. He withdrew $1,500 per month in anticipation of profits. The businesses net income for the year amounted to $24,300.

Prepare a statement of capital for Mr. Rodriguez, for the calendar year. (Show the additional investment as an increase in the January 1 capital balance. Do not label the results of this addition.)

EXERCISE 2-6

Allison Jones is the owner of a dry cleaning business. Prepare an **account form Balance Sheet** as of June 30 of the current year, based on the following information:

Cash	$3,230.00
Accounts Receivable	
Albert Costume Co.	165.00
Cave Beauty Parlor	90.00
Furniture and Fixtures	1,700.00
Cleaning Equipment	1,500.00
Accounts Payable	
Evans Supply Co.	900.00
Radiant Co.	500.00
Allison Jones, Capital	5,285.00

EXERCISE 2-7

Samuel Bland is the owner of a car wash business. Prepare an **account form Balance Sheet** as of September 30 of the current year, based on the following information:

Cash	$ 4,430.00
Accounts Receivable	
ZZZ Trucking Co.	327.00
Anny Car Service	175.00
Car Wash Equipment	9,300.00
Accounts Payable	
CW Supply Co.	245.00
Equipment Repairs, Inc.	1,200.00
Samuel Bland, Capital	12,787.00

EXERCISE 2-8

Using the data provided in Exercise 2-6 prepare the **report form Balance Sheet**.

EXERCISE 2-9

Using the data provided in Exercise 2-7 prepare the **report form Balance Sheet**.

EXERCISE 2-10

Ramirez Cruzado is the owner of a private car service business. On October 1 of the current year, Mr. Cruzado has the following **assets**, **liabilities**, and **owner's capital**:

Cash in Bank	$ 5,475.00
Accounts Payable	
Rental Sales, Inc.	1,245.00
Automobiles	15,400.00
Ramirez Cruzado, Capital	?
Auto Repair Equipment	2,500.00
Office Machines	900.00
Accounts Receivable	
City-Wide Co.	375.00
Alan Banndt, Inc.	420.00
Furniture and Fixtures	1,205.00

Prepare an **account form Balance Sheet** for Mr. Cruzado.

EXERCISE 2-11

Rita Antoninado is the owner of the City Beauty Parlor. On December 1 of the current year, Ms. Antoninado has the following **assets**, **liabilities**, and **owner's capital**:

Cash in Bank	$6,345.00
Accounts Payable	
Beauty Supplies Co.	2,255.00
Beauty Parlor Equipment	5,650.00
Rita Antoninado, Capital	?
Furniture and Fixtures	3,750.00
Office Machines	300.00
Accounts Receivable	
Selma D. Qunine	45.00
Stylish Model Agency	620.00

Prepare an **account form Balance Sheet** for Ms. Antoninado.

Chapter 3 Recording Business Transactions

EXERCISE 3-1

1. What are daily business transactions? Where are records of daily business transactions recorded?
2. What are the three kinds of information that every business transaction should have? What changes can result from every business transaction?
3. Where are business transactions recorded? How many sides does each individual record contain? What are the three things that may appear on each side of the record?
4. On which side of the account is an increase (decrease) in an asset shown? Where does the beginning balance appear?
5. On which side of the account is an increase (decrease) in capital shown? Where does the beginning balance appear?
6. On which side of the account is an increase (decrease) in a liability shown? Where does the beginning balance appear?

Exercise 3-1 continued

7. On which side of the account is revenue recorded to? What effect does revenue have on permanent capital?

8. On which side of the account is an expense recorded to? What effect does an expense have on permanent capital?

9. On which side of the account is the proprietor's drawing account recorded to? What effect does it have on permanent capital?

10. Explain the advantage of using the three- or four-column ledger account rather than the "T" account form.

11. What is a journal? What advantages does the journal provide that the ledger doesn't? Why must the ledger be used, even after the introduction of the journal?

12. Why is posting necessary? What are the two things that posting tells the accountant?

13. What is the purpose of preparing the trial balance? How frequently should it be prepared? Why?

EXERCISE 3-2

Use the following Expanded Accounting Equation form:

	Assets				=	Liabilities	+	Capital
Cash +	Accounts Receivable +	Furniture & Fixtures +	Office Equipment +	Office Supplies =		Accounts Payable +		B. Greedlindt, Capital
	(Example)	+ 500.00				+ 500.00		

For each of the business transactions listed below, indicate the appropriate records affected by placing the dollar amounts and direction of the changes in the appropriate columns.

The Betsy Greedlindt Delivery Service had the following **business transactions** during the current month:

1. Betsy Greedlindt invested $9,000 cash in the business.

2. The proprietor bought a desk top calculator for use in the office, paying cash of $35.

Exercise 3-2 continued

3. A customer, Andrea Hayes, borrowed $150 from the proprietor, who took the money out of the business.
4. Ms. Greedlindt bought office supplies from the B. Browny Stationery Co. for $200. Ms. Greedlindt agreed to pay for these supplies next month.
5. The proprietor sent a check for $75 to B. Browny Stationery Co. in part payment of the $200 outstanding debt.
6. A customer, Andrea Hayes, paid $80 of her debt to the business.
7. The proprietor purchased six chairs, costing $300 from the AA Furniture Co. on credit.
8. Ms. Greedlindt took home office supplies valued at $15 for her own use.

EXERCISE 3-3

Use the following Expanded Accounting Equation form:

							=	Liabilities	+	Capital
		Assets								
	Accounts		Automobile		Auto	Office		Accounts		A. Smith,
Cash +	Receivable +			+	Supplies +	Supplies =		Payable	=	Capital
	(Example)				+ 200.00			+ 200.00		

For each of the business transactions presented below, indicate the appropriate records affected by placing the dollar amounts and direction of the changes in the appropriate columns.

Alexandrea Smith is the owner of the Fast and Friendly Car Service. The following business transactions occurred during the current month:

1. Ms. Smith invested $12,500 cash in the business.
2. Received a check for $125 from ABC Bank for amount owed to the car service.

Exercise 3-3 continued

3. Purchased a used automobile for $3,200 paying cash.
4. Purchased gasoline and oil for $25 cash.
5. Purchased office supplies for $135 from the ABC Stationery Co. on account.
6. Sent a check for $300 to Legent Auto Repair Co. in full payment of an outstanding obligation.
7. Purchased letterhead stationery for $75 cash.
8. Took home office supplies valued at $25 for her own use.

EXERCISE 3-4

From the following Balance Sheet record the beginning balances on to **"T" Accounts**.

Albert Z. Randolph
Balance Sheet
April 1, 200-

Assets			Liabilities and Capital		
Cash		$10,200.00	Accounts Payable		
Accounts Receivable			Fabbs		
R. Cling, Inc.	$220.00		Supply Co.	$300.00	
C. Gable, Co.	280.00	550.00	Ed & Co.	175.00	$475.00
Office Supplies		150.00	Albert Z. Randolf,		
Office Equipment		2,000.00	Capital		12,375.00
Total Assets		$12,850.00	Total Liabilities		
			and Capital		$12,850.00

EXERCISE 3-5

From the following Balance Sheet record the beginning balances on to **"T" Accounts**.

Cynthia B. Stempler
Balance Sheet
June 1, 200-

Assets			Liabilities and Capital		
Cash		$9,300.00	Accounts Payable		
Accounts Receivable			Ardleys & Son	$500.00	
Able Co.	$900.00		Ryantal, Inc.	200.00	$700.00
D. Kleindt, Co.	550.00	1,450.00	Cynthia B. Stempler,		
Store Supplies		200.00	Capital		13,450.00
Furniture & Fixtures		3,200.00	Total Liabilities		
Total Assets		$14,150.00	and Capital		$14,150.00

EXERCISE 3-6

Use the following Expanded Accounting form. Record the beginning balances to "T" accounts for the month of January of the current year:

	Assets					=	Liabilities	+	Capital
Cash	+ Accounts Receivable +	Furniture & Fixtures +	Beauty Equipment +	Beauty Supplies =			Accounts Payable	+	G. Cransdale, Capital
4,000.	2,500.	1,800.	1,300.	165.			2,000.		7,765.

Record each of the business transactions presented below to the appropriate ledger account:

Gerrard Cransdale is the owner of a small unisex beauty parlor. The following business transactions took place during the current month.

200-

Jan 1 Bought chairs and a reception table from the R & V Equipment Co. for $1,200 on account.

2 Purchased 5 hair dryers for $750 cash.

3 Bought cream rinse and shampoo from Able Beauty Supplies. Inc. for $150 on account.

4 Returned a defective chair valued at $100 to the R & V Equipment Co. Mr. Cransdale reduced his obligation to the company to the extent of the value of the item returned.

5 Sent a check for $250 in part payment of an outstanding obligation to the Riverside Supply Co.

6 Purchased curling irons and other equipment for $300 cash.

7 Contributed a desk worth $175 to the business.

8 Received a check from Cynthia Rayes for $55. This check represented the payment of an outstanding obligation from a customer.

EXERCISE 3-7

Use the following Expanded Accounting Equation form. Record the beginning balances to "T" accounts for the month of February of the current year:

	Assets				=	Liabilities	+	Capital
Cash +	Accounts Receivable +	Furniture & Fixtures +	Beauty Equipment +	Beauty Supplies =		Accounts Payable +		B. Swainberger, Capital
5,600.	3,400.	2,100.	3,800.	425.		1,250.		14,075.

Record each of the business transactions presented below to the appropriate ledger account.

Blanche Swainberger is the owner of a beauty salon. The following business transactions occurred during the month of February.

200-

Feb 1 Sent a check for $65 to Right-As-Rain Shampoo Co. in payment of an outstanding bill.

2 Received a check from Edith Ramirez for $95 in payment of a past due bill.

3 Purchased beauty supplies from a local vendor, paying $125 cash.

4 Received a $200 refund check for Beauty Equipment returned.

5 The proprietor contributed a display showcase valued at $400 to the business.

6 Bought various items of beauty equipment at a cost of $950 from the B & B Equipment Co. on account.

7 Sent a check to Alliance Beauty Co. for $550 in payment of an outstanding obligation.

8 Received checks from various customers amounting to $420.

EXERCISE 3-8

Use the following Expanded Accounting form. Record the beginning balances to "T" accounts for the month of March of the current year:

Date		Assets					= Liabilities +	Capital
		Cash +	Accounts Receivable +	Furniture & Fixtures +	Office Equipment +	Office Supplies =	Accounts Payable +	W. Debbs, Capital
Bal.		6,500	2,350	3,300	900	325	2,350	11,025

Record each of the business transactions presented below to the appropriate ledger account:

Wendell V. Debbs is the owner of the Debbs Real Estate Agency. The following business transactions took place during the month of March.

200-

Mar 1 Received a check for $250 from Luis Greene in part payment of an amount due.

2 Purchased office supplies paying $75 cash.

3 Mr. Debbs contributed a sofa to the business that was valued at $450.

4 Sent a check for $1,250 to E. Smithe, Inc. in full payment of an outstanding obligation.

5 Returned a typewriter previously purchased. The refund amounted to $150.

6 Purchased a word processor from M&M Machine Co. for $1,300 on credit.

7 The proprietor invested $1,500 in the business.

8 Received a check from a customer for $750.

EXERCISE 3-9

Use the following Expanded Accounting Equation form. Record the beginning balances to "T" accounts for the month of April of the current year:

Date		Assets					= Liabilities +	Capital
		Cash +	Accounts Receivable +	Furniture & Fixtures +	Office Equipment +	Office Supplies =	Accounts Payable =	R. Cohens, Capital
Bal.		7,500	3,150	4,000	1,275	625	3,350	13,200

Record each of the business transactions presented below to the appropriate ledger account:

Ruth Ann Cohens is an attorney at law. The following business transactions took place during the current month:

200-

Apr 1 Received a check from Lofler Storage Co. for $900 in payment of their outstanding balance for services previously rendered.

2 Sent a check to Baily Book Co. in payment for legal books previously purchased. The amount of the check was $350.

3 Purchased a receptionist's desk and chair from ABC Furniture Co. for $500 on account.

4 Purchased stationery and other supplies for $125 cash.

5 Returned a typewriter valued at $250 and received a cash refund.

6 Purchased an electronic typewriter for $650. Sent a check for $175 with the balance payable to Able Office Machine Co. within 30 days.

7 Ms. Cohens invested a desk valued at $300.

8 The proprietor took a chair from the business valued at $130.

Chapter 4 Recording Adjusting, Closing, and Reversing Entries

EXERCISE 4-1

1. What is the purpose in recording adjusting entries? When are these entries usually recorded? Who is called upon to record these entries?
2. Differentiate between a business that is on the "accrual basis" and a business on the "cash basis."
3. What is an accrued expense? accrued revenue?
4. What is a deferral? What account is created as a result of the deferral of an expense? How is that account classified?
5. What is deferred revenue? Illustrate a situation calling for the deferral of revenue. What is the name of the account set up?
6. What is the concept of matching costs and revenue? Why is this concept important? How do accruals and deferrals relate to the matching concept?
7. What two other account titles might the account supplies be called? How are these accounts classified?
8. What is a worksheet? What business form becomes the basis for the preparation of the worksheet? Where is the information for the preparation of the worksheet obtained?
9. What is a chart of accounts? How is the chart of accounts organized?
10. When are closing entries recorded? Why are closing entries recorded? What is the temporary account that is established for the sole purpose of recording the closing entries?
11. What are the steps in the accounting cycle?
12. What are reversing entries? When are reversing entries recorded? Why are reversing entries made?

EXERCISE 4-2

Record the following adjusting entries in two-column general journal form. Assume that the accounting period ends on December 31 of the current year, and that all adjusting entries are made as of that date.

1. The balance in the Supplies account was $840. A physical count of the supplies on hand indicate that $575 worth of supplies remained at the end of the year.
2. Rent for the month of December, amounting to $350, had not been paid by December 31 of the current year.
3. The balance in the prepaid insurance account amounted to $1,200. It was determined that $375 worth of insurance was used up for the current year.
4. Accrued salaries for the week amounted to $550.
5. Income received but not earned from rental income amounted to $900.
6. Store Supplies Expense account had a balance of $1,375 at the end of the year. A physical count indicated that $350 worth of supplies remained on hand at the end of the year.

EXERCISE 4-3

Record the following adjusting entries in two column-general journal form. Assume that the accounting period ends on December 31 of the current year, and that all adjusting entries are made as of that date.

1. Office Supplies according to the trial balance had a balance of $9,275. A physical inventory at the end of the year indicated that the cost of supplies on hand amounted to $5,300.
2. Although the telephone bill has not arrived by the end of the month, the accountant anticipates the bill for the month at $95.
3. Salaries are paid for the five day work week ending on Friday. The last payroll period in the old year is on Friday, January 1. If the daily payroll amounts to $230, what is the adjusting entry to be made on December 31?
4. The balance in the insurance expense account at the end of the year amounted to $900. It was determined that the unexpired insurance amounted to $300.
5. The monthly rent expense amounted to $300. The rent expense for the months of October, November, and December have not yet been paid.
6. Interest income earned, but not yet received for the four months ending December 31 amounted to $450.

EXERCISE 4-4

On January 4 of the current year, a business acquired a step van at a total cost of $15,650. This van has an estimated useful life of 5 years. At the end of five years, it is expected to have a scrap value of $650. Record the adjusting entry at December 31 to recognize the first year's depreciation.

EXERCISE 4-5

On July 2 of the current year, a printing press was purchased at a total cost of $5,300. This equipment has an estimated useful life of 10 years, with a residual value of $500. Record the adjusting entry at December 31 to recognize the first year's depreciation since the date of purchase.

EXERCISE 4-6

The following selected account balances appeared on the January 31 trial balance, before adjusting entries are made for the month.

	Debit	Credit
Prepaid Advertising	900.00	
Supplies	2,100.00	
Office Equipment	7,920.00	
Unearned Interest Income		1,000.00
Salaries Expense	1,600.00	

The following information is to be used to prepare the necessary adjusting entries for the month of January:

Exercise 4-6 continued

1. The prepaid advertising represented the first three months of the calendar year.
2. An inventory of supplies on hand at January 31 amounted to $800.
3. The office equipment has an expected useful life of 12 years with a scrap value of $720.
4. Unearned interest income that was earned for the month of January amounted to $400.
5. Accrued salaries not recorded at January 31 amounted to $540.

EXERCISE 4-7

The following unadjusted trial balance for Bonita Wein appears below:

Bonita Wein
Trial Balance
June 30, 200-

Cash	$3,600.00	
Accounts Receivable	2,000.00	
Supplies	1,500.00	
Insurance	500.00	
Office Equipment	500.00	
Delivery Equipment	1,700.00	
Accounts Payable		$3,550.00
B. Wein, Capital		3,000.00
B. Wein, Drawing	300.00	
Income from Services		4,600.00
Salaries Expense	600.00	
Rent Expense	300.00	
Utilities Expense	150.00	
	$11,150.00	$11,150.00

Based on the unadjusted trial balance for the month ending June 30 and the information for adjustments appearing below, prepare an eight-column worksheet.

Adjustment information:

a. $600 worth of supplies were used.
b. Depreciation of office equipment for the month amounted to $25.
c. Depreciation of delivery equipment for the month amounted to $35.
d. Interest expense incurred for the month, but not yet payable amounted to $40.
e. $50 of the insurance was used up.
f. Accrued salaries amounted to $150.

EXERCISE 4-8

The following unadjusted trial balance for Spencer Greene appears below.

Spencer Greene
Trial Balance
December 31, 200-

Cash	$30,000.00	
Accounts Receivable	2,100.00	
Office Supplies	1,400.00	
Furniture and Fixtures	8,000.00	
Accumulated Depreciation		2,000.00
Accounts Payable		13,000.00
S. Greene, Capital		7,800.00
S. Greene, Drawing	7,000.00	
Income from Services		39,500.00
Income from Commissions		2,500.00
Salaries Expense	12,000.00	
Rent Expense	3,000.00	
Utilities Expense	1,000.00	
Miscellaneous Expense	300.00	
	$64,800.00	$64,800.00

Based on the unadjusted trial balance for the year ending December 31 of the current year and the adjusting information appearing below, prepare an eight-column worksheet.
Adjustment information:

a. The inventory of office supplies at December 31 amounted to $550.
b. The annual depreciation of the furniture and fixtures amounted to $1,000.
c. Accrued salaries amounted to $225.
d. Unearned income from services amounted to $1,200.
e. Income from commissions earned but not recognized or received amounted to $450.

EXERCISE 4-9

Based on the completed worksheet to Exercise 4-7:

1. Record the trial balance, balances into ledger or "T" accounts.
2. Journalize and post the adjusting entries.
3. Journalize and post the reversing entries.

EXERCISE 4-10

Based on the completed worksheet to Exercise 4-8:

1. Record the trial balance, balances into ledger or "T" accounts.
2. Journalize and post the adjusting entries.
3. Journalize and post the reversing entries.

Chapter 5 Accounting for a Trading Business

EXERCISE 5-1

1. What is the primary difference between a service business and a trading business? What is the revenue account for a trading business called?
2. What kinds of accounts are unique to a trading business? Why are these accounts needed in a trading business?
3. Classify the following accounts:
   Merchandise Inventory
   Merchandise Purchases
   Purchases Returns and Allowances
   Income from Sales
   Sales Returns and Allowances
   Purchases Discount
   Sales Discount
4. What does the expression "2/10, n/30" mean?
5. What is the difference between "cost of goods available for sale" and "cost of goods sold"?
6. What is the difference between freight on purchases and freight on sales?
7. What is the difference between Merchandise Inventory, January 1, 2002 and Merchandise Inventory, December 31, 2001?
8. What does the beginning Merchandise Inventory become at the end of the fiscal or calendar year? How is this change recorded?
9. Knowing the cost of goods available for sale, how would the accountant determine the cost of goods sold?
10. How does the closing process for a trading business differ from the closing process of a service business?

EXERCISE 5-2

Goods are sold on account for $3,000, terms 2/10, n/30. Assume that the goods are paid for within the discount period. Make the following entries on the books of the seller: (1) the recording of the original sale and (2) the receipt of cash.

EXERCISE 5-3

Merchandise is sold on March 15 for $2,500 with terms of 2/10, 1/15, n/30. The goods are paid for on March 28.
  Determine the amount of cash to be received by the seller.
  Record the journal entry on the books of the seller to reflect the receipt of the money on March 28, and record the journal entry made on the books of the buyer to reflect the payment made.

EXERCISE 5-4

Adams Company had beginning merchandise inventory valued at $39,000. Net purchases during the year amounted to $168,000. A physical inventory taken at the end of the year was determined to be $35,000. Determine: (1) the cost of goods available for sale, and (2) the cost of goods sold.

EXERCISE 5-5

During the current year the Sherman Company had net sales amounting to $196,000. The ending merchandise inventory was $32,000. The beginning inventory amounted to $29,000 with net purchase of $45,000 made during the year. Determine: (1) the cost of goods available for sale; (2) the cost of goods sold, and (3) the gross profit on sale.

EXERCISE 5-6

At the end of the accounting period the following information is available with reference to a trading business:

Sales, $300,000; Sales Returns and Allowances, $5,000; Sales Discount, $3,000; Merchandise Inventory (beginning), $50,000; Merchandise Purchases, $200,000; Purchases Returns and Allowances, $10,000; Purchases Discount, $3,000; Freight on Purchases, $1,000; Merchandise Inventory (ending), $100,000; Selling Expenses, $50,000; General & Administrative Expenses, $50,000.

Determine: (1) Net Purchases; (2) Cost of goods available for sale; (3) Cost of goods sold; (4) Gross profit on sales.

EXERCISE 5-7

The partial trial balance for the end of the current year appears below:

	Debit	Credit
A. Business, Drawing	17,000.	
Merchandise Inventory (beginning)	20,000.	
Income from Sales		150,000.
Sales Returns and Allowances	600.	
Sales Discount	1,000.	
Merchandise Purchases	90,000.	
Purchases Returns and Allowances		400.
Purchases Discount		1,600.
Freight on Purchases	300.	
Rent Expense	16,000.	
Salaries Expense	32,000.	
Selling Expenses	3,500.	
General and Administrative Expenses	13,500.	

A physical inventory taken at the end of the year amounted to $27,000.

Determine: (1) Net Purchases; (2) Cost of goods available for sale; (3) Cost of goods sold; (4) Gross profit on sales.

EXERCISE 5-8

Using the information provided in Exercise 5-6, prepare the following general journal entries:
(1) Adjust the beginning Merchandise Inventory
(2) Set up the ending Merchandise Inventory
(3) Record the appropriate closing entries.

EXERCISE 5-9

Using the information provided in Exercise 5-6, prepare a multiple-step Income Statement for the end of the current calendar year.

EXERCISE 5-10

Using the information provided in Exercise 5-7, prepare the following general journal entries:
(1) Adjust the trial balance Merchandise Inventory.
(2) Set up the ending Merchandise Inventory.
(3) Record the appropriate closing entries.

EXERCISE 5-11

Using the information provided in Exercise 5-7, prepare a multiple-step Income Statement for the end of the current year.

EXERCISE 5-12

The Local Store's Trial Balance appears below:

The Local Store
Trial Balance
December 31, 200-

	Debit	Credit
Cash	1,400.	
Merchandise Inventory	17,440.	
Store Supplies	815.	
Prepaid Insurance	1,230.	
Store Equipment	12,125.	
Accumulated Depreciation-Store Equip.		2,590.
Accounts Payable		2,670.
Alvin Local, Capital		32,065.
Alvin Local, Drawing	16,230.	
Income from Sales		95,215.
Sales Returns and Allowances	735.	
Discount on Sales	975.	
Merchandise Purchases	57,170.	
Purchases Returns and Allowances		370.
Discount on Purchases		960.
Transportation on Purchases	650.	
Salaries Expense	18,815.	
Rent Expense	6,000.	
Advertising Expense	285.	
	133,870.	133,870.

Exercise 5-12 continued

The following information was available as of December 31, 200-, the end of the calendar year:

a. Ending merchandise inventory, $16,990.
b. Store Supplies Inventory, $165.
c. Expired insurance, $1,010.
d. Estimated annual depreciation of store equipment, $1,435.
e. Accrued salaries amounted to $1,200.

Directions:

1. Prepare an eight (8)-column worksheet.
2. Record the appropriate adjusting entries in general journal form.
3. Record appropriate closing entries to the general journal.
4. Record appropriate reversal entries, dated January 1, to the general journal.

Chapter 6 Special Journals and Controls

EXERCISE 6-1

1. What are two reasons for using special journals?
2. What kinds of transactions are recorded in the Sales Journal?
3. What transactions are posted daily from the Sales Journal? Where are these accounts specifically found? What is the purpose for, and form of the summary entry in the Sales Journal?
4. What is the function of the **controlling account?** What is the purpose of the **subsidiary ledger?**
5. What kinds of transactions are recorded in the Cash Receipts Journal? Which column(s) are posted daily? Which column(s) are posted in summary at the end of the month?
6. What kinds of transactions are recorded in the Purchases Journal? Which columns are posted daily? in summary? What is the advantage of the summary entry from this journal at the end of the month?
7. What kinds of transactions are recorded in the Cash Payments Journal? Which columns are posted daily? in summary? What is the advantage of the summary entry from this journal at the end of the month?
8. What is the purpose in preparing a schedule of accounts receivable and a schedule of accounts payable? What kind of accounts will no longer appear in the general ledger? What accounts mirror the subsidiary ledgers?
9. What kinds of transactions will be recorded in the general journal when the four special journals are being used? What is a bracket entry? When is a bracket entry necessary?
10. What additional special journals may an organization use in addition to the four special journals previously mentioned?

EXERCISE 6-2

The following business transactions took place during the month of June, of the current year, for the Ryan Drygoods Co.

200-
June 4 Sold various sheets and pillow cases to the Pillow Place, Inc. for $305, terms: n/30. Sent invoice #101.
7 Sold bath mats and shower curtains to Evander's Bath Shop, for $850, terms: n/30. Sent invoice #102.
10 Sold soap dishes, and assorted shower rings to A,B,C, Shower, Inc. for $225, terms: n/30. Mailed invoice #103.
15 Sold various curtain rods and rings to Evander's Bath Shop for $240, terms: n/30. Issued invoice #104.

Directions:

1. Rule Sales Journal.
2. Set up an Accounts Receivable ledger with all necessary accounts as needed.
3. Set up General Ledger accounts for Accounts Receivable and Sales.
4. Journalize and post the daily transactions listed above.
5. Journalize and post the summary entry.
6. Prepare a schedule of accounts receivable.

EXERCISE 6-3

The following business transactions took place during the month of September, of the current year, for the Evanrude Company.

200-
Sept 1 Sold merchandise to A. Gray for $400, terms: n/10. Issued invoice #207.
4 Sold merchandise to Jones & Son, Inc. for $370, terms: n/30. Issued invoice #208.
7 Sold goods to A. Gray for $900, terms: n/10. Issued invoice #209.
16 Sold merchandise to J. Smith for $350, terms: n/30. Issued invoice #210.

Directions:

1. Rule Sales Journal.
2. Set up an Accounts Receivable ledger with all necessary accounts as needed.
3. Set up General Ledger accounts for Accounts Receivable and Sales.
4. Journalize and post the daily transactions listed above.
5. Journalize and post the summary entry.
6. Prepare a schedule of accounts receivable.

EXERCISE 6-4

Rule a sales journal and a five-column cash receipts journal as illustrated in Chapter 6. Record the following business transactions to the appropriate journal, and post to the appropriate ledger accounts on a daily basis:

Exercise 6-4 continued

200-

Jan 2 Sold goods to A. Able for $200; terms: n/10.
5 Sold goods to B. Baker for $500; terms: n/10.
7 Weekly cash sales amounted to $1,700.
12 Received a check from A. Able in payment of her 1/2 obligation.
14 Borrowed $500 from Safety National Bank, giving our written promise to repay the obligation in sixty days.
15 Received a check from B. Baker in payment of his obligation of 1/5 that was due today.
17 Sold merchandise to A. Able for $475; terms 2/10, n/30.
19 Received a check for $2,100 representing cash sales for the last twelve days.
26 Received a check in payment of A. Able's obligation of 1/17.
29 Sold goods to A. Able for $380; terms 2/10, n/30.
31 Cash sales for the past twelve days amounted to $2,400.

Prepare the summary entries for the Sales and Cash Receipts Journal. Post to the appropriate ledger accounts in the general ledger. Prepare a schedule of accounts receivable.

EXERCISE
6-5

Rule a sales journal and a five-column cash receipts journal as illustrated in the chapter. Record the following business transactions to the appropriate journal, and post to the appropriate ledger accounts on a daily basis:

200-

Aug 1 The beginning cash balance was $8,000 (show in ledger account and "short" in the cash receipts journal).
4 Sent a bill to Henry James for $300; terms: 2/10, n/30.
7 Cash sales for the week ending 8/7 amounted to $1,200.
8 Sold goods to Long Co. for $900; terms 2/10, n/30.
11 Received a check from Lender Co. in payment of an outstanding promissory note due today for $500.
13 Received a check from Henry James in payment of his 8/4 obligation.
21 Cash sales for the two weeks ending today amounted to $2,600.
29 Received a check from Long Co. in payment of the 8/8 obligation.
30 Sold goods to Henry James for $750; terms: 2/10, n/30.
31 Sent a bill to Long Co. for $250; terms: 2/10, n/30.

Prepare the summary entries for the Sales and Cash Receipts Journal. Post to the appropriate ledger accounts in the general ledger. Prepare a schedule of accounts receivable.

EXERCISE
6-6

Rule a multiple-column purchases journal as illustrated in the book. Record the following business transactions to the purchases journal and post to the appropriate accounts daily. At the end of the month record and post the summary entry.

Exercise 6-6 continued

200-

Mar 2 Purchased merchandise from Adam Talcott Co. for $350; terms: n/10.

4 Purchased store supplies from Davis Stationers, Inc. for $75; terms: n/30.

7 Received a bill from Fancy Freight Co. for freight charges of $45 on purchase of merchandise made on March 2.

18 Bought a desk and chair from Greenery Furniture Co. for $2,050; terms: n/30.

30 Received invoice #7650 from Adam Talcott Co. for merchandise purchased for $900; terms: n/30.

Summarize the purchases journal and post to the appropriate ledger accounts. Prepare a schedule of accounts payable.

EXERCISE 6-7

Rule a multiple-column purchases journal as illustrated in the book. Record the following business transactions to the purchases journal and post to the appropriate accounts daily. At the end of the month record and post the summary entry.

200-

Apr 1 Bought merchandise from S & W Co. for $735; terms: n/10.

5 Received invoice #234B from Albert Gates for $375; terms: n/10.

8 Received invoice #75432 from ABC Freight Co. for $27. This invoice represents freight charges related to purchase of 4/1.

12 Purchased an electronic typewriter from R. Victor, Inc. for $450; terms: n/30.

27 Bought six cases of rexograph paper from Stationery Supply Co., for $360; terms: n/10.

Summarize the purchases journal and post to the appropriate ledger accounts. Prepare a schedule of accounts payable.

EXERCISE 6-8

Rule a purchases journal and a five-column cash payments journal as illustrated in Chapter 6. Record the following business transactions to the appropriate journal and post to the appropriate ledger accounts on a daily basis:

200-

May 2 Received invoice #4456A, dated May 1 from Stanley Co. for $650. This invoice represents merchandise purchased with terms of 2/10, n/30.

5 Received a bill from United Freight Co. for $67. This represents freight charges on the purchase of merchandise from Stanley Co. Payment is to be made by May 10.

8 Sent a check to Stanley Co. for $300 in part payment of the invoice dated May 1.

Exercise 6-8 continued

200-

May 9 Paid the Always Open Realty Co. the month's rent amounting to $800.

10 Sent a check for the balance due on the invoice of May 1 owed to Stanley Co.

14 Purchased Office Supplies from Anchor Stationers, paying by a check amounting to $75.

17 Purchased merchandise for $375 from Callahan Co., terms: 2/10, 1/15, n/60.

23 Purchased merchandise from Stanley Co. for $850. Sent a check in payment of the purchase.

30 Sent a check to Callahan Co. in payment of the invoice dated May 17.

Summarize the purchases journal and the cash payments journal. Post the summary entries to the appropriate ledger accounts. Prepare a schedule of accounts payable.

EXERCISE 6-9

Rule a purchases journal and a five-column cash payments journal as illustrated in Chapter 6. Record the following business transactions to the appropriate journal, and post to the appropriate ledger accounts on a daily basis:

200-

Oct 1 Paid the Ambassador Realty Co. the month's rent amounting to $900.

3 Purchased supplies from Reliable Supply Outfitters, Inc. for $225; terms: 2/5, 1/10, n/30.

5 Purchased merchandise for $650. and issued a check in payment.

7 Sent a check for Reliable Supply Outfitters, Inc. in payment of the October 3 purchase.

9 Purchased goods from XYZ Co. for $660; terms: 2/10, n/30.

11 Bought office supplies from Dante Office Supply Co., for $125; terms: Cash.

12 Sent a check for the office supplies purchased on October 11.

18 Sent a check in payment of the goods purchased on October 9.

21 Sent a check in payment of the freight charges for the goods purchased on October 9. The check was made payable to Local Freight Handlers, Ltd. in the amount of $65.

24 Received a bill from the Constant Cleaning Service for $185. for cleaning services rendered the previous week.

Summarize the purchases journal and the cash payments journal. Post the summary entries to the appropriate ledger accounts. Prepare a schedule of accounts payable.

EXERCISE 6-10

Record the following daily business transactions to a two-column general journal. Assume that the business uses the four primary special journals discussed in this chapter.

1. Sent a note for $300 to R. Brown in payment of our outstanding promise due today. The terms of the note called for payment in 60 days.
2. Received a credit memo for $70 from our creditor which authorized the return of goods previously purchased from Gabor Bros.
3. Received a promissory note for $500 from Revere Co. in payment for an invoice dated last week.
4. Issued a credit memo for $65 to Alice Field for defective merchandise she returned.

EXERCISE 6-11

Using the four special journals, and a two-column general journal, record the following selected business transactions:

200-

Jan 1 Sold goods to Alvin & Sons, $135; terms: 2/10, n/30.

3 Issued a credit memo for $5 to Alvin & Sons for defective goods returned today.

4 Purchased merchandise from Selby Supply Ltd. for $300; terms: 2/5, 1/10, n/30.

5 Received a bill from Able Freight Co. for freight charges amounting to $15 for merchandise purchased on 1/4.

6 Sent a check in payment of bill received from Able Freight Co.

7 Cash sales for the week amounted to $1,300.

9 Received a check from Alvin & Sons in payment of the invoice issued on 1/1. (Note the transaction of 1/3.)

11 Purchased a filing cabinet from Standard Office Equipment Co. for $75; terms: n/30.

13 Sent a check to Selby Supply Ltd. in payment of 1/4 purchase.

15 Sold an extra desk and chair to R. Lamb for $125. Ms. Lamb agreed to pay for the items in 25 days.

18 Sold merchandise to Delvalle Co. for $250; terms: 2/10, n/30.

21 Purchased office supplies paying $75.

23 Sent a check for $700 in payment of January rent.

26 Received a check from Delvalle Co. for $100 on account.

29 The proprietor, Robin Bentley took $500 out of the business to pay her home rent for the month of February.

31 Sold goods to various cash customers for $750.

Pencil foot, rule, and summarize the special journals. Indicate which columns of the special journals are to be posted at the end of the month. Use a checkmark to indicate which columns are not to be posted at the end of the month.

EXERCISE 6-12

Using the four special journals, and a two-column general journal, record the following selected business transactions:

200-
Nov 2   Sold goods to Acme Bros. $350; terms: 2/10, n/30.
3   Issued a credit memo for $25 for goods sold to Acme Bros. on November 2.
5   Purchased goods from Ryan Co. for $600; terms: 2/5, 1/10, n/30.
6   Received a bill from XYZ Freight Co. for freight charges amounting to $35 for merchandise purchased on 11/5.
7   Sent a check in payment of yesterday's freight charges.
8   Cash sales for the week amounted to $2,300.
9   Received a check from Acme Bros. in payment of the invoice of 11/2. (Note the transaction of 1/3.)
11   Purchased a paper cutter from Standard Office Equipment Co. for $45; terms: n/30.
12   Received a credit memo from Ryan Co. authorizing the return of defective goods valued at $60.
13   Sent a check to Ryan Co. in payment of 11/5 purchase.
15   Sold an extra desk and chair to R. Stern for $125 cash.
18   Sold merchandise to Valley Bros. for $550; terms: 2/10, n/30.
21   Purchased office supplies paying $75.
23   Sent a check for $700 in payment of January rent.
26   Received a check from Valley Bros. in full payment of 11/18 sale.
29   The proprietor, Robert Davids took $300 out of the business to pay his outstanding credit card bill for the month of November.
30   Sold goods to various cash customers for $970.

Pencil foot, rule, and summarize the special journals. Indicate which columns of the special journals are to be posted at the end of the month. Use a checkmark to indicate which columns are not to be posted at the end of the month.

Chapter 7 Accounting for Cash— Special Controls

EXERCISE 7-1

1. What kind of asset must a business continuously safeguard, regardless of the size of the business? Why? How is this accomplished?
2. When opening a business checking account, what is the purpose of the following items: signature card; deposit slip; bank statement; authorized signature.
3. What is the reason for the preparation of the bank reconciliation statement? How frequently is it prepared? Where is the information for its preparation obtained?

Exercise 7-1 continued

4. What are the steps taken in the preparation of the bank reconciliation statement? What information does the checkbook provide toward the preparation of the bank reconciliation statement? What information does the bank statement provide to expedite the preparation of the bank reconciliation statement?

5. What is the purpose in establishing the petty cash fund? Why is this system in use if the business concern uses a checking account? How frequently is the fund replenished? What is the justification for replenishing the fund?

6. What is the purpose of the voucher system? What special journals are replaced by the use of the voucher system? How does the use of the voucher system provide special controls which safeguard cash?

7. What is the purpose of the unpaid voucher file? Why is the accounts payable subsidiary ledger not necessary when using the voucher system?

EXERCISE 7-2

A business's checkbook balance on June 30 was $9,111.45. On July 2 you received the commercial bank's bank statement. The bank statement balance on June 30 revealed a bank balance of $12,751.61. In comparing the bank statement with the business's checkbook, the following information was discovered:

1. Monthly service charge, $3.62
2. Outstanding checks, $5,142.65
3. Deposit in transit, $1,498.87

Prepare a bank reconciliation dated June 30 of the current year, based on the above information.

Prepare the necessary journal entries resulting from the preparation of this bank reconciliation.

EXERCISE 7-3

A business's checkbook balance on April 30 was $442. The statement received from the bank showed a balance of $301. The following additional information was discovered:

1. Service charge, $2.00
2. Outstanding checks, $194.00
3. Deposit in transit, $316.00
4. A check paid by the bank for $31.00 was incorrectly recorded in the checkbook as $13.00.

Prepare a bank reconciliation dated April 30 of the current year, based on the above information.

Prepare the necessary journal entries resulting from the preparation of this bank reconciliation.

EXERCISE 7-4

Rule a petty cash book as illustrated in Chapter 7. Record the necessary journal entries (in general journal form) as well as those entries that would normally be recorded to the petty cash book. When recording the general journal entries, indicate which special journal would be used (as part of your explanation).

200-

Aug 4 Wrote and cashed check #2345 for $100 to establish the petty cash fund.

6 Issued petty cash voucher #101 in payment for sales slip books for use in the store. The amount of the voucher was $27.50.

9 Issued voucher #102 in payment for printer toner cartridge costing $12.75.

15 Issued voucher #103 for $22 in payment for stamps purchased at the US Post Office.

18 Issued voucher #104 in payment for carfare to an employee delivering a package to a customer. The amount of the voucher was $4.00.

21 Issued voucher #105 for $24.50 in payment for freight charges to be billed to the miscellaneous expense.

22 Summarized the petty cash book and wrote check #2406 to replenish the fund.

23 Decided to increase the petty cash fund by an additional $25. Wrote check #2411 to increase the fund.

EXERCISE 7-5

Rule a petty cash book as illustrated in Chapter 7. Record the necessary journal entries (in general journal form) as well as those entries that would normally be recorded to the petty cash book. When recording the general journal entries, indicate which special journal would be used (as part of your explanation).

200-

Nov 3 Wrote check #407 for $125 to establish the petty cash fund.

7 Issued petty cash voucher #1 for $5.40 payable to Halston Freight Co. Ltd. for freight charge on goods sold to a customer.

10 Issued petty cash voucher #2 for $25 payable to A-1 Hardware Co. for repair of entrance door lock. Charged the maintenance expense account.

13 Issued voucher #3 for $44 in payment for postage stamps purchased yesterday.

14 Issued voucher #4 for $23 for pricing labels purchased for use in the store, from Nagel Store Supply Co.

16 Issued voucher #5 for $10 in payment for office supplies purchased from Buyrite Stationers, Ltd.

17 Issued voucher #6 for $15 payable to the U.S. Post Office for assorted stamps purchased today.

18 Summarized the petty cash book and wrote check #443 to replenish the fund.

19 Decided to increase the petty cash fund by an additional $25. Wrote check #450 to increase the fund.

EXERCISE 7-6

Rule a voucher register and check register as illustrated in Chapter 7. Record the following selected transactions to the appropriate registers.

200-
Mar 1 Prepared voucher #301 for purchase of goods from Bradley, Inc., terms: n/10, for $500.

5 Prepared voucher #302 for advertising expenses amounting to $700, payable to Aldon Ad Agency.

7 Issued check #456 in payment of voucher #302.

10 Issued check #457 in payment of voucher #301.

12 Prepared voucher #303 payable to H&H Freight Co. for $90. This bill is payable in 20 days for freight on purchase of last month.

15 Prepared voucher #304 payable to All-County Realty Co. for $350. This represents the store rent for the current month.

15 Wrote a check #458 in payment of voucher #304.

17 Received a bill from Howard Jay Co. for $580. This bill represented the purchase on merchandise with terms of 2/10, n/30. Prepared voucher #305.

22 Issued check #459 in payment of salaries expense amounting to $700. This check was in payment of voucher #306 issued today.

26 Issued check #460 in payment of voucher #305.

30 Summarize and indicate the summary notations to both registers.

EXERCISE 7-7

Rule a voucher register and check register as illustrated in Chapter 7. Record the following selected transactions to the appropriate registers.

200-
Feb 3 Issued voucher #101 for $3,000 for goods purchased from Greene Manufacturing Co., terms: 2/10, n/30.

5 Issued voucher #102 payable to ABC Stationery Co. for $200, terms: 2/10, 1/15, n/30. This purchase represented various kinds of office supplies acquired.

7 Issued voucher #103 for $500. This represented the rent for the month of February that was payable to Regis Realty, Inc.

9 Wrote check #901 in payment of voucher #103.

12 Wrote check #902 in payment of voucher #101.

15 Prepared voucher #104 in payment of semi-monthly salary expense that amounted to $1,500. Issued check #903 in payment of this voucher.

19 Purchased a desk and chair for $650. Prepared voucher #105 payable to Stanley Furniture Co., terms: n/30.

27 Wrote check #904 in payment of voucher #102.

28 Summarize and indicate the summary notations to both registers.

Chapter 8 Accounting for Receivables and Payables

EXERCISE 8-1

1. What are two ways in which goods and or services may be sold in the normal course of business? Which method is preferred? Why?
2. Explain the direct write-off method of recognizing bad debts. When is this method used? What are the advantages and disadvantages in using this method?
3. When using the direct write-off method of recognizing bad debts, what is the entry that is made when a customer who was previously written-off suddenly pays the debt?
4. Explain the net sales method of recognizing bad debts. When is this method used? What are the advantages and disadvantages in using this method?
5. When using the net sales method of recognizing bad debts, what is the entry that is made when a customer who was previously written-off suddenly pays the debt, or a part of it?
6. Explain the aging of accounts receivable method of recognizing bad debts. What is the advantage of using this method over the direct write-off, or the net sales methods? What are the disadvantages in using this method?
7. When using the aging of accounts receivable method of recognizing bad debts, what is the entry that is made when a customer who was previously written-off suddenly pays the debt or a part of it?
8. What is the difference between the adjusting entry made using the net sales method and the aging of accounts receivable? Which of the two methods is more accurate? Why?
9. What is a promissory note? What is the note called in the hands of the maker? What is the note called in the hands of the recipient?
10. What is the advantage of accepting or requiring a written promise rather than an oral promise? How does an interest-bearing note differ from a non-interest-bearing note?
11. How many days are there in a "banking year?" What relationship remains constant when using the 60-day method of determining interest?

EXERCISE 8-2

Record the following transactions using the two-column general journal.

200-
Jan 4 Sold merchandise to Unreliable Co., for $950, terms: n/30.
     6 Sent a credit memo to Unreliable Co. authorizing the return of damaged merchandise with a value of $75.
Feb 9 Received a check from Unreliable Co., for $375, in part payment of January 4 sale.
Apr 3 Determined that the balance owed us by Unreliable Co. will be uncollectible. Decided to write off the accounts receivable using the direct write-off method.
May 9 Received a check for $200 from Unreliable Co. in part payment of the past due obligation that was written off on April 3.

EXERCISE 8-3

The balance in the accounts receivable account at the end of the accounting period consisted of a debit balance of $3,525. The balance in the allowance for bad debts account was a credit balance of $95. It was determined (using the net sales method) that of the total sales ($98,320) approximately 1/2 of 1% will prove to be uncollectible.

1. Using the net sales method, prepare the general journal entry that would be made at the end of the accounting period.
2. Using the aging of accounts receivable method, prepare the general journal entry that would be made at the end of the accounting period. Use the percentage provided above as if determined from an aging table.
3. Record the necessary entry in the general journal to recognize the write-off of J. Driskal's account for $300.
4. Record the receipt of $200 as a result of a check received from J. Driskal.

EXERCISE 8-4

Based on the aging of receivables method of recognizing bad debts record the necessary adjusting entries based on the information presented in each situation.

1. The allowance account before adjustments has a credit balance of $850. The analysis of uncollectible accounts anticipates a write-off of $8,675.
2. The allowance account before adjustments has a debit balance of $375. The analysis of uncollectible accounts anticipates a write-off of $6,900.

EXERCISE 8-5

Using the formula P × R × T = I or the 60-day method of determining interest, determine the interest for each of the following notes:

Face Amount	Number of Days	Interest Rate	Face Amount	Number of Days	Interest Rate
1. 3,000	60	6%	6. 3,000	60	3%
2. 3,000	360	6%	7. 3,000	60	9%
3. 3,000	30	6%	8. 3,000	60	12%
4. 3,000	90	6%	9. 3,000	30	3%
5. 3,000	120	6%	10. 3,000	90	9%

EXERCISE 8-6

Using the formula P × R × T = I or the 60-day method of determining interest, determine the interest for each of the following notes:

Face Amount	Number of Days	Interest Rate	Face Amount	Number of Days	Interest Rate
1. 4,500	60	6%	6. 4,500	60	3%
2. 4,500	45	6%	7. 4,500	60	9%
3. 4,500	30	6%	8. 4,500	60	12%
4. 4,500	90	6%	9. 4,500	90	3%
5. 4,500	15	6%	10. 4,500	30	9%

EXERCISE 8-7

An interest-bearing promissory note dated April 3 of the current year bearing interest at a rate of 9% and due in 60 days is sent to a creditor. The face value of the note is $1,500.

1. Determine the due date of the note.
2. Determine the total interest that will be earned on the note.
3. Record the general journal entry for the issuance of the note.
4. Record the general journal entry for the payment of the note.

EXERCISE 8-8

Based on the information provided in Exercise 8-7, assume that the note is discounted at a bank by the creditor after being held for 20 days, at a rate of 12%.

1. Determine the maturity of the note.
2. Determine the net proceeds resulting from discounting the note.
3. Determine the general journal entry when the note is discounted.
4. Determine the entry to be made on the creditor's books on the maturity date of the note.
5. Assuming that the customer does not pay the note and the bank charges a protest fee of $8, record the general journal entry on the creditor's books.

EXERCISE 8-9

A short term loan is taken at a local bank. The bank requires its customer to sign a promissory note, which is then discounted by the bank. The face of the note is for $2,500 with a 90-day maturity and a rate of interest of 9%.

1. Determine the due date of the note if it is dated November 11.
2. Determine the net proceeds of the note.
3. Record the general journal entry for the resulting discounting of the note.
4. Determine the part of the interest that is an expense in the old year, and the new year.

EXERCISE 8-10

Record the following transactions in general journal form:

200-
Jun 3 Received a $3,600, 60-day 8% note dated today from Anchor Co.

28 Discounted Anchor Co. note at a discount rate of 10%.

Aug 2 Note due today from Anchor Co. is dishonored. Bank debits our account for the maturity value of the note and a protest fee amounting to $6.

22 Received amount owed us from Anchor Co. and interest from date of default at a rate of 12%.

Chapter 9 Accounting for Long-Life and Intangible Assets

EXERCISE 9-1

1. What is the difference between a current asset and a long-life asset?
2. When a current asset is used up, what does it usually become? Why?
3. Why must a long-life or fixed asset be handled differently from a current asset?
4. Why is the useful life of a plant asset important? How is the loss in value of a plant asset determined? What is a plant asset's depreciable value? How is depreciable value determined?
5. What is the most common form of depreciation used? What form of depreciation is not based on time, but on use of the plant asset?
6. What is accelerated depreciation? What are the two common methods used? Which accelerated depreciation method uses the straight-line method to determine the annual depreciation rate?
7. According to the "cost principle," what are the only times that the value of the plant asset itself is eliminated from the books of account?
8. Prior to the sale of a plant asset, what must be calculated to the date of the sale? What may be recognized as a result of the sale or disposal of a fixed asset?
9. Distinguish between accounting for a trade-on allowance for similar assets and not similar assets using the income tax method.
10. What is depletion? How does it differ from depreciation? What kind of items are subject to depletion? What is amortization? What kinds of items are subject to amortization?
11. What is the difference between a capital expenditure and an expense?

EXERCISE 9-2

A machine having an original cost of $12,000 is said to have a scrap value of $1,200. The expected useful life is 4 years.
Determine:

1. The annual rate of depreciation (expressed as a %), using the straight-line method;
2. The depreciable value of the asset;
3. The amount of annual depreciation expense to be recognized;
4. The first year's depreciation and the resulting book value of the asset assuming that the asset was acquired 6 months into the new year;
5. The depreciable value of the asset after the first year's depreciation.

EXERCISE 9-3

On July 3 of the current year equipment is purchased with an original cost of $49,500. The useful life of the equipment is 6 years with estimated residual value of $1,500.
Determine:

Exercise 9-3 continued

1. The annual rate of depreciation (expressed as a percentage), using the straight-line method;
2. The depreciable value of the asset;
3. The amount of annual depreciation expense to be recognized;
4. The first calendar year's depreciation to be recognized and the resulting assets book value;
5. The book value of the asset after $2^1/_2$ years.

EXERCISE 9-4

Assume that the asset in Exercise 9-3 has a useful life of 1,200 machine hours and a residual value of $1,500.

Determine:

1. The depreciable value of the asset;
2. The rate of depreciation per machine hour;
3. The entry and the depreciation recognized after 250 hours of use;
4. The book value of the asset after 950 hours of use;
5. The book value of the asset after 1250 hours of use.

EXERCISE 9-5

Based on the information presented in Exercise 9-2, determine:

1. The double-declining balance method rate of depreciation;
2. The first full year's depreciation using the DDB method*;
3. The second full year's depreciation using the DDB method*;
4. The third full year's depreciation using the DDB method*;
5. The fourth full year's depreciation using the DDB method*;
6. The residual value of the asset after it has been fully depreciated under the DDB method*.

* Double-declining balance method

EXERCISE 9-6

Based on the information presented in Exercise 9-2, use the double-declining balance method, assuming that the asset was acquired nine months into the calendar year (assume a calendar year accounting period).

Determine:

1. 1st year's depreciation;
2. 2nd year's depreciation;
3. 3rd year's depreciation;
4. 4th year's depreciation;
5. Remaining depreciation;
6. Residual value.

EXERCISE 9-7

Based on the information presented in Exercise 9-3, use the double-declining balance method and calculate the annual depreciation for the asset acquired on July 3 (assume a calendar-year accounting period).

EXERCISE 9-8

Based on the information presented in Exercise 9-2, answer the numbered items assuming the use of the sum-of-the-years'-digits method of calculating depreciation.

EXERCISE 9-9

Based on the information presented in Exercise 9-3, answer the numbered items assuming the use of the sum-of-the-years'-digits method of calculating depreciation.

EXERCISE 9-10

A truck is acquired at a cost of $37,500 with an expected useful life of 7 years, with anticipated scrap value of $1,500. Determine the first two years' depreciation of the asset acquired at the beginning of the calendar year by: a) the straight-line method; b) the double-declining balance method; c) the sum-of-the-years'-digits method.

EXERCISE 9-11

A van has an original cost of $48,000, a useful life of 5 years, and an anticipated scrap value of $3,000. The asset is sold after $3^1/_2$ years for $8,400.
   Determine:

1. The annual straight-line depreciation;
2. The adjusting entry for depreciation in the fourth year, prior to the sale of the asset;
3. The entry to record the sale of the asset on July 2.

EXERCISE 9-12

A new mainframe computer with a selling price of $30,000 is purchased. When the new mainframe computer is purchased, a trade-in allowance of $6,750 is given for an old mainframe computer that originally cost $24,000 and has an accumulated depreciation of $18,000 to the date of trade-in. The remaining cost of the new mainframe computer is paid for in cash. (a) In general journal form, prepare the entry for the trade-in using the income tax method. (b) Assuming a trade-in allowance of $44,000, prepare the general journal entry using the income tax method.

EXERCISE 9-13

A farmer has 25,000 acres of farmland under cultivation. This land is leased at an annual cost of $750,000 for a 10-year period. It is estimated that the land over the leasehold will yield 18,750,000 pounds of produce.

Determine:

1. The amount of depletion to be recognized per pound of produce grown;
2. The depletion to be recognized if the harvest in the first year yielded 2,450,000 pounds.

EXERCISE 9-14

The research and development costs associated with a patent amounted to $75,000. It is expected that this patent will have a useful life of 15 years. What is the annual amortization on the patent to be recognized? What is the general journal entry to record the annual amortization?

EXERCISE 9-15

Purchased a franchise for $25,000 to operate an ice cream concession for 10 years. At the same time paid an additional $5,000 for an option to renew the franchise after 10 years.

Determine:

1. The annual amortization to be recognized over the 10 years;
2. What entry must be made when the option is not exercised.

EXERCISE 9-16

Major structural repairs amounting to $170,000 caused the estimated useful life of the plant to increase by 10 years. The original cost of the plant was $500,000 and it had been depreciated using the straight-line method for 25 years. Residual value was estimated to be insignificant, thus ignored. The accumulated depreciation through the prior year amounted to $250,000.

Determine:

1. The annual depreciation recognized prior to this year's capital expenditure;
2. The book value of the plant asset after recording the capital expenditure;
3. The depreciable value of the plant asset after recognizing the capital expenditure;
4. The remaining useful life of the plant asset as a result of the capital expenditure;
5. The new annual depreciation expense to be recognized as a result of the capital expenditure.

Chapter 10 Accounting for Inventories

EXERCISE 10-1

1. What is merchandise inventory? When is the physical count taken for the purpose of determining the merchandise inventory? What is the difference between the ending merchandise inventory for year X1 as compared to year X2?
2. Why is it necessary to take a physical inventory when accounting in a trading business?
3. Why is it important to state properly the value of the ending inventory when preparing an income statement for a trading business?
4. What effect does an overstatement of ending inventory have on: cost of goods sold; net income; current assets; proprietor's capital?
5. What effect does an understatement of ending inventory have on: cost of goods sold; net income; current assets; proprietor's capital?
6. What is the difference between a periodic and a perpetual inventory system? Which system is appropriate when a physical inventory is being taken once a year?
7. Why is the perpetual inventory system said to be a more accurate method of determining the cost of goods sold?
8. What is the stock record card? Which inventory system uses the stock record card? When the stock record card is used, what new ledger accounts are used on the books?
9. Define the following inventory methods: weighted average; FIFO method; LIFO method.
10. What is the purpose of the gross profit method and the retail method? What benefits are derived from using either method?

EXERCISE 10-2

A sporting goods store uses the periodic system of accounting for inventory. The following represents the units and unit costs for the basketballs in inventory and acquired during the year:

Beginning Inventory	30 units at $ 9.50
First Purchase	80 units at 10.00
Second Purchase	40 units at 10.50
Third Purchase	50 units at 11.00

Determine the value of the ending inventory and the cost of goods sold, assuming that goods are sold in the order of acquisition, based on the following information:

Ending Inventory (Units)	Ending Inventory	Cost of Goods Sold
(a) 30 units	$	$
(b) 55 units		
(c) 65 units		

**EXERCISE
10-3**

The beginning inventory and purchases of a product are presented below:

Beginning Inventory	15 units at	$19.
Purchase	20 units at	20.
Purchase	16 units at	18.
Purchase	15 units at	16.

The physical inventory taken at the end of the accounting period determines an ending inventory of 16 units. Using the periodic inventory system, determine the cost of the ending inventory and the cost of goods sold according to each of the following methods:

Inventory Method	Ending Inventory	Cost of Goods Sold
FIFO	$	$
LIFO		
Weighted Average		

**EXERCISE
10-4**

The following transactions relating to the purchase and subsequent sale of merchandise took place during the month of April for the current year.

200-
Apr 1   Beginning balance of inventory consisting of 200 units at $2.50 per unit.
    5   Purchased 100 units at $2.80 per unit.
    8   Sold 250 units.
  12   Purchased 200 units at $3.00 per unit.
  21   Sold 150 units.
  26   Purchased 100 units at $3.10 per unit.
  30   Sold 75 units.

Directions:

1. Rule a stock record card similar to the one illustrated in Chapter 10.
2. Record the above transactions to the stock record card, determining the appropriate balances after each transaction. (Assume a FIFO inventory method is in use.)
3. Prepare general journal entries for the above transactions. Assume that the unit selling price for each item sold was $5.50.

**EXERCISE
10-5**

The following transactions relating to the purchase and subsequent sale of merchandise took place during the month of April for the current year.

200-
Apr 1   Beginning balance of inventory consisting of 200 units at $2.50 per unit.
    5   Purchased 100 units at $2.80 per unit.
    8   Sold 250 units.
  12   Purchased 200 units at $3.00 per unit.
  21   Sold 150 units.
  26   Purchased 100 units at $3.10 per unit.
  30   Sold 75 units.

Exercise 10-5 continued

Directions:

1. Rule a stock record card similar to the one illustrated in Chapter 10.
2. Record the above transactions to the stock record card, determining the appropriate balances after each transaction. (Assume a LIFO inventory method is in use.)
3. Prepare general journal entries for the above transactions. Assume that the unit selling price for each item sold was $5.50.

EXERCISE 10-6

Using the information provided in Exercise 10-5, assume that the inventory system in use is the periodic inventory system. Assume further that the weighted average method is used to assign costs.
   Determine:

1. The value of the ending inventory;
2. The cost of goods sold;
3. The gross sales for the month.

EXERCISE 10-7

Using the information provided in Exercise 10-5, assume that the inventory system in use is the periodic inventory system. Assume further that the LIFO method is used to assign costs.
   Determine:

1. The value of the ending inventory;
2. The cost of goods sold;
3. The gross sales for the month.

EXERCISE 10-8

Using the information provided in Exercise 10-5, assume that the inventory system in use is the periodic inventory system. Assume further that the LIFO method is used to assign costs.
   Determine:

1. The value of the ending inventory;
2. The cost of goods sold;
3. The gross sales for the month.

EXERCISE 10-9

Using the lower of cost or market rule, determine the value to be assigned to the ending merchandise inventory. Since the present inventory is carried on the books at its original cost, it may be necessary to make an adjusting entry to recognize the lower of cost or market rule on the books. Should such an entry be necessary, make it in general journal form.

Exercise 10-9 continued

Items	Quantity	Unit Cost Cost	Unit Cost Market	Lower of Cost or Market
Basketballs	22	$ 9.00	$ 8.50	$
Baseballs	40	1.45	1.65	
Tennis Rackets	30	33.00	29.00	
Tennis Balls	60	1.25	1.10	———
			Total	

EXERCISE 10-10

Using the lower of cost or market rule, determine the value to be assigned to the ending merchandise inventory. Since the present inventory is carried on the books at its original cost, it may be necessary to make an adjusting entry to recognize the lower of cost or market rule on the books. Should such an entry be necessary, make it in general journal form.

Items	Quantity	Unit Cost Cost	Unit Cost Market	Lower of Cost or Market
Dress Jeans	100	$ 20.50	$20.00	$
Work Jeans	150	10.00	10.50	
Casual Jeans	400	15.00	16.00	
Jeans Jacket	250	21.00	20.00	———
			Total	

EXERCISE 10-11

The accountant for the AAA Trading Source, Inc. uses the gross profit method to determine the value to be assigned to the ending inventory. The following information is available:

Beginning Merchandise Inventory $ 35,400.
Net Purchases for the year   144,600.
Net Sales for the year   270,000.

During the previous year, the actual net sales amounted to $250,000 and the actual cost of goods sold amounted to $160,000. Use the gross profit method to determine:

1. The gross profit rate;
2. The value of the ending inventory;
3. The cost of goods sold for the year;
4. The gross profit on sales for the year.

EXERCISE 10-12

The accountant for a local retailer uses the gross profit method to determine the value to be assigned to the ending inventory. The following information is available:

Beginning Merchandise Inventory $ 15,600.
Net Purchases for the year   92,000.
Net Sales for the year   145,300.

Exercise 10-12 continued

During the previous year, the actual net sales amounted to $120,600 and the actual cost of goods sold amounted to $65,124. Use the gross profit method to determine:

1. The gross profit rate;
2. The value of the ending inventory;
3. The cost of goods sold for the year;
4. The gross profit on sales for the year.

EXERCISE 10-13

In order to facilitate the determination of the value of the ending merchandise inventory, the accountant utilizes the following information and the **retail method** of inventory determination:

	Cost	Retail
Beginning Merchandise Inventory	$ 32,600.	$ 58,900.
Net Merchandise Purchases	124,750.	204,300.
Net Sales		229,800.

Determine:

1. The cost of the ending inventory;
2. The cost of goods sold.

EXERCISE 10-14

In order to facilitate the determination of the value of the ending merchandise inventory, the accountant utilizes the following information and the **retail method** of inventory determination:

	Cost	Retail
Beginning Merchandise Inventory	$ 12,300.	$ 20,900.
Net Merchandise Purchases	142,700.	230,700.
Net Sales		228,600.

Determine:

1. The cost of the ending inventory;
2. The cost of goods sold.

Chapter 11 Accounting for Payroll

EXERCISE 11-1

1. What is payroll? What are the different ways employees are compensated?
2. What are payroll deductions? What is the difference between gross pay and net pay (take-home pay)?
3. What are the typical payroll deductions that are made from an employee's wages? What is the purpose of the Employee's Withholding Allowance Certificate (Form W-4)? When is Form W-4 prepared and by whom?

Exercise 11-1 continued

4. What is Social Security tax (FICA tax)? What is the current rate and FICA tax ceiling? Why is this tax called a nonprogressive tax?

5. What is federal income tax? Who pays this tax? Why is this tax known as a progressive tax? What are the three factors that determine the amount of federal income tax that is being withheld from an employee's salary?

6. What are state and local income taxes? What factors determine the amount of state and local income taxes that are withheld from an employee's salary?

7. What is state disability insurance? What is the current rate in New York State? Who is responsible for paying this cost?

8. What are voluntary deductions? What effect does voluntary deductions have on an employee's net pay?

9. What forms or records does the accountant prepare and maintain to keep track of employee payroll information? How and why are these forms prepared? What role does the federal, state, and local governments play in the use of these records?

10. Explain the purpose and calculation of unemployment compensation taxes. When does the federal government allow a credit, or reduction in the federal unemployment tax rate?

11. What are the various ways in which employees earn wages? If an employee is paid on a hourly basis, when, and at what rates does this employee become eligible for overtime pay?

12. When does an employee receive the W-2 Form (Wage and Tax Statement)? What is the purpose of this form? Where is the information needed to complete this form obtained?

EXERCISE 11-2

The following weekly wages were earned for the week ending December 13, 2003. Next to the total wages appears the cumulative wages to date, excluding the current week. Determine, based on the current rate and ceiling, the amount of Social Security tax and Medicare tax to be withheld from each employee's earnings for the week.

Employee	Wages	Cumulative Earnings	FICA Tax	Medicare Tax
1. A. Adams	$ 587.75	$28,760.10		
2. B. Bell	850.00	41,650.00		
3. C. Campbell	965.00	87,285.00		
4. D. Daily	1,200.00	88,800.00		
5. E. Ellen	1,500.00	31,500.00		

EXERCISE 11-3

The following weekly wages were earned for the week ending December 24, 2003. Next to the total wages appears the cumulative wages to date, excluding the current week. Determine, based on the current rate and ceiling, the amount of Social Security tax and Medicare tax to be withheld from each employee's earnings for the week.

Exercise 11-3 continued

Employee	Wages	Cumulative Earnings	FICA Tax	Medicare Tax
1. F. Friend	$ 650.00	$33,150.00		
2. G. Ginger	910.00	46,410.00		
3. H. Handle	1,050.00	84,150.00		
4. I. Irving	1,175.00	86,925.00		
5. J. Jones	850.00	86,350.00		

EXERCISE 11-4

Determine for each of the following employees their federal withholding tax, using the withholding tables provided in Chapter 11.

Employee	Status	Exemption	Gross Pay	Federal Withholding Tax
A. Allen	M	3	$650.00	
B. Brown	S	1	550.00	
C. Cole	S	0	875.00	
D. Dole	M	5	785.00	
E. Evans	M	1	665.00	

EXERCISE 11-5

Determine for each of the following employees their federal withholding tax, using the withholding tables provided in Chapter 11.

Employee	Status	Exemption	Gross Pay	Federal Withholding Tax
F. Fried	S	3	$385.00	
G. Grande	S	3	650.00	
H. Howard	M	2	925.00	
I. Inings	M	4	805.00	
J. James	S	1	765.00	

EXERCISE 11-6

Determine for each of the following employees their New York State and New York City withholding taxes, based on the tables provided in Chapter 11.

Employee	Status	Exemption	Gross Pay	NYS Withholding Tax	NYC Withholding Tax
A. Allen	M	3	$650.00		
B. Brown	S	1	550.00		
C. Cole	S	0	875.00		
D. Dole	M	5	785.00		
E. Evans	M	1	665.00		

EXERCISE 11-7

Determine for each of the following employees their New York State and New York City withholding taxes, based on the tables provided in Chapter 11.

Employee	Status	Exemption	Gross Pay	NYS Withholding Tax	NYC Withholding Tax
F. Fried	S	3	$385.00		
G. Grande	S	3	650.00		
H. Howard	M	2	925.00		
I. Inings	M	4	805.00		
J. James	S	1	765.00		

EXERCISE 11-8

Prepare a payroll register similar to the one illustrated in this chapter. Use the payroll information determined from supplementary Exercises 11-4 and 11-6. Calculate the FICA tax based on current rates, assuming that this payroll register is for the week ending May 4 of the current year. No employees have exceeded the ceiling on the Social Security tax.

EXERCISE 11-9

Prepare a payroll register similar to the one illustrated in Chapter 11. Use the payroll information determined from supplementary Exercises 11-5 and 11-7. Calculate the FICA tax based on current rates, assuming that this payroll register is for the week ending July 26 of the current year. No employees have exceeded the ceiling on the Social Security tax.

EXERCISE 11-10

Referring to the completed supplementary Exercise 11-8, prepare the necessary general journal entries to remit the appropriate taxes to the various taxing authorities at the end of the month. Assume that the completed payroll register represents the only payroll for the month of May of the current year.

EXERCISE 11-11

Referring to the completed supplementary Exercise 11-9, prepare the necessary general journal entries to remit the appropriate taxes to the various taxing authorities at the end of the month. Assume that the completed payroll register represents the only payroll for the month of July of the current year.

EXERCISE 11-12

The following employees had cumulative earnings for the first quarter of the current year as shown on their individual cumulative earnings reports. The state experience rating for this company for unemploy-

Exercise 11-12 continued

ment insurance purposes is 3.7%. Determine the federal and state unemployment tax that must be remitted to the respective taxing authorities at the end of the first quarter of the current year.

Employee	Cumulative Earnings	FU Tax	SU Tax
A. Albert	$6,452.00		
B. Bailey	7,452.85		
C. Cable	3,654.35		
D. Dallas	8,654.05		
E. Elston	5,985.00		

EXERCISE 11-13

The following employees had earnings for the second quarter of the current year, and cumulative earnings for the year as listed. The state experience rating for this company for unemployment insurance purposes is 3.7%. Determine the federal and state unemployment tax that must be remitted to the respective taxing authorities at the end of the second quarter of the current year. (Note: The calculations for this exercise represent the second quarter for Exercise 11-12.)

Employee	2nd Quarter Earnings	Cumulative Earnings	FU Tax	SU Tax
A. Albert	$6,300.00	$12,752.00		
B. Bailey	7,650.00	15,102.85		
C. Cable	3,350.75	7,005.10		
D. Dallas	6,975.00	15,629.05		
E. Elston	6,012.80	11,997.80		

EXERCISE 11-14

Calculate the gross pay for the following employees based on the hours worked and their hourly rate. Distinguish between regular and overtime earnings.

Employee	Total Hours	Hourly Rate	Regular Earnings	Overtime Earnings	Gross Pay
A. Austin (M,3)	43	6.25			
B. Bentley (S,1)	46	7.00			
C. Corvette (M,4)	38	7.50			
D. Datsun (S,0)	45	5.75			
E. Edsel (M,2)	48	8.00			
F. Ford (S,2)	40	6.00			

EXERCISE 11-15

Based on the gross pay determined for the employees in supplementary Exercise 11-14, prepare a payroll register for the week ending June 15 of the current year. After completing the register, record in general journal form the entries needed to pay the payroll and remit the various taxes to the taxing authorities. Use the various tables presented in Chapter 11.

Chapter 12 Partnership Accounting

EXERCISE 12-1

1. What are the disadvantages to the sole proprietorship form of business organization? What are the advantages to the partnership form of business organization?
2. What are the characteristics of a partnership? Explain.
3. How may a partnership be financed? How are the assets contributed to a partnership by the individual partners valued? How is each partner's investment in the partnership recognized?
4. How is the distribution of income and losses in a partnership determined? If the articles of partnership does not mention the distribution of profits, what will the courts decide in the event of a dispute?
5. How might the introduction of a new partner to a partnership be handled by the existing partners to the partnership? How is the withdrawal of a partnership handled by the partners?
6. What are the steps taken in the liquidation of a partnership? How does a partnership liquidation differ from a partnership dissolution?
7. How does the partnership drawing account differ from the drawing account of a sole proprietorship?
8. When is the account "Loss and Gain on Realization" used? Where is the balance in the account closed to? Why?
9. In a partnership liquidation, how is the capital deficit of one partner handled by the remaining partners to the partnership?

EXERCISE 12-2

Able and Baker decide to enter into a partnership. The assets contributed by Able consist of cash amounting to $900; accounts receivable, $18,900 with an allowance for bad debts of $600; inventory, $36,000; and store equipment, $19,000 which had been previously depreciated for $1,500.

The partners agree to accept the above assets with the following adjustments: The allowance for bad debts is to be increased to $1,000. The inventory will be valued at its current replacement cost of $45,000. The store equipment is to be valued at its fair market cost of $15,000. Record the general journal entry necessary to recognize Able's investment in the partnership.

EXERCISE 12-3

Mary and Rose decide to enter into a partnership devoted to selling ladies accessories. Mary contributes various items from her previous sole proprietorship. Her contribution consists of the following: cash, $1,200; accounts receivable, $21,000; an allowance for bad debts, $2,000; furniture and fixtures, $40,000; accumulated depreciation, $18,000; accounts payable, $700.

Mary and Rose agree to accept the items noted at their face value, with the following exceptions: the net receivable value to be $18,500,

Exercise 12-3 continued

and the furniture and fixtures to be valued at current replacement cost of $28,000.

Record the general journal entry necessary to recognize Mary's investment in the partnership.

EXERCISE 12-4

The partnership of Roberts, Stevens, and Taylor had a net income for the current year amounting to $61,900. The capital balances of the partners at the beginning of the year were $23,000, $26,000, and $32,000, respectively. The balances in the partners' drawing accounts were $11,000, $13,200, and $12,000, respectively. The articles of partnership calls for 10% interest on the beginning of the year capital balances and salary allowances of $11,000, $14,000, and $12,000, respectively. The profit and loss sharing ratio is 30:30:40.

Using a chart similar to the one illustrated in Chapter 12:

1. Determine the distribution of net income to each partner.
2. Record the entries necessary to transfer the net income and the balance in the drawing accounts to the partners' capital accounts.
3. Prepare a capital statement dated December 31 of the current year.
4. Assuming a net income of $27,100, determine the distribution to be made to each partner.

EXERCISE 12-5

Tinker and Chance form a partnership and invest $60,000 and $30,000, respectively. Their profit and loss sharing ratio is 60:40. The partnership agreement calls for each partner to receive a 5% interest on their capital balances and a salary allowance of $3,000, and $6,000 respectively. At the end of the first year of operation, the partnership had a net income of $60,000.

Using a chart similar to the one illustrated in Chapter 12, determine the distribution of net income to each partner. Prepare the general journal entry to transfer the net profit to each partner's capital account. Assume that during the year Tinker withdrew $10,000, and Chance withdrew $8,000 in anticipation of profits. Determine the new balance in the capital accounts following the closing of the drawing account balances.

EXERCISE 12-6

Partners Mutt and Jeff have respective capital balances of $45,000 and $30,000. Their partnership agreement calls for each partner to receive 8% interest on their capital balances, and salary allowances of $24,000, and $18,000, respectively. Their profit and loss sharing ratio is 45:55. The partnership net income before salary allowance or interest on capital balances amounted to $60,000.

Using a chart similar to the one illustrated in Chapter 12, determine the distribution of net income to each partner. Prepare the general journal entry to transfer the net income to each partner's capital account.

EXERCISE 12-7

Stevens, Taylor, and Umanski are partners with capital balances of $60,000, $35,000, and $40,000, respectively. Profit and losses are shared equally. Umanski retires from the firm. Record the entries for Umanski's retirement for each of the following separate circumstances:

1. Umanski's interest is sold to Vance, a new partner, for $48,000.
2. One-half of Umanski's interest is sold to each of the remaining partners for $24,000.
3. Umanski receives $46,000 of partnership funds for his interest. The remaining partners absorb the bonus paid to Umanski.
4. The partnership buys out Umanski paying $36,000. The excess is shared by the remaining partners according to their profit and loss sharing ratio.

EXERCISE 12-8

Revelation and Stewart are partners with respective capital balances of $20,000 and $30,000. Their profit and loss sharing ratio is $66^2/_3 : 33^1/_3$. The partnership agrees to admit Turnbull as a partner. Turnbull is to contribute $40,000 cash and is to share in the firm's profit and losses equally. The existing assets of the partnership are not to be revalued. Although Turnbull is contributing only $40,000, she will be receiving a capital balance of $45,000. Make the general journal entry necessary to admit the new partner.

EXERCISE 12-9

Hanley, Issacs, and James are members of a partnership who share profits in the ratio of 50:30:20, respectively. The current balance sheet has the following balances: cash, $15,000; other assets, $80,000; accounts payable, $20,000; Hanley, Capital, $15,000; Isaacs, Capital, $40,000; James, Capital, $20,000.

Record the necessary general journal entries to recognize the following separate liquidations of the partnership:

1. Assume that other assets are sold for $70,000.
2. Assume that other assets are sold for $40,000.
3. Assume that other assets are sold for $20,000.
4. Assume that other assets are sold for $90,000.

EXERCISE 12-10

The partnership of Jame, Karol, and Lorraine dissolve and liquidate their partnership at the end of the previous month. The partner's respective capital balances amounted to $50,000, $70,000, and $120,000. Their balance sheet at the time revealed cash of $30,000, other assets of $250,000, and current liabilities amounting to $40,000. The partnership's profit and loss sharing ratio was 20:20:60.

Record the necessary general journal entries to recognize the following separate liquidations of the partnership:

1. Assume that other assets are sold for $300,000.
2. Assume that other assets are sold for $100,000.
3. Assume that other assets are sold for $40,000.
4. Assume that other assets are sold for $30,000.

Chapter 13 Corporate Accounting

EXERCISE 13-1

1. How is a corporation defined? What are the advantages of a corporate form of business organization over a sole proprietorship, or a partnership? What are the disadvantages?
2. What is the capital section of a corporation called? What does this section consist of? What is the definition of the components of this section?
3. What are the steps necessary in forming a corporation?
4. What rights do stockholders of a corporation have?
5. What is the job of the corporate directors and officers of the corporation?
6. What kinds of stock may a corporation issue? What is the advantage and disadvantage of each form of stock?
7. Distinguish between issued stock, outstanding stock, and treasury stock.
8. What is a discount on preferred stock? What is a premium on preferred stock?
9. How are profits of a corporation distributed? What is the obligation of the corporation to distribute profits?
10. How does the balance sheet of a corporation differ from the balance sheet of a sole proprietorship, or partnership.

EXERCISE 13-2

The Everyday Corporation was incorporated to do business in New York State on June 1 of the current year. The corporation incurred the following organizational costs:

Attorney fees (with a market value of $2,000) paid for with the acceptance of 1,500 shares of $1 par common stock.

Paid the state $250 for incorporation fee.

The accountant accepted 1,000 shares of $1 par common stock for services that would normally be billed $950.

Prepare the general journal entry necessary to record these transactions and to amortized organization costs for the first year, assuming that the company elects to amortize this cost over five years.

EXERCISE 13-3

Sterling Corporation has issued outstanding participating preferred stock of 1,000 shares of 8%, $100 par, and 10,000 shares of no-par common stock. The preferred stock is entitled to participate on a share by share basis for dividends beyond those payable to the preferred stockholder and a $2 dividend to the common stockholder. The directors declare a dividend of $39,000 for the current year.

Determine the amount of dividend per share on (a) the preferred stock, and (b) the common stock.

Record the general journal entry for the declaration and the subsequent payment of the dividend. (Set up separate liability accounts to distinguish the two classes of stock to receive dividend payments.)

**EXERCISE
13-4**

The Crown Company has 8,000 shares of outstanding stock of $50 par value cumulative preferred stock and 20,000 shares of $10 par value common stock. The company declared a cash dividend amounting to $120,000. The common stockholder participates in initial dividend at the same rate as the preferred stockholder. Subsequent dividends are distributed based on the ratio of the total par value of each class of stock.

1. If no arrearage on the preferred stock exists, how much in total dividends per share is paid to each class of stock?
2. If one year's dividend arrearage on the preferred stock exists, how much in total dividends, and in dividends per share, is paid to each class of stock?
3. Assume that no arrearage on the preferred stock exists but that the stock is fully participating. How much in total dividends, and in dividends per share, is paid to each class of stock?

**EXERCISE
13-5**

The stockholders' equity section of the Fleetwoody Corporation's balance sheet at the beginning of the current fiscal year appears below:

8% Preferred Stock, $50 Par Value, 8,000 shares authorized; 6,000 shares issued and outstanding	$300,000
Paid-in Capital in Excess of Par Value-Preferred Stock	42,000
Common Stock, $20 Par Value, 100,000 shares authorized; 40,000 shares issued and outstanding	800,000
Retained Earnings	320,000

During the current year, the following transactions occurred:

200-

Apr 10 Issued 9,000 shares of common stock for $22 cash per share.

23 Repurchased 4,000 shares of common stock for the treasury at $23 per share.

May 2 Shareholders donated 1,800 shares of common stock to the corporation.

14 Sold one-half of the treasury shares acquired April 23 for $25 per share.

14 Sold the donated shares at $25 per share.

July 15 Issued 1,000 shares of preferred stock to acquire special equipment with a fair market value of $62,000.

Prepare general journal entries to record the foregoing transactions.

**EXERCISE
13-6**

The Hilltop Corporation, Inc. was organized on July 1 of the current year with an authorization of 10,000 shares of $5 no-par value preferred stock ($5 is the annual dividend) and 40,000 shares of $10 par value common stock.

Exercise 13-6 continued

Record in general journal form the following transactions that affected stockholders' equity:

200-

July 1 Issued 7,000 shares of preferred stock for $51 cash per share and 12,000 shares of common stock at $16 cash per share.

10 Issued 1,500 shares of common stock in exchange for equipment with a fair market value of $27,000.

15 Sold, 2,000 shares of preferred stock for cash at $50 per share.

31 Closed the $39,000 net income for July from the Income Summary Account to Retained Earnings.

Following the preparation of the general journal entries, prepare the stockholders' equity section of the balance sheet for July 31.

EXERCISE 13-7

The capital section of the Anytime Corporation at December 31 of the current year appears below:

Common stock, $100 par value, 20,000 shares authorized; 10,000 shares issued and outstanding	$1,000,000
Premium on Common Stock	150,000
Preferred Stock, 6%, $50 par value, 2,500 shares issued and outstanding, fully participating	125,000
Premium on Preferred Stock	12,500
Retained Earnings	746,000
	$2,033,500

Record the following transactions in general journal form:

200-

Mar 1 Sold, 1,000 shares of common stock for $120 per share.

15 Purchased 100 treasury shares, common, for $121 per share.

Jun 12 Declared a dividend totaling $80,000.

30 Declared and issued a 1% stock dividend on common stock. The common stock market value is $122 per share.

Aug 1 Sold 50 shares of the treasury stock for $123 per share.

Answer Key for Supplementary Exercises

Chapter 1
Exercise 1-1	There are no key figures. **1.** 5, 7, 8; **6.** $1,600 Income
Exercise 1-2	There are no key figures. 7 Assets, 2 Liabilities, 1 Capital
Exercise 1-3	There are no key figures. 6 Assets, 3 Liabilities, 1 Capital
Exercise 1-4	**1.** 1,500; **2.** 7,750; **3.** 5,000; **4.** 7,100; **5.** 14,500
Exercise 1-5	**1.** 4,780; **2.** 800; **3.** 3,705; **4.** 11,296; **5.** 1,140
Exercise 1-6	No key figure
Exercise 1-7	No key figure

Chapter 2
Exercise 2-1	No key figure
Exercise 2-2	Net Income $5,555.
Exercise 2-3	Net Income $2,870.
Exercise 2-4	Robert Rockwell, Capital (Dec. 31) $15,290.
Exercise 2-5	Emanuel Rodriguez, Capital (Dec. 31) $37,190.
Exercise 2-6	Total Assets – $6,685.
Exercise 2-7	Total Assets – $14,232.
Exercise 2-8	Same key figure as Exercise 2-6
Exercise 2-9	Same key figure as Exercise 2-7
Exercise 2-10	Total Assets – $26,275.
Exercise 2-11	Total Assets – $16,710.

Chapter 3
Exercise 3-1	No key figure
Exercise 3-2	Betsy Greedlindt, Capital $8,985.
Exercise 3-3	Alexandrea Smith, Capital $12,475.
Exercise 3-4	No key figure
Exercise 3-5	No key figure
Exercise 3-6	Gerrard Crandsale, Capital $7,940; Cash, $2,755.
Exercise 3-7	Blanche Swainberger, Capital $14,475; Cash, $5,575.
Exercise 3-8	Wendell V. Debbs, Capital $12,975; Cash, $7,825.
Exercise 3-9	Ruth Ann Cohen, Capital $13,270.

Chapter 4
Exercise 4-1	No key figure
Exercise 4-2	1. Supplies Expense $265; 3. Prepaid Insurance Balance $825; 6. Supplies Expense Balance $1,025.
Exercise 4-3	No key figure
Exercise 4-4	$3,000.
Exercise 4-5	$240.
Exercise 4-6	No key figure
Exercise 4-7	Net Income, $2,650.
Exercise 4-8	Net Income, $22,875.
Exercise 4-9	No key figure
Exercise 4-10	No key figure

Chapter 5
Exercise 5-1	No key figure
Exercise 5-2	Discount taken, $60.
Exercise 5-3	Discount taken, $25.
Exercise 5-4	Cost of goods sold, $172,000.

Exercise 5-5	Gross profit on sales, $154,000.
Exercise 5-6	Gross profit on sales, $154,000.
Exercise 5-7	Gross profit on sales, $67,100.
Exercise 5-8	No key figure
Exercise 5-9	No key figure
Exercise 5-10	No key figure
Exercise 5-11	No key figure
Exercise 5-12	Net income, $24,610.

Chapter 6

Exercise 6-1	No key figure
Exercise 6-2	Total credit sales, $1,620.
Exercise 6-3	Total credit sales, $1,858
Exercise 6-4	No key figure
Exercise 6-5	No key figure
Exercise 6-6	No key figure
Exercise 6-7	No key figure
Exercise 6-8	No key figure
Exercise 6-9	No key figure
Exercise 6-10	No key figure
Exercise 6-11	No key figure
Exercise 6-12	No key figure

Chapter 7

Exercise 7-1	No key figure
Exercise 7-2	Corrected balance, $9,107.83.
Exercise 7-3	Corrected balance, $423.
Exercise 7-4	Replenished the fund, $90.75.
Exercise 7-5	Replenished the fund, $122.40.
Exercise 7-6	No key figure
Exercise 7-7	No key figure

Chapter 8

Exercise 8-1	No key figure
Exercise 8-2	No key figure
Exercise 8-3	Uncollectible amount, $491.60
Exercise 8-4	Adjusting amount, **1.** $7,825.; **2.** $7,275.
Exercise 8-5	**5.** $60; **6.** $15; **10.** $67.50
Exercise 8-6	**5.** $11.25; **6.** $22.50; **10.** $33.75
Exercise 8-7	Amount paid, $1,522.50.
Exercise 8-8	Cost of discounting the note, $20.30.
Exercise 8-9	Cost of discounting the note, $56.25.
Exercise 8-10	No key figure

Chapter 9

Exercise 9-1	No key figure
Exercise 9-2	Annual depreciation, $2,700.
Exercise 9-3	Annual depreciation, $8,000.
Exercise 9-4	Depreciation per machine hour, $40.
Exercise 9-5	DDB rate, 50%
Exercise 9-6	1st Year's Depreciation, $4,500.
Exercise 9-7	DDB rate, $33\frac{1}{3}\%$
Exercise 9-8	SYD fractions $\frac{4}{10}, \frac{3}{10}, \frac{2}{10}, \frac{1}{10}$
Exercise 9-9	SYD fraction $\frac{6}{21}, \frac{5}{21}, \frac{4}{21}, \frac{3}{21}, \frac{1}{21}$

Exercise 9-10	No key figure
Exercise 9-11	Annual S/L depreciation, $9,000.
Exercise 9-12	No key figure
Exercise 9-13	No key figure
Exercise 9-14	No key figure
Exercise 9-15	No key figure
Exercise 9-16	No key figure

Chapter 10

Exercise 10-1	No key figure
Exercise 10-2	No key figure
Exercise 10-3	No key figure
Exercise 10-4	No key figure
Exercise 10-5	No key figure
Exercise 10-6	**1.** $352.08
Exercise 10-7	**1.** $385
Exercise 10-8	**1.** $312.50
Exercise 10-9	No key figure
Exercise 10-10	No key figure
Exercise 10-11	No key figure
Exercise 10-12	No key figure
Exercise 10-13	No key figure
Exercise 10-14	No key figure

Chapter 11

Exercise 11-1	No key figure
Exercise 11-2	**1.** $36.44, $8.52; **4.** $00.00, $17.40.
Exercise 11-3	**1.** $40.30, $9.43; **4.** $4.65, $17.04.
Exercise 11-4	A. Allen, $42.00; B Brown, $61.00.
Exercise 11-5	F. Fried, $18.00; G. Grande, $59.00; H. Howarrd, $91.00; J. Jennings, $55.00; J. Jones, $108.00.
Exercise 11-6	A. Allen-NYSWT, $23.10; NYCWT, $14.55.
Exercise 11-7	F. Fried-NYSWT, $7.90; NYCWT, $5.25.
Exercise 11-8	No key figure
Exercise 11-9	No key figure
Exercise 11-10	No key figure
Exercise 11-11	No key figure
Exercise 11-12	A. Albert-FUT, $51.62; SUT, $238.72.
Exercise 11-13	A. Albert-FUT, $4.38; SUT, $20.28.
Exercise 11-14	A. Austin Gross Pay, $278.13.
Exercise 11-15	No key figure

Chapter 12

Exercise 12-1	No key figure
Exercise 12-2	Able, Capital $76,700.
Exercise 12-3	Mary, Capital $47,000.
Exercise 12-4	No key figure
Exercise 12-5	Tinker profit, $26,490.; New Capital Balance, $82,490.
Exercise 12-6	Mutt profit, $5,400. New Capital Balance, $78,000.
Exercise 12-7	No key figure
Exercise 12-8	No key figure
Exercise 12-9	No key figure
Exercise 12-10	No key figure

Chapter 13

Exercise 13-1   No key figure
Exercise 13-2   Amortization, first year—$640.
Exercise 13-3   No key figure
Exercise 13-4   No key figure
Exercise 13-5   No key figure
Exercise 13-6   No key figure
Exercise 13-7   No key figure

GLOSSARY

ACCELERATED DEPRECIATION. The recognition of a greater amount of depreciation in the early years of use for a fixed plant asset and reduced amounts in the later years.

ACCOUNT. An individual record of specific things that a business owns (assets) and owes (liabilities) as well as a recognition of ownership (capital).

ACCOUNTING. The art of organizing, maintaining, recording, and analyzing financial activities.

ACCOUNTING EQUATION. The relationship between assets, liabilities, and capital of a business organization. The equation states: Assets = Liabilities + Capital.

ACCOUNTS PAYABLE. A current liability that is evidenced by an oral Promise to Pay made to the creditor.

ACCOUNTS PAYABLE CONTROL ACCOUNT. A general ledger account that mirrors the value of the subsidiary accounts payable ledger. The purpose of this control account is to provide a balance that is equal to the total of the balances of the subsidiary ledger.

ACCOUNTS PAYABLE LEDGER. A subsidiary ledger that contains various creditor accounts. All credit transactions from the purchases journal and the cash payments journal, as well as certain transactions from the general journal, are posted daily to the various creditor accounts in the subsidiary ledger.

ACCOUNTS RECEIVABLE CONTROL ACCOUNT. A general ledger account that mirrors the subsidiary account receivable ledger. The purpose of the control account is to provide a balance that agrees with the total balances of the individual ledger accounts in the subsidiary ledger.

ACCOUNTS RECEIVABLE LEDGER. A subsidiary ledger that contains individual customer accounts. All transactions involving customers are posted daily from either the sale or the cash receipts journal and under certain circumstances from the general journal to the individual customer accounts in the accounts receivable ledger.

ACCRUAL. An accumulation of assets or expenses or revenue items as well as liabilities whose value has been incurred but no cash has yet been transferred.

ACCRUAL BASIS. A method of recognizing the receipt of cash when it is earned rather than when the cash is actually received and of recording an expense when it is actually incurred rather than when the cash is disbursed. When a sale of a product or a service is made on credit, this transaction is recognized as revenue even though the cash is not received until a later time. Most businesses are on the accrual basis.

ACCRUED REVENUE. Revenue that has been earned but not yet received. This allows the company to match revenue earned in the same accounting period in which the associated costs were incurred.

ADJUSTING ENTRIES. Journal entries recorded in order to reflect properly the appropriate balances in the various ledger accounts for a specific accounting period. The entries are usually prepared at the end of the accounting period. However, they could be prepared at any time that the accountant feels it would be appropriate to do so.

AGENCY RELATIONSHIP. A relationship in which a person is authorized by a principal to make contracts with a third party on the principal's behalf. The agent is a principal's representative; therefore, any contracts entered into by the agent are binding upon the principal.

AGING OF ACCOUNTS RECEIVABLE METHOD. A method that is used to record adjusting entries at the end of the year to recognize and provide for the write-off of uncollectible accounts. A comparison of this method with the direct-write-off and the net sales methods shows that the aging method is by far the most accurate.

AMORTIZATION. The systematic write-off of the cost of an intangible asset over its economic life.

ARTICLES OF INCORPORATION. The charter under which the corporation conducts business in the particular state in which it is incorporated as well as in other states.

ARTICLES OF PARTNERSHIP. A contract prepared by individuals or entities prior to the beginning of a partnership. Information as to the sharing of profits and losses, as well as other aspects of the partnership, should be included in this partnership agreement.

ASSET. Anything that is owned and has money value.

AUTHORIZED STOCK. Those shares of stock that the articles of incorporation permits a corporation to sell.

BAD DEBT. An expense that a business recognizes as a result of a customer's failure to pay an obligation usually arising as a direct result of a prior credit sale. The expense is established when it is reasonably determined that the customer will not pay the obligation.

BALANCE. A term referring to the value or worth, expressed in monetary terms, of a specific ledger account. An individual account may be said to have a "debit" balance, a "credit" balance, or "no" (zero) balance.

BALANCE SHEET. A financial statement that shows the financial position of a business at a moment in time. It is a detailed presentation of the assets, liabilities, and owner's equity. It is a detailed accounting equation, in which the total value of the assets is equal to the total liabilities plus proprietor's capital.

BANK RECONCILIATION. The process by which an account's balance as per the banks records is brought into agreement with the balance per the depositor's records. The form used to reconcile the balances is known as the bank reconciliation statement.

BANK RECONCILIATION STATEMENT. A statement prepared once a month to bring about an agreement between the checkbook balance and the bank balance.

BANK STATEMENT. A record that is sent by the bank, usually on a monthly basis, to indicate the bank's record of the activities within an individual checking account. The activities recorded on the statement include deposits, paid checks, various bank charges, collections made by the bank to the customer's account, and payments authorized from the customer's account.

BOARD OF DIRECTORS. The elected officials of a corporation who oversee the operations of the firm and appoint the various officers who actually run the corporation. The board is elected by the stockholders of the corporation. Usually only the common stockholders have voting rights.

BOOK VALUE. The original cost of a fixed asset, less the accumulated depreciation.

BOSTON LEDGER. A three-column ledger account. The money columns include a debit column, a credit column, and a balance column. The advantage of this form of ledger account is that a running balance may be maintained in the account after each transaction has been recorded in it.

BRACKET ENTRY. An entry recorded in a two-column general journal that represents the need to post to a subsidiary ledger account as well as the corresponding control account in the general ledger. A bracket entry is also known as a "double-posting entry."

BUSINESS ENTITY CONCEPT. The accounting principal that says a business is separate and apart from the individual(s) who own it. The assets of the owner(s) should not be combined with the assets of the business.

BUSINESS TRANSACTIONS. Any business activity that affects what a business owns or owes, as well as the ownership of the business.

CALLABLE STOCK PROVISION. A provision that enables an issuing corporation to buy back its stock at a stated price, which is usually above the original purchase price of the stock. The callable provision is at the option of the corporation, but the provision is stated on the stock certificate.

CAPITAL. The ownership of the assets of a business by the proprietor(s).

CAPITAL EXPENDITURE. A material expenditure for an asset that will be used for more than one year, that increases the value or useful life of a fixed asset.

CAPITAL IMPROVEMENTS. Expenditures (costs) made to fixed assets in order to increase the useful lives of the assets over several accounting periods. Examples include the installation of a new engine in an old truck or the addition of a room to a building.

CASH. An asset consisting of coins, bills, money orders, checks, certificates of deposit, or treasury bills.

CASH BASIS OF ACCOUNTING. An accounting system that recognizes the revenue when the cash is received and recognizes the expense when the cash is disbursed. It does not match the expense with the related revenue produced during the same accounting period. This system is mainly used by individuals for income tax purposes.

CASH DISCOUNT. A reduction in price offered by a seller to a buyer as an incentive to pay the obligation to the seller before the buyer is actually required to do so.

CASH PAYMENTS JOURNAL. A journal that records all transactions involving the payment of cash regardless of the reason.

CASH RECEIPTS JOURNAL. A journal that records all transactions involving the receipt of cash regardless of source.

CHARTER. The articles of incorporation as approved by a particular state.

CHART OF ACCOUNTS. The table of contents of a ledger. The chart of accounts is a listing of the account pages and account titles found in the ledger. It is traditionally set up in the order of the accounting equation. The first section consists of the assets followed by liabilities, permanent capital, and temporary capital accounts.

CHECK REGISTER. A register replacing the cash payments journal when the voucher system is in use. It serves the same function as the cash payments journal, except that the account in this register is debited to vouchers payable.

CLOSE CORPORATION. A corporation that is owned by a few individuals such as the immediate members of a family.

CLOSING ENTRIES. Journal entries usually prepared at the end of the accounting period to eliminate the balances in the temporary capital account and to transfer these balances to the income summary account and eventually to the permanent capital account.

CLOSING THE LEDGER. The process by which the temporary capital accounts are eliminated. The closing process involves sending the balances from the respective temporary capital accounts to an account entitled income summary.

COMMISSION BASIS. A form of employee compensation. It is usually calculated as a percentage of the value of an item that is sold by the employee.

COMMON STOCK. A class of stock that usually sells for a price considerably less than other classes of stock. It has voting rights and the right to share in the distribution of income by the corporation in the form of dividends.

COMPOUND JOURNAL ENTRY. A journal entry in which there is more than one debit or credit entry as part of the transaction. If the compound entry contains two debits and one credit, the total value assigned to the debits must agree with the value of the credit entry, as required by double-entry accounting.

CONTINGENT LIABILITY. A liability that will be incurred only if a particular event takes place. The commitment of the endorser of a discounted note is to pay the discounter the maturity value of the note in the event the maker defaults on the note. If the maker defaults on the note, the contingent liability becomes an actual liability.

CONTRA-ACCOUNT. Any account that offsets a related account to reflect the proper amount on the financial statements. An example of a contra-account is the sales returns and allowances account that offsets the sales account.

CONTRA-ASSET ACCOUNT. An account that has a credit balance and reduces an asset account to reflect the proper amount on the balance sheet. The accumulated depreciation account and the allowance for bad debts accounts are examples of contra-asset accounts.

CONTROL ACCOUNT. An account that presents a summary of a group of accounts found in a subsidiary ledger. The accounts receivable and the accounts payable accounts found in the general ledger are examples of control accounts.

CONVERSION CLAUSE. A provision on a stock certificate that allows a stockholder to convert the stock owned to another class of stock.

COPYRIGHT. The exclusive right granted by the federal government to authors, artists, and composers to publish and sell their intellectual work. This right expires 50 years after the death of the originator.

CORPORATION. An artificial being, invisible, intangible, and existing only in contemplation of the law. It is a legal entity separate from its owners.

COST PRINCIPLE. The cost assigned to an asset, including the purchase price, transportation charges, installation charges, and any other costs associated with placing the asset into use by the organization.

CREDIT. The right side of a ledger account. It represents a position or location within a specific account.

CREDIT BALANCE. The balance of an account whereby the total credit amounts exceed the total debit amounts.

CREDIT MEMORANDUM. A document authorizing the buyer to return goods to the seller. A buyer must request permission to return goods to a seller. This permission is granted and evidenced by the credit memorandum. The effect of the credit memorandum is to reduce the obligation of the buyer by crediting the account receivable. If the goods have been paid for prior to their return, then the buyer receives a refund.

CREDITORS. Individuals or companies that are owed obligations by others. A creditor is normally known as an accounts payable, if the form of the obligation is evidenced by an oral promise.

CUMULATIVE EMPLOYEE EARNINGS RECORD. A record maintained to accumulate the weekly earnings of each employee. The record is summarized quarterly and enables the determination of each employee's cumulative earnings at any given point in time.

CUMULATIVE PREFERRED STOCK. The right that a preference stockholder has in receiving dividend distributions owed from prior years, as well as from the current year, before any distribution is made to other classes of stock.

CURRENT ASSETS. Assets that can reasonably be expected to be used up or converted into cash or sold within one year or less.

CURRENT LIABILITIES. Debts that are payable within one year or the current accounting period, whichever is longer.

DEBIT. The left side of a ledger account. It represents a position or location within a specific account.

DEBIT BALANCE. The balance that results when total debit amounts exceed total credits.

DEFERRAL. The postponement of the recognition of either an expense or a revenue item.

DEPLETION. The pro-rata allocation of the cost of land (through direct ownership or lease) to the units of natural resources removed from the land.

DEPOSITS IN TRANSIT. Deposits that have been sent but not yet received by the bank.

DEPOSIT SLIP. A form prepared in order to place money into a checking account. The resulting balance after the deposit is made is then used to pay checks that are issued on that particular account. The primary way to get money into a checking account is through the preparation of the deposit slip.

DEPRECIABLE VALUE. The original cost of a fixed asset, less the residual value of the asset. Depreciable value represents the total cost of the asset that is subject to depreciation.

DEPRECIATION. The systematic and rational allocation of the cost of an asset over its useful life.

DIRECT WRITE-OFF METHOD. A method of not recognizing the expense of an uncollectible account (bad debt) until it can be determined that the debtor will not be able to pay it. This method does not necessarily match the expense associated with the uncollectible account in the same period as the revenue was earned.

DISCOUNTING NOTES. The process involving the sale of a promissory note to a bank or financial institution prior to maturity. The bank deducts from the maturity value of the note an interest charge based on the period of time the note is to be held by the bank and the rate of interest the bank charges.

DISSOLUTION. The result of any charges in the composition of a partnership. This necessitates the preparation of a new article of partnership so that the business may be reorganized and continue in operation.

DIVIDENDS. A corporation's distribution of income to the stockholders of the corporation. The form of the dividend may be either in cash or in additional shares of stock.

DOUBLE-DECLINING BALANCE METHOD. An accelerated method of depreciation that uses a rate twice as high as the straight-line method. The rate is applied to the remaining balance (book value) of the asset every year.

DOUBLE-ENTRY ACCOUNTING. A method of accounting in which for every debit entry, there must be a corresponding credit entry of the same amount. Every business transaction *must* be represented by double-entry accounting. There must be at least two changes.

DOUBLE TAXATION. The taxing of corporate dividends twice—once in the form of corporate income tax and once as income tax paid by the stockholders receiving the dividends.

DRAWING ACCOUNT. A temporary capital account set up in the name of the sole proprietor or the partner from which the owner can withdraw money or take other assets in anticipation of profit.

EMPLOYEE'S WITHHOLDING ALLOWANCE CERTIFICATE. A form filled out by an employee when he or she begins work for a company. This form, also known as a "W-4," asks for the number of withholding exemptions the employee wishes to take. The payroll department uses this information to determine how much income tax to withhold from the employee's salary.

EQUITY. The ownership of or financial rights to business assets. The right side of the accounting equation—Liabilities + Capital—is known as the equities of the business, thus the accounting equation could be expressed as "Assets = Equities."

EXCHANGE OF ASSETS. A business transaction in which one asset is acquired by the giving up of another asset.

EXPENSES. The costs of doing business. These are costs that must be incurred in order for an organization to generate revenue. A retail store must incur the expense of renting the store in order to operate the business.

EXPERIENCE RATING. The unemployment compensation tax rate assigned to an employer by the state, based on how stable a work force the employer has maintained.

FICA. The Federal Insurance Contributions Act. This act established the Social Security system. The FICA, or Social Security tax, is one of a number of deductions taken from an employee's salary.

FIFO. First in, first out. It is a method of assigning costs to an inventory of merchandise. The first goods received are charged against the earliest sales of the merchandise.

FIXED ASSET. An asset that has an expected useful life of one year or more. Fixed assets are also referred to as "plant assets" or "property, plant and equipment."

FOOTING. The process of adding a column of numbers. Since this activity is usually done in pencil, it is commonly called "pencil footing."

FOUR-COLUMN LEDGER ACCOUNT. The money columns include a debit column, a credit column, a debit-balance column, and a credit-balance column. The advantage of this form of ledger is that a running balance may be maintained in the account after each transaction has been recorded in it. It is most commonly used in those organizations that utilize accounting posting machines.

FRANCHISE. A right or privilege to sell or distribute a product in accordance with special conditions.

FREIGHT-ON PURCHASES. An expense related to the cost of acquiring goods for resale. Other terms frequently used include freight-in or freight-inward. Any transportation charge related to the cost of acquiring goods to be resold is charged to this account.

GOODWILL. The dollar value assigned to the business's managerial skills and reputation. It is usually recognized at the time the business is sold.

GROSS PAY. The earnings of an employee prior to deducting any required taxes.

GROSS PROFIT METHOD. A method of estimating the cost of goods sold and the ending inventory for an accounting period based on the relationship that a prior year's gross profit, had to net sales. A percentage is determined based on a prior year's gross profits and net sales and used for the current year's calculation.

GROSS SALES. The balance in the sales ledger account before any consideration is made for possible sales returns that are recorded to a separate account.

HOURLY EMPLOYEE BASIS. A form of employee compensation under which an employee is paid a specific rate of pay for each hour worked.

INCOME STATEMENT. A financial statement that presents revenue and expenses and the net income or loss for a specific period of time.

INCORPORATORS. Those individuals who bring about the formation of the corporation. They consist of major stockholders of the corporation.

INDEPENDENT CONTRACTORS. Individuals or businesses that are not directly employed by a firm, but used to do specific activities for the firm, usually on an irregular basis.

INTANGIBLE ASSETS. An asset that cannot readily be seen or touched. Examples of intangible assets are copyrights, franchises, patents, and trademarks. Intangible assets have no physical substance, but are of value to the owners' of the organization.

INTEREST-BEARING PROMISSORY NOTE. A note that has a specific rate of interest indicated on its face. When the note matures, the maturity value of the note is its face value plus the interest earned.

INTERIM STATEMENT. A statement prepared for any period of time less than a complete accounting period.

INTERNAL CONTROLS. Procedures designed to safeguard assets of a business organization, generate appropriate accounting data, and ensure efficient productivity.

INVESTMENTS. Assets that are not used in the operation of a business, and are not expected to be converted into cash within one year.

ISSUED STOCK. Those authorized shares that have been sold by the corporation to the stockholders.

JOURNAL. A book of original or first entry. All business transactions are first recorded in a journal. The basic two-column journal provides for entering business transactions in dated order. All parts of the transaction are recorded in the journal and provision is made for an adequate explanation.

LEASEHOLD. Real estate held by a tenant as a result of a lease.

LEDGER. A book of secondary or final entry. Within the ledger are individual accounts. The term "ledger account" refers to an individual account in the ledger. A ledger may be a computer printout, a bound book, or a looseleaf-type book.

LIABILITIES. The ownership of the assets of an organization by its creditors. The ownership extends to the creditors' right to collect what is due them prior to any distribution to the owners of the business.

LICENSE. *See* patent.

LIFO. Last in, first out. It is a method of assigning costs to goods sold based on the most recent costs being charged against the most recent sales of the merchandise.

LIMITED LIFE. A term that usually refers to an asset which is expected to have a useful life of less than one year.

LIQUIDATION. The winding up of an organization. This process involves the conversion of all assets to cash, payment of creditors, and return of investment to the owners of the organization.

LONG-TERM LIABILITIES. An obligation that is not expected to mature and become payable within one year. A mortgage notes payable is an example of this type of liability.

LOWER OF COST OR MARKET RULE. A rule requiring the recognition of a permanent reduction in the value of inventory due to physical deterioration of an asset, a permanent price decline in terms of the replacement cost, or obsolescence. Inventory is valued at its actual cost or the current replacement cost (market price), whichever is lower.

MATCHING PRINCIPLE. A fundamental concept in the accounting profession in which revenue earned is recorded in the same period as the costs to produce the revenue were incurred. Through the process of recording adjusting entries the principle of matching costs and revenue is accomplished.

MATURITY VALUE. The principal and interest that the note earns on the due date of the note.

MERCHANDISE INVENTORY. Goods on hand at the end of an accounting period. The value of the inventory is determined by taking a physical inventory. This inventory consists of goods previously purchased but not sold during the current accounting period. The ending inventory becomes the beginning merchandise inventory at the beginning of the new accounting period. During the new accounting period no adjustments are made to this account on the books.

MERCHANDISE PURCHASES. Goods that a trading business purchases for the purpose of resale. During the year this account is treated as an asset. However, its location on the chart of accounts indicates that it is actually an expense, the assumption being that since the goods were bought for resale they represent expenses. Those goods that were actually sold become part of the calculation of cost of goods sold, which is an expense category.

MONETARY PRINCIPLE. An assumption made by the accounting profession that the dollar is a stable unit of value in measuring economic transactions.

MONEY VALUE. The assignment of a value expressed in monetary terms for all things within the accounting environment.

NEGOTIABILITY OF STOCK. The ability to transfer ownership of a corporation through the sale of stock.

NET EARNINGS SUMMARY. A temporary capital account that is used to close out all other temporary capital accounts at the end of the accounting period.

NET PAY. The actual amount of money an employee takes home after deductions are made from the employee's gross pay.

NET PROCEEDS. The amount of money the endorser of a discounted note receives from the discounter when the note is discounted.

NET SALES. The results of subtracting sales returns and allowances and sales discounts from the sales account. These sales represent the actual sales that remained sold.

NONCUMULATIVE STOCK. A class of preferred stock that does not participate in dividends that were not paid in previous years.

NONPROGRESSIVE TAX. A tax that is *not* based on the amount of money that an individual earns.

NOTES PAYABLE. A written promise evidencing a debt. This debt may either represent a current or a long-term liability, depending on when the obligation becomes due.

NOT-FOR-PROFIT CORPORATIONS. Corporations that are organized for altruistic purposes—usually for charitable or research activities—and merely use the corporate form of organization in doing their business. Due to the nature of the organizations they are not usually subject to corporate income tax.

OBSOLESCENCE. The condition whereby an asset is no longer useful to an organization because of technological improvement or business reorganization of the process the asset was previously used for.

ORGANIZATIONAL COSTS. These costs consist of legal, accounting, and any additional fees that must be paid before a business is incorporated.

ORGANIZATIONAL STRUCTURE. The chain of command as established by management. The various authorities and responsibilities are usually illustrated by an organizational chart.

OUTSTANDING CHECK. An item on a bank reconciliation that represents checks issued to the payee, but not yet paid by the bank and therefore not shown on a bank statement.

OUTSTANDING STOCK. Those shares of stock that have been issued and remain in the hands of the stockholders.

OVERTIME. Compensation calculated at $1\frac{1}{2}$ times an employee's hourly rate of pay for each hour worked beyond a normal five-day, forty-hour workweek.

OVERTIME EARNINGS. Earnings based on the number of hours worked beyond the normal workweek and on the overtime rate. *See also* overtime rate.

OVERTIME RATE. A rate paid for services over the "normal" workweek of 40 hours. The rate is determined by an agreement between the employer and either the employee or his or her union. The minimum rate is calculated at $1\frac{1}{2}$ times the regular rate of pay.

OWNERSHIP. The right to dispose of property as well as determine its use.

PARTICIPATING PREFERRED STOCK. A class of stock that participates in any additional dividend paid after the other classes of stock have received dividends comparable to that originally paid to the preferred stockholder.

PARTNERSHIP. An organization of two or more individual entities that agree to join forces for the common purpose of earning a profit within a business environment.

PAR VALUE. An arbitrary money value assigned to a share of stock. It does not necessarily have any relationship to the actual worth of the stock.

PATENT. A right given to an individual or a group to use a particular process or invention. Sometimes referred to as a "license."

PAYROLL. A list of all employees and their respective salaries for a given period.

PAYROLL REGISTER. A record of the total hours employees' worked during a given payroll period. This book contains employees' names, total earnings, and the various deductions that have been taken from gross pay to arrive at net pay for all employees on the register.

PERIODIC INVENTORY METHOD. The taking of a physical count of the merchandise on hand at the end of an accounting period.

PERMANENT CAPITAL. The owner's equity in a business organization that is not expected to change other than as a result of an increase or decrease in the owner's investment in the business.

PERMANENT INVESTMENT. An investment designated by management or the proprietor to remain with the company until the dissolution of the company. The term usually refers to investments made by proprietors at the beginning of the company's operations.

PERPETUAL INVENTORY SYSTEM. The continuous taking of a physical count of the goods available for sale. This system is usually used only by those concerns that sell high-ticket, low-volume goods.

PETTY CASH BOOK. A book maintained to record the outlay of cash from the petty cash fund.

PETTY CASH FUND. A small amount of money, usually fifty to one hundred and fifty dollars, set aside to pay for insignificant expenditures for which a check would not be accepted or appropriate.

PETTY CASH VOUCHER. A document prepared evidencing the outlay of a small sum of money that is signed by the person receiving the money from the petty cashier.

PHYSICAL DETERIORATION. The wearing out of a plant asset due to its use.

PIECEWORK BASIS. A form of employee compensation based on employee productivity. An employee is paid a predetermined fee for each operation completed or unit of work done in the manufacturing process.

POST-CLOSING TRIAL BALANCE. A trial balance that is prepared after closing the ledger. Temporary capital accounts having no balance after the closing entries have been posted, will not be found in the post-closing trial balance.

POSTING. The process of transferring debits and credits from one of the five journals to the appropriate ledger account.

POST REFERENCE COLUMN. A column in a ledger account used to indicate the source of an entry and, conversely, a column in a journal indicating the ledger account an entry was posted to.

PREEMPTIVE RIGHTS. A stockholders' right to maintain the same percentage ownership in the stock of a corporation when additional shares of stock are issued by the corporation.

PREFERENCE STOCK. A class of stock that has certain guaranteed rights, such as a percentage dividend, the receipt of dividends prior to a distribution to other classes of stock, or preference in the event of a liquidation. The purchase price of a preference stock is usually considerably higher than that of common stock.

PREPAID EXPENSE. An asset account. It is an item that is normally considered to be an expense, but because it is paid in advance, it is classified as an asset. At such time as the value of the asset has been used up, an adjusting entry will convert this prepaid expense (asset) to an actual expense.

PROFIT. The excess of revenue after subtracting expenses.

PROFIT AND LOSS SHARING. A plan outlined in the partnership agreement for distributing profits and losses among its members. If the partnership agreement is silent as to the method of distribution, the law will interpret this to mean that each partner shares equally in the profits and losses of the company.

PROFIT CORPORATION. Any corporation that is organized for the purpose of generating profits.

PROMISSORY NOTE. An unconditional written promise to pay a stated sum of money upon demand, or at a future determinable date. It is usually prepared and signed by the debtor and given to the creditor.

PROPERTY, PLANT, AND EQUIPMENT. Assets that have a useful life of more than one year and are used in the continuing operations of the organization.

PURCHASES DISCOUNT. A reduction in price taken by a buyer as a result of a discount being offered by a seller. On the books of the buyer, this discount represents a decrease of cost.

PURCHASES JOURNAL. A journal that records all purchases on credit.

PURCHASES RETURNS AND ALLOWANCES. A contra or negative account. This account offsets the merchandise purchases account. When goods previously purchased are returned, the entry for the return causes a credit to be recorded in this contra-account.

REPLENISH THE FUND. The replenishment of a petty cash fund for funds withdrawn from it. This process involves the preparation of a check and the recognition of the expenses that caused the fund to become depleted.

RESIDUAL VALUE. The value of a fixed asset after it has been fully depreciated. It is an estimate of what the asset will be sold for when it is no longer usable.

RETAIL METHOD. A method of estimating the cost of goods sold and the ending inventory using a ratio of the total cost of goods available for sale compared with the total selling price of all the goods. This ratio is then applied to each dollar of sales to determine the cost of goods sold and the gross profit.

REVENUE. Sales of a product or service resulting in the receipt of assets such as cash or accounts receivable that will eventually have an effect on the owner's equity.

REVERSING ENTRIES. Entries recorded at the very beginning of the new accounting period representing the exact opposite of the adjusting entry recorded at the end of the previous accounting period.

A reversing entry is necessary any time an adjusting entry sets up an account that will not be closed at the end of the accounting period and produces an account with a balance that does not normally appear on the books during the year. An adjusting entry for accrued salaries creates the account salaries payable. Since this account is neither closed at the end of the period or normally carries a balance during the year, a reversal entry is called for.

SALARY ALLOWANCE. A fee paid to a partner of a company for services rendered as provided in the terms of a partnership agreement. This distribution is made before any other distribution of the profits or losses are made to the other partners in the company.

SALES DISCOUNT. A reduction of sales price offered by a seller to a buyer. The difference between the amount owed by the customer and the amount of cash received is known as the sales discount, assuming the customer has taken the discount offered.

SALES JOURNAL. A journal that records all sales of goods and services on credit.

SALES RETURNS AND ALLOWANCES. A contra-revenue account that specifically offsets the sales account. Any time goods previously sold are returned to the seller, the return is recorded as a debit to the sales returns and allowances account.

SCHEDULE OF ACCOUNTS PAYABLE. A listing of the balances in the subsidiary accounts payable ledger. The total of this schedule must agree with the balance in the control account in the general ledger.

SCHEDULE OF ACCOUNTS RECEIVABLE. A listing of the balances of the subsidiary ledger account. This schedule is used to verify the accuracy of the control account in the general ledger. The total of the schedule must agree with the balance in the accounts receivable control account.

SCRAP VALUE. Represents the value of the fixed asset after it has been fully depreciated. It is an estimate of what the asset will be sold for when it is no longer usable.

SEPARATE LEGAL EXISTENCE. The legal existence of a company which entitles a company to own assets, incur debts, or enter into contracts.

SIGNATURE CARD. A card required to open a checking account. The signatures of the authorized signers of an organization's checks are listed on this card.

SOLE PROPRIETORSHIP. A business formed by one individual.

STATE DISABILITY INSURANCE. A fund established by the state to pay benefits to individuals who become disabled. The money from this fund is provided by employees through a payroll deduction unless by union agreement the cost of this insurance is to be paid by the employer.

STATED VALUE. An arbitrary value assigned to no-par stock. It has an effect similar to that of a par-value stock.

STATEMENT OF CAPITAL. A financial statement that shows the change in the value of the ownership in a business over a period of time. The change in capital is due to income or loss and withdrawals by the owner over a period of time.

STOCKHOLDERS' EQUITY. The ownership of the assets of a corporation as evidenced by transferable shares of stock. On the balance sheet, the stockholders' equity section consists of the stock sold by the corporation and the retained earnings (income retained by the corporation).

STOCK-RECORD CARD. A ledger account that is used to keep track of merchandise that is received and issued. It also contains information as to the unit cost of goods received and issued.

STRAIGHT-LINE METHOD. The most common method of depreciation used by companies to reflect the deterioration of assets. The total cost of the asset less any salvage value is divided by the useful life of the asset to determine the annual depreciation cost. The name given to the method results from the fact that the annual depreciation recognized each year is the same amount for a given plant asset.

SUBSIDIARY LEDGER. A detailed record of individual customer or creditor accounts which when totaled equal the control account in the general ledger. A subsidiary ledger can be set up for any group of accounts in which detailed information is needed and yet does not have to be shown in the general ledger other than in the form of a control account.

SUM-OF-THE-YEARS'-DIGITS METHOD. An accelerated method of recognizing depreciation. The rate used is a fraction that has as its numerator the remaining life of the asset and as its denominator the sum of all the years' depreciation.

TAKE-HOME PAY. The net salary earned by an employee after all payroll deductions.

TEMPORARY CAPITAL. Those capital accounts that will be eliminated at the end of the accounting period. Temporary capital accounts include revenue, expenses, and proprietor's drawing accounts. These accounts are classified as temporary because they are closed out to income summary at the end of the accounting period.

TEMPORARY INVESTMENT. Money or other assets that are lent by the proprietor and are expected to be returned to him by the business. This temporary investment is usually recorded to the proprietor's drawing account as a credit entry.

TERMS. The means or method of the payment of an obligation. Terms are established by the seller and are included on the invoice.

TRADE-IN ALLOWANCE. A reduction in the purchase price of a new plant asset in exchange for the asset being replaced.

TRADEMARK. A symbol, name, or other device designating the origin or ownership of a unique product. A trademark is legally reserved for exclusive use by the owner.

TREASURY STOCK. Shares of stock of the corporation that have been purchased on the open market by the corporation. These shares do not have voting rights or dividend rights while in the hands of the corporation.

TRIAL BALANCE. A record that may be prepared at any moment in time to prove the accuracy of the ledger. By taking a listing of the balances in the individual ledger accounts, the total of these debit and credit balances should agree. If the totals agree, the ledger is said to be in balance.

UNEARNED REVENUE. An advance payment for services that still must be performed. Unearned revenue represents a liability or obligation of the company receiving the payment for a service not yet rendered.

UNEMPLOYMENT COMPENSATION TAXES. Taxes levied against employers by federal and state governments to provide for compensation to unemployed workers.

UNITS OF PRODUCTION. A depreciation method based on use rather than time. The following formula is used:

$$\frac{\text{Cost} - \text{Salvage Value}}{\substack{\text{Estimated Total Number of} \\ \text{Units to be Produced}}} = \text{Depreciation per Unit of Measure}$$

The resulting rate is then multiplied by the number of units produced each year in order to determine the annual depreciation expense.

UNLIMITED LIABILITY. A characteristic of a sole proprietorship or partnership organization that allows creditors to settle their debt by claiming the personal property of the owners of the business when business assets are inadequate to settle the obligation.

UNPAID VOUCHER FILE. A file containing unpaid vouchers that is organized according to the due date of the specific voucher.

UNRECORDED EXPENSES. Expenses incurred but not recorded. Usually these expenses will be recorded when paid. In order to adhere to the concept of matching costs and revenue, it is necessary to record the unrecorded expenses as an adjusting entry at the end of the accounting period.

UNRECORDED REVENUE. Services that have been rendered but not yet billed. By the end of the accounting period an adjusting entry should be made to recognize this revenue even though it has not actually been received in the form of cash, thus converting unrecorded revenue to recorded revenue.

VOUCHER. A document that contains specific information dealing with the recognition and subsequent payment of an obligation.

VOUCHER REGISTER. A register taking the place of the purchases journal when the voucher system is used by the organization. All prepared vouchers are recorded in the voucher register, and subsequent payments are listed in the register for information purposes.

VOUCHER SYSTEM. A method of establishing control over the making of expenditures related to the payment of liabilities. All transactions that will eventually result in the payment of cash must first be recorded as liabilities using the various books of the voucher system.

WAGE AND TAX STATEMENT. A document indicating an employee's total earnings during the calendar year and also the total taxes withheld from his or her salary. It is prepared by an employer at the end of every calendar year and sent to the employee shortly thereafter. This form, which is also known as a "W-2" form, is used in the preparation of an individual's personal income tax return.

WEIGHTED AVERAGE METHOD. A method of assigning a cost to the ending inventory and to goods sold by determining an average unit cost for all the goods that are available for sale during the accounting period.

WORKSHEET. An expanded trial balance. The purpose of the worksheet is to enable the accountant to prepare easily the adjusting entries as well as various financial statements, including the income statement, statement of capital, and balance sheet.

INDEX

MOVE TO THE HEAD OF YOUR CLASS
THE EASY WAY!

on's presents THE EASY WAY SERIES—specially prepared by top educators, it maximizes
ctive learning while minimizing the time and effort it takes to raise your grades, brush up on the
cs, and build your confidence. Comprehensive and full of clear review examples, **THE EASY
Y SERIES** is your best bet for better grades, quickly!

541-1976-1	Accounting the Easy Way, 4th Ed.—$14.95, Can. $21.95
541-1972-9	Algebra the Easy Way, 4th Ed.—$13.95, Can. $19.50
541-1973-7	American History the Easy Way, 3rd Ed.—$14.95, Can. $21.00
641-0299-0	American Sign Language the Easy Way—$14.95, Can. $21.00
120-9134-5	Anatomy and Physiology the Easy Way—$14.95, Can. $19.95
120-9410-7	Arithmetic the Easy Way, 3rd Ed.—$13.95, Can. $19.50
641-1358-5	Biology the Easy Way, 3rd Ed.—$13.95, Can. $19.50
641-1079-9	Bookkeeping the Easy Way, 3rd Ed.—$14.95, Can. $21.00
120-4760-5	Business Law the Easy Way—$14.95, Can. $21.00
641-0314-8	Business Letters the Easy Way, 3rd Ed.—$13.95, Can. $19.50
641-1359-3	Business Math the Easy Way, 3rd Ed.—$14.95, Can. $21.00
120-9141-8	Calculus the Easy Way, 3rd Ed.—$13.95, Can. $19.50
641-1978-8	Chemistry the Easy Way, 4th Ed.—$14.95, Can. $21.95
641-0659-7	Chinese the Easy Way—$14.95, Can. $21.00
641-2146-4	Earth Science The Easy Way—$14.95, Can. $21.95
641-1981-8	Electronics the Easy Way, 4th Ed.—$14.95, Can. $21.00
641-1975-3	English the Easy Way, 4th Ed.—$13.95, Can. $19.50
120-9505-7	French the Easy Way, 3rd Ed.—$14.95, Can. $21.00
641-0110-2	Geometry the Easy Way, 3rd Ed.—$14.95, Can. $21.00
120-9145-0	German the Easy Way, 2nd Ed.—$14.95, Can. $21.00
641-1989-3	Grammar the Easy Way—$14.95, Can. $21.00
120-9146-9	Italian the Easy Way, 2nd Ed.—$13.95, Can. $19.50
120-9627-4	Japanese the Easy Way—$14.95, Can. $21.00
641-0752-6	Java™ Programming the Easy Way—$18.95, Can. $25.50
641-2011-5	Math the Easy Way, 4th Ed.—$13.95, Can. $19.50
641-1871-4	Math Word Problems the Easy Way—$14.95, Can. $21.00
120-9601-0	Microeconomics the Easy Way—$14.95, Can. $21.00
641-0236-2	Physics the Easy Way, 3rd Ed.—$14.95, Can. $21.00
641-2263-0	Spanish Grammar—$14.95, Can. $21.95
641-1974-5	Spanish the Easy Way, 3rd Ed.—$13.95, Can. $19.50
120-9852-8	Speed Reading the Easy Way—$13.95, Can. $19.50
120-9143-4	Spelling the Easy Way, 3rd Ed.—$13.95, Can. $19.50
120-9392-5	Statistics the Easy Way, 3rd Ed.—$14.95, Can. $21.00
641-1360-7	Trigonometry the Easy Way, 3rd Ed.—$14.95, Can. $21.00
120-9147-7	Typing the Easy Way, 3rd Ed.—$18.95, Can. $26.50
120-9765-3	World History the Easy Way, Vol. One—$15.95, Can. $22.50
120-9766-1	World History the Easy Way, Vol. Two—$14.95, Can. $21.00
641-1206-6	Writing the Easy Way, 3rd Ed.—$14.95, Can. $21.00

Barron's Educational Series, Inc.
250 Wireless Boulevard • Hauppauge, New York 11788
In Canada: Georgetown Book Warehouse • 34 Armstrong Avenue, Georgetown, Ontario L7G 4R9
RRON'S www.barronseduc.com $ = U.S. Dollars   Can. $ = Canadian Dollars

es subject to change without notice. Books may be purchased at your local bookstore, or by mail from Barron's. Enclose check
oney order for total amount plus sales tax where applicable and 18% for postage and handling (minimum charge $5.95 U.S.
Canada). All books are paperback editions.   (#45) R 6/03